MODERN
SOCIOLOGICAL
THEORY

are to be returned on or before
the last date below.

MODERN SOCIOLOGICAL THEORY

MALCOLM WATERS

SAGE Publications

London · Thousand Oaks · New Delhi

First published 1994

SAGE Publications Ltd
6 Bonhill Street
London EC2A 4PU

SAGE Publications Inc
2455 Teller Road
Thousand Oaks, California 91320

SAGE Publications India Pvt Ltd
32, M-Block Market
Greater Kailash – I
New Delhi 110 048

British Library Cataloguing in Publication data

Waters, Malcolm
    Modern Sociological Theory
    I. Title
    301.01

ISBN 0–8039–8531–2
ISBN 0–8039–8532–0 pbk

Library of Congress catalog card number 93–86214

Typeset by Photoprint, Torquay, Devon
Printed in Great Britain by The Cromwell Press Ltd,
Broughton Gifford, Melksham, Wiltshire

Contents

Preface

This book seeks to aid the good teaching of sociological theory. It does so by trying to establish that there is a theoretical tradition in sociology to which students can be exposed. It rejects the notion that theory can be understood as a series of discrete schools or compartmentalized individual theorists. Theory is a developing set of arguments and debates which focuses on common questions. And while there may be disparate, and perhaps irreconcilable, approaches to answering these questions, the disagreements and debates all take place within a common universe of discourse. The book argues that the contours of that universe are given in four concepts which theory must always address: agency, rationality, structure, and system. It tries to show, first, that these are the foci of theoretical debate, and second, that these baseline concepts are always mobilized in seeking to theorize such substantive phenomena as power or gender.

I believe that the book is also challenging. It aims neither to reduce theory to oversimplified and programmatic formulae nor to provide an entertaining read, although it might do either of these by accident. Rather it seeks to stick to the facts of theory and to present it at the level its authors would wish to have it presented. Because the book seeks to condense and precis, rather than to simplify, some the material is inevitably difficult. It is probably therefore much more suitable for graduate and senior undergraduate students than for those at the very beginning of their academic experience.

Most of my debts are diffuse rather than particular. My colleagues in the Department of Sociology at the University of Tasmania are a continuing source of support and intellectual stimulation. I should mention my persistent arguments with Stephen Crook and Jan Pakulski as a more precise source for ideas. Perhaps more importantly, my students in our third-year core-theory course, Modern Sociological Analysis, have been the victims of my numerous attempts to rehearse the contents of the book over a period of some twelve years. They have been more than forbearing, although they have certainly been that, and have made proactive, positive, and sometimes provocative contributions. My 'Scottish' mates, John Holmwood and Sandy Stewart, remain influential, and I must thank Stephen Mennell for insisting that I should discover the theory of Norbert Elias. Lest I come to be regarded as the enemy of all bureaucrats, Stefan Rucinski kept the Faculty of Humanities and Social Sciences running while its Dean was busy writing. Rowena Stewart and Christina Parnell have provided unstinting administrative assistance.

I actually began the writing while I was a Bye Fellow at Robinson College, Cambridge in 1991. I owe a great debt of gratitude to the Master and Fellows of the College for their generous hospitality and for the stimulating environment which they provided. Particular thanks must go to my sponsor, Peter Kornicki, and to the then Junior Bursar, Cdr George Coope, who went far beyond the call of duty in helping to provide facilities. I must also thank the librarians at Robinson, at the Faculty of Social and Political Studies, and at the Institute of Criminology, who all went out of their way to assist.

The editorial staff at Sage, that leading publisher of social science, have been as helpful and positive as can be. Karen Phillips commissioned the work and assisted in the early stages, while Louise Murray saw it through to the end. Stephen Barr kept a dispassionate watching brief throughout. Sage's anonymous referees in Britain and the USA have made a major contribution to the final product. I trust that they will notice the effects of their advice even if they cannot be acknowledged on an individual basis.

The book incorporates some material that I have published elsewhere in earlier versions. Parts of chapter 8 are modified elements of 'Patriarchy and Viriarchy', *Sociology* 23 (2): 193–211 (1989a); the second half of chapter 9 is abstracted and modified from *Class and Stratification*, Melbourne: Longman Cheshire (1990) and from 'Collapse and Convergence in Class Theory', *Theory and Society* 20: 141–72 (1991); and a further small part of the chapter is modified from *Postmodernization*, London: Sage (1992) (written with Stephen Crook and Jan Pakulski).

Writing so long a book as this provides such a burden and disruption to domestic life that, at one stage during its production, I felt obliged to promise my wife, Judith Homeshaw, that I would in future stick to journal articles. It is a measure of the extent to which she shares my academic commitment that she has already let me off that particular hook. Without the pleasures of the family life we share with Penny and Tom, writing this book would have been quite impossible.

Acknowledgements

Figures 2.2, 4.1 and 4.2 are reprinted by permission of the publisher from *The Constitution of Society* by Anthony Giddens, Oxford: Blackwell. Figures 5.3 and 5.4 are reprinted by permission of the publisher from *The American University* by Talcott Parsons and Gerald M. Platt, Harvard University Press, Cambridge, Mass., copyright © 1973 by the President and Fellows of Harvard College. Figure 5.5 is reprinted by permission of the publisher from Jeffrey C. Alexander, *Theoretical Logic in Sociology, Vol. 1: Positivism, Presuppositions and Current Controversies*, University of California Press, Berkeley and Los Angeles, copyright © 1982 The Regents of the University of California.

1 General theory in sociology

Sociology can fairly make a claim to the status of an established academic discipline for two reasons: first, it has a widely acknowledged theoretical tradition; and, second, it makes a serious attempt at methodological rigour in the conduct of research. However, it is theory which defines the discipline because theory sums up what sociology can say to its audience about the social world. Methodology, by contrast, is merely a set of rules for deciding what one can say and the status of what one has said, a means to an end. Theory must always be the central and irreducible goal if sociology is to take a significant place within the development of human self-knowledge and the guidance of human society. If sociology sacrifices theory to interpretation it drifts towards the opinionism of journalism or history; if it chooses empiricism it drifts towards the tautologism and dehumanization of behaviourist psychology or economics; and if it retreats into philology or epistemology it drifts towards the scholasticism of philosophy or theology.

Sociological theory is neither a unified nor a completed project. It is differentiated into specialized foci of interest which are only partially linked together. In physics there is now very real hope for the unification of particle theory with theories of the cosmos which hitherto have provided the ultimate divide between a micro- and a macro-universe. In sociology no such hope is yet available for a resolution of its special dualities: action and structure, materialism and idealism, individualism and holism, rational instrumentalism and communicationism, and value-neutrality and value-relevance. Indeed it would be possible to construct a book which focused precisely on these oppositions as prevailing debates. Such a book might argue that these debates need to be resolved if sociological theory is not to be counted as a failure. But theorizing is a process rather than an accomplishment and, so long as these oppositions are mobilized in addressing substantive concerns, sociological theory can progress in the way that physics manifestly has.

It is precisely on substantive concerns that this book focuses. It addresses the things which sociological theory can say, its substantive topics and the claims it makes about them, rather than the explanatory dualisms which might frustrate such an endeavour. Somewhat surprisingly these topics are relatively few in number and this fact alone speaks positively to a measure of theoretical integration in a discipline so young. Theoretical sociologists, one can argue, communicate with one another within a field of common discourse, even if not a field of common agreement – they use a shared system of concepts to focus on topics of common interest. In identifying these topics of common theoretical interest this book specifically rejects arguments that sociological theory should be understood as a multiplicity of competing, or even conflicting, schools of thought or paradigms, each of which has a finished argument. Argumentative competition is precisely the social process by which theorizing is achieved.

One of the reasons why theory in sociology has a common but broad agenda is that it has a relatively unified theoretical heritage, although not an absolutely unified one. It stands between, say, psychology or economics on one hand, which can point to the single figure of a Freud or a Marshall as the originating point for their theoretical development, and history or political science on the other, for which it would be difficult to identify any small group of defining and founding theorists. The topics and approaches of sociology are broadly traceable to the work of three major, late-nineteenth-century figures, Karl Marx, Max Weber and Émile Durkheim, only the last two of which regarded themselves as sociologists, and only Durkheim exclusively so. Although it is high time that sociology went beyond a simple reading of the classics, we need nevertheless to emulate their originality and their broad compass. So we shall remind ourselves continuously throughout this book that the topics that we currently consider came from these sources.

This introduction is divided into three sections. The first focuses on what theory is and how it is practised. The second sidesteps into a textual, although not a pedagogical, irrelevancy, an identification of the main approaches to sociological theory, which shows the links between more recent theorizing and the classics. This is provided as a scheme against which the somewhat unusual organization of the book can be referenced, allowing the reader to 'check back' when a particular theorist or theoretical tradition (an 'ism') is encountered and to locate it in relation to other developments. The third section identifies the main thrust of the book, the central concepts of sociological theory which are covered in each of the chapters.

The practice of sociological theory

In sociology, the word 'theory' is used much as it is used in everyday life. We can take the definition given in the *Concise Oxford Dictionary* as an indicator of its everyday meaning: 'Supposition explaining something, esp. one based on principles independent of the phenomena etc. to be explained' (1964: *s.v.* Theory). The *Shorter Oxford Dictionary*, which as it happens is rather longer, has the space to offer several definitions, including one which might suit more precisely an academic discipline such as sociology:[1] 'A scheme or system of ideas or statements held as an explanation or account of a group of facts or phenomena; . . . a statement of what are held to be the general laws, principles, or causes of something known or observed' (1973: *s.v.* Theory). In sociology the phenomena to be observed, quite obviously, are social phenomena, that is, its theory focuses on the relationships and interaction (other-related practices) between human beings.

We can now move on to use these definitions to isolate the special characteristics of theory as opposed to other sociological practices. Theory in sociology includes any intentionally constructed set of statements which can meet the following criteria:

- They must be abstract, that is, they must be separated from the social practices which they address. Theory usually achieves abstraction by the development of technical and arcane concepts which are used only within the sociological community.
- They must be thematized. A specific thematic argument must run through the set of statements giving them coherence and force.
- They must be logically consistent. The statements must not contradict one another and, if possible, should be deducible from one another.
- They must be explanatory. Theory must constitute a thesis or argument about social phenomena which can account for their form, or substance, or existence.
- They must be general. They must, in principle, apply to, and be able to account for any and all instances of the phenomena which they seek to explain.
- They must be independent. They must not be reducible to the explanations participants themselves offer for their own behaviour.
- They must be substantively valid. They must be consistent with what is known about the social world both by its participants and by sociologists and other social scientists. At a minimum there must be 'rules of translation' which can connect the theory with other bodies of knowledge.

For any practising theorist, theory is a developing set of ideas which seeks maximally to meet these criteria but which may only be a partial contribution to a more communal theoretical enterprise.

This does not mean that theory looks the same everywhere in sociology. There are, in general, three types of theory: formal, substantive and positivistic. *Formal* theory is the most inclusive. It seeks to produce a scheme of concepts and statements within which society, or human interaction in its entirety, can be explained. Often such theory is paradigmatic in character, that is it seeks to set the entire agenda for future theoretical practice against the claims of opposing paradigms.[2] Such theory is also often 'foundational' in character, that is, it seeks to identify a single set of principles which are the ultimate foundation for social life and by which everything can be explained.[3] Chapters 2–5 of this book concentrate on formal and foundationalist theory.

Substantive theory, by contrast, is much less inclusive. It seeks not to explain all things but either specific, but very generally ramifying, events or specified types of social process. The former includes theories of the emergence of industrial society, or of the maintenance of capitalism, while the latter might include theories of worker alienation, political domination, class subordination, religious commitment, or 'deviant' behaviour. Chapters 6–9 describe the most general examples of substantive theory in sociology.

Positivistic theory[4] seeks to explain empirical relationships between variables by showing that they can be deduced from more abstract theoretical statements. It explains very specific statements indeed. Because positivistic theory is so focused on specific empirical relationships its findings have not proved to be influential. Consequently they are not canvassed widely in this book, although some examples are discussed in chapter 3.

We now know, in formal terms at least, what theory is and what its varieties are. We can therefore move on to ask how it is done or practised or what its methodology is. A simple answer is to say that theory is done by reading, thinking, writing, publishing and arguing, but not necessarily in this order. More helpfully, theorizing might generally be regarded as a process of scholarship, as opposed to research, which is advanced by one or more of the following strategies:

- Proposing or advancing a political or practical agenda. Here the sociologist often seeks to reveal the true or genuine nature of society to open up possibilities for changing it. Major examples are feminist sociological theory (chapter 8) and critical theory (chapter 5) which seek to emancipate sections of humanity from dominating structures.
- Standing opposed to prevailing theoretical arguments. Here the theorist engages in a critique of extant theory and offers an alternative. The classical example is Durkheim's critique of Spencer (see chapter 9). More recently, Giddens' structuration theory (see chapter 7) was developed because Giddens believed that structural-functionalism and Marxist structuralism (see chapter 4) took insufficient account of human motives and their consequences.
- Synthesizing received theoretical wisdom. This involves a reading and interpretation of major theoretical contributions in order to discover commonalities and convergences between them. A relatively early example is Parsons' synthesis of Marshall, Pareto, Durkheim and Weber into a 'voluntaristic theory of action' (see chapter 2). In the contemporary period, Alexander seeks to synthesize the contributions of Marx, Durkheim, Weber and Parsons, and Habermas goes even wider to include also Mead, Schütz, Lukács, and several linguistic philosophers (see chapter 5).
- Accommodating research findings. Although accomplishing an interchange between theory and research is one of the 'parenthood' statements of sociology, the actual practice is all too rare. Two more or

less isolated examples are: the use of findings from small groups research to construct a scheme of 'functional imperatives' for society by Parsons and Bales (see chapter 4); and Goldthorpe's argument that there are seven classes, which is based on findings from social mobility research (see chapter 9).

- Hunting basic formalities. This is a reductionist strategy in which the theorist seeks to discover a simple, very formal set of axiomatic (self-evident) principles by means of which all social life can be explained. Early exponents of the strategy were Weber and Simmel, while more recent ones include Homans and Elster (see chapter 3).
- Making sense of great events. Arguably the main impetus for the origins of theory was the emergence of capitalist industrial society. The transition was so enormous that intellectuals were virtually obliged to theorize in order to make sense of the changes.

This wide range of alternative strategies suggests that sociological theory might be characterized by substantive diversity. This is indeed the case and the next section identifies the main approaches.

Approaches to sociological theory

We have said that sociological theory is only a relatively unified body of knowledge. There are in fact a number of interweaving strands or themes in its development. This section is a 'road map' which seeks to simplify the maze. It relies explicitly on a scheme developed by Alexander (see pp. 152–5 and the diagram in figure 5.6) which asks what the main pre-suppositions or assumptions of theory are. A simplified version of the scheme, redrawn for present purposes, is given in figure 1.1. The scheme makes two distinctions and intersects them to produce four types of theorizing. The first distinction relates to what the theorist believes are the elements which make up the social world, the elements of which it is constituted. The theorist can take the view either that the social world consists of the creations, interpretations, meanings, and ideas of thinking and acting subjects (subjective); or the view can be that the human condition is characterized by an immutable and common set of constraints in which there is no opportunity for choice or intention (objective). The second distinction relates to the type of explanation offered by the theorist. In the first type of explanation, the social world is 'reduced to' the characteristics of each of its individual participants, to their isolated meanings or interests (individualistic). The second type of explanation makes reference to wholes, either to collective systems of ideas or to shared material conditions (holistic). The four types of theorizing which the scheme yields are:

- *constructionism* (subjective/individualistic), which seeks to understand individual and intersubjective meanings and motives – here human

Nature of constitutive elements

		Subjective	Objective
Terms of explanation	Individualistic	Constructionism	Utilitarianism
	Holistic	Functionalism	Critical structuralism

Figure 1.1   *The types of sociological theorizing*

beings are regarded as competent and communicative agents who actively create or construct the social world;
- *utilitarianism* (objective/individualistic), which seeks to explain behaviour on the basis of an explicit calculus of individual interests and the means to realize them – here human beings are regarded as calculating and maximizing, always seeking advantages at the expense of others;
- *functionalism* (holistic/subjective), which examines social arrangements in terms of their contribution to the meeting of imperatives specified by an overarching shared normative system – here human beings are regarded as religious and cultural conformists who cannot survive without social and moral support; and
- *critical structuralism* (holistic/objective), which traces the development through time of underlying, material structures and their effects on individuals, societies and cultures – here human beings are regarded as the victims of their socioeconomic and historical location which manipulates and twists them into distortions of their true selves.

Three developmental phases can be specified for each of these traditions: a classical phase in which the basic topics of interest are identified; a modern phase in which each theoretical position is elaborated and developed; and a contemporary or postmodern phase in which the tradition is subjected to a combination of revision and pastiche. The skeleton of these developments is set out in figure 1.2. The figure also identifies some cognate disciplines which are similar to each of the four types of sociological theorizing and which should further assist in recognizing the differences between them.

These four types of theorizing represent sociological traditions which are being reformulated in the contemporary period but which connect back to classical antecedents in the work of Marx, Weber, Durkheim and others. These developments can now be sketched and the leading practitioners identified. Towards the end of the section we can also trace developments in feminist theory which developed separately from sociological theory but now has a pronounced influence upon it.

Core proposal	Theory type	Classical	Modern	Contemporary	Cognate disciplines (similar methodology and pattern of explanation)
Agency	Constructionism	Weber	Symbolic interactionism	Structuration theory	Cultural anthropology
		Simmel	Phenomenology/ ethnomethodology		History
System	Functionalism	Spencer	Structural-functionalism	Neofunctionalism	Darwinian biology
		Durkheim			Ecology
Rationality	Utilitarianism	Marshall	Exchange theory	Rational choice	Neoclassical economics
		Pareto		Public choice	Behavioural psychology
Structure	Critical structuralism	Marx	Critical theory	Communicationism	Structuralist linguistics Political economy Cultural studies
		Engels	Structuralist Marxism	Poststructuralism	Psychoanalytic psychology

Figure 1.2 *Development and types of sociological theory*

Constructionism

The constructionist strand in sociological theorizing can be traced to the late-nineteenth-century and early-twentieth-century German theorists, Georg Simmel and Max Weber. They offer broadly similar arguments which draw on distinctions made in German philosophy between the natural and the cultural sciences. They insist that human behaviour is fundamentally different from the behaviour of natural objects. Human beings are always agents in the active construction of social reality – the way they act depends on the way in which they understand or give meaning to their behaviour. So sociological observers must interpret, that is give meanings to, the meanings established by participants.

Simmel influenced early-twentieth-century American sociological thought, most particularly a constructionist tradition developed at the University of Chicago by George Herbert Mead. The school of thought originated by Mead, called symbolic interactionism, is a social psychology which argues that relationships between actors are established in patterns of linguistic communication. Communication is the medium by which society gets inside each actor and is thus why understandings come to be shared and society emerges.

Weber's influence was felt more effectively in mid-century European sociology, particularly in the work of Alfred Schütz. Schütz read Weber from the viewpoint of the European philosophical tradition of phenomenology, which is associated with Bergson and Husserl, to establish a *phenomenological sociology*. Phenomenological sociology concentrates on the ways in which actors interpret the social world by turning sense-data into typifications or mental pictures. Schütz examines the ways in which individual typifications can be linked intersubjectively and the connections between a sociologist's typifications and actors' typifications.

A radicalized American version of phenomenology, which developed in the 1970s, is *ethnomethodology* which argues that it is impossible to typify the social world in a scientific way and that therefore it must be interpreted by sociologists in exactly the same way that actors do it.

A second set of constructionist arguments seeks to move out from individual motives and reasons to examine large structures. Some examples slide towards other perspectival streams – the work of Parsons became the main example of functionalism, and Habermas has managed to remain in the critical-structuralist camp. However there is one example which remains close to its origins. In the contemporary or postmodern period this main contribution is the *structuration theory* produced by the British sociologist Anthony Giddens. Structuration theory tries to show that there is a connection between interpretive action and the emergence of stable, large-scale social systems. For Giddens these are the unintentional consequence of the ways in which actors' draw on established ways of doing things in order to realize their personal objectives.

Functionalism

Functionalism originated with Herbert Spencer, the nineteenth-century English social theorist, who first proposed that society was much like a biological organism. It had evolved to the point at which each of its component 'organs' was making a positive contribution to the survival and maintenance of society. However, the critical and most influential founding functionalist is Émile Durkheim, a French theorist, who re-analysed Spencer's argument. Durkheim's key thesis is that the parts of society are integrated by a shared consciousness, a *conscience collective*. Social action can be explained by the contribution it makes to this shared consciousness which is religious or moral in character.

The major mid-twentieth-century development of functionalism is *structural-functionalism*, which emerged from a reading by Talcott Parsons, an American, of the works of Weber, Durkheim, Marshall and Pareto. Parsons originally argued, in a constructionist way, that these converged on a theory of social action which he termed 'voluntarism' – here there was a common set of shared norms, as in Durkheim, but actors could choose between them, as in Weber. However, he progressively moved more and more towards Durkheim's position, arguing that society needs the functional contributions of certain types of structure if it is to continue as a system. He further argues that the direction in which the structure changes is determined by the contents of culture, a common normative system.

After Parsons died, in 1979, structural-functionalism disappeared under the weight of an overwhelming positivistic criticism which denied the utility of the scheme in empirical research. However, this approach has experienced something of a revival in the late 1980s under the influence of the American theorist Jeffrey Alexander, whose rereading is known as *neofunctionalism*. Neofunctionalism makes a play for a multidimensional social theory, which would encompass all of the strands of theorizing discussed in the present summary. It also claims that Parsons came closest to producing such a multidimensional theory.

Utilitarianism

The foundations of utilitarian sociological thought are to be found in the nineteenth-century British classical economics of Alfred Marshall. Marshall explained human activities in relation to 'wants', personal desires or objectives, and introduced the key concept of utility to indicate the relative values of social objects which an actor might pursue. A more sociological foundation is to be found in the theories of his contemporary, the Italian political economist Vilfredo Pareto, who first specified the problem of whether collective arrangements could emerge from the pursuit of individual gratification.

The specifically sociological development of these ideas can be found in *exchange theory* which is associated with George Caspar Homans, the mid-twentieth-century American historian and social psychologist. Homans sought to establish that stable, institutionalized relationships could emerge from interactions between actors seeking to realize their goals. He was able to establish successfully that want-satisfaction could not take place in isolation from other actors.

More recent developments concentrate on the problem identified by Pareto and these are known as *rational choice theory*. There are two variants. *Game-theoretic Marxism*, as argued by Jon Elster and John Roemer, focuses on whether individual members of the working class can ever see it to be in their interests to engage in revolution. *Public choice theory* focuses on the question of how the state can emerge from individual interests and how state actors will act to maximize their interests when it does. They are linked by the common problem of how rational individuals can be persuaded to engage in the pursuit of collective enterprises which may involve individual costs.

Critical structuralism

There are two, related, sociological strands in the theory of the nineteenth-century German political economist Karl Marx and his collaborator

Friedrich Engels. The first is that the history of human societies is the history of its underlying structure of material relationships. The second is that human beings are fundamentally expressive and creative but this true nature is suppressed by the weight of material history. Material history remoulds both general ideas and the individual consciousness.

The first strand is most highly developed in the mid-twentieth-century French *structuralist Marxism* of Louis Althusser and Nicos Poulantzas. Structuralist Marxism proposes that historical transformations are the product of a coalescence of contradictions in the structures of the economic base, the state, and ideology. In this argument the individual actor is viewed as a puppet dangling on the strings of history without autonomy or volition. The second strand has a longer history which can be subsumed under the label critical theory and which includes Weberian as well as Marxist themes. The focus here, in the work of the Italian and Hungarian Marxists Antonio Gramsci and György Lukács, and the Frankfurt School of Social Research, all of which developed in the inter-world-war period, is on the ways in which ideologies are constructed, the ways in which they can dominate the consciousness, and the ways in which they can be resisted.

In the contemporary period structuralist Marxism has virtually been eclipsed. It has been displaced by a radical *poststructuralism*, originating in France, and associated in sociology with the work of Michel Foucault, but made most explicit in the literary theory of Jacques Derrida. Post-structuralism in effect reproduces constructionism but in a radical and critical direction. Meanwhile the critical theory tradition itself has reached a highly developed stage in what might be called the *communicationism* of the German social philosopher, Jürgen Habermas. Habermas tries to link together the arguments of Marx, Weber, Mead, Schütz and Parsons to suggest that the social arenas of intersubjectivity and interpretation are being colonized and repressed by the arenas of commercialism and bureaucracy.

Feminism

Although feminist theory has developed independently of the mainstream of sociological theory, it too has passed through a series of phases (discussed in detail in chapter 8). In broad terms they are as follows. The first phase of feminism was associated with the first wave of the women's movement which sought female suffrage and participation in the labour force. It can be called *liberal feminism* because it concentrates on issues to do with equality of opportunity. The second and modern phase of feminism concentrates on the concept of patriarchy, taking the view that society is entirely suffused by gender-structured power relations. This is a *socialist feminism*, and often a Marxist feminism, because it argues that society must be entirely reconstructed if gender equality is to be accomplished. An emerging paradigm in the contemporary phase is a *radical feminism* which accepts that gender differences are structural and intractable. It argues for either a reconstruction of gender in terms of either physiology or psychology or sexual preferences or for a withdrawal by women from associations with men. Representatives from each of these traditions can be encountered in chapter 6.

The main concepts

Sociology is a broad church. Not only is there diversity in sociological theory but also in the possible ways in which one can categorize theoretical orientations. Some surveys of theory are organized historically while others identify theoretical 'schools' or traditions. This book takes the unusual approach of seeking to identify the main conceptual topics of sociological theory and assessing what can be said about them. The first four of these topics are identified as foundational within each of the four theoretical approaches identified above. They are 'agency' (constructionism), 'rationality' (utilitarianism), 'system' (functionalism) and 'structure' (critical structuralism). However, none of these conceptual topics is the exclusive property of the approach for which it is the foundation. Therefore within each of the chapters which deal with them we consider a range of theoretical analyses. For example, the chapter on agency reviews the theories not only of Mead, Schütz and Giddens but also the functionalist view of agency offered by Parsons and the critical theoretical view of Habermas.

The substance of each of these four topics is as follows:

Agency

This topic lies within the arena of human subjectivity. It concerns what happens in the consciousness when an individual undertakes to act in the social world. It includes the meanings that subjects give to their behaviour and their reasons or motives for acting. The topic of agency also extends to the ways in which meanings are communicated within interaction and to the ways in which stable intersubjective social worlds are thus established. The chapter on agency concentrates on the work of sociologists who argue the need to interpret meanings and motives in the way that subjects do themselves. Here society is viewed as a human construction which constantly shifts and changes with the subject's perceptions and motivational inputs. It also examines arguments which seek to show how collective arrangements can emerge from individual agency.

Rationality

An exclusive focus on agency presents the methodological problem of reliably getting into the mind of the subject. Some theorists have argued

that this can only be done in the limited sector of action which we call
rational, that is, with respect to behaviour which is specifically directed to
the accomplishment of a conscious objective. In this chapter we examine
these limited theories as well as others which make the assumption that all
behaviour is governed by rationality. These assume that all behaviour is
goal-directed and constructed on the basis of calculating self-interest. A
particular problem which faces all arguments about rationality is that of
explaining behaviour which provides gains only at the level of the
collectivity and costs to the individual.

Structure

The topic of structure is possibly the least graspable of the ones on view
here. Structure refers to patterns in social arrangements which underlie the
immediacy of experience. For some sociologists structure is an analytic
abstraction from subjective experience. However, the theorists who have
most to say about structure are those who argue that it has an ontological
status which privileges it over agency. In these formulations, structure
determines the content of conscious experience so that the subject and its
agency disappears. Such structures are variously argued to be located in
the unconscious mind, in material relationships, or in the symbolic
relationships of myth or language.

System

Many sociological theorists are impressed by the fact that collective social
arrangements appear to have a logic and direction which appears to be
independent of the subjective intentions of participants. These social
arrangements take the form of integrated wholes which receive the
description of system. Theorists interested in systems examine the ways in
which the parts of a system fit together in such a way that each part appears
to contribute to the maintenance of the whole and therefore cannot be
analysed separately.

The second set of four conceptual topics is probably much more controversial. This is because they are substantive rather than formal and there is
much more argument about the central substantive topics of sociology. The
four are: 'culture and ideology', 'power and the state', 'gender and
feminism', and 'differentiation and stratification'. They are included on the
basis that they are: general – they are an aspect of every element of social
life; pervasive – they must be accounted for in any theory which claims to
be complete; controversial – they are the focus of current debates; and
central – they are pivotal in analysing any substantive arena of social life.
On these criteria they win out against several other candidates, including
race, ethnicity, deviance and religion. Religion and deviance are subordinate to other topics covered – religion is considered under culture and

system, and deviance, to an extent, under agency. Sociological theories of race and ethnicity are simply underdeveloped and insufficiently influential.

Culture and ideology

Here we concentrate on culture as a collective phenomenon. Culture consists of generally shared visions of meaning, value and preference. The specific focus of the chapter is on the segment of culture which consists of idea systems and is often called 'ideology'. The chapter examines the origins of the concept of ideology and, in particular, theoretical arguments which stand opposed to constructionism. These propose that culture must be understood as determined by social relationships which are suffused by materialism and power. In these arguments then, material relationships determine cultural ideas which in turn enter the consciousness of individuals. Ultimately this means that individuals will conform to material forces, even where these forces are exploitative. So in the most extreme ideological arguments, both agency and rationality are 'explained away'.

Power and the state

Theories of ideology, then, offer an argument that individual interests and objectives can be confounded by effective ideas. Some of the positions in the debate which surrounds this argument can also be subsumed under the conceptual heading of 'power'. If people act against their own individual wants or interests it must be because they are constrained to do so. These constraints can variously be understood: as intentionally constructed and put into effect by other individuals (constructionist or utilitarian); as the result of a set of very abstracted agreements about how a society should be coordinated (functionalist); or as the outcome of deep-seated and largely unrecognized realities (critical structuralist).

Gender and feminism

For much of the history of the development of sociological theory gender remained unspecified. Although it is now recognized to be a necessary and important topic for theory it remains unintegrated relative to other topics. Sociologists are simply not very successful, for example, in connecting arguments about gender with arguments about class differentiation or arguments about agency. Most of these other accounts are written as if gender is unimportant. This is partly because the theories of gender which are available tend to originate in the feminist movement rather than within academic sociology. The key foci for such theories are accounts of gender differences and accounts of gender inequality and oppression. The general tendency of sociological theory has been to despecify gender as an inevitable and natural concomitant of sex and to view it as a social construction, although there are some recent developments which seek to reverse this trend.

Differentiation and stratification

This topic refers to the ways in which the social world divides into parts or elements which are kept separate from one another by boundaries. There are two main processes by which this division occurs. It occurs on the basis of the performance of different activities on the part of each of the units which make up society. This is called functional or structural differentiation. It also occurs on the basis of domination or ranking by one or more units over one or more others. There are several dimensions on which this stratification process can occur but the form which receives the most theoretical attention is the division of society into classes.

It bears restating that this book is organized not in terms of schools of thought but in terms of the main conceptual topics or themes of sociological theory. However some chapters reflect a tracing of a theme through a main tradition. For example, the chapter on system has an extensive coverage of functionalist sociology tracing the development of the term system from Durkheim, through Parsons and Alexander, but ending with Habermas. Other chapters are more eclectic, taking elements from traditions across the theoretical spectrum. The chapters on culture, power, gender and differentiation take this form. However, we begin with a chapter which is unified to a relative degree around the interpretivist tradition on the topic of agency.

Notes

1 The otherwise excellent *Penguin Dictionary of Sociology* offers no entry for the word 'theory'.

2 For examples, see the sections of this book on Althusser (chapter 4), Giddens (chapters 2 and 4), and Parsons (chapters 2, 4 and 5).

3 For an analysis and critique of foundationalism in sociology see Crook (1991).

4 Positivism is a philosophy of science which insists that the only reality is that which can be observed. It underlies the empiricism which dominates contemporary American sociology.

2 Agency: meaning and motives in social arrangements

If you ask someone why they do something, why they engage in a particular piece of social behaviour, they will usually answer by giving you a reason. So a politician runs for office because she wants to serve the public; a man marries because he is in love; a student puts in extra work in order to achieve a better grade or mark. These reasons capture the idea of agency, the idea that people set goals for themselves and act in relation to these goals in an intentional way. In acting in relation to goals they give meaning to their behaviour. Their behaviour makes sense to them and, when they give explicit reasons or accounts, their behaviour can also make sense to other people.

All this is largely an uncontroversial matter. People in everyday life routinely operate this way and just about all sociologists, as well as historians, political scientists and others, accept that people do. Moreover, in everyday life, as well as in much history and political science, the accounts or reasons which people give for their behaviour are accepted as absolutely valid explanations for that behaviour, assuming the person not to be lying. However, for sociologists (as well as many economists and others) this issue is entirely problematic. While most sociologists accept that subjective meanings may well be a fact, the reasons or accounts which people give for their behaviour are only interesting to some sociological theorists. Within this group, a much smaller group of sociologists regards reasons or accounts as valid and necessary components of theory.

The process of acting in relation to a set of meanings, reasons or intentions is known as agency. A stress on agency implies that individuals are not the products or even the victims of the social world but rather that they are thinking, feeling and acting subjects who create the world around them. They may do this either intentionally and unintentionally but they do it above all by giving meaning to their own behaviour and to the behaviour of others. Large-scale social arrangements are seen as emerging out of complex processes of interaction in which meanings are negotiated, contested, and at least to some extent, shared. So the institutions of the social world are not just givens but human accomplishments.

A more formal statement of agency is given by Giddens whose own theory is dealt with in detail towards the end of this chapter. He defines agency as: 'the stream of actual or contemplated causal interventions of corporeal beings in the ongoing process of events-in-the-world' (1976: 75, italics deleted). Agency, he says, involves a stress on the practical activities of human beings in intentionally constructing their social world. However, it also involves the notion that individuals make choices about the 'interventions' in which they engage and thus that the future of the social world is indeterminate. He stresses (1976: 77) that while one would certainly wish to examine purpose and intention, such purposes may not necessarily be realized and indeed that interventions have many consequences which are unintended.

In summary, the primary characteristics of theories of human agency are the following:

1   They treat human beings as intelligent and creative subjects who are, above all, in control of the conditions which affect their social lives.
2   Human beings endow behaviour with meaning. It is a significant task of sociology to penetrate and understand such meanings. Sociology must therefore be a 'hermeneutic' discipline which investigates 'action'.
3   Human action is motivated – meaning is given to it in terms of the way in which the individual mentally projects action through time in order to achieve goals. These motives are accessible to the sociologist by means of verbalized accounts or reasons for behaviour.
4   The substance of the social world is human interaction, a constant process of intersubjective negotiation of meanings by the use of words, gestures and other symbols.
5   Regular patterns emerge within human interaction so that not all aspects of meaning have to be constantly renegotiated. These emergent patterns constitute the taken-for-granted, large-scale arrangements of social life.
6   Nevertheless, the stress in theories of agency is on giving descriptions and explanations of immediate and everyday social experience, often from the point of view of specific individuals or types of individual, rather than on theorizing enduring, large-scale structural arrangements.

This chapter focuses on theories which emphasize all or most of these principles. The first section examines briefly the founding arguments of Weber, who stresses the interpretation of meaning, and Simmel, who stresses the analysis of the formal properties of interaction. Simmelian sociology is then traced through the symbolic interactionist tradition which emerged in the USA in the first half of the twentieth century. Weberian hermeneutic sociology finds its modern expression in a phenomenological philosophy of social science proposed by Schütz which, in turn, provides a departure for a fully-fledged, antiscientific analysis of meanings known as ethnomethodology. Each of these modern developments constitutes a radical form of agency theory in which large-scale social arrangements (e.g. social structures) are bracketed as having no force. However, Weber's understandings of agency in particular can be developed as an explanation for the existence of social structures. Such expanded statements of agency are traced through the work of three theorists, Parsons, Habermas and Giddens.

Founding arguments

Sociological arguments about agency have their origins in an intellectual debate which emerged in late-nineteenth-century German intellectual life. The vigorous materialist arguments of Marx (see chapter 4) had challenged an idealist tradition established by the great philosopher Hegel, which argued that each period of history needed to be understood as being guided by its own unique and essential spirit or set of ideas. The historiography of the period argued that it was this analysis of the prevailing spirit of the times which distinguished the human sciences from the natural sciences. Here we cover the work of two great thinkers who find each of these positions to be unsatisfactory because each in its way denies human freedom and creativity. Weber and Simmel seek to interpose themselves between materialism and idealism and to establish that society emerges neither from spirits not economic structures but rather from human intentions.

Weber: it all means something to someone

The major classical source for theoretical statements of agency is Weber's analysis of social action and his elaboration of the methods by which human action can be analysed and understood (1978: 4–22). Weber begins with three key definitions which are linked together. First he defines sociology as: 'a science concerning itself with the interpretive understanding of social action and thereby with a causal explanation of its course and consequences' (1978: 4). Here he is proposing an interpretive sociology, one which seeks to *understand* meanings. Note the central formulation which makes theories of agency different from other sociological theories – the argument that the causes of an event can be discovered in the meanings attributed to it by participants.

Another critical feature is that the subject matter of sociology is argued to be *social* action – agency theories are frequently described as theories of social action. Action occurs wherever: 'the acting individual attaches a subjective meaning to his behavior' (1978: 4). Thus the subject matter of sociology is defined by the agent. Further: 'Action is "social" in so far as its subjective meaning takes account of the behavior of others and is thereby oriented in its course' (1978: 4). So, the issue of whether action is social or not is established in the mind of the actor rather than by the observer – action does not have to be directed towards other people in order to be social, and can in fact be quite solitary, it merely has to take the actions of others into account.

Max Weber (1864–1920)

Weber is widely regarded as a founding figure, often as *the* founding figure, of sociology. He set an agenda for the discipline in a wide-ranging series of studies of religion, economics, political relations, law and methodology. Surprisingly, the only major work he published during his lifetime was *The Protestant Ethic and the Spirit of Capitalism* in 1905. His essays and other writings were collectively published posthumously, in 1922, as *Wirtschaft und Gesellschaft* (Economy and Society). His writings reflect the personal commitments of his merchant-turned-bureaucrat-turned-politician father and his ascetically religious mother. Paradoxically, the best of his writings appeared after a major psychological breakdown which occurred in 1897, that was coincident with his father's death, and that led to continuous mental disturbance. The writings constitute a lifelong debate with Hegelian idealism on one hand and Marxist materialism on the other. Weber was an establishment academic, holding professorships at the Universities of Freiburg, Heidelberg and Munich. He represented Germany at the peace negotiations at Versailles in 1918 and took a hand in the drafting of the 'Weimar Constitution' which established a democratic republic in Germany after the First World War.

Sources: *Penguin Dictionary of Sociology* (1984: *s.v.* Weber, Max); Beilharz (1991: 224–30); Ritzer (1992: 112–13)

Meaning clearly takes a central place in this analysis and Weber embarks on an extensive treatment of it. He begins by saying that there are two kinds of meaning which sociologists may explore: the meaning which actors actually give within their lived experience; and the typical meaning which an observer may ascribe to hypothetical types of actor. Under the latter regime one can explore typical meanings for, say, mail deliverers as they place letters in boxes, and one can do this without refering to any particular individual person.

The meanings attached to a given piece of action are most intelligible to the sociologist, and their intepretation is most certain, when action is at its most rational. Rational action occurs when a person is trying to achieve certain ends by selecting appropriate means for their realization according to the facts of a situation (1978: 5). Sociologists will have difficulty in interpreting irrational or emotional action, so Weber recommends the construction of a hypothetical rational course of action and then the comparison of the actual action with this construction.

In making this distinction between rational and other kinds of action Weber formalizes a scheme of the possible types of social action which may occur. The scheme identifies four types of social action:

- Instrumentally rational action (*Zweckrationalität*): action that is the means by which individuals can attain calculated, short-term, self-interested goals. An example of such action might be speculative investment in the stock market, or the persuit of members of the opposite sex for purposes of sexual gratification alone.

*   Value-rational action (*Wertrationalität*): action determined by a conscious belief and commitment to a higher order value such as truth, beauty or justice, or a belief in God. Weber recognizes that action of this type is relatively rare. However, examples might include accepting work as a teacher at a low salary because one believes in the value of education, or making a donation to charity.
*   Affectual action: action determined by feelings, passions, psychological needs, or emotional states. Examples include acts of physical aggression, sexual acts, and temper tantrums.
*   Traditional action: action which is habituated so that it is performed because it has always been performed in a particular way. The utterance of a particular set of words at a marriage ceremony or the act of driving on a particular side of the road might be examples. The great majority of human behaviour falls into this category of habituated action.

Not all of these types of action are equally susceptible to interpretive understanding. It will be remembered that Weber's definition of sociology involves the 'interpretive understanding' (*Verstehen*) of human action. There are two possible ways of accomplishing such understanding. The first is 'direct observational understanding' (*aktuelles Verstehen*). This is the kind of immediate understanding which is normally experienced in everyday life when we know instantly what a person is doing although we may not know why they are doing it. For example, we know what a mail deliverer is doing when placing papers in a mailbox.

However, this is only a limited form of understanding. An adequate sociology must seek explanatory understanding (*erklärendes Verstehen*) in which the actor's motive is revealed: 'A motive is a complex of subjective meaning which seems to the actor himself or to the observer an adequate ground for the conduct in question' (1978: 11). Both traditional action and affectual action stand at the margin of action which can be regarded as meaningfully oriented. They can only be subjected to direct understanding and not to explanatory understanding. Because value-rational action is rare, the chief focus of interest for the sociologist must therefore lie with instrumentally rational action.

The rational understanding of motive is achieved where the sociologist is able to locate the action in an intelligible and wider context of meaning. So we would normally understand the mail deliverer's motivation in terms of the payment of wages and possibilities for human subsistence in an industrial society. The difficulty is, and Weber was quick to recognize this, that we might not be correct – the mail deliverer could conceivably be a person of independent means who enjoys outdoor exercise, wants to do something useful, and donates all income received to charity. Wherever possible, the sociologist's interpretation needs to be verified by comparison with the actual course of events – in the extended example used here this might involve following a number of mail deliverers around and watching what they did with their wages. Clearly, and as Weber admits, this is possible in only the rarest of circumstances. Instead sociologists must rely, if possible, on comparing a very large number of social processes, both historical and contemporary. Failing this they must fall back on the unreliable assurances of the mental experiment.

It is at this point that Weber distinguishes between the criteria for meaning adequacy and causal adequacy. The establishment of motive is adequate to the establishment of the meaning adequacy of a theory of a social process. Meaning adequacy is established when the relationship between the component elements of a course of conduct are recognized as a 'typical' complex of meaning according to the way in which we usually think and act. Causal adequacy, by contrast, is established when the relationships between the elements of a course of conduct can be shown to occur frequently or, preferably, invariably. A correct causal interpretation (note the conjunction of the two words) occurs when both criteria have been met, that is when a relationship between statistically regular overt actions and the motives which lie behind them have been established.

Within all this Weber claims the establishment of a peculiar sociological methodology which is distinct from the way in which meaning is observed and established in everyday life. In everyday life one engages in the direct understanding of the actual meaning of all types of social action which needs only to be adequate in practical terms; but in sociology one engages in an explanatory understanding of the motives for rational action which must be both causally and meaningfully adequate. In this he sets himself against his contemporary Simmel whom he accuses of failing to draw a distinction between subjectively intended and objectively valid meanings (1978: 4). As we shall see, Simmel does rather take meanings for granted but nevertheless manages to make an important contribution to theories of agency by stressing the importance of interaction.

Simmel: impressionistic theory

For Simmel social processes are fundamentally psychological processes. The precondition for the existence of society is consciousness on the part of individuals that they are tied to other individuals. In a passage reminiscent of Weber, Simmel claims that: 'what palpably exists is indeed only individual human beings and their situations and activities: therefore the task can only be to understand them, whereas the essence of society, that emerges purely through an ideal synthesis and is never to be grasped, should not form the object of reflection directed toward the investigation of reality' (Simmel in Frisby 1981: 40). The reality of social processes, what Simmel calls 'sociation', is located in the mind, so that society is a unity of cognition, a product of the fact that each individual is party to a common set of knowledge. Simmel (1959a: 342–56) gives three sets of grounds for this proposal:

- Our knowledge of the psychological disposition of other people is inevitably incomplete. So we are obliged to think about others in terms of an abstracted set of common characteristics. We must assume that all teachers or all bureaucrats, for example, are similar in specific ways. Further we must assume that all individuals are related to each other in typical ways. So, every individual conceives of society as unified.
- The individual not only thinks of others as typical but is treated by others in similar terms. In certain circumstances such perceptions reach the level of pure objectivity as in the case of monetarized capitalist culture in which, apart from those in the leading positions, individuals are reduced to objective and anonymous producers and consumers.
- There is a harmony between the individual's capacities and the place occupied in society. Social inequality is therefore a reflection of natural individual differences.[1]

Georg Simmel (1858–1918)

Born in Berlin, Germany, Simmel was by religion a Christian but by ethnicity a Sephardic Jew. The latter serves to explain why, despite enjoying a considerable intellectual reputation, he was ascribed only a marginal academic career. Most of his posts were either honorary or dependent on 'soft' money. He eventually took up a Chair of Philosophy at the University of Strasbourg in German Alsace in 1914, but that too was in an academic wilderness. Simmel's status as a sociologist has always been controversial, partly because it was only in the middle part of his career that he explicitly claimed to be writing sociology. He is otherwise known as a philosopher or psychologist. His best-known books of the middle period are *The Philosophy of Money* and *Sociology*. He is the founder of a 'formal sociology' in which the objective is to taxonomize the various possible forms of social life rather than to analyse substantive instances.

Sources: *Penguin Dictionary of Sociology* (1984: *s.v.* Simmel, Georg); Beilharz (1991: 202–8); Ritzer (1992: 158–9).

Here, then, Simmel gives grounds for the idea that the origins of society lie in the minds of its participants from which it grows like a field of wheat. Let us now consider the processes by which this emergence occurs. If society is contained in the minds of individuals it cannot be an external objective unity but can only be an aggregate of the parts which make it up.

These parts are the actions of individuals which themselves comprise two inseparable elements: a content, that is, 'an interest, a purpose or a motive'; and 'a form or mode of interaction among individuals through which, or in the shape of which, that content attains social reality' (1959b: 315). The motivations which propel life (e.g. hunger, love, religiosity, technology, intelligence) are not strictly social until they operate to transform isolated individuals into interactive relationships.

Simmel insists that sociology should concentrate on these forms of interaction, which might be defined as the repeated and universal patterns of behaviour through which various contents are expressed. Although Simmelian sociology is therefore often described as 'formal sociology' he does not provide the systematic classification of social forms which one might expect. Indeed his sociology is frequently described as fragmentary or impressionistic or even a series of snapshots (e.g. Frisby 1981) which while rich in insights is short on programmatic organization. However, Levine (1959) gives an indication of the implicit classification of social forms, which Simmel might have proposed, as follows:

- forms of interactive process, e.g. imitation and differentiation within social processes of fashion;
- social types, e.g. aristocracy;
- developmental patterns, e.g. the relationship between group size and the development of individuality.

There is no doubt that between Weber and Simmel, Weber has been more influential in the development of sociological theory. This is because Weber is willing to address typical complexes of meaning in such large-scale human constructions as bureaucracy and capitalism, for example. He does not, as Simmel does, insist on the reduction of such structures to the psychological processes of the individual actors involved. The structures can be analyzed independently of an analysis of actors. This means that Weber has influenced not only agency theories but theories which seek to treat social structures as independent realities. Simmel's influence, on the other hand, has been slight, fleeting and indirect. It nevertheless has considerable importance in underpinning those social psychological theories which focus resolutely and exclusively on agency. One of these, symbolic interactionism, was a dominant theoretical orientation in American sociology during the first half of the twentieth century and we now move on to address it.

Symbolic interactionism: the self-made society

Simmel's influence was carried into American sociology through Park, who was one of his students. Park founded what has become known as the Chicago school of urban sociology which followed many of Simmel's views of the city as an anonymous and threatening social environment by undertaking studies of its disorganizing social effects. These studies were essentially descriptive accounts of particular forms of interaction, including insightful but unvalidated reports of meaning-endowment by participants. They included studies of juvenile gangs, poverty, vice, and the experiences of new migrants. Few, if any, would have met Weber's criterion of causal adequacy. More importantly, while at the University of Chicago, Park came into contact with the psychologist Mead and doubtless introduced Simmel's work to him (see Rock 1979: 44–58). Mead's interpretation of Simmel was to become the central foundation for a theoretical tradition which came to be called symbolic interactionism. This is the view that society is constituted by an exchange of gestures and language (symbols) which stand for mental processes.

Mead: common-sensing

Mead's spectacular insight is that the critical differentiating factor between human societies and the societies of (other) animals is language. Animals are able to have conversations by means of gestures which act as direct stimuli but this does not constitute communication. Rather the behaviour of, say, a male ape beating his chest is a signal that he is about to act aggressively. Another ape may back off from his territory in response to the stimulus but does not understand or interpret the behaviour by ascribing meaning or motive to it.

Mead, then, indicates a subsequent intermediate stage in linguistic development in which utterances take on a gestural status. So, signal words, which are phonetically and semantically differentiated begin to be used as human society emerges. Such signals as 'help' or 'back off' still survive in human language and become most apparent within what Weber calls affectual action, behaviour with a high emotional content. But Mead still does not wish to describe this signal language as communication.

George Herbert Mead (1863–1931)

Mead was born to a Protestant Minister's family in Massachusetts, USA. He studied at Harvard and also at Leipzig and Berlin, where he came under the influence of the psychologist Wilhelm Wundt. Although he never took a postgraduate degree, he taught social psychology at the University of Chicago from 1892 onward. In a life of little formal accomplishment Mead never published a book. Nevertheless he was hugely influential and his lectures were collected and published posthumously. He is the founding figure in the social psychologistic branch of sociology called symbolic interactionism.

Sources: *Penguin Dictionary of Sociology* (1984: *s.v.* Mead, G.H.); Coser (1977: 333–55); Ritzer (1992: 332)

Communication only genuinely occurs where each of the parties not only gives meaning to their own behaviour but understands or seeks to understand the meaning the other gives. Each person places themself in the place or position of the other person. Such sharing of meaning can only be accomplished where language develops to the point of propositional or syntactic differentiation (Habermas 1987: 5) and thus becomes truly symbolic in character. It becomes the abstracted reference to a shared complex of meaning. So marriage guidance counsellors, for example, seek to encourage spouses to move beyond emotional gesture and to seek to give each other reasons for their own behaviour and statements about why they understand the other's spouse to be behaving as they do – the counsellor seeks to bring about correspondence between self-understanding and the other's understanding of oneself.

Habermas (1987: 11–12) identifies two functional tendencies in this argument about language and communication and its relationship to human development. First, it offers the clear advantage that human beings can pause, reflect on and work out the consequences of a particular course of action by imagining themselves in the mind of the other without having actually to take the other's place. So they can orient their behaviour to the most positive set of of consequences. Second, the fact that people are engaged in complex interactions of meaning with others puts pressure on them to adapt rapidly to the expectations of others. Human society thus develops as a communication community.

This perspective on human society which emphasizes the importance of language in establishing mutual understanding is summarized by Blumer (1969: 2) in a famous statement of three premises of symbolic inter-actionism:

- human beings act toward things on the basis of the meaning which things have for them (by 'things' he means physical objects, other people, social institutions, and abstract ideals or values);
- the meaning of such things is derived from, or arises out of, the social interaction that one has with one's fellows; and
- these meanings are handled in, and modified through, an interpretive process used by the person in dealing with the things he encounters.

A more complete and developed summary of symbolic interactionism is offered by Meltzer et al.:

> The influence that stimuli have on human behavior is shaped by the context of symbolic meanings within which human behavior occurs. These meanings emerge from the shared interaction of individuals in human society. Society itself is constructed out of the behavior of humans, who actively play a role in developing the social limits that will be placed upon their behavior. Thus, human behavior is not a unilinear unfolding towards a predetermined end, but an active

constructing process whereby humans endeavor to 'make sense' of their social and physical environments. This 'making sense' process is internalized in the form of thought: for thinking is the intra-individual problem-solving process that is also characteristic of inter-individual interaction. In thinking, then, there occurs an interaction with oneself. . . . [A]ny complete understanding of human behavior must include an awareness of this covert dimension of activity, not simply the observation of overt behavior. [1975: vii]

Mead on socialization: playing the game

So what sets symbolic interactionism apart from structuralist sociologies is the notion that human beings are creative agents, and what sets it apart from behaviouristic social sciences is its stress on mental processes. Because these internal or psychological processes are held to be critical, we now turn to an examination of Mead's analysis of them (1934: 164–226).

The central concept in Mead's symbolic interactionism is the self. As Rock (1979: 102) indicates the self is virtually held to be the only 'real' sociological object, all others being epiphenomenal. The self is structured by language. Human beings use both the terms 'I' and 'me' to describe the self and these represent two of its phases or moments. The 'I' is the thinking and acting subject, the creator and initiator, literally, the ego. The 'me' is the objective self, the self upon which the 'I' reflects, it is the self thought of in other situations and in other times and places, both real and imagined. Most importantly it is the aspect of self which is an expression of the gaze of others upon it – in Cooley's terms it is the 'looking-glass self'. So society flows into the individual via the 'me' and is simultaneously constructed and reconstructed by the 'I'. In an important sense the interaction which symbolic interactionists discuss is an internal conversation between the 'I' and the 'me' in which the expectations of society are reconciled with individual demands and expressions. Above all this is a conscious psychological process.

We can now turn to Mead's analysis of the emergence of the self (1937: 150–64). A developed and complete self is that in which one can be relatively sure that the meaning given to a symbol is about the same as that given by others – that is, a developed self is one which both contains and creates society. The first stage in the development of such a capacity can be found in the behavioural patterns of children. The earliest forms of *play* consist of unorganized imitations in which they take on different roles, those of, say, mother, driver, or police officer. In so doing they call out in themselves the responses which others call out in themselves so sociability begins to be established.

The second stage of the organized *game* is rather more complicated. Here, in a game of tea parties or football, for example, the child must be prepared to take the role of (i.e. put itself in the place of) all others in the game and indeed must know the relationship between them. So in a game of football, in order to play competently, one must simultaneously be aware of what each member of both one's own and the opposing teams are likely to do. The relationships between roles are established in rules and children spend much time and energy in negotiating rules, that is, in creatively establishing the objectivity of society.

The self reaches its most advanced stage of development when it is able to integrate the orientations of the others with which it interacts into a general set of standards of behaviour, when it takes the role of the *generalized other*. It no longer views self and society as separate but becomes an individual reflection of the society around it. It feels itself to be part of the group, and it knows how people in that situation ought to act and do act. The generalized other becomes part of an extended conversation with the 'I' and the 'me' and indeed in the most socially integrated of selves becomes coterminous with the 'me'.

Recent developments: divided communication

Symbolic interactionism of the type inspired by Mead flourished at the University of Chicago in the period up to the Second World War. However, as a nonempiricist social psychology it fared less well in the post-War period in the face of the twin threats of a scientistic behaviourist psychology and a vigorous structural-functionalist theoretical orientation in sociology. Symbolic interactionism responded by dividing into separate schools – the Chicago school led by Blumer remained true to Mead's vision of a philosophical and interpretivist social psychology, while the Iowa school led by Kuhn embraced the exacting and empiricist dictates of behaviourist psychology (see chapter 3).

Meltzer et al. (1975: 61–7) summarize the differences between the two in the following way. Blumer sees human behaviour as unpredictable and indeterminate so that individuals can be viewed as creative innovators. Blumer establishes this indeterminacy in terms of the relationship between the 'I' and the 'me' which now takes on a more Freudian flavour (see chapter 4).[2] The 'I' is emotional, impulsive and energetic, while the 'me' is the representative of society which gives direction to the 'I'. Indeterminacy arises from the impulsiveness of the 'I'. By contrast, for Kuhn, humanity takes on an 'oversocialized' character (see Wrong 1976) as the 'I' becomes subsumed by the 'me'. The self is socially determined and its behaviour thus predictable because the individual is held simply to internalize norms.

Thus Blumer views human action as a process of construction in which the individual reflects upon environmental stimuli and considers whether to act upon them in terms of their possible consequences and their relationship to various possible projects. Individuals are conceived of as making or creating the roles they perform as the consequence of tentative and exploratory processes of interpretation. Within the Iowa approach, stimuli are not interpreted and considered, they merely act as triggers which 'release' (to use Blumer's term) behaviour from pre-existing psychological structures. Individuals do not create roles but simply play them according to expectations absorbed from social structure.

Goffman: all the world's a stage

The most influential of the modern symbolic interactionists is the resolute non-theorizer,[3] Goffman (1959), who takes most of his guidance from the Chicago school of symbolic interactionism. For Goffman the individual is indeed a creative executor of roles, but to such an extended degree that the individual is held to put on special performances whenever a role is played. Social life is a theatre in which, while the parts may all look the same, there are different calibres of performance. Thus Goffman insists on a perspective which he describes as dramaturgical. Each social situation is viewed as a theatrical stage in which real-life drama is literally performed by literal actors. Upon the theatrical stage interaction takes place among three parties: the performing actor playing a role; the other characters in the play; and the audience. In real-life drama the three parties are collapsed into two – other characters are also the audience. Nevertheless, in the ordinary situations of real life, actors perform roles in such a way as to present a particular impression of themselves and must act in particular ways if that impression is to be sustained.

Erving Goffman (1922–82)

Born in Alberta, Canada, Goffman studied at Toronto and Chicago. He later held professorships at Berkeley and Pennsylvania. He is often regarded by others as a symbolic interactionist, although he tended to regard himself as an anthropologist. He is well known for his studies of everyday life and especially the everyday lives of the excluded and oppressed. His best-known books are *The Presentation of Self in Everyday Life*, *Asylums*, *Stigma*, and *Frame Analysis*.

Sources: *Penguin Dictionary of Sociology* (1984: *s.v.* Goffman, Erving); Ritzer (1992: 357)

This process of 'impression management' is central in Goffman's argument. The symbolic interactionists are particularly concerned with linguistic utterances. However, for Goffman this form of expression, the expression that a person *gives* is a much too narrow description of communication. He is rather more concerned with the expression that a person *gives off*, which includes a wide range of symptomatic action including body language, gesture, dress, display of possessions, arrangement of physical objects, location and so on. The person will use these to control the definition of the situation: so in bat and ball games (cricket or baseball) pitchers/bowlers who are not competent with the bat will, when batting, rehearse shots in order to try to convince the opposing team that they can in fact bat. In dramaturgical terminology these constitute the 'front' or front of stage, the expressive equipment which defines the situation.

There are three main components of front: the 'setting' which consists of the scenery, including furniture, decor and other 'props' (e.g. the account-ant's computer, the academic's bookshelves); appearance, which includes such fixed characteristics as age, gender and race, as well as the flexible elements of dress, and which inform about the actors status; and manner, particular signals of how the person expects to behave (e.g. an affectionate manner will indicate an expectation of intimate behaviour).

Naturally, the existence of a front stage will also imply a backstage, an area to which actors can retire to relax and regroup, and also prepare and rehearse the performances which will be required in the front. So, in English middle-class homes, if the living and dining rooms are front, the kitchen, toilet and bedroom are backstage.[4]

Goffman also discusses the way in which actors in ordinary situations will call on members of their team to support the impression that they are trying to sustain. However, his greater interest lies in actions which accidentally or intentionally discredit the actor by disrupting the perform-ance. These may include slips by the performing actor, what might be described as the 'farting in church' syndrome, but they will also include intentional disruptions accomplished by those who deny the moral recti-tude of a particular definition of the situation – the political heckler is an obvious example. Surviving such threats involves several defensive arts of impression management: dramaturgical loyalty, or 'the show must go on', which means not giving away backstage secrets between performances; dramaturgical discipline which means keeping enough psychological dis-tance from the role performed that one can control its performance and not betray the internal terrors of 'stage fright'; dramaturgical circumspection, choosing where and when to perform, and choosing one's audience, in order to achieve maximum effect; and allowing tolerant members of the audience sufficient social space to allow them tactfully to ignore indis-cretions.

The question often arises as to whether Goffman can properly be classified as a symbolic interactionist There are two sets of grounds for supposing that he should be. The first is the early influence on him of such committed symbolic interactionists as Blumer and Hughes at Chicago. The second is that the central theoretical construct in Goffman is the self, as is convincingly argued by Lofland (1980). Lofland shows that Goffman's concept of self has two components. The first is the official self, that which is located in the social situation. It is external to the person and resides in the pattern of social control which is exerted in relation to the person. This official self is constituted as a role or roles and awaits the person to be put on like a suit of clothes. There is, of course, a different suit of clothes, a different self, for each situation or encounter. The second component is the performing or role-playing or impression-managing self. This self, familiarly, is impulsive and energetic with changing moods and emotions.

The slips and disruptions described by Goffman in his dramaturgical analogy tend to reveal this underlying true and vulnerable self which if exposed will lapse into 'silent irritability' (Lofland 1980: 41). Moreover, the official and performing selves seldom fit perfectly so that social life is a matter of constant negotiation between them. The performing self strives to hold up the mask of the official self with varying degrees of success but simultaneously chafes at its constraints on creative expression.

So far then, the two aspects of self parallel those described by Mead – the official self corresponds with the 'me', indeed Goffman describes it as a '*me* ready-made' (in Lofland 1980: 40), and the performing self with 'I'. But Lofland also argues that a third notion of self is implied by Goffman's interpretation. This is a kind of spiritual or natural self which Lofland describes as the soul or, more formally, as selfhood or personal identity. This identity is asserted against the controls of all the official selves in which one engages – it is not the self which performs but the self that resists performance, the self that asserts individuality against conformity. Thus, perhaps like Marx, Goffman views human beings as repressed seekers of freedom and dignity.

A second emergent orientation to realism in Goffman's theoretical approach, argue Crook and Taylor (1980), is a shift in the direction of structuralism. The dramaturgical perspective discussed above, which is initially employed by Goffman as a metaphor or analogy, eventually develops into an organized set of frameworks which people draw upon to make sense of their experience. These frameworks impose themselves upon the individual urging or demanding that social life be experienced in particular ways and certainly limiting the range of ways in which it can be experienced. Thus rituals, play, games, and fabrications tend to repeat themselves in form and character. Goffman builds up a model of frames within frames in which each frame keys (i.e. unlocks at the level of meaning) the ones it contains in a microscopic direction, and each is transformed into a new set of meanings in a macroscopic direction. So the frame 'Waters' reading' might contain the frame 'Goffman's sociology' which in turn frames 'everyday dramaturgical rituals' which might in turn frame 'domestic social life' which itself frames 'biological reproduction'. Goffman appears to accept the notion that at the most microscopic level there are realities which cannot be contradicted, certainly the material constraints of the physical world constitute a primary frame which does not key any deeper frame and can only be transformed without unresolved contradiction.

Becker: deviant sociology

Nowhere has the influence of symbolic interactionism been more strongly felt than in the analysis of deviance. Until the 1960s the predominant sociological theory of deviance was anomie theory. Deriving from the work of Durkheim (see chapter 9) it argued that some people became deviant, while others did not, because their location in society meant that they were less exposed to its dominant norms and values and were thus free to constitute norms and values of their own. 'Society', needing to maintain itself, would then mobilize systems of social control and resocialization to bring the recalcitrants back into line. The underlying notion within such a view was that deviants were different sorts of people from 'normals', they were disadvantaged. Because symbolic interactionism theorizes from the point of view of individual perceptions and meanings and because of its focus on the use of language, it was able to penetrate this idea and turn it on its head.

A key figure in this revolutionary form of analysis is Becker (1963) who starts from the commonplace that different groups regard different acts as deviant and moves on from this to the position that deviance must be related to perception rather than to motivation. The central fact of deviance is that it is created not by the way in which the individual acts but by society. If deviance consists in breaking rules then it is social groups which create deviance by making those rules: 'From this point of view, deviance is not a quality of the act the person commits, but rather a consequence of the application by others of rules and sanctions to an "offender" ' (1963: 9, italics deleted). But the application of rules and sanctions is a form of symbolic interaction, that is, it involves the use of language. In engaging in such action groups give a meaning to rule-breaking by applying a 'label' to its perpetrator. Because only some rule-breaking behaviour will be noticed and actually labelled, Becker wants to maintain a distinction between rule-breaking and deviance. Deviance is rule-breaking to which a label has successfully been applied.

Howard S. Becker (b. 1928)

Becker studied within the symbolic interactionist tradition with Everett Hughes at Chicago. His main contributions have been to the sociologies of education and deviance.

Since to apply a label also lends legitimacy to the application of sanctions, labels must be forced on people. So power differentials become critical in who gets to apply deviant labels and who is labelled and in which way. People who are privileged, white, male, older, etc. will apply labels, while people with complementary characteristics are more likely to be labelled. The label then takes on a reality status of its own. It sets the deviant apart from conventional society and sets up clusters of people with similar deviant labels, exposing the deviant to deviant socializing experiences (e.g. in prisons or mental hospitals) and denying them access to material means of supporting a normal status. It also allows normals to interpret suspicious behaviour on the part of the labelled deviant as confirmation of the label. Labelling thus forces the individual to take on a new, deviant identity – the application of the label becomes a self-fulfilling prophecy.

Becker was not alone in accomplishing the shift in our perspective on deviance, nor has labelling theory stood the test of time. After all it could not account for the origins of deviance itself but only for its institutionalization and perpetuation. Becker nevertheless continues rightly to insist that deviance can only properly be understood within an interactionist perspective. It is socially constructed within the interaction between rule-breakers and rule-enforcers. Much of the criticism has focused on the fact that rule-enforcers and labelled rule-breakers have usually been different types of person and that deviance is therefore integrally related to wider structures of power not given within the perceptions of the individual (see e.g. Taylor et al. 1973).

Phenomenology: seeing things

The fact that symbolic interactionism took Simmel as its starting point tended to isolate early American theory from the theoretical discourses of mainstream sociology in the modern period, which often takes the form of a debate between Durkheimian, Weberian and Marxian inspirations. The contribution of agency theory to this debate more often takes place under Weberian auspices and one specific route for the influence of Weber is via phenomenological sociology. Phenomenological sociology argues that social science can take as its subject matter only our immediate experience of the social world received through sense data as a series of phenomena.

Schütz: a meaningful theory

Aside from Weber, the origins of the approach lie in the phenomenological philosophy of Husserl and, to a lesser degree, Bergson. Husserl's phenomenology eschews the concern with the structure of language familiar within Anglo-Saxon analytic philosophy and concentrates rather on the ways in which human beings sense and make sense of reality. Within phenomenology reality can only be appearance and experience – the only grasp we can have on reality is via our senses. So reality can only exist in visual, audial, tactual, oral, and olfactory sense data. The inrush of sense data is continuous through time and is interrupted only by sleep, and then only partially. So we 'make sense' of the data by mentally slicing them up and allocating them to discrete categories, such as 'car' or 'stock market crash' – and these are phenomena. Phenomenological philosophy reflects on the processes by which human beings create categories of reality and allocate particular sense data to them.

Phenomenological sociology then, by extension, examines the ways in which individuals apprehend sense data about the social world and allocate these data to categories as social phenomena. More importantly it seeks to analyse whether these categories are shared between the members of society and, if so, the ways in which they come to be shared. In engaging in just such a project Schütz (1972) seeks to apply the phenomenological insights of Husserl to the sociological insights of Weber. Schütz accepts that Weber was on the right track but that there are some problematic aspects of his conception of action as subjectively meaningful behaviour which require refinement.

Alfred Schütz (1899–1959)

Schütz was born in Vienna and studied at his home university. In 1939 he emigrated to the USA where he took up an academic post at the New School for Social Research in 1943. However, for most of his life he was only an amateur or part-time academic, combining his academic career with banking. Although his major work *The Phenomenology of the Social World* was published in 1932 it was not published in English translation until 1967.

Sources: *Penguin Dictionary of Sociology* (1984: s.v. Schutz, Alfred); Ritzer (1992: 376–7)

First, he questions Weber's idea that the meaning of action is identical with the motive for action (1972: 19). It is perfectly possible, say at the end of a day, to sit back and reflect on some of one's particular actions during the day, actions which Weber would have decided were habitual or affectual, and feel that they are indeed meaningful. They are meaningful because they make sense with the course of one's life experience. So most action, and not merely rational action, is in fact meaningful. Second, Schütz (1972: 19–24) argues convincingly that Weber says little or nothing about the way in which we come to know the meanings endowed by others. It is, of course, perfectly possible to misunderstand or to be deceived by others, but the simple fact is that most of the time others will not be trying to express their motives or intentions to us at all. The conclusion is that while we can know what others are doing it is very unlikely that we will know why they are doing it. The meaning of others' actions in the sense of motive is unavailable to us.

This leads Schütz into a critique of Weber's concept of *Verstehen*. In *erklärendes Verstehen* (explanatory understanding) sociologists are supposed to locate the actor's motive within a typical complex of meaning which seems to be an adequate set of grounds for the act. But this complex of meaning has two aspects, neither of which is accessible to the sociological observer: first, it is the culmination of a series of past events, engaged in with unknown others, which in some sense 'bring it about'; and second, it is intended to have consequences in the future, also in relation to unknown others.

Schütz (1972: 69–71) proposes a solution along the following lines. There is no meaning in actual lived experience. The attribution of meaning to behaviour is subsequent to it: 'The reflective glance singles out an elapsed lived experience and constitutes it as meaningful' (1972: 71). The subject (mentally) gazes on the continuous flow of action through time and recognizes that a piece of it is discrete and thus becomes an 'act'. But Schütz must now ask the question as to what gives each act a specific meaning differentiating it from all other acts. We can do this because we continuously categorize our experience into schemes so that we can allocate the act upon which we reflect to a particular scheme. Thus schemes are constituted and reconstituted by the very process of classifying acts as members of them. To give an example 'getting fuel' might always have consisted of 'buying oil' but if I do something new and chop my own wood, and interpret that as 'getting fuel', then the scheme 'getting fuel' itself changes.

Schütz now turns to the issue of motive and here what he calls the 'time-stream of consciousness', the continuous process of the human biography through time, becomes paramount. The term 'motive' covers two quite separate aspects indicated by the notions of past and future discussed above. From the actor's point of view motives temporally located prior to the act are 'because-motives'. To be a genuine because-motive it must be a prior experience. Thus the expression 'I am cutting wood because it will keep me warm' does not indicate a genuine because-motive but the expression 'I am cutting wood because I ran out of oil' does – the oil-running-out precedes the wood-cutting but the keeping-warm occurs after it. The former phrase is an example of the second type of motive, an 'in-order-to' motive, one which refers to a future state of affairs and has a teleological or intentional content – one cuts wood in order to keep warm. The in-order-to motive is in fact the projection of the completed act into the future. Self-understanding involves recognition of the act within both types of motive.

Having established the primitive terms of meaning and motive, Schütz must now turn to the fundamental problematic – the existence of society. He first addresses this via the hypothetical of a two-person interaction. The initial basis of sociality is that each ego (self) recognizes that alter (the other) also reflects on and attributes meaning to their own action. This raises the question of perceiving the meaning that alter gives and here Schütz is obliged to introduce language into the proposal. Alter can express the meaning of an act to ego by the use of signs, that is by symbolic representations, which refer to previous shared experiences. An exchange of signs between ego and alter can establish shared understandings of various degrees. This is most complete in the we-relationship in which both ego and alter can simultaneously and identically grasp the meaning of an act. This intersubjectivity is accomplished when ego's in-order-to-motive becomes alter's because-motive and vice versa. For example, if I ask my spouse what is for dinner I do so in order to know what to expect and my spouse answers because I have sought the information. We can do this because we: 'anticipate that [alter] will be guided by the same types of motives by which, in the past, according to my stock of knowledge at hand, I myself and many others were guided under typically similar circumstances' (1962: 23).

However, the social world is extended in time and space and does not consist in mere face-to-face interaction. To live in it one must grasp not only the meanings given to it by those we interact with ('consociates'), but also those given by others one cannot meet ('contemporaries'), those who once lived ('predecessors') and those who will live in the future ('successors'). These will most frequently be types of person rather than actual individuals. As one moves from consociates, to contemporaries, to predecessors, to successors, and ultimately to human beings in general, the degree of specificity with which one is able to understand the meanings they endow declines. Nevertheless, taken together, they go to make up the lifeworld (*Lebenswelt*) of each individual.

Note that in each of the preceeding paragraphs reference is made to types or typifications. These take a central place in Schütz's argument. In all situations in which we attempt to discern the meanings of others we construct in our minds 'course-of-action types' in which we relate typical because-motives to typical acts and in turn to typical in-order-to motives. But if we link such types to the typical underlying motives of an actor then we are constructing personal types. The more distant the inhabitants of our *Lebenswelt* are (i.e. contemporaries, predecessors, etc.) the more invariant and inflexible will be the motives which we attribute to them. So, one will assume that one's spouse will be able to act flexibly in a wide variety of ways but that a mail deliverer will act only within a narrow range of expectations.

So far we have examined Schütz's arguments about the way in which actors understand themselves and each other in the common-sense world of everyday life. However, this *Lebenswelt* is regarded by him as only one version of reality, one province of meaning, and he must also address the question of how the inhabitants of a second province of meaning, that of social science, can practise *Verstehen* on the inhabitants of the first. His answer is that the process is similar (1962: 40–4). The social scientist constructs a set of course-of-action types based on observation and then brings them together in the form of a typical actor with a consciousness relevant to the situation under investigation. The social scientist has created mental puppets or homunculi which can then be manipulated. Where several such types are constructed reciprocity of perspectives is assumed. In such a constructed social world rational motives can indeed be imputed.

The type constructs of the *Lebenswelt* are based on subjective meanings and can therefore be designated as 'first order constructs' but the types of social science which provide objective meanings are based on these and are therefore of a 'second order'. Second order constructs, in order to remain consistent with first order ones, must meet the following rules of translation:

- They must meet the highest standards of clarity, parsimony and analytical separation and must accord with the principles of formal logic. (First order constructs are distinguished precisely because they do not meet this criterion.)
- They must always make reference to subjective interpretation when offering explanations of observed facts.
- They must be constructed in such a way that if a real actor performed a real act in the manner indicated by the construct, that actor and other actors would understand what was going on.

Berger and Luckmann: building society

A more sociological and less philosophical restatement of Schützian phenomenology is given by Berger and Luckmann (1967). They start from the premise that human beings construct social reality in which subjective processes can become objectified. In a hypothesized primitive situation, the process begins with a habitualization of a piece of action which allows the actor and other actors to notice that it has repeated and regular characteristics. In phenomenological terms, actors will now be able to typify that action and the motives which they suppose are attached to it. They will, assert Berger and Luckmann, assume from the beginning that there will be reciprocity of typification and will begin to model their own behaviour upon each other. These typifications will minimally focus on language, labour, sexuality and territoriality. But the types of action will only accomplish reality status when they are perceived as real by third parties. Berger and Luckmann formulate this process loosely in the phrase: 'the institutional world . . . is now passed on to others' (1967: 76). Presumably this 'passing on' must involve communication and/or socialization but how this is accomplished with third parties who have not been involved in constructing the original typifications is not made clear. In any event, this osmosis results in an institutional world of reciprocal typification of habitualized action between types of actor (1967: 72) which has the characteristics of objectivity and historicity. However, the relationship between individuals and institutions is a 'dialectical' (interactive) one expressed in a formula with three moments: 'Society is a human product. Society is an objective reality. Man is a social product' (1967: 79, italics deleted). These dialectics are mediated, on one hand, by knowledge laid down in the memory during experience and, on the other, by roles which individually 'represent' the institutional order.

There is more to Berger and Luckmann's story than this, however. In a functionalist claim, they state that having been constructed society now

---

Peter L. Berger (b. 1929)

An American, Berger studied at the New School for Social Research in New York City with Alfred Schütz and was for a time a professor in a seminary in Connecticut. He is now a travelling, freelance lecturer and speaker.

Source: Cuzzort and King (1980: 268)

---

requires to be legitimated (explained and justified), that is, all the differentiated and localized worlds of meaning need to be held together (1967: 79).[5] They indicate four 'levels' of legitimation but the most senior and salient of these is the fourth level, the level of symbolic universes, that are: 'bodies of theoretical tradition that integrate different provinces of meaning and encompass the institutional order in a symbolic totality' (1967: 113). This solves the problem of the meaning of the individual's participation in society ('social integration') and the problem of fit between institutions ('system integration'). Although they fight shy of the word, it is clear that this over-arching canopy of legitimation is religious in character. They do, however, continue to stress that the symbolic universe is a social construction with a history and not a structural given.

Ethnomethodology: not taking the taken-for-granted for granted

This section examines an argument on agency which developed in the USA in the 1960s and 1970s. It insisted on privileging the agent's point of view in such an emphatic way that it developed a radical critique of sociology in particular and academic life in general. In line with the general pattern of political protest which prevailed in universities at the time, ethnomethodologists did not merely argue their position but often engaged in practical disruptions of academic meetings and of university departments in order to make their point that traditional sociological theories were elitist and false.

The negatives of positivism

Ethnomethodology is essentially the child of Schützian phenomenology. It elevates the 'reflective glance' that Schütz sees as essential in providing meaning to behaviour to the centre of sociological investigation. Garfinkel (1967), the founding figure in the tradition, seeks to direct empirical study at routine and commonplace activities of everyday life. He argues that their central characteristic is their 'reflexive' character. By this he means that the way in which people act out and organize their social arrangements is identical with their procedures for giving accounts of those arrangements. To give an account is to reflect on behaviour and to seek to make it understandable, or meaningful, to oneself and to others. Human beings are argued to do this on a continuous basis and, in so doing, continuously and practically to create and remake the social world. In giving accounts and creating the world human beings are regarded as essentially competent and skilled in accounting for the settings of everyday social experience. Ethnomethodologists seek to use this competence to expose the taken-for-granted understandings about how the social world works which other sociologists are argued to leave uninterpreted.

Harold Garfinkel (b. 1917)

An American, Garfinkel studied at Princeton and spent much of his academic career at the University of California at Los Angeles. He is regarded as the founding figure of ethnomethodology, although he actually wrote relatively little.

The accounts which participants give are seldom if ever finished and complete. Those giving the accounts ('reporters') signal their assumption that some things can be understood, without being made explicit, by using 'et cetera' clauses. Likewise listeners ('auditors') will wait for an explanation eventually to be made rather than demanding it immediately. So accounts will be built up serially over a period of time as particular elements of it become relevant to the interests of reporter or auditor. This means that accounts, and the actions upon which they reflect, cannot be judged against any ideal or sociological standard of rationality. Rather they are rational or sensible or objective in terms of the spatial, temporal and organizational location within which they occur. In Garfinkel's terms, accounts are 'indexical' rather than 'scientifically objective' expressions – their meanings and their rationality is tied to the context of their use (1967: 3–4).

In summary, the argument so far is that the meaning of action is given in its accountability and that the rationality of accounts is implied by the context in which they are given. This presents a problem: indexical expressions are a rich, indeed the only, source of information about social life but they are not objective expressions in the formal scientific sense. Social science promises that indexical expressions can be transformed into objective ones, but on every occasion on which it attempts to do so the transformation fails to be accomplished according to the rules which social science sets itself. So indexical expressions 'present immense, obstinate, and irremediable nuisances' in imposing rigour and logic on actual human action (Garfinkel 1967: 6). Wherever social scientists attempt to make such a transformation, in sample surveys for example, they must fall back on 'all other things being equal' or 'this is the case for all practical purposes' clauses to cover their failures.

Garfinkel is thus able to draw a comparison between everyday reasoning which is practical, skilled and accomplished, and social science reasoning which is problematic, difficult and, at best, a qualified failure. Therefore, the only way in which the sociologist can reveal the facticity of social experience is to approach it as would an anthropologist. That is, the sociologist must seek to understand situations, in the terms in which participants give accounts of them, by calling to our attention the reflexive or accounting practices themselves. Sociologists must somehow induce participants to give accounts and thus to reveal the contextually rational properties of their social arrangements.

The incompatibility between indexical and objective expressions is, as is noted above, an incompatibility between the rationality which resides in the province of meaning of the *Lebenswelt* and that which resides in the scientific province of meaning. In some measure these overlap – there is a series of what Garfinkel calls everyday rationalities which are also found in science. In fact he identifies ten of these, the flavour of which may be gathered from the following examples: categorizing and comparing situations with experience; searching for the most effective means to achieve a goal; and employing of rules of procedure to decide whether a judgement is correct. But there are also four purely scientific rationalities (1967: 267–8): consistency of the relationship which a person establishes between means and ends, with the principles of formal logic; clarity and precision in defining terms; clarity and precision in specifying relationships between variables; and consistency between one's beliefs about the situation and established scientific knowledge. Garfinkel asserts that any attempt to put the scientific rationalities into practice in everyday life would result in disruption: for example, the expectation that each person should define precisely the meaning of the terms they use would make everyday discourse impossible. Unlike Schütz, Garfinkel sees no possibility of translation between the constructs of everyday life and those of science because the existence of the scientific rationalities precludes it.

Folk sociology

Garfinkel's proposed solution is an ethnomethodology, the use of folk or people's own methods in sociology, as a replacement for the supposed rigours of positivistic and quantitative empiricism on one hand and grand theories of structure on the other: 'I use the term "ethnomethodology" to refer to the investigation of the rational properties of indexical expressions and other practical actions as contingent ongoing accomplishments of organized artful practices of everyday life' (1967: 11). He specifies (1967: 31–4) five 'policies' which ethnomethodology should follow:

- Any and all social settings, whether trivial or self-important, are open to investigation because each of them is the practical accomplishment of its members; neither nuclear physics nor cabinet meetings have any greater facticity than a casual street corner encounter.

- The presentation of arguments, demonstrations, statistics, etc. are achievements which are contingent on the social arrangements within which they are produced; they are 'glosses' or frontstage talk which cover and protect underlying troubles, problems and compromises; ethnomethodology must in all circumstances penetrate these glosses.
- The rationality, objectivity, effectiveness, consistency, etc. of an activity are not to be judged according to standards imported from another situation (e.g. science, sociology or formal logic) but as contingent upon the situation in which the activity occurs.
- A situation is orderly in so far as participants are able to give mutually intelligible accounts of it to one another.
- All forms of inquiry consist in organized and artful practices – so there is no difference in principle between sociological accounts and every-day accounts.

Ethnomethodology seeks to reveal the underlying, unspoken, unmentionable social realities over which actors gloss when they speak to one another. In seeking to do this Garfinkel proposes methods that might in other contexts be regarded as unethical. He quite explicitly seeks to disrupt the continuity of reflexive behaviour:

> [I]t is my preference to start with familiar scenes and see what can be done to make trouble. The operations that one would have to perform in order to multiply the senseless features of perceived environments; to produce and sustain bewilderment, consternation, and confusion; to produce the socially structured effects of anxiety, shame, guilt, and indignation; and to produce disorganized interaction should tell us something about how the structures of everyday activities are ordinarily and routinely produced and maintained. [1967: 37–8]

This confusion is induced in participants by undertaking field research in which 'breaching' or norm-disruptive experiments occur. Some examples of breaching experiments are: investigators acting like lodgers when living with their own families; investigators attempting to overpay for shop purchases; and investigators taking the role of social security officials and alternating 'yes' and 'no' answers to clients' questions, whatever is asked. Once one has produced bewilderment and anxiety in the participant one must oblige the giving of an account which does not gloss but reconstructs the natural facts. In so doing the respondent must be allowed neither to 'play games' nor to call on others for support.

It might be argued that once ethnomethodology has sown confusion among those it studies, its job is done. It has demonstrated that the stable social order which we all enjoy is indeed a constructed and fragile reality to which we all conspire and which is capable of being undone by 'calling the game'.[6] However, as Denzin (1971: 272–3) argues, ethnomethodology offers very real insights into the ways in which organizations work, especially those which process people. Ethnomethodologists have discovered, for example, that organizations will generate fictitious records to convince superior authorities of the amount of work they do. Even where the records are not fictitious, they are a glossing of rumour, gossip, hearsay and error. Comparable organizations differ in the ways in which they classify similar events, not only such difficult ones as suicide, mental illness and juvenile delinquency, but even such straightforward ones as birth and death. In part this is a consequence of the classifications being open-ended rather than exclusive. Ambiguous or difficult cases can be accommodated in a discretionary way. In so doing organizations create the meanings of deviance and assign individuals to deviant categories.

All of the above arguments about agency bracket the large-scale social arrangements that we refer to as 'organizations' or 'structures' or 'systems'. These are held simply to be other ways of describing human interaction, the only reality there is for an agency theorist. They are held to have no separate existence of their own and thus can have no causal force upon individuals. We can now move on to examine three statements of agency which undertake no such bracketing, those of Parsons, Habermas and Giddens. These view systems and structures as the product of human construction.

Parsons: volunteering for action

When symbolic interactionism was in its heyday and Anglo-Saxon sociology had scarcely heard of Weber or Durkheim or Marx, a young American academic completed his graduate education at the Universities of London and Heidelberg and there encountered the works of great European thinkers. This man was Parsons, whose central interest was the emergence of industrial capitalism and the way that this development had been misinterpreted in classical economics as a simple and individualistic flowering of utilitarian rationality (Menzies 1977).[7] He set out to show that human behaviour could be conceived not merely as the rational pursuit of individual success but as framed within a series of general human possibilities and ideals. Parsons sought to demonstrate this by showing that the theories of great thinkers were converging on such a view. In so doing, he transformed Anglo-Saxon sociology, not merely because it had now to consider Parsons' own argument but because he forced it to come to terms with those social theorists who had influenced him.

Parsons argues that classical theories of action converge on the notion of guiding norms, a common value system, that actors contribute to and within which they make guided choices. The convergence occurs within the following theoretical antecedents:

- the classical economics of Marshall (see chapter 3), which introduces the notion of 'wants adjusted to activities' and which Parsons interprets both as a rejection of the strictly utilitarianist view that wants are entirely individualistic and the promotion of 'an integrated value system common to large numbers' (1937: 704);
- Pareto's distinction between logical and nonlogical action (see chapter 3), which is an implicit distinction, respectively, between rational behaviour in the pursuit of instrumental ends, and value-guided behaviour;
- the move in Durkheim (see chapter 5) from determination by the material constraints of population density to a stress on the significance of religion and the *conscience collective*, that is, to a notion of society as a moral or normatively guided community;
- Weber's attack on Marxist historical materialism, in which he asserts the efficacy of religious ideas as an autonomous source of social change (see chapter 9) and also his distinction between instrumental rationality and value-rationality (see above).

The action theory on which European thought was argued to be converging is developed as follows (1937: 43–51). Action is made up of component elements, each of which is a 'unit act'. Each unit act involves:

- an agent or 'actor';
- an 'end' or goal to which the act is oriented;
- a 'situation', comprising: 'means', elements of the situation over which the actor has control; and 'conditions', over which there is no control; and
- a 'normative orientation' which specifies a range of alternative ends and means which are appropriate to a situation.

However, within the course of a few pages, Parsons slips into what has become the conventional description of the unit act, in which it is said to be composed of 'ends, means, conditions and guiding norms' (1937: 48). Nevertheless the principal implication is that action is always normatively oriented. Actors voluntaristically select ends and means from among those which are normatively prescribed. However, they must adjust the level of goal-realization in relation to conditions:

> Action must always be thought of as involving a state of tension between two different orders of elements, the normative and the conditional. As process, action is, in fact, the process of the alteration of the conditional elements in the direction of conformity with norms. . . . Thus conditions may be conceived at one pole, ends and normative rules at the other, means and effort as the connecting links between them. [Parsons 1937: 732]

The question now arises as to what sorts of norms or values are available to actors in making their voluntaristic choices. The available choices are limited to combinations of five dilemmas that Parsons calls the 'pattern variables' (Parsons et al. 1951: 76–98). Indeed the definition of a pattern variable asserts that it is: 'a dichotomy, one side of which must be chosen by an actor before the meaning of a situation is determinate for him, and thus before he can act with respect to that situation' (1951: 77).

The five pattern variables are:

- affectivity versus affective neutrality: whether the actor should gratify personal emotional impulses or accept the discipline of the group;
- self-orientation versus collectivity-orientation: whether primacy should be given to personal individual interests or to collective social interests;
- universalism versus particularism: whether all the objects (other actors or collectivities) in the situation should be treated in accordance with a general norm or in terms of their particular relationship to the actor;
- ascription (quality) versus achievement (performance): whether the objects in a situation are to be treated in terms of what they *are*, in terms of what is intrinsic to them, or in terms of what they *do*, the outcomes of their action;
- diffuseness versus specificity: whether to respond to the total range of actions performed by the object or to a narrow and restricted sector of that range.

A curious aspect of this early work of Parsons is that he insists that actors make choices between alternatives made available in the normative order when he has already admitted that norms structure conditions. This problem might best be illustrated by means of the example of an academic relating to a student. An academic might choose to be affective, self-oriented, particularistic, ascriptive and diffuse, and there are academics who have so chosen, but they are usually sanctioned until they conform to norms of neutrality, collectivity-orientation, universalism, achievement and specificity, or excluded from the academic system. There is no choice for an actor in the role of academic other than to demonstrate at least minimal commitment to the latter.

This constraint in the nominally voluntaristic theory of action causes Parsons to drift towards the diminution of agency in his later work. At some points he takes a structuralist turn (see chapter 4) but the main direction is towards a normative or religious determinism in which action is conflated to the cultural system (see chapter 5). His own claims notwithstanding, Parsons turns out not really to be an agency theorist at all.

Habermas: arguments resolved

Here we enter our first encounter with the person regarded by many as the leading theorist of the contemporary or postmodern period, Habermas.[8]

We shall also meet him in the chapters on Culture and System. However, his theory is fundamentally grounded in agency, in actors' choices about how they establish their social relationships. He bases this position initially in the work of Weber and ultimately in Mead, although he is able to incorporate a much wider range of influences.

Habermas begins by outlining four possible sociological models of action (agency):

- *The teleological (strategic) model* Here the actor is said to be motivated by an orientation to success, choosing between alternative courses of action in relation to a short-run purpose (*telos*) or goal, located in the material world. The various attempts at employing such a model are reviewed in chapter 3.
- *The normative regulation model* Here the actor is guided by values and norms shared between the members of a social group – the actor is motivated by conceptions of what ought and ought not to be done. The best-known examples are the structural-functional theories (including Parsons') reviewed in chapter 4.
- *The dramaturgical model* Here the actor is claimed to express the contents of the subjective consciousness to an audience of other actors. The work of Goffman and Becker discussed above are the main examples.
- *The communicative model* Here actors are conceptualized as being engaged in relationships with other actors in facing practical problems: 'The actors seek to reach an understanding about their action situation and their plans of action in order to coordinate their actions by way of agreement' (1984: 86). They reach understanding by using speech. The examples which influenced Habermas are the theories of the symbolic interactionists and phenomenologists (see above).
(Habermas 1984: 85–101; White 1988: 37–9)

Habermas provides two principal critiques of these models. First, no single model exhausts the possibilities of human action – each of the types of action specified is a possibility. Second, only the first model appears to make any claim about the rationality of human agency, understood as the application of reason to courses of action. Habermas wants to extend this conception of rationality to each of the other three models. In particular he wants to develop and to explore the rationality of communicative action in order to balance the narrow and one-sided view of rational action as solely purposive or instrumental. In so doing he will seek to use communicative action as an ideal reference point in order to mount a critique of modern society. The telos of communicative action is to reach understanding.

On the basis of a reading of postWittgenstinian linguistic philosophy,[9] Habermas insists that the basic truth or correctness or morality of any action is neither absolute nor arbitrary but is defined by the social context in which it is established (Pusey 1987: 75–85). Truth and morality are human social constructions, they are the consequences of agency. But this agency is intersubjective, involving interaction with others. The interaction is mediated through linguistic utterances or 'speech-acts'. Through speech, actors will seek to reach such understandings on three dimensions:

> As the medium for reaching understanding, speech acts serve: (a) to establish and renew interpersonal relations, whereby the speaker takes up a relation to something in the world of legitimate social orders [e.g. as we try to do in preaching or adjudicating or protesting politically]; (b) to represent (or presuppose) states and events, whereby the speaker takes up a relation to something in the world of existing states of affairs [e.g. as we try to do in teaching or speaking in a seminar or speaking as a journalist]; (c) to manifest experiences – that is, to represent oneself – whereby the speaker takes up a relation to something in the subjective world to which he has privileged access [e.g. as we try to do in expressing romantic love or communicating comradeship or in saying why we appreciate the beauty of a painting or of a landscape]. [1984: 308]

Habermas is saying, then, that when actors seek to communicate they will simultaneously make reference to each of these three standards – they will judge or evaluate each other's speech acts on the basis of whether they are morally correct, factually true and subjectively sincere.

These evaluations are made through a process of *argumentation* (1984: 18–25). Argumentation is a situation in which competing validity claims are tested against each other on each of the three dimensions of morality, truth and sincerity. Argumentation reproduces social life both by grounding it in relation to communicative criteria and by serving as a context for learning. In reproducing understanding, by this means, actors constitute and reconstitute for themselves a world of consensus and understanding. For this world of understanding Habermas employs the Schützian term, lifeworld (*Lebenswelt*).

Habermas can now move to a redefinition of Weber's concepts of action in order to reveal different meanings of rationality. Speaking roughly, in everyday life there are two ways in which we can assess whether an action is rational: (a) whether it can succeed in manipulating physical or social objects; or (b) whether it can be assessed as normatively correct or intersubjectively true. The validity criterion for such actions, of which speech acts will make up the greater part, is, in the case of (a), success in reaching objectives. However, in the case of (b), the validity criterion is a capacity to withstand contesting validity claims within a process of argumentation in which the object is to reach consensus between the participants. The first type (a) Habermas describes as cognitive-instrumental action and the second (b) he describes as communicative action.

As figure 2.1 shows, Habermas further differentiates success-oriented actions into those oriented to physical objects and impersonal events

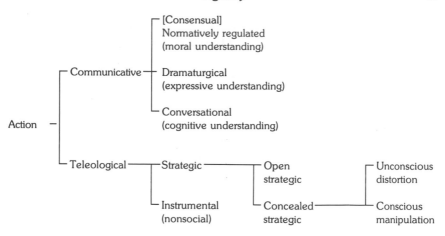

Figure 2.1 *Habermas' taxonomy of action (Habermas 1984: 285, 329, 333)*

(instrumental) from those oriented to influencing the decisions of a rational other (strategic). His main types, communicative and strategic action are then further decomposed. Two of the more interesting aspects of this taxonomy are: the tripartite division of communicative action which parallels Parsons' middle period (see chapter 5); and the notion of unconscious distortion which implies possible incompetence on the part of the actor.[10] Both teleological and communicative action are held to be rational, and may be considered as refinements of Weber's concepts of instrumental rationality and value-rationality (see above) respectively, but will allow Habermas to consider the rationalization of society in all its manifestations and not merely in instrumental terms (see chapter 5).

Giddens' structuration theory: society by accident

Parsons and Habermas tend towards a conflation of agency with system, as is discussed in chapter 5. Parsons' volunteer gets oversocialized and becomes the subordinate of a dominating and quasi-religious culture; while Habermas' lifeworld becomes colonized by state and commercial interests which insist on steering it in directions they prescribe. Among contemporary theorists, only Giddens manages to conflate structures and systems to agency. He does so by means of the unique device of viewing structures as the accidental or unintentional consequence of agency – what he calls structuration. We can now consider his argument about agency in detail before examining his notion of structure in chapter 4.

Interpretation rules, OK?

Throughout this chapter we have returned to the criticism that theories which stress agency have strengths in explaining individual behaviour, and

---

Anthony Giddens (b. 1938)

Giddens was born in North London, England. He studied at the University of Hull and the London School of Economics, where he wrote a Master's thesis on the sociology of sport. His first teaching post was at the University of Leicester, England, with Ilya Neustadt and Norbert Elias. He moved to the University of Cambridge as a Fellow of King's College, eventually to become Professor of Sociology. He holds a similar, simultaneous appointment at the University of California, Santa Barbara. He has published over twenty books. Among other distinctions, Giddens is joint founder, with David Held and John Thompson, of Polity Press, which has become a major social science publisher, and he is one of only a few sociologists ever to have been elected to a Fellowship of the British Academy.

Source: Bryant and Jary (1991)

---

even in explaining mutual interactive behaviour, but enormous difficulties in coming to terms with explaining the apparently external, objective and constraining realities of society writ large. So the symbolic interactionists ignore it, the phenomenologists assume that they have explained it without succeeding in so doing, and ethnomethodology virtually denies its existence. The most recent, arguably the most successful, and certainly the most influential attempt to bridge the gap between agency and social structure is offered in the theory of structuration proposed by Giddens. Giddens is unique among agency theorists because although he begins his work with a reading of constructionist sociologies, including those of Weber, Schütz and Garfinkel, he also has a demonstrated familiarity with a wide range of social theory, including the work of Durkheim, Marx, Parsons and Habermas. Unlike other agency theory, the theory of structuration seeks explicitly to link constructionist sociology with these structuralist and functionalist arguments.

In general Giddens (1976: 23–70) applauds the Schützian attempt to reconstitute the philosophical basis of social science (see above). Interpretive (i.e. constructionist) sociologies, he argues, establish successfully that the sciences of the human world are different from the natural sciences by showing that human beings competently accomplish that world rather than it being pregiven. The use of language is an essential element in this accomplishment because it is the medium by which meanings become shared. Moreover, successful methodological practices in social science can only be similar to everyday methodologies because this is the only way in which one can grasp meaning and motive.

However, Giddens agrees that interpretive sociologies do indeed have some of the shortcomings which are mentioned in the critical conclusion to the present chapter. They concentrate too heavily on the meanings at the expense of the material conditions of social life; they do not examine power differences and divisions of interest; and they concentrate on motives and reasons rather than causes. His first thrust in seeking to solve these problems is to separate the notion of agency from intention – intention (i.e. in-order-to-motive, see p. 33) only becomes an issue when individuals engage in the retrospective glance or give accounts. While individuals are typically expected to engage in responsible retrospective monitoring of their action, this has little to do with its explanation. Instead, Giddens argues, we should concentrate on the production and reproduction of society, its *structuration*.

When actors create society they do not do so from scratch but draw upon pregiven resources. There are three kinds of such resources: meanings (things known, the stock of knowledge), morals (value systems), and power (patterns of domination and divisions of interest). Here Giddens first offers the dual view of social life on which he continues to insist throughout his work. All large-scale social phenomena are indeed patterns of interaction but they can also be thought of as structures.[11] They are structures, that is they are systematic, regular and permanent, in so far as actors reproduce them into the future.

Giddens generally endorses the constructionist notion that the human sciences are fundamentally different from the natural sciences. The latter must engage in only a singular act of establishing the meaning of such objects as atoms or genes. But the human sciences must engage in a 'double hermeneutic', that is, they must seek the meaning for events for which a meaning has already been established by participants. However, the fundamental methodology is not, as Schütz has it, the translation of sociological types into lay understandings, but the mediation of everyday concepts into scientific ones. This is, for Giddens, essentially unproblematic in terms of validation, so the essential prerequisite remains that the social scientist needs to grasp everyday understandings.

Giddens sums up his sociological approach in a set of 'new rules of sociological method' (1976: 160–2) a phrase which intends an opposition to Durkheim's classical manifesto (1964). The nine 'rules' are subdivided into four categories.

The subject matter of sociology
- Society is not a pregiven objective reality but is created by the actions of its members.
- The act of creation of society is necessarily a skilled performance.

The limits of human agency
- Actors are not free to choose how to create society but are limited by the constraints of their historical location which they do not choose.
- Structure has the dual capacity both to constrain and to enable (provide resources for) human agency. The focus for sociology is structuration: the processes by which structures are constituted through action and action is constituted structurally.

- Every human action or structure involves three aspects: meanings, norms and power.

Sociological methodology

- Sociologists cannot avoid using their own experience as a basis for the understanding of social life and indeed should embrace this necessity.
- Sociologists must 'immerse' themselves in the situations they analyze.

Sociological concept formation

- Concept formation involves a double hermeneutic. Sociologists need to guard against slippage in the precision of their own concepts as they become appropriated for use in everyday life.
- In sum, the primary tasks of sociology are the redescription of social settings in a scientific metalanguage and the confirmation of the principle that society is the product of human agency.

Acting out structures

This, then, is Giddens' general approach. We can now move on to examine the formal details of the theory. His written work is highly repetitive and these details can be established by a reading of any one of several major books (e.g. 1976: 93–129; 1979: 49–130; 1982: 1–39; 1984: 1–40, 162–226, 281–354). Here we shall concentrate on the origins of the term in his early analysis of class (1981) and his formal and synthetic restatement of the theory (1984). His introduction of the term structuration in 1973 was made, he says: 'without reflecting at that time upon its likely importance as a general concept in social theory' (1991a: 202). But the term was soon to develop into 'an ontological framework for the study of human social activities' (1991a: 201), in other words a general theory.

Somewhat surprisingly, Giddens (1973: 105) finds the suggestion for application for the term structuration in Marx. Marx had written about the way in which economic differences between capitalists and workers presuppose social relationships between them (see chapter 9). Giddens' focus of interest is: 'the modes in which "economic" relationships become translated into "non-economic" social structures' (1973: 105, italics deleted). However, because Giddens wants to stress Weber's approach to class, he translates Marx's definition of class relations as property differences into Weber's notion of differential market capacity (see chapter 9). He is now able to say that there are two ways in which different market capacities become translated into the real social groups which we call classes. These he calls mediate and proximate structuration. Mediate structuration is contained in the processes by which membership in social classes is reproduced – the sociological shorthand for this phenomenon is 'mobility chances'. Where actors operate to close off mobility chances, classes become structurated, that is boundaries are established between them – so some actors will use property to structurate an upper-class boundary, others will use credentials and skills to structurate a middle-class boundary. The notion of proximate structuration focuses on the issue of

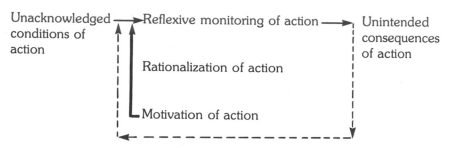

Figure 2.2   *Giddens' model of the actor (Giddens 1984: 5)*

class boundaries at the level of personal interaction. It includes such elements as the different types of work assigned to different occupations, authority differences, and differences in styles of life and consumption patterns which make inter-class interaction difficult.

Even though this was not intended as a general theoretical statement, the elements of the emerging argument were present: actors are seen to be taking pregiven resources and using them to reproduce interaction patterns over time, thus lending structural quality to their behaviour. Already Giddens is seeking to integrate constraint with enablement.

Giddens begins his more formal general statement of the theory of structuration (1984: 5–14) with his model of the agent (represented diagramatically in figure 2.2). He describes it as a 'stratification model' because it conceives of the actor as a series of layers of consciousness. The most conscious or 'aware' level is that at which actors monitor the flow of their own activities (i.e. by the reflective glance [see p. 33]) and those of others (by *Verstehen* [see p. 19]). Actors routinely maintain a theoretical understanding of action by means of language – so this consciousness can be described as discursive. Below the discursive level is the level of rationalization of action, understandings of meanings which are kept tacitly in the actor's mind, and which constitute a 'practical consciousness' of how to act in the world (Garfinkel's taken-for-granted reality [see p. 36]). The elements of practical consciousness can rapidly be raised to the discursive level should the actor be asked to give an account and so the two levels are not radically distinct. However, taken together they are indeed distinct from the third level, the arena of unconscious motives and cognition. This contains the orientational disposition of the actor, the motivational plan or life-goals. This third level is separated from the other two by the Freudian barrier of repression (see chapter 4).

The contents of figure 2.2 refer to the intentional elements of the agent, they constitute the flow or *durée* of everyday life. However, intentionally oriented actions may also have unintended consequences and these may feed back to become the unacknowledged conditions of future acts. They provide the limits or boundaries, the constraints within which human action takes place. Giddens identifies three research situations in which such consequences can be analysed (1984: 13–14). The first situation is where an act initiates a sequence of acts which together produce a consequence without the actor being aware of the sequence. The second is where one act is part of a contemporaneous complex of acts which together produce a consequence without the actor being aware of the general pattern of activities. The third is the feedback situation mentioned above in which the actor is unable to acknowledge that consequences become conditions because of their long separation in time and space. The example of the poverty cycle, given by Giddens elsewhere (1979: 79) illustrates this process: material deprivation (child) → poor schooling → low-level employment → material deprivation (adult). He is saying that conditions of material deprivation lead to actions which might be described as a low level of educational and occupational performance which lead to future conditions of further material deprivation.

Conclusion

Summary

1　The founding arguments of agency theory come from Weber and Simmel. Weber, in particular, established that action, defined as meaningful, motivated, other-oriented behaviour, is the proper subject matter of sociology. It can be studied using acts of interpretive understanding. However, a truly explanatory form of interpretive understanding is only possible where action is instrumentally rational, that is, where the actor is oriented to a short-term, material goal.

2　The symbolic interactionism of Mead identifies language as a key foundation for social life. Society is constituted in a self-reflective process in which the individual identifies with society via what Mead constructs as the 'generalized other', a typification of all social norms and arrangements.

3　Schütz criticizes Weber's restriction of meaningful action to rational action as too restrictive – all action can be made meaningful by the attribution of motive within the reflective glance. However, Schütz insists that sociology should be restricted to the interpretation of the 'lifeworld' of immediately lived experience because only within the 'lifeworld' and its typifications can we be sure that we genuinely understand motives.

4　Schütz's epigones, Berger and Luckmann, and Garfinkel, take his arguments in different directions. Berger and Luckmann argue that the more meanings are shared, the more they come to be seen as real, external and constraining. Garfinkel, on the other hand, argues that the attribution of meanings in everyday life is so contextualized that abstract and scientific concepts cannot be used to analyse it.

5　Both Parsons and Habermas begin by theorizing agency but later subordinate it to systems. Parsons suggests that within any 'unit act' actors select within a specified range of alternative goals and therefore that action is 'voluntaristic'. Habermas partitions action into two main types, communicative and strategic, but insists that each is rational and therefore penetrable by the observer.

6   Giddens is the only agency theorist who can genuinely explain structures without conflating agency to them. He does this by employing the unique device of viewing structure as the unintentional consequence of action. Under this regime, the skills and creativity of actors, as well as their rationality, become irrelevant to the process.

Critique

The key criticism which applies to all pure theories of agency is that because they link or even reduce social processes to the contents of the mind they must typically analyse not much more than interpersonal interaction. However, the complexities and scale of such social phenomena as bureaucracies, class systems, religions, or states render them irreducible to aggregates of meaning-endowments other than in the most simplistic terms.

Symbolic interactionism, for example, remains acomparative and ahistorical, a social psychology with sociological sympathies but not remotely a complete sociology. Even in these terms, however, it is vulnerable. In reducing society to the internal 'self' it places its objects outside the realm of scientific-empirical analysis. The contents of the minds of others are only accessible by self-reflection, that is by the projection of one's own experience on to the apparent experience of others. The symbolic interactionist can only estimate an explanation at the level of motive but cannot validate that explanation. Although Goffman's frame analysis has been cautiously hailed as a possible way out of this subjective relativism it remains firmly fixed at the level of adducing the structure of meanings rather than the structure of society. It translates dramaturgy into a semiology rather than into a mainstream theoretical sociology. Goffman can only address what he and other symbolic interactionists have always addressed.

In view of this one might ask why symbolic interactionism has been so successful. The reasons may be to do with temporal and cultural context. As is indicated above, the perspective became dominant in the USA in the first half of the twentieth century. This was a period in which neither Weber nor Durkheim had been translated into English and in which Marx was an ideological pariah. Moreover, symbolic interactionism suited a culture that stressed the creative capacities of the individual and that sought to construct the individual as responsible for its actions rather than the consequence, much less the victim, of society. There are also more positive grounds for its success. Symbolic interactionism was at some levels subversive, managing to undermine the precious impressions people had of themselves and showing that the stigmatized (deviants, ethnic minorities, the poor, etc.) were not moral inferiors but victims of power plays by dominant groups and no different in their humanity than were the powerful. Symbolic interactionists, Goffman chief among them, were often clever and insightful, and their insights, especially as concretized in terminology (e.g. 'impression management', 'labelling'), continue to suffuse general sociology to this day.

Like Weber and Goffman, Schütz is trapped in the double bind of agency theory. If he theorizes at the level of the self or mind he only has a social psychology and has difficulty in moving beyond it to examine intersubjectivity and the sociological abstractions he calls types. However, in establishing intersubjectivity he is forced to reference it against systems of signs, 'stocks of knowledge' and the shared circumstances of the past. In so doing he presupposes cultures, social realities that stand prior to and are independent of individual subjectivities. He may wish to reduce these cultural realities to the contents of the mind but cannot do so without denying the possibility of intersubjectivity.

Despite this philosophical bent, if one were choosing the best example of a phenomenological social theorist one would elect Schütz rather than his students, Berger and Luckmann. Schütz at least seeks to address the problem of the process of intersubjective validation, while Berger and Luckmann gloss this problem by assuming that the process is unproblematic. This leads them into greater difficulty. In proposing over-arching structures, they are caught in a bind between viewing them as intentional creations or as functional imperatives. The former is clearly unrealistic – it would be absurd to view Christianity or Hinduism as something constructed to a human purpose – and they are forced to retreat to an unwitting functionalism.

By contrast, ethnomethodology can be said to take an emphasis on agency to its extreme. Not only are social arrangements human creations, they are deliberate and intentional human creations which provide a gloss and stability to cover up 'genuine' uncertainty and disorder. Moreover, intersubjectivity is not held to reside in shared understandings but in an agreement not to reveal disagreement and misunderstanding. So the incapacity to address large-scale structures and processes is more profound in ethnomethodology than in other agency theory. The implications for the possibility of a sociology are also more pronounced.

Giddens' structuration theory takes a central place in agency theory.[12] Aside from being the most recent heir to the agency tradition, it clearly places agency back in the mainstream of sociological theorizing, an accomplishment for which its author must receive considerable credit. Structuration theory is agency theory at its best and only the best example of an approach can be the legitimate focus of criticism of that approach. In a number of ways then, structuration theory deserves critical treatment. We may identify six main areas of criticism, most of which focus on the central issue of the emergence of structure (see pp. 104–7).[13]

1   The notion of structure is itself unclear as Held and Thompson (1989)

point out. Giddens insists that he means rules and resources but these terms are not used in any familiar way, nor are they explicated sufficiently. Beyond this, however, lies a more important issue, that of where the rules and resources are located or, in more formal terms, what their reality status is. Giddens, it will be remembered, gives us two such locations: in memory traces; and as instantiated in interactive practices. These different locations provide us with two very different, dare one say dualistic, notions of structure. 'Memory traces' is redolent of the unconscious structuralism of Lévi-Strauss, whom Giddens acknowledges, and Freud, whom he does not, except that Giddens has it as a tacit rather than an unconscious structuralism. 'Instantiation' is pure agency theory, similar to symbolic interactionism, in which structure is viewed as emergent from the conscious practices of actors. These must be regarded as radically opposed ideas of structure.

2 Solving the problem of dualism by the use of the conjunction 'and' is common practice in Giddens' reasoning. A repeated and pervasive example is that in which he argues that structure is dualistic because it is both enabling 'and' constraining. The terms not only have different meanings but actually contradict one another. The term 'enabling' presumably means offering a range of meanings, values, and means within which the actor can choose in following a course of conduct. But presumably that choice must be limited, in other words highly constrained, otherwise there would be no sense in using the term structure.

3 This leads to the further question of who or what does the choosing, that is, to Giddens' theory of the agent. If structure consists in memory traces within the practical consciousness of the actor then the argument must be that structure actually constitutes the actor. If the actor is not separate from structure, the ontological status of the freely acting individual must be in doubt.

4 Giddens' argument only gives the appearance of the reduction of action to structure. What is in fact occurring, not withstanding all claims to conceptualizing duality, is a reduction of structure to action/agency. If we accept that structure is indeed located in memory traces and instances of action then it is indeed being located at the level of agency and nothing more.

5 Taken together, the previous two criticisms indicate a pervasive circularity in Giddens' reasoning. The form of the argument is that structure structurates action, which instantiates and reproduces structure, which structurates action and so on, and that this all occurs simultaneously. This is another aspect of the earlier criticism of solving dualism by terminological fiat. More importantly, it is also an aspect of the reduction of structure to action. The circularity can and does only occur at the level of the actor and within the actor's consciousness. It is a circularity between reflexive monitoring, the location of action on one hand, and practical consciousness, the location of structure on the other.

6 Paradoxically, in all this individualistic reductionism, the aspect of the actor which might actually provide an identity to the individual disappears. The third and most unconscious level of the agent, the level of unconscious motives and cognition, appears to be of independent origin and also to be determinative in figure 2.2, and yet it is not discussed in relation to structure, structuration, and so on elsewhere in the analysis.

The difficulty in previous agency theories, according to Giddens, is that each accepts that social existence is constituted as a dualism of action and structure. His solution is to propose that action and structure be regarded as a duality, that is as simultaneous aspects of a single phenomenon. This might, at first blush, be regarded as an attempt to solve the problem by terminological fiat. But we have seen that Giddens goes much further than this in teasing out the analytic connections between action and structure. Nevertheless, if structure exists only when it is instantiated in interaction, then there seems to be no good reason for having a different word for it. Indeed, if we accept Giddens' statement that the dualism is unwarranted then sociological theorizing might be better served if dualistic terminology itself were abandoned. He appears to have recognized the problem but not to have escaped the theoretical formulation which has produced it.

Further reading

Max Weber's basic definitions can be found in *Economy and Society* (1978) and Simmel's are in *Georg Simmel 1858–1918*, edited by Kurt Wolff (Simmel 1959a, b). An excellent secondary analysis of Weber is given by Frank Parkin in *Max Weber* (1982) and a philosophical restatement and extension of his position can be found in Peter Winch's *The Idea of a Social Science* (1958). David Frisby's *Sociological Impressionism* (1981) is much the best secondary source on Simmel.

Mead's writings are collected in *Mind, Self and Society* (1934). Meltzer et al.'s *Symbolic Interactionism* (1975) is the best summary of the tradition, while its origins and reception are traced by Paul Rock in *The Making of Symbolic Interactionism* (1979). Goffman's point of departure is *The Presentation of Self in Everyday Life* (1959) and his most developed argument is in *Frame Analysis* (1974). Commentaries and debates are collected by Jason Ditton in *The View from Goffman* (1980).

The most accessible of Schütz's writings are probably the first few of his *Collected Papers* (1962) although *The Phenomenology of the Social World* (1972) is much more integrated. For Berger and Luckmann see *The Social Construction of Reality* (1967) or Berger's introductory statement, *Invitation to Sociology* (1966). Garfinkel's collected papers are in *Studies in Ethnomethodology* (1967) but there is a more useful general collection edited by Roy Turner, *Ethnomethodology* (1974).

Further reading on Habermas and Parsons is recommended elsewhere.

However, for excellent introductions see Michael Pusey's *Jürgen Habermas* (1987) and Guy Rocher's *Talcott Parsons and American Sociology* (1974). Students of Giddens should read at least three of his works: *The Class Structure of the Advanced Societies* (1981), *New Rules of Sociological Method* (1976), and his formal theoretical statement, *The Constitution of Society* (1984). The best collection of commentaries is probably the one edited by Bryant and Jary, *Giddens' Theory of Structuration* (1991).

Notes

1 We concentrate here on exegesis rather than criticism but Simmel's views about social inequality are very obviously flawed and reflect the prevailing ideology among privileged groups in nineteenth-century European society.

2 The parallel with Freud is not exact. Blumer's 'I' resembles Freud's id rather than ego, while the 'me' resembles the superego. The closest parallel to the ego in Blumer might be the self. For a detailed discussion of Freud see chapter 4.

3 Goffman's claims about his writing are invariably modest. He does not claim to be doing grand theory nor even to be saying everything there is to say about the social. Rather he offers only a perspective on a neglected aspect of social life. Nevertheless his writing is influential enough to be included here.

4 There are quite clear cultural differences regarding this distinction. It is significant that Goffman's theoretical statements are based on ethnographic studies of Hebridean crofters. In contemporary middle-class America, front areas have extended to kitchen, bathroom, etc. and far less of a distinction is maintained in domestic life.

5 Against themselves they do later say that the integration of institutions is not a functional imperative for the social processes that produce them (1967: 82).

6 In making this claim Garfinkel almost certainly underestimated the power and constraint which social reality exercises over the individual. If ethnomethodological investigators were continually to practice breaching experiments their violation of shared definitions of reality would result in the application of material or physical sanctions. Ethnomethodology is correct in estimating social reality to be fragile at the level of interaction but its force at the level of collectivities and general processes is far more difficult to disrupt.

7 For a biographical note on Parsons see p. 143.

8 For a biographical note on Habermas see p. 162.

9 Ludwig Wittgenstein was a British analytic philosopher whose main claim was that the meaning of any word is given by the way in which it is actually used.

10 Habermas himself denies this implication.

11 The relationship between action and structure is analagous for Giddens to the relationship between speech and language (1976: 118–20). Note, however, that Giddens is firmly in the interpretive/agency camp – action is real but structure is an abstraction or element of analysis.

12 This critique is in large measure the outcome of many years of conversation with John Holmwood and Sandy Stewart. For a detailed exposition of their critique of Giddens see their *Explanation and Social Theory* (1991).

13 The secondary literature on the theory of structuration is becoming considerable. Excellent collections, each of which includes a magnanimous reply by Giddens, are Bryant and Jary (1991), Clark et al. (1990), and Held and Thompson (1989).

3 Rationality: the maximization of individual interest

Within the right-wing ideologies which have emerged in the market democracies towards the end of the twentieth century an understanding of human behaviour as motivated by the maximization of individual interests has become a relative commonplace. These ideologies (variously called economic rationalism, supply-side economics, new rightism, Reaganomics, Rogernomics, or Thatcherism) are underpinned by the theory that human beings have individualized material interests, that these interests take precedence over commitments to such general values as justice or welfare, and that they also take precedence over such nonmaterial interests as personal development, intellectual stimulation, aesthetic appreciation, and the pursuit of community. Because they are indeed ideologies, and not mere theory, they also evaluate human behaviour as well as entire societies in terms of their material success. Success is accomplished by maximizing material advantage over competitors not only by achieving the highest level of efficiency in production but also by exploiting others as much as possible, while remaining as unexploited as possible oneself. Such exploitation can be established either within an employment relationship or within a bargaining or trading relationship.

In many ways the trading relationship is the paradigm for formal sociological theories emphasizing rationality as the primary defining characteristic of human society. In such a view, the members of society are frequently conceived of as being in possession of valuables with varying levels of scarcity which they can barter with one another. These valuables include such predictable items as property, both productive property and property for consumption, and skills and credentials, but also such other social valuables as approval, affection, prestige, political support, sexual responsiveness, and labour power. Such valuables will have varying degrees of scarcity. They will be provided to other people only in so far as others provide wanted valuables to oneself. So, for example, a person might be viewed as offering sexual responsiveness to another in exchange for material security. Human society is conceived to emerge from a multitude of such exchanges either explicitly or tacitly understood.

The link between theories emphasizing rationality and the theories emphasizing agency discussed in the previous chapter is clear. Indeed rationality theories may be considered as a subtype of agency theory. Like agency theory they are individualistic rather than holistic, that is they view macrostructural social phenomena as emerging from human interaction – there is no sense in rationality theory that such large-scale phenomena are pregiven. The special assumption they make is that human beings have an acquisitive and success-oriented nature which focuses on immediate returns. This is held to be so even in cases where individuals make an apparent sacrifice for the benefit of others. A soldier who risks 'certain' death to rescue others might be seen as trading life against the return of immense prestige and social approval, the mantle of heroism. Likewise, the religious martyr is maximizing the chance of the greatest reward of all, an eternity in paradise.

In making such assumptions, rationality theories solve the meaning-validation problems which we have seen are associated with *Verstehen*, at least in their own terms. It will be remembered that *erklärendes Verstehen* is held by Weber only to be achievable where action is rational in instrumental or value terms. Traditional (habitual) and affective actions are accessible only by means of *aktuelles Verstehen* which has no social-scientific status. In one sense, then, Weber's definition of the subject matter of sociology is exceedingly narrow, because by his own admission most action in everyday life is habitual in character. Likewise, phenomeno-logical and ethnomethodological sociologies focus only on behaviour which receives the meaning-accolade of the reflective glance or account. We have seen that Giddens' solution is to dispense with rationality altogether and to be prepared to examine the unintended consequences of human action. By absolute contrast, the theories examined in the present chapter 'solve' Weber's problem by extending instrumental rationality to include the other three types and therefore the entire gamut of human action. The problem of the validation of *Verstehen* is thus solved because all human action has the same meaning, it is conceived of as oriented to the maximization of instrumental interests.

In summary, then, rationality theories are those which give primacy to all or most of the following features:

1   Human beings seek to maximize the gratification they receive from the social world. These 'interests' in relation to the social world have an objective character.
2   Each member of society is in control of a supply of social valuables. Valuables consist of items with both material and psychological consequences. Individual gratification is maximized to the extent that the supply of valuables under the individual's control is maximized and, correspondingly, that the need or demand for valuables is minimized.
3   Interaction with others in the social world is conceived as a series of trading negotiations or games which are competitive in character. The object of social participation is to increase the supply of social valuables through this process of interaction. This may involve simply the exchange of valuables with a view to profit or may involve a more complex attempt to use the supply one has in order to control, coerce

and/or exploit the other. In many theories of rationality the total costs to all participants set against the total benefits are held to amount to zero – that is, the game is a 'zero-sum' game. This means that self-advantage automatically implies disadvantage for the other.

4   Human behaviour is thus held to be rational because individuals engage in a continuous calculation of returns to engagement in a particular piece of action against the costs of that engagement.

5   Because human wants and gratifications are relatively unchanging, stable interaction patterns emerge which offer regular exchanges that are understood by the participants to be normative in character, i.e. morally correct. These stable exchange patterns, taken together, constitute large-scale phenomena. To reverse the reasoning, macro-structural phenomena can always be reduced to rationalized exchanges between individuals. The technical term for describing such a position is 'methodological individualism'.

6   However, emergent structural arrangements are not the main focus of interest for theories of rationality. Rather, the general tendency is to research and analyse small-group interaction, or hypothetical small-group interaction, and then to expand the results to the level of empirical generalization. These empirical generalizations become the building blocks for theory.

7   There is a general convergence between sociological theories of rationality and both economic theory and game theory because each stresses the maximization of individual advantage within a rational calculus of action.

Because of this convergence we find many of the founding arguments of rationality theory in classical economic theory. Perhaps the most sociologically accessible (and because of Parsons [1937] the most sociologically familiar) of these are the work of Marshall, the nineteenth-century, Cambridge economist, and Pareto, the Italian political economist. However, economically-minded, rational exchange of scarce items is not the only foundation for theories of this type. Items become defined as valuable not only because they are scarce but also because they are wanted. The behaviouristic psychology of Skinner provides a foundation for establishing wants by means of behavioural exchange.

Sociological theories of rationality follow one of three streams. First, the direct heir to psychological behaviourism is the exchange sociology of Homans and its later development by Blau, Emerson and others. Second, there is a direct application of the private-choice notions of economic theory in the noneconomic sphere contained in what has been called public-choice theory. Last, there is what might be described as the high point of sociological reasoning in a theoretical development which combines elements of exchange theory with Marxist accounts of exploitation and game theory. This is called rational-choice theory or game-theoretic Marxism or analytic Marxism. This chapter surveys each of these in turn.

Founding arguments

The most significant statements about rationality are made by adherents to the tradition described in the introduction to this book as utilitarian theory, that is, theorists who argue that social life is both subjective and instrumental or material in character. In nineteenth-century society, which was increasingly materialistic and individualistic in its cultural orientations, such an approach took an easy foothold. However, it did so among social scientists who defined themselves as economists rather than sociologists. The two most influential of these are Marshall (often regarded as the founder of modern economics) and Pareto. Each of these sought to establish the character of individual human purposes or goals. More recently, in the twentieth century, the American psychologist Skinner has sought to demonstrate the way in which commitment to purposes or goals becomes individually fixed.

Marshall: you can always get what you want

Marshall's economic theory (1961) begins with the concept of wants. Within his naïve, nineteenth-century conception of human evolution, in primitive societies wants first arose from needs. The most basic set of wants was therefore oriented to basic food, clothing, shelter, etc. In this early stage, these wants gave rise to corresponding activities, such as hunting, building, and weaving. But as society developed, the relationship reversed and activities began to give rise to wants. For example, the possibilities which arose from the skills developed in weaving gave rise to the possibility of wanting clothes for their beauty or their fashionability.

Alfred Marshall (1842–1924)

An Englishman, Marshall studied at Cambridge, where he first took a lectureship in moral science. He was appointed to a chair of political economy at Bristol before returning to Cambridge as Professor of Political Economy in 1885. He is credited with formalizing the classical economics of Adam Smith and David Ricardo. His *Principles of Economics* is a foundational text for the discipline whose name it bears.

Source: *Penguin Dictionary of Economics* (1984: s.v. Marshall, Alfred)

The connection between this conception of wants and the sociological notion of exchange is the concept of 'utility'. Whereas a want is a psychological predisposition of the actor, utility is the way in which the actor orients towards an item or object in the world. The utility of an object is the extent to which it can satisfy a want. Individuals will demand (that is they will seek to engage in an exchange in order to get) those goods which have maximum utility.

However, utility is not an immutable property of the object demanded – it varies according to the amount of it one already has. Marshall hereby introduces one of the fundamental laws of economics, the law of diminishing utility: 'The total utility of a thing to anyone (that is, the total pleasure or other benefit it yields to him) increases with every increase in his stock of it, but not as fast as his stock increases' (1961: 93, italics deleted). In contemporary economics this is known as 'the law of diminishing marginal utility' because the utility of the last purchase made is less than the one before it. Under this law, marginal utility eventually can fall to zero or even below it (as in the case of the last piece of chocolate candy which makes one sick) in which case the person will cease to engage in exchange relationships (i.e. stay away from the chocolate shop).

Marshall's interest in utility is purely an economic one, he wants to understand the way in which the prices at which items are exchanged are established. The price a person is willing to pay for an item (i.e. the amount of money or barter items one is willing to exchange for it) depends on the utility of the item. Given diminishing marginal utility, the price one is willing to pay for each marginal item, assuming the individual's supply of money to be fixed, will also diminish at the margin. If the price is low the individual will buy a large amount, and if the price is high the individual will buy a correspondingly smaller amount.

Three further factors enter into the individual's calculation of whether or not to purchase. The first is the factor of elasticity of wants, the question of how sensitive is one's propensity to satisfy wants in response to changes in price. For some items wants are said to be relatively inelastic while others are elastic. For example, if one owns a car, the want for fuel is relatively inelastic, one will tend to continue to buy fuel in similar quantities whether the price rises or falls. But the want for, say, a car CD player is relatively elastic – a rise in price will tend to deter purchase and a fall in price will tend to induce it. Second, a person may defer gratification by putting off the purchase of an item with greater utility until a future date. However, because they are giving up the immediate gratification which can come from the object, utility will be discounted by a corresponding amount at the time of purchase. Third, the price which is paid is usually less than the value or utility of an item – for example, one might be paying twenty per cent of one's salary for housing when one would be willing, if necessary, to pay fifty per cent. The difference is a surplus and the surplus generated on inelastic items (necessities) tends to be transferred to the purchase of elastic items (luxuries).

Here, then, Marshall provides us with the first element of a rationalistic theory of society, the idea of utility. Utility is significant because it provides a standard against which each individual can calculate the value of any item involved in an exchange. The concept applies not only to wants but to the items one might offer in exchange for the satisfaction of wants. One can compare the utility of holding on to an item with the utility of having the want satisfied by another person and then choosing to exchange or not to exchange on the basis of maximum advantage. It is clear from this that Marshall conceives of human beings as rational maximizers, a view which continues to pervade rationality-based theories of society including contemporary economics.[1]

Pareto: inescapable logic

Pareto and Marshall were contemporaries and while neither had any influence on those other contemporaries considered to be more cogent founders of sociological theory, Durkheim, Marx, Simmel and Weber, it is clear that there was some exchange of ideas – Parsons (1937: 13) tells us that Pareto was 'almost certainly' influenced by a reading of Marshall. The key area of overlap between them is Marshall's concept of utility as the basis for the rational calculation of individual advantage. Pareto begins here but then takes the important step of generalizing individual utility to the level of the societal community, thereby establishing himself as a true sociologist.

Vilfredo Pareto (1848–1923)

Pareto was born in Paris of a noble Italian father and a French mother. He was educated at Turin Polytechnic, as an engineer, before becoming director of a railway company. He did not receive his first academic appointment until made an extraordinary Professor of Economics at Lausanne, Switzerland, in 1893. His first publications were in that 'dismal science' but he published the *Tratato di sociologia generale* (Treatise on General Sociology) in 1916. He returned to Italy late in his life under the sponsorship of the Fascist regime established by Benito Mussolini.

Sources: *Penguin Dictionary of Sociology* (1984: *s.v.* Pareto, Vilfredo); *Penguin Dictionary of Economics* (1984: *s.v.* Pareto, Vilfredo); Coser (1977: 387–428)

Pareto (1966: 99–102) begins, then, at the level of individual utility but is dissatisfied with the one-sidedness of the concept. Utility has a short-term and instrumental character. An item has utility if its use is convenient for a human being. But within this notion there are two types of utility – economic utility, which focuses on material well-being, and moral utility, which focuses on moral development. For example, attendance at religious worship on a routine and regular basis has moral utility because of its instrumental relationship to, say, personal salvation. However, he remains concerned that the concept is still too economic and instrumental in character. So he proposes the use of the term 'ophelimity' instead.

Ophelimity means that an item satisfies some human need or desire. The term thus allows the sociologist to escape from the problem of having to specify objectively the interests of a particular person or group. Just as there can be economic and moral utility, there can also be economic and moral ophelimity.

Pareto has decided, then, that while human beings indeed undertake rational economic action in pursuit of material and moral interests that this is not a complete representation of their action. He is able to move on to offer a classification of action which in some respects parallels Weber's (see chapter 2). For Pareto (1966: 143–9, 183–209), there are three types of human action:

- The relatively unimportant category of instinctive or habitual actions.
- Logical actions, which in current terminology would be called rational actions. These are actions based on ophelimity in which the observer can reconstruct the actor's relationship between means and ends. The most penetrable of these will be actions based on economic rationality.
- Nonlogical actions, where the actor believes that an appropriate means–ends relationship has been established but where this makes no logical sense to an observer. Such actions are most usually those for which the logic has been established by means of a reflective glance (see above, pp. 33–4). Here the actor imposes a logical scheme on past acts which have no logic in their formulation.

Pareto criticizes the mainly economic theories which seek to analyze only logical actions and proposes instead to embark on an analysis of nonlogical actions.

Nonlogical actions are further subdivided. If we compare human societies, Pareto (1966: 215–50) argues, we will find both common uniformities and individual variations. If the variations are stripped away, the uniformities can be considered as universal 'residues' of human action and can be distinguished from 'derivations', the socially constructed varieties of human social life. The residues are surprisingly multitudinous so they are classified into six groups. Some of the most important of these are:

- the 'instinct of combinations', the inclination to recognize that objects are associated with one another;
- the 'persistence of aggregates', the inclination to recognize the continuity of human associations across time; and
- 'sociality', the tendency for human beings to live in society and to subordinate themselves to it.

Derivations, by contrast, include variations in human knowledge, in authority patterns, and in the degree of consensus in a society.

It would now appear that, unlike Marshall, Pareto's main concern is with nonrational (nonlogical) action, and even with logical action in pursuit of desires, in preference to a concern with rational action in the pursuit of material interests. This is not so. Nonlogical action is, for Pareto, an inferior form of action which is progressively being excluded by the steady march of evolution. Concrete human society is a combination of sentiments, interests, and logical reasoning, as well as of derivations from these residues, but it is only in terms of interests and logical reasoning that society can be governed. Pareto can thus establish a critique of public policy which is based on what is good for society as a whole rather than for its individual members. For example, a government which embarks on a war of territorial conquest may legitimate this action on the nonlogical grounds of establishing the power and identity of the nation. Indeed, such a government might seek to justify itself further by saying it is good for the individual members of the society. But, assessed in logical terms, the war should perhaps not be pursued, because it involves deep sacrifice for the individual members of society (loss of life, property, etc.).

Pareto (1966: 253–6) insists, then, that social scientists should not confuse the maximum utility *of* a community (as a whole) with maximum utility *for* a community (as an aggregate of individuals). He further insists that the latter is the sole reasonable basis for public policy, at least partly because nonlogical action is impenetrable for the policy analyst. Rather public policy, always and inevitably, intervenes in and decides between the realization of individual utilities. Successful public policy establishes a calculus of individual utilities which it should explicitly seek to maximize across the population.

This formulation has entered contemporary social science parlance as the concept of 'Pareto optimality' and it takes a significant place, as we shall see, in what has become known as 'public choice theory'. Pareto is the first to admit that the complete accomplishment of optimality is impossible (1966: 300). One cannot make ultimate and absolute judgements of what is good and bad for individuals all the way into an infinite future. Rather one must investigate the proximate (immediate and material) consequences of human action. In this formulation, such notions as the 'ideal society' or the 'just society' are the property of poets and metaphysicians. After all, logicality is the dominant social orientation, as he argues in a passage which stands opposed to the Marxist claim of the possibility of a proletarian revolution:

[T]he workers prefer the tangible benefits of higher wages, progressive taxation and greater leisure – a preference they exercise while freely entertaining myths of their own: the myth of the holy proletariat, the myth of the inherent evil of the capitalist system, and the myth of an ideal government under worker-soldier soviets, and so on. [1966: 302]

We shall later consider whether Pareto optimality is itself a myth.

Skinner: society written on a clean slate

Both Marshall and Pareto take the view that human behaviour needs to be analysed in terms of the gratification of material wants. However, they leave untheorized, outside of Pareto's almost structuralist statement of the universality of certain human wants (the residues), the basis on which wants emerge and are maintained. Moreover, they are unable to give an account of why wants become translated into certain types of action and not others. For example, robbing-a-bank might be a more rational way of feeding one's family, on a balance of risks, than working-in-a-sweatshop, and we might reasonably ask why the latter is more frequently chosen than the former. The general set of statements which is employed to answer these questions comes from Skinner, a twentieth-century behaviourist psychologist.

B.F. Skinner (b. 1904)

An American, Burrhus Frederick Skinner is the founder of the behaviourist school of psychology. He later generalized his arguments to a general philosophy of society, for example, in *Beyond Freedom and Dignity* in which he proposed that human society could be changed by the modification of individual behaviour.

Skinner (1953; 1974) dismisses almost all of the arguments reviewed in the other chapters of this book, including subjectivism and structuralism, as mere speculation. For him, theories which stress agency cannot be accorded scientific validity because the contents of another's mind are inaccessible, and social structures are mere abstractions in the mind of the observer. Rather, human experience must be seen as essentially organic – everything which is known is known through the body and the only information which the brain can receive is that which can be transmitted through the nervous systems of the body. The gratification of wants must therefore be mediated organically.

Nevertheless, the basis for Skinner's theoretical statement is indeed a rationalistic one (1974: 39, 46). He begins, much like Marshall, with the view that many items in the environment of the human organism are critically necessary for its survival, including food, water, fuel, and shelter. Behaviour which reduces threats to organic survival, that is, which procures necessary items, is strengthened or reinforced by that conse-quence. There are two types of such behaviour: reflex behaviour which is involuntary and automatic and, more important and interesting, operant behaviour, which is a product of the will. Operant behaviour is argued by Skinner to be conditioned, that is, to have been reinforced by events in the external environment. A positive reinforcer strengthens the behaviour that produces it (e.g. eating reduces hunger and is therefore likely to be repeated); a negative reinforcer strengthens any behaviour that stops or prevents it (e.g. subzero temperatures will tend to make one take shelter).

Skinner (1974: 49–52) is now in a position to say what wants are. They are simply shortages of the things we need to survive. Human beings will behave in such a way as to minimize shortages. This fact can and will be used by other people in the environment to shape and maintain certain behaviours. Such responses as the provision and withholding of food or affectionate embraces can be employed as stimuli to accomplish certain responses, especially, for example, on the part of children.

Skinner (1953: 91–106) can now distinguish between the types of stimulus which are required to induce a particular behaviour, on one hand, and those needed to get it done skilfully, on the other. Getting-something-done can be accomplished by consistent reinforcement. But getting-something-done-skilfully requires differential reinforcement, that is variation in the intensity, timing and scheduling of reinforcement. So, when a behaviour is performed skilfully, reinforcement needs to be immediate and intense in order to maximize skilful performance. Maintaining behaviour over time requires what Skinner calls variable-interval reinforcement (1953: 116) that is reinforcements must occur relatively frequently but at time intervals which are unpredictable by the recipient.

There remains an obvious problem. Human beings do not only engage in activities which meet survival needs. 'Playing chess' or 'reading a book on sociological theory' have no immediate relationship to survival, yet human beings can be gratified by their performance. Skinner (1953: 107–10) begins to solve this problem by conceiving of each behavioural event as composed of three items: the stimulus, a signal in the environment which requests or elicits behaviour; the response, the behaviour itself; and reinforcement. Under 'intermittent reinforcement' (e.g. variable-interval reinforcement) a response will tend to occur when the stimulus is introduced even when there is no reinforcement, that is, the stimulus–response relationship starts to be valued positively in itself. It is not merely the positive reinforcements or the aversion of negative ones which alone are gratifying. We do not look forward to meal times simply because of hunger, nor to seeing our conjugal partners after work each evening because this will assist in perpetuating the species. These stimuli, and the complex ones which are inductively built upon them, are gratifying in themselves.

The process of 'induction' is one in which stimuli with common properties elicit similar responses. The degree of similarity of response varies according to the degree of similarity of the stimuli. So, we might 'explain' enjoying a chess game in terms of the similarity of its stimuli to those obtained in other competitive activity more closely related to survival, hunting for example. In some circumstances the environment will narrow down those aspects of the stimulus to which a response is required by extinguishing responses to all other aspects. This is especially so in the case of of the complexities of language – human beings are conditioned to respond predictably to the tone, phonetics, semantics, and syntax of language in all their multiple combinations. For Skinner, meanings become unproblematically external. Where an act is a stimulus its meaning is the response it elicits; where it is a response the meaning is determined by the stimulus.

For Skinner, then, human behaviour is determined environmentally. The human individual is understood to seek to satisfy wants which indicate shortages of the things it needs to survive. The environment 'uses' this dependency to condition the individual's behaviour in specific directions. The individual is, in this theoretical approach, more than any other a *tabula rasa* (clean slate) on which the social environment is written in large letters. Non-survival-based gratifications are also induced in the individual by the conditioning effect of the environment. Some of us enjoy Brahms and others enjoy Springsteen as stimuli because we are conditioned to such gratifications.

The enormous lacuna in Skinner is the assumption of the neutrality of the environment which, incidentally, leaves a useful intellectual space for the establishment of a sociology of large-scale structures. In his view such structures must be seen either as self-generating or as nonexistent. However, of more immediate concern is whether a sociological theory can be built upon assumptions derived from Skinnerian and economic theory in which human beings are conceived of as rational maximizers of gratification. Exchange theory attempts to do just this.

Exchange theory: trading associations

The first attempt to introduce rationalistic assumptions into sociology came in the mid-twentieth century in the shape of exchange theory. Exchange theory combined an economic model of human behaviour with the Skinnerian notion of conditioning, to try to show that stable social norms can emerge as the consequence of individual interests. The originator of the tradition is Homans who, in the 1950s and 1960s, engaged in a vigorous debate on just this issue with Parsons (see chapter 5), a departmental colleague at Harvard.

Homans: fair exchange

Emerson (1981: 31–4) identifies three distinctive, core assumptions in exchange theory:

- The focus is on the costs and benefits people obtain in social inter-action. There are many types of social valuable, including goods, money, praise, esteem, approval and attention, but they have the common characteristic that people will actively try to obtain or produce them. So a core assumption is that people will (often or always) act rationally to maximize benefit (i.e. reinforcement, value, utility, reward or payoff).

- The value of items is variable but they all follow the single principle of diminishing marginal utility (in exchange theory, called the principle of satiation or value adaptation).
- The benefits an individual receives in social interaction are contingent upon the benefits which the individual provides to others. To receive benefits there must be an exchange process which is social and interactive in character. Society is therefore to be understood as a network of benefit flows.

George Caspar Homans (1910–89)

An American, Homans began his career as an historian before encountering sociology and anthropology under the influences of Lawrence Henderson and Elton Mayo at the Harvard Business School in the 1930s. After the Second World War he joined Talcott Parsons in the multi-disciplinary Department of Social Relations at the same University. He publicly and vehemently opposed Parsons' grand theoretical sociology, proposing instead a positivistic and individualistic version of exchange theory.

Sources: *Penguin Dictionary of Sociology* (1984: *s.v.* Homans, George); Ritzer (1992: 426–7)

Nowhere is the merger of psychology with economics more apparent than in Homans' exchange theory but he most explicitly acknowledges his debt to Skinner. Skinner bases his analysis of human behaviour on laboratory studies of animals, mainly pigeons and rats. Homans, who is the originating figure in the exchange theoretical tradition in sociology, also finds the transfer of findings between species nonproblematic. Whereas much animal behaviour is reflex in character, some, especially the behaviour which can be induced in laboratory animals, is operant behaviour which is similar to the operant behaviour of humans. Indeed, Homans is happy to summarize Skinner's analysis, much in the fashion of the above section, as a basis for his own approach to social behaviour (1961). However, there is a significant difference between the two analyses. We have seen that Skinner gives the environment God-like characteristics of omnipotence and inscrutability so that it takes on the character of an invisible hand. In Homans the environment is populated by actors not unlike oneself, each seeking to control or condition the situations in which they find themselves in order to maximize advantage. Such situations are conceived as interactions between pairs of individuals in which each seeks to control the flow of rewards to their own advantage. Indeed, in a playful twist, Homans reconceptualizes Skinner's animal laboratory as an inter-action situation between a pigeon and an experimental psychologist in which the pigeon gives findings to the psychologist as a reward for the provision of food, and thus conditions the psychologist's behaviour. Homans does not comment on who gets the better of the deal.

Homans confines his analysis to what he calls everyday or subinstitu-tional social behaviour, that is to interpersonal interaction. The behaviour in which he is interested (1961: 2–3) has three signficant characteristics:

- It is social in the sense that when an individual acts, the performance will be rewarded or punished by the behaviour of another person.
- The other person must be the direct source of reinforcement which must not be mediated through some larger structure.
- The behaviour must be actualized rather than merely ideal or expected.

Homans would thus argue that his is not a grand theory in the accepted sense of seeking to explain everything. He does not seek, for example, to examine the ways in which rules are established and institutionalized or the way in which whole societies change.

Homans' intention is to establish some propositions about exchange between human beings which hold universally and he aims to do this at the most elementary or primitive level. So he begins (1961: 30–41) by defining some primitive terms: an 'activity' is a type, but not a concrete instance, of behaviour; a 'sentiment' is a particular type of activity which expresses or symbolizes internal attitudes and feelings; and 'interaction' occurs when two individuals mutually direct their activities. Activities are variable in terms of their 'frequency' and their 'value', where the latter indicates the strength of the reinforcement. The term 'value' is identical with the economist's term 'utility' (1961: 41). Homans now applies these terms to a hypothetical and primitive situation of exchange between two individuals ('Person' and 'Other') who trade approval in exchange for assistance.

There are five basic propositions which Homans deduces from such a situation. If there is a long history of assistance–approval exchange (Person asks Other for help, Other gives it, and then Person thanks Other) then Person is typically more likely to ask for assistance in the future.

- The more similar the present situation is to past ones in which rewards have been received, the more likely the activity is to be performed.

Also the more Person expresses thanks and appreciation to Other, the more likely Other is to offer assistance.

- The more frequently that activity is rewarded, the more likely it is to be performed.

Also, if Person is the only individual who seems to appreciate Other's help, the more likely Other is to give that help.

- The more valuable is the reward for an activity, the more often it will be performed.

However, the continuous expression of thanks by Person to Other will cause Other to regard those thanks as worthless and indeed possibly as a nuisance.

- The more frequently that an activity has been rewarded in the recent past, the less valuable each subsequent reward becomes (i.e. marginal utility declines).

Thus far, the argument appears to be an obvious derivation from Skinner and Marshall – individuals are only going to act if they get rewards but some care must be exercised by those involved in interaction because rewards can lose their value. As exchange procceds, however, the participants will engage in two kinds of calculation. They will first calculate what it costs them in material and psychic terms to provide rewards to others. And they will also calculate the profit they amass from rewards received. Generally, they will be looking for a rough balance between these, that is for distributive justice (1961: 75) and thus another proposition emerges – if Other thinks that Person does not appreciate the assistance given to a sufficient degree, Other is likely to react in an emotional way.

- The more disadvantaged a person is in terms of distributive justice, the more likely are sentiments of anger.

It is clear from the above that Homans concentrates his analysis at the level of two-person interaction. However, he is not unmindful of the need to explain social phenomena of large complexity, scale and endurance. He sets out an agenda for the elaboration of exchange theory into this 'institutional' realm which has become the holy grail for other exchange theorists keen to defend themselves from charges of psychologism (1961: 378–98). Small-scale and large-scale social phenomena are different, he argues, only in terms of their level of complexity and not in terms of the fundamental processes which constitute them. There are two forms to this complexity. The first is that behaviours tend to become maintained not by a primary reward received directly from another but by such generalized reinforcers as money and status. Second, the reward can be received in a roundabout or indirect way. The stability of such exchanges is established in norms and patterns of authority which, as it were, are built upon previous elementary exchanges. Norms, for example, are expectations built upon the frequency of exchange processes of particular types. A manager who does not wear a suit is not immediately threatened by a loss of pay but does experience social disapproval. Social disapproval is a generalized mediator which conveys the message that benefits may disappear.

The example of a manager wearing a suit is that of a simple institution. The next question is the one about the way complex and elaborate institutions emerge. Homans is clearly a social constructionist in the fashion of Giddens or Berger and Luckmann (see chapter 2): 'the secret of society is that it was made by men, and there is nothing in society but what men put there' (1961: 385). The origins of complex contemporary society lie, then, in a hypothetical small-scale primitive unit exhibiting mainly elementary levels of social behaviour, that is, engaging in direct exchange. If the society develops some kind of surplus (e.g. of food, money or military personnel) institutional elaboration can begin. Such elaboration must be understood to be intentional: 'some man or group of men within the society . . .is apt to invest [the surplus] by trying out some new set of activities that departs from the original or primeval institutional pattern' (1961: 386). This new pattern inevitably extends beyond immediate relationships and involves intermediaries. There must be sufficient capital to maintain the loyalty of intermediaries until the returns from the new investment flow in. The capital must consist of such generalized reinforcers as money, social approval, or control of the means of violence. The more investment there is, the more elaborate is the chain of interdependence, the more specialized are the roles within the network, the greater is the level of mutual dependence, and so the greater the inclination to follow norms or authoritative commands which hold the network together. In all circumstances there will be no institutional development unless there is a pay-off both for the original investor and for the participants in maintaining it.

Emerson: unfair exchange

Homans' agenda for the development of institutions is, by his own admission, speculative, resembling 'a primitive orgy after harvest' (1961: 378). A very much more systematic conceptualization of the development of large-scale social institutions is given by Emerson (1981). Emerson's critical move is to take exchange theory beyond the dyad (two-person interaction). The key problem in the analysis of the diad is that it assumes monopolies of supply ('resources') on the part of each member which precludes exploitation and thus power differentiation. In order to raise the level of analysis, Emerson introduces the concept of an exchange network, which consists of two or more connected exchange relationships. The most simple example is a triad (three-person interaction) in which the relationship A-B and the relationship B-C are connected through B. The connection is positive or cooperative where increases in the A-B exchange promote increases in the B-C exchange, for example, where A is an employer, B is a worker/consumer, and C is a producer of commodities.

The connection is negative or competitive where increases in the A-B exchange reduce the level of B-C exchange, for instance, where both A and C are employees and B is an employer. Within this simple example, the position of B in a negatively connected network is powerful because, other things being equal, the resources B controls are relatively scarce – there are two suppliers of labour but only one supplier of wages. Where this occurs, the powerful individual is in a position to exploit others and to build up surplus, anger about distributive justice notwithstanding.

Emerson thus conceives of social structure as a series of interconnected networks within which strategically located individuals are able to build up the supply of, and to monopolize, resources. However, the conception remains wedded to the notion of interpersonal exchange of benefits and, as Homans shows, not all behaviour is constructed in this way. It is Blau (1964) who offers a general argument about the translation of microstructures of exchange into stable macrostructures.

Blau: power attracts

Like Homans and Emerson, Blau begins at a primitive level, the level of why people associate with each other at all. For Blau this is obvious, human association can be intrinsically rewarding: 'Most human pleasures have their roots in social life' (1964: 14). But participating in human associations can also bring costs and the distribution of costs and benefits is seldom even – people do things for each other, calling these things favours or help or assistance without any immediate or apparent return. However, normally they receive social approval in return or at least anticipate that the other person will be in a position to do them a favour at some point in the future. Social life is therefore characterized by a surface altruism which masks hedonism and egoism. However, hedonism and egoism focus on diverse objects and this places people in positions to trade the resources that they do not want for those that they do. In all circumstances, then, argues Blau, human association implies exchange.

Peter M. Blau (b. 1918)

Blau was born in Vienna, Austria but emigrated to the USA in 1939. He took his PhD at Columbia in 1952. He is at least as well known for his contributions to organization theory and the measurement of occupational status and mobility as for theory.

Source: Ritzer (1992: 528)

The force which propels the formation of associations is 'social attraction'. Blau generally wishes to use this terms in its widest possible sense – being drawn to another person whether because of that person's intrinsic attractiveness or because that person can offer extrinsic advantages.

However, the formation of an association depends not only on being attracted by others but also on being attractive to others. Once mutual attraction is established, social exchange can begin. Unlike Emerson, Blau is willing to admit the possibility of power differences in dyadic exchange. They occur where one person is in an exchange deficit and can only support the continuation of the exchange by subordinating themselves to the other. The other can accept a power credit, a power to command which can then be used in other exchanges. So people are powerful to the extent that others are dependent upon them.

The differentiation of power promotes two dynamic forces which operate to establish collective social organization. The first is legitimation. The fact that people are willing to subordinate themselves in return for social benefits indicates approval of the exercise of power. To the extent that they communicate and express this approval the power is legitimated. The legitimation of power allows the organization of collective effort in the pursuit of objectives. However, where the power exercised is perceived as exceeding the value of the benefits received, a second dynamic force comes into play, opposition. Here people will express and communicate disapproval to one another. However, this is also a source of collective organization because people will form such oppositional organizations as social movements, political parties, and unions to order to make their opposition effective.

Here Blau makes his critical link between 'microstructures' (interacting individuals) and 'macrostructures' (interrelated groups). The first step in the argument is to say that there are parallel processes in the two types of structure – just as individuals work together, so do groups, and just as one individual may oppose another, the same may be said of groups. The grounds for this appear to be that processes of social exchange are universal to all interaction situations. This allows Blau to say that people share common values and that these consensual values become the mediating link between situations where there is no direct contact. The critical mediating values are those of integration (shared bonds of understanding and common standards of valuation which allow the development of such media of exchange between groups as money), differentiation, legitimation and opposition.

Public choice: power to the people who have power

Social exchange theory seeks mainly to understand why individuals behave the way they do rather than seeking to explain society. Its principal minimum statement about collective organizations is that they emerge as the consequence of individual rational behaviour. Maximally, it suggests that collective organizations are the deliberate and intentional product of individual behaviour, that is, that collective organizations further the interests of individuals. We can now consider a set of theoretical arguments which proceeds from the opposite direction. It asks why collective organizations behave in the way that they do. As might be expected, it argues that collective organizations act rationally to maximize benefits but, in so doing, it does not assume coincidence between individual and collective rationalities. Indeed, its principle focus is the way that organizations must seek to reconcile these often conflicting rationalities. The arguments are known as public choice theory and, because the theory originates in political science, rather than sociology, they focus on behaviour of governments and other political organizations.

The basic orientation of public choice theory is the view that political behaviour is not in principle different from economic behaviour. Like economic theory it takes the view that the elements of theory are individuals rather than collectivities: 'The building blocks are living, choosing, economising persons' (Buchanan 1978: 5). Moreover, as Buchanan (1978) argues, individuals are defined as the sum of their preferences. So assuming that individuals are different, their preferences must also differ. However, many aspects of social life are collective and public rather than private and individual. This raises the central problem of public choice theory alluded to above, that of how different individual preferences can be reconciled in formulating projects, the consequences of which will be experienced by all the members of a political community. Indeed, within public choice theory this becomes the precise function of government.

Olsen; Buchanan: the illogic of collective action

The philosophical underpinning for this central problematic comes from Olsen (1965). Olsen starts with the simple premise that the purpose of collective organizations is to further the interests of their members. He looks for the severest test of his argument by choosing organizations in which the interests of members might be expected to be shared: unions, farmers' cartels, shareholders' associations, and the state (for whose members the common interest is good government). Each of these requires a reconciliation of individual interests and common interests. We can take the state as our main example. For citizens, the common interest is the provision of certain services, say defence, economic management, and education. However, each individual's interest presumably lies in the minimization of economic cost in the form of financial contributions to the state, that is each individual will seek to become a 'free rider', to hitch a lift without paying the fare. As Olsen cogently points out, no matter how developed the sense of patriotism or nationalism, in no society in history has any state managed to survive on voluntary, philanthropic contributions. Rather the reconciliation between the individual and the collectivity has been accomplished by the inevitable and compulsory measure of taxation.

The reason the state must rely on taxation is because it is providing 'public goods', that is goods and services which: 'must be available to everyone if they are available to anyone' (1965: 14). If it were possible to deny services to those who did not contribute then the contributions could indeed be made voluntary. Contributions could also be voluntary if the group was small because the contributor could expect a share of the collective gain which was perceptible and appreciable. However, even in small groups, where contributions are noncompulsory, the fulfilment of collective interests can be expected to be suboptimal other than where each member contributes an equal amount. Indeed, smaller contributors may be expected to exploit larger ones. The larger the group becomes, the greater the level of suboptimality so that very large or latent groups (e.g. social classes, women, consumers, taxpayers, racial minorities) have no widespread tendency to act to further their common interests. The only large groups which can operate successfully are those which can secure nonvoluntary commitments including the state, unions and professional associations.

If Olsen is correct when he says: 'rational, self-interested individuals will not act to achieve their common or group interests' (1965: 2, italics deleted), the problem arises of explaining those collective institutions which palpably exist – if every member wants to be a free rider, how can contributions be mobilized? Buchanan (1978) would argue that Olsen is engaged in a false construction of the problem, that is, he assumes that the exchange between the individual and the collectivity is taking place in an unconstrained way outside of any norms or rules. In fact, organizations, including states, typically are intentional constructions and are therefore constitutional. Human beings come together to create organizations uncertain about what the individual consequences will be. Rational negotiation will lead them to a position which establishes a set of rules in which the outcome will, in some sense, be fair or just. They will institutionalize a set of norms which ensure, as far as possible, that contributions and benefits will, within reason, be balanced. Indeed, if properly thought out, such constitutions will even ensure that majority rule does not allow for exploitation of the minority. Thus, in Buchanan, the USA has a normatively preferable constitution to that of Britain because of the constraints it places on majority voting by separating powers.

Arrow; Niskanen; Downs: rational dictatorship

The economist Arrow (1963) lays out some of the conditions which such a constitution, or in his own terms a social welfare function, would have to meet. They are as follows:

- The aim of the society is to maximize social utility or welfare within known technological and resource constraints. A social welfare function would consist of a ranked list of priorities in the public goods provided in the society, known as a preference schedule.

- There must be a positive association between individual preferences and collective preferences. So if a public good rises in every individual's preference schedule it would also rise in the collective schedule.[2]
- The function must be independent of irrelevant alternatives, i.e. preferring one good will not be affected by one's preference for other goods.
- The social welfare function is not to be imposed dictatorially.

Arrow then enters a complex logical proof to demonstrate that the four conditions are not mutually compatible. Like Olsen, Arrow is forced to fall back on compulsion and to sacrifice the last condition. He must construct the state as omniscient and impartial, that is, the assumption is made: 'that full information is available to society (or the social decision-maker) concerning all individual preferences, and that social welfare will be maximized by reference to rules strictly adhered to' (Rowley 1978: 33). As Rowley says, the reality is that individual preferences are neither widely known nor especially stable even if it were in principle possible to know them all. Nevertheless, for Arrow: 'the problem is to counsel not citizens generally but public officials' (1963: 107, italics deleted) and indeed such counselling should prescribe different (i.e. collective welfare) values than those values of individual interest which might be advised to a private citizen.

Few public choice theorists now accept that the state can be impartial and omniscient. Indeed, the tendency has been increasingly to regard the bureaucrat not as an ethical arbiter seeking constantly to optimize collective welfare but rather as a rational maximizer operating much in the way that other actors are believed so to do. The leading proponent of this view is Niskanen (1971). In his view, bureaucrats must be understood as managers, similar to managers in the private sector, except that whereas private sector managers are motivated by an orientation to the survival and profitability of the firm, bureaucrats are oriented to the survival and growth of the bureau. In everyday terms, bureaucrats normally seek to maximize the total budgets of their bureaux. However, under Pareto optimality (see p. 63) there ought to be a singular and important constraint on this maximizing behaviour, that the budget must be equal to or greater than the minimum total cost of providing the service which the bureau is set up to supply (Niskanen 1971: 42).

Niskanen compares the behaviour of bureaux under the aegis of this motivational assumption with the behaviour of firms under conditions of changes in the level of costs, and changes in demand for services. Under all conditions, in the model which he uses, the output and budget for a bureau are either equal to or (more frequently) greater than the output and budget for a firm operating in a competitive environment. This is not normatively acceptable under the criterion of Pareto optimality so Niskanen is led to a radical ideological position which is now commonly associated with public choice theory. This is that the state should be reorganized so that it approximates more closely the motivational and structural characteristics of business. So bureaux need to be turned into competitive suppliers of services and bureaucrats need to be allowed personally to profit from their efficient supply. If one follows this path of reasoning to its ultimate conclusion, the most effective way to render the supply of services competitive and profitable is to privatize them as far as possible.

If bureaucrats and citizens are cynical, public choice theorists would say realistic, maximizers, what then must politicians be like? In Downs' economic model of democracy (1957) they too are maximizers of self-interest. They never seek office out of a desire to implement policy but only to attain the income, status and power which come from high office (1957: 28). Policy formulation is based on the prospect of winning elections – governments are vote maximizers in a context of utility-maximizing voters. When it comes to policy-making, a government subjects each issue to a hypothetical (or actual) poll of voters and 'always chooses' the majority preference. If it fails to do so it will be defeated (Downs 1957: 54–5). However, it can only do this under conditions in which it is certain of its optimality calculation, either because of effective polling or because the majority of voters is passionately committed on an issue. In response the opposition has two possible strategies: it can match the government's policies or it can represent a coalition of minorities by attacking the government's policies without offering an alternative.

Here Downs enters a critique of democracy, again under the criterion of Pareto optimality. Under conditions of certain knowledge and unequal incomes, governments will tend to redistribute income from the minority rich to the majority poor. However, this is suboptimal because the highly taxed rich will make decisions about their income based on economic utility – they will work less, move their wealth offshore, etc. However, where knowledge is uncertain (i.e. where the wishes of the majority are less clear) the government is less likely to interfere in the economy to redistribute income and so government is likely to be 'smaller'. The normative implication is that uncertainty needs to be maintained by the persuasions of government propaganda because this will empower the privileged in a political sense and thus maintain economic incentives to output and efficiency.

Coleman: rogue organizations

A sociological version of public choice theory, which also incorporates some of the elements of exchange theory, is proposed by Coleman (1990). Indeed Coleman uses exchange theory to solve the central problem of public choice theory. Collective institutions in that theory are taken to be a priori, almost Kantian constructions, in relation to which individuals must decide whether to make or not to make a contribution. Coleman begins rather at the level of the individual actor and seeks to undestand how collective institutions can emerge not from material transfers between the individual and the collectivity but from material transfers between individuals.

Coleman's primitive terms are similar to those of exchange theory. Actors have two principal characteristics: first, they have control over certain resources and, second, they have an interest in resources. The single principle of action which links these characteristics together is that they will act so as to maximize the realization of their interests (1990: 37). However, because the resources one controls and one's interests almost never coincide, practices of interest maximization will serve to establish relations of interdependence between actors – that is, the realization of one's own interests depends on access to resources under the control of others. It follows that there can be three types of action:

- processes of consumption, controlling and using one's own resources (a trivial type of action which does not give rise to social processes);
- processes of exchange, employing one's resources to gain control of the resources of others; and
- unilateral transfer of resources, giving up control of resources to other people because one conceives that it is in one's best interests to do so.

Note that the third of these seeks to resolve the problems of the free rider or the contributor's dilemma, which is central to public choice theory, by asserting the coincidence of individual with collective interests. More importantly, it allows Coleman to move from an analysis of primitive individual actors, engaging in immediate and instrumental interest maximization, to an examination of enduring relationships. Again, three such relationships are important:

- *Relations of trust* These occur within the context of exchange. Because exchanges will typically take place over time, actors will take the risk of a return on their investment of resources at some future date. For each of the actors within an exchange relationship there is an overarching interest in maintaining it by repeated reciprocation. They give rise to the generalized social resources which are called obligations.
- *Authority relations* In many instances actors will unilaterally transfer rights to the control of resources to a single authority figure as a means to ensuring equivalent contributions by other members of a collectivity. (Olsen's taxation example is an instance of such a process.) Although Coleman does not use the term, the generalized social resource thus produced is usually called power.
- *Norms* This term denotes situations in which individual rights of self-control are surrendered to the collectivity. They specify what each individual must contribute to the collectivity. Here the generalized social resource produced might be termed value-commitment (although, again, this is not Coleman's terminology).

The generation of such resources, what Coleman calls social capital, allows the construction of corporate actors. Much as is suggested by Buchanan, Coleman stresses the importance of constitutions, which are the most prominent formal expressions of norms in this process. Political constitutions, in particular, specify the relationship between individual freedom to act and collective control. The exact balance between contribution and benefit is seldom Pareto-optimal but rather reflects the differing levels of power which each participating actor has in writing the constitution. Power differentials will also be reflected in the ways in which control of the corporate entity is distributed between the actors who make it up. Nevertheless, Coleman's view of the the development of collective actors is positive, in the sense that he believes that they do, and indeed must, represent the aspirations to interest realization of their participating actors.

This now becomes an argument about human evolution. The development of human society is characterized by the proliferation of purposively constructed, corporate actors (states, businesses, etc.) which progressively displace 'natural', corporate actors based on primordial relationships (families, tribes, communities, etc). Individual human actors decreasingly interact with one another not on behalf of their individual interests but as representatives of corporate actors. This 'new social structure' must be understood not as a pattern of interest maximization between purposeful human actors but as such a pattern established between corporate actors which are 'legal' but not real persons. This gives Coleman grounds for a critique of modern society in which corporations are viewed as rootless rogues bent on an irresponsible pursuit of self-interest and in which the personal and collective interests of individuals are subordinated.

Rational choice: games Marxists play

Just as Olsen posed fundamental questions for theories of government, so also did his statements about the impossibility of collective commitment to public goods pose problems for Marxists. In the same way as rationally maximizing citizens would seek to become 'free riders' on the backs of their fellow citizens, all rationally maximizing members of the working class would allow others to fight the revolution for them: 'a worker who thought he would benefit from a "proletarian" government would not find it rational to risk his life and resources to start a revolution against the bourgeois government' (Olsen 1965: 106). In so far as Marx seeks to explain class action in terms of the pursuit of material interests, his theory, argues Olsen, is inconsistent because material interests are always expressed individually rather than collectively. Olsen discusses the way Lenin and Trotsky anticipated his own argument by arguing for Bolshevism, the need for a compact, highly disciplined and motivated, revolutionary elite to exploit weaknesses in the fabric of capitalist society and to install socialism from above. Such a development is explicable within public choice theory in terms of Downs' arguments about the rationally maximizing behaviour of politicians. Lenin and Trotsky were doubtless also motivated by the pursuit of the personal rewards of the power and status which come with high office.

It will also be remembered that a critical element in Olsen and in Downs is uncertainty. The higher the level of uncertainty about outcomes, the less likely is an individual calculus of rationality to produce commitment to the collectivity. In the Marxist scenario the level of uncertainty is held to be extreme. Not only are the chances of successful proletarian revolution on the slim side, even where bourgeois society is in a state of disorganization, but workers are held to be uncertain about what their true material interests are – there is a problem of false consciousness.

The branch of Marxist thought which seeks to deal with this problem is known as analytic or game-theoretic Marxism. Its chief architects are Elster and Roemer, although Elster has recently moved beyond Marxist theory to develop a stand-alone theory of rational choice. Roemer has had a considerable influence on Wright's theory of class (see chapter 9) but, generally, the highly individualistic and rationalistic assumptions of analytic Marxism are rejected by traditional Marxists.

Elster: the revolutionary's dilemma

To its credit, analytic Marxism has always sought to address its problems in terms of a worst-case scenario in which uncertainty is maximized. The scenario is drawn from the theory of games. The elements of game theory are that there are always two or more players, each player can choose between two or more strategies, and the choices generate differential rewards. A critical element is that the rewards vary with the choices made by all players, that their decisions are interdependent, and that each must anticipate the moves of all the others (Elster 1989a: 28). The most well-known and well-used game-theoretic problem is known as the Prisoner's Dilemma. In its most simplified form the problem of the Prisoner's Dilemma is as follows:

> Two prisoners, suspected of having collaborated on a crime are placed in separate cells. The police tell each of them that he will be released (4) if he denounces the other and the other does not denounce him. If they both denounce each other, both will get three years' imprisonment (2). If he does not denounce the other, but the other denounces him, he will get five years (1). If neither denounces the other, the police have sufficient evidence to send each to prison for one year (3). [Elster 1989a: 29n; numbers indicate rank ordering of individual payoffs with 1 the worst]

Each prisoner will immediately suppose that the other will confess and denounce, in which case their own dominant strategy will be to confess and denounce. Each gets three years. If they had kept silent, they would each have got one year. The situations discussed by Olsen and others extend the Prisoner's Dilemma game to multiple players, to what Parfit (1986) calls the Contributor's Dilemma (where the individual has to decide about contributions to the production of public goods) and the Samaritan's Dilemma (where a decision has to be made about whether or not to help another person). Each example shows that individual maximization produces a worse individual outcome.

Jon Elster (b. 1940)

Elster was born in Norway but went to live in the USA, where he is Professor of Political Science at the University of Chicago. He retains the position of Research Director at the Institute for Social Research, Oslo.

Elster, who is the most important game-theoretic Marxist, insists on the position that actors are individual rational maximizers and also wishes to find a solution to the Contributor's Dilemma in terms of collective class action. He warns us against sliding into the position of arguing that, where players knowingly do worse for themselves than they could have done, their action is not really rational. This would be a slide into a notion of collective rationality when rational-choice theory is predicated on individual and instrumental rationality (1989a: 29). For an action to be rational it must have the following characteristics: first, the action must be the best means of realizing the actor's wants; second, the wants must be optimal to the actor's well-being as far as the actor can tell; and third, the actor must collect an optimal (in terms of the balance between costs and benefits) amount of evidence in support of each of these views.

Elster's formulation of the Contributor's Dilemma problem is as follows: 'The group has a collective action problem if it is better for all if some do it than if nobody does, but better for each not to do it' (1989a: 126). He solves it by assuming that the game is not resolved in a single move. When a given group faces repeated instances of a problem of collective action, they will learn about what constitutes their best interests, they will learn to trust each other's cooperation and to fear each other's future withdrawal. There are some stringent conditions under which this will occur: the participants must have foresight, they must care about the future; the potential gains from cooperation must be substantial and visible and the gain from noncooperation rather smaller; and each individual must be confident that others in the group are operating on the basis of a similar, rational and knowledgeable set of beliefs.

More concretely, Elster argues that collective action emerges from a mixture of motivations, many of which are nonrational. The typical complexes are as follows:

- *Individualists* These correspond with the description above. In repeated moves they calculate the future benefits of cooperation and costs of retaliation.
- *Collectivists* These engage in collective action because it is intrinsically rewarding. They may enjoy the sociability and camaraderie of collective action or they may regard it as a route to personal development. The focus is on the process itself rather than outcomes of the process.
- *Utilitarians* Like individualists, utilitarians are rational maximizers. However, rather than maximizing their own individual benefits, they are oriented to benefits for the collectivity.
- *Idealists* These are sacrificers rather than maximizers. They calculate what the ideal collective situation would be and then act accordingly.
- *Followers* People who look at what others are doing and go along with it because it seems to be a reasonable thing to do. These are motivated by norms of fairness or justice.
  (Elster 1989a: 52–60, 133; 1989b: 34–49)[3]

In a concrete situation of primitive decisions about collective action the process might be begun by the few collectivists and/or idealists. This might trigger a positive reaction from the utilitarians by raising their consciousness about alternative possibilities for the common good. This, in turn, would multiply activism, raising fears of retaliation for the individualists and setting new norms for the followers.

To return to the central Marxist problem of collective class action, this process, argues Elster, is more likely to occur for a class of workers when:

- It becomes aware of the collective gains which are possible within an alternative pattern of social organization and that, on a per capita basis, these gains are much greater than it receives in current circumstances.
- There are clear possibilities for individual participants with differing types of motivation to communicate with each other. Under this condition, activists (collectivists and idealists) can communicate the possibility of progress on the common good to utilitarians and beyond.
- There is a low rate of turnover of personnel within the class. This increases the repetition rate for collective action dilemmas and persuades individualists towards calculation of future costs and benefits.
- A set of means appears to be available by which the present situation might be reversed and where the employment of these means involves minimal cost to individuals (after Lash and Urry 1984: 38).

Roemer: towards socialist exploitation

After his initial brush with the Marxist problem of collective action, Elster turns increasingly towards the general contribution which rational choice can make to the theory of society and we shall move to a consideration of these arguments towards the end of this section. Before we do, there needs to some consideration of another game-theoretic reinterpretation of a different aspect of Marx's thought. Although it does not lie strictly within the realm of rational choice theory, Roemer's version of analytical Marxism (1981; 1982) complements and supports it. This is because it too seeks to remedy the deficiencies of the labour theory of value[4] as the source for revolutionary action and it also draws on the techniques, if not the complete substance, of formal economics.

Roemer's revelatory discovery is that exploitation is not confined to situations in which there is an exchange of labour for wages. He begins with a model of a simple situation of own-account producers producing at a level adequate to subsistence and trading with each other in order to accomplish it. They differ only in their amount of capital, but greater capital offers greater production opportunities. Those with more capital can produce the exchange value they need in order to subsist with less labour than those with little or no capital. So, while ownership of the means of production remains paramount, it provides not for the exploitation of wage-workers by capitalists but for exploitation at the point of exchange between producers. It also allows the identification of exploitation within noncapitalist institutions (i.e. where there is no profit-taking).

While there is exploitation in this simple model there are, as yet, no classes. Roemer now adds a labour market to the model and classes emerge. They emerge as the consequence of optimizing behaviour on the part of participants – some see advantage in selling their labour power rather than working for themselves, others optimize by hiring labour, and so on. Classes articulate with the pattern of exploitation so that hiring labour always implies exploiting while selling-labour-power always implies being exploited. Roemer calls this the 'Class Exploitation Correspondence Principle'.

Before traditional Marxists should draw some solace from this principle, Roemer moves on to show that classes can also emerge where there is no labour market. He accomplishes this by introducing a credit market into the model so that capital can be lent between producers. Again, producers will decompose in terms of three optimizing strategies – lending, borrowing or neither – and Roemer is able to show likewise that this produces classes (financiers, debtors, etc.) and that there is an ineluctable correspondence between class membership and position in the pattern of exploitation. He finally closes the circle by demonstrating an isomorphism between labour-market-based class and exploitation and exploitation based on the credit market. If there is an isomorphism then the full panoply of Marxian relations of class and exploitation can emerge without there being an exchange of labour power for wages.

One of the constraints Roemer imposes on this model is a prohibition on the accumulation of capital. He now moves on first to relax this constraint, and then other constraints on forms of capital holding, shared production, and the possibility of substitution between the factors of production. In order to sustain the exploitation model he has proposed, he must now reject the traditional Marxist notion that the value of a commodity is contingent on the labour embodied in it. Rather, the reverse is true, that is, the value of labour depends on the price the market sets for it and, by extension, on the market for its products. He also introduces the notion of differential skills at this point, finding that it is possible for those with high skills to accomplish wealth independently of both their class position and whether they are exploiter or exploited.

Having displaced the central concept of the labour process from Marx, Roemer now proposes a theory of exploitation based principally on property relations. He conceives property relations in game-theoretic terms in which there are two players but these are collective players or 'coalitions'. If a coalition is receiving less of a payoff than it can expect under the terms in which the game is specified, it is exploited, and vice versa. The terms of three different games are specified: feudal, capitalist and socialist exploitation.

The pattern of exploitation in feudal property relations is relatively straightforward to ascertain (1982: 199–202). If a coalition would be better off by withdrawing from the game then it is exploited, if it would be worse off it is an exploiter. In so far as serfs cultivate their own family plot and also cultivate the aristocrat's land, they are clearly exploited. If they withdrew they could engage in cooperative economic production, devoting the whole of their labour power to it. For this reason, the game of feudal exploitation can only be sustained if the exploiting player coerces participation by the exploited in a trade of (more valuable) agricultural labour for (less valuable) military protection. Serfs would be better off trading for military protection in a free market.

Whereas feudal exploitation depends on constraints on individual freedom to withdraw, the specification of capitalist exploitation is made in terms of ownership of private property (1982: 202–8). If a coalition would be better off withdrawing and taking with it an equal per capita share of all the alienable private property available in the game, then that coalition is exploited. If it would be worse off, then it is an exploiter. It will be remembered that property ownership defines exploitation because it provides production opportunities, which in turn provide subsistence on the basis of differential labour inputs. If feudal exploitation depends on constraints on trade, capitalist exploitation depends on barriers to ownership of private property.

To analyse socialist exploitation, Roemer reintroduces the issue of differential skill. Differential skill must also be modelled into some games of capitalist exploitation (see 1982: 208–11) but the pure case in which property differences are prohibited but skill differences remain is the more interesting. If a coalition can withdraw from the game taking with it its per capita share of the total skills in the society and be better off, then it is being exploited. If it would be worse off, then it is an exploiter. Roemer is careful to point out that it is thus appropriate to speak of socialism even while there is exploitation. Under socialism each contributes on the basis of ability and receives a fair return for work performed. By contrast, under communism, where there would be no exploitation, each person contributes on the basis of ability but receives on the basis of need. In practice, the state socialist societies which were institutionalized for much of the twentieth century exhibited both socialist exploitation and a further form, status exploitation. The latter was akin to feudal exploitation in that the holders of positions of power used coercion to enforce special payments to those positions (1982: 243).

Elster again: mixing cement

The link between Roemer and Elster can now be made apparent. Roemer is modelling the way situations are, the conditions of exploitation which might or might not become apparent. Elster is theorizing processes of reproduction and transformation of situations, the grounds on which individuals might seek to remove or overcome exploitation which is socially unnecessary, that is, which can be removed without depleting overall welfare. Of the two, Elster's argument is the more general because it seeks to address the fundamentals of human cooperation. Indeed, all his work appears to be directed at resolving the Hobbesian problem of order, the issue of why human society is characterized not by the restless pursuit of self-interest but rather by extended stretches of cooperation and harmony. In his most recent work he turns away from problems of Marxism to address this much more general issue explicitly and we move on to consider this venture into grand theory.

Elster addresses two concepts of social order: that of the predictability of patterns of behaviour and that of cooperation (1989b: 1–2)[5]. Much of what we have so far discussed in Elster is the attempt to solve the problem of cooperation, but here we concentrate on the issue of order as predictability in social life. We can privilege this over the problem of cooperation because, as we have seen, cooperation presupposes an opportunity to appeal to norms or ideals or collective interests which override individual ones.

One of the advantages of rational choice theory is that its claims are modest. It does not claim to explain all things but merely those which meet the standard of rationality. Much behaviour is admitted to be irrational and can stem from the indeterminacy of the situation, from irrational beliefs, from inadequate evidence, or from unrealistic wants. Consequently, once Elster moves beyond the realm of rationally motivated behaviour he is at something of a loss. For example, he describes a wide range of social norms (1989a: 113–23; 1989b: 215–47) and even describes their beneficial consequences in terms of predictability and cooperation. But these consequences are unintended and, functionalist explanations being unacceptable, he cannot offer an account of why norms should be maintained. Nor indeed can he explain their existence, saying only that

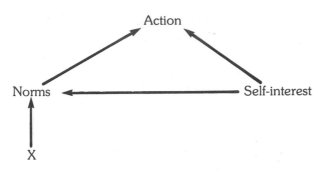

Figure 3.1   *Elster's theory of the determinants of action*
(Elster 1989b: 151)

they must: 'result from psychological propensities about which we know little.' He confesses: 'Although I could tell a story or two about how norms might have emerged, I have nothing to say about how they actually did emerge' (1989a: 123).

This admission is all the more extraordinary in view of Elster's account of social action which assigns a central place to norms. This account is broadly couched in terms of the diagram in figure 3.1. Action is shown as the consequence both of naked self-interest and of self-interest mediated by norms. Norms are in part the conseqence of self-interest because people subscribe to and adhere to norms which favour their self-interest. However, norms cannot entirely be reduced to self-interest, as the above discussion of collective cooperation shows. Rather they are the consequence of a residual factor, the 'X' factor which, according to Elster, is beyond current understanding.

This self-confessed lacuna becomes an even more relevant issue when we examine Elster's analysis of society, although, because Elster is such a resolute methodological individualist, the term 'society' may be too strong a description. He insists: 'There are no societies: only individuals who interact with each other' (1989b: 248). Societies are defined, behaviouristically and individualistically, by a coefficient of cohesion (the number of transactions between individuals within a particular territory divided by the total number of transactions in which they are involved). A society is any area in which there is a local maximum of cohesion so that slightly smaller and slightly larger areas have marginally lower levels (1989b: 249). Superimposed on societies are cultures, bounded densities of tradition and norms, but which are not necessarily coterminous with them. Superimposed on societies and cultures are states, which might be thought of as territorial densities of power. As might be expected, Elster offers no explanation for either cultures or states but he does seek to show why individuals interact consistently with each other and in an orderly way. There are three universal, principally psychological, processes, which form the 'cement of society': envy, opportunism and credibility.

Elster appears to regard envy as a fundamental of human nature (1989b: 252–63). It is born in emotional comparisons of oneself with others, at least partly because there seems to be no other way in which one might assess oneself. The primary concern of envy is self-respect, that is, an attempt to bring others to one's own level, rather than attainment of the level of others. This is because bringing others down to one's own level allows one to cast the blame on them. Only by fixing blame for one's own failure on others does that failure become psychologically acceptable. Envy-avoidance motivates social practices of uniformity and the punishment of public forms of deviance. It therefore operates in the direction of conformity and extrudes an, albeit odiferous, social adhesive.

The palliative for envy is opportunism. Here Elster (1989b: 263–72) wants to discuss opportunism as the pursuit of self-interest irrespective of any law or morality. Opportunism disrupts conformity – it allows people 'corruptly' to buy their way around norms which constrict initiative, and it can also beat out favouritism and discrimination. However, in the long term, large-scale corruption will disrupt and unravel the social norms which make society predictable and thus possible. The optimal level of corruption appears to be a moderate and relatively constant one, about that found, say, in Thailand or the USA (1989b: 271), rather than episodic and high levels similar to those found in, say, late-twentieth-century Zaïre or, in less extreme terms, Italy.

The last, and conceivably most important, ingredient in the cement of society is credibility (1989b: 272–87). Here Elster refers to the issue of whether the communications one makes about future intentions can be trusted. There are five generalized techniques which tend to improve credibility:

- *Investment in bargaining power*   The accumulation of resources which can be used as bases for negotiation. Clearly the more power one has the more credible one's word becomes, especially if one's word involves threats.
- *Precommitment*   Prior public statements, often written as contracts, indicating future threats or promises and often indicating penalties for noncompliance.
- *Long-term self-interest*   Foresight among all parties to a negotiation that a given course of action will have future costs and benefits of particular kinds.
- *Social norms*   The invocation of norms of honesty, justice, fairness, etc.
- *Investment in reputation*   The creation of an established reputation for irrationality which increases the credibility of threat because it implies both noncalculation of costs and denial of norms.

Elster concludes by discussing the effects of social change on possibilities for credibility. Change, and such other processes as social mobility, reduce the contributions which long-term self-interest and social norms can be expected to make to credibility, because neither can successfully be assessed under radically altered circumstances. However, this comment too may have its limitations, this time the limitations of tautology. After all, is Elster not simply saying that the more things change, especially in unknown directions, the less predictable they are likely to be?

Conclusion

Summary

1   From independent points of view, Marshall and Pareto establish the idea that individuals act rationally to maximize their own individual advantage. Individuals calculate whether or not to engage in any action on the basis of the extent to which their wants will be satisfied by it. The 'good' society occurs where individual wants are satisfied to the greatest extent. While Marshall and Pareto argue that such wants are inherent or natural, Skinner argues that they are conditioned in the individual by other people in the social environment.

2   Homans and other exchange theorists show that the satisfaction of wants takes place in the context of negotiation and interaction with other people. Interactions are trading situations in which each individual tries to invest as little as possible in order to achieve the maximum return. Collective phenomena can be explained as ways of establishing norms of exchange.

3   However, there is a fundamental theoretical flaw in these arguments which is recognized by public choice theorists and game-theoretic Marxists. The debate centres on the fact that if each individual seeks to maximize their own interests at least cost then there is no incentive for any individual to contribute to collective action. Public choice theorists concentrate on whether government is possible and generally conclude that it is but only in so far as it is based on benevolent dictatorship and the principle that government agencies make a social profit, that is they contribute more individual welfare to society than they create individual cost. Likewise, the conclusion for game-theoretic Marxists is that working-class political action can only occur where there is a vanguard leadership group.

4   There nevertheless remain many collective organizations which meet none of these criteria. Here such rational choice theorists as Elster must accept that rational behaviour is limited to quite specific situations and that much irrational behaviour must remain unexplained.

Critique

As Hindess (1988: 93) points out, the chief advantages which general theories based on rationality can claim are parsimony and explanatory power. Coleman (1990: 37) is possibly the least reticent in making such a claim, and his position might roughly be generalized to all of the theories considered in this chapter. He writes:

> One property of the theoretical system developed here is parsimony. Actors are connected to resources (and thus indirectly to one another) through only two relations: their control over resources and their interest in resources. Actors have a single principle of action, that of acting so as to maximize their realization of interests.

It is this single principle which gives theories based on rationality both their weakness and their strength. Their strength is their ability to develop formal, propositional, often mathematical, models of human behaviour which bear a family resemblance to the similar models constructed by economists. However, the key weaknesses are: how much of social life can be considered to be consistent with the assumption of rationality; and, for those parts that are indeed considered to be rational, the extent to which rationality theory can explain variations in social arrangements. We can now make some more elaborate points of criticism in relation to these general questions.

1   There can be no argument about the fact that human beings reflect upon the world around them, make choices in relation to the possibilities that the world offers, and act intentionally in relation to those choices. It is also unquestionable that the pursuit of those choices might be thought of as the maximization of interest or utility. However, to claim that these processes constitute a scientifically based, rational calculus might be unacceptable. It assumes, for example: that the individual is knowledgeable about the consequences of employing a particular set of means; that actors will take steps to acquaint themselves with the range of means which are available; that they are capable of translating generalized desires into specific targets; and that they are capable of projecting a sequence of events which, if followed, will lead to the realization of that target. Moreover, it assumes actors to be proactive rather than reactive; to be empowered relative to the physical and social environment; and to know what their interests are. At best these assumptions are warranted only within theories of rational action which propose short-run material ends that are instrumentally realizable. However, even within such a notion of bounded rationality, the assumption that choices are made rationally rather than on some other basis is only a methodological convenience and not a deduced theoretical principle.

2   As Homans, Elster and others are the first to admit, much human action certainly is not rational. The types of action described by Weber as habitual, affectual, and value-rational are not susceptible to analysis by theories based on an assumption of instrumental rationality. As Weber tells us, most human action falls into the traditional or habitual

category, that is, it consists in routinized and unreflective norm-following. Nonrational and irrational behaviour can only be analyzed by comparison with rational behaviour. This means that rationality theories frequently are self-limiting theories – they restrict themselves to primitive or elementary arenas of social life and often have real difficulty in dealing with complexity.

3   Even if we accept the value of examining the elementary bases for social behaviour, the parsimonious explanatory power of rationality theory is available only by virtue of being constituted as a tautology. Rationality theory argues that a particular course of action is under-taken because it contributes to the realization of an interest. However, there is no autonomous indicator of that interest. It must be abstracted from the course of action which, consequently, must be said to be explaining itself.

4   Tautology also lets rationality theory off the hook of the falsifying case. Because interests are both abstracted from and are explanations of action there can be no 'in principle' instance in which an explanation is unavailable. Thus rationality theory is successful in terms of its capacity to generalize, but any particular explanation is trivial and uninteresting. The courses of action, 'Hitler murders Jews', 'workers submit to capitalism', and 'juveniles steal cars for joy-riding' each receive a trivial explanation of the form, 'because they wanted to' or 'because they could get something out of it' or 'because it was in their interests to do so'.

5   Rationality theory thus lends an unconstrained character to sociological explanation in which social life appears to be indeterminate. This might best be illustrated by the contradictory directions in which public choice theory apparently leads. Olsen, Arrow and others would argue that the only way to provide public goods in the face of rationalizing free riders is to move towards (benign) dictatorship, but Niskanen and Downs would argue that the maximizing behaviours of politicians and bureau-crats prevent an optimal distribution of public goods. Each position is consistently deducible from an assumption of interest-maximizing rationality.

6   It follows that the provision of particular explanations for the various and complex forms of social existence requires a specification of interests which is autonomous relative to the course of action which it explains. The only possible source for statements of interest is social location, that is, one must say that the individual is located at the intersection of a series of social rights and obligations which are external. However, to do so would be to violate the principle of methodological individualism on which rationality theories insist. It would privilege social structures, argued to exist prior to and indepen-dently of the intentions of individuals.

7   However, ultimately, this feared path is the one rationality theorists are forced to tread. They must do one of three things: they must commit

the sophistry of arguing that individuals will see the surrender of resources to the collectivity as being in their own interests (the Coleman solution); they must deny the existence of the social by proposing gross psychological reductionism and thus accept explanatory failure (the Elster solution); or they must accept the reality of society and its effectivity in constituting interests (the Weber solution). However, to do the last would take one out of the realm of rationality theory. This is the sociologist's dilemma.

Further reading

An excellent summary of exchange theory is Emerson's 'Social Exchange Theory' (1981). More recent developments and debates are summarized in Cook et al., 'Exchange Theory' (1990). Homans makes his formal, founding statement in *Social Behaviour* (1961). A critical treatment can be found in Ekeh's *Social Exchange Theory* (1974).

The central problems for public choice and rational choice theory are set out in Olsen's *The Logic of Collective Action* (1965). The most sociological version of public choice theory is Coleman's *Foundations of Social Theory* (1990), although it is rather daunting in its scale. Game-theoretic Marxism is neatly summarized and criticized by Lash and Urry in 'The New Marxism of Collective Action' (1984). The most accessible of Elster's numerous books is *Nuts and Bolts for the Social Sciences* (1989a), while *The Cement of Society* (1989b) is more serious if a little more difficult. An excellent and wide-ranging critique of both positions can be found in Hindess, *Choice, Rationality and Social Theory* (1988).

Notes

1 Marshall, like the Scottish moralist philosophers who preceded him, was a utilitarian in the literal philosophical sense, that is, he believed that the maximization of the satisfaction of each individual set of wants would automatically lead to maximum satisfaction of wants for all. The 'greatest good for the greatest number' understood in material terms is his value-criterion for a good society. As Parsons (1937: 241) indicates, the utilitarian formulation relies on huge assumptions at the level of social relations including: 'rationality of action, mobility of resources, independence of wants [from] the processes of their satisfaction, competition and substantial equivalence in exchange possible only through the elimination of force and fraud and other milder forms of coercion, perhaps even of certain forms of the exercise of power short of coercion.'

2 Rowley interprets this as the condition of Pareto optimality:

It prescribes for a socially optimal allocation of resources the efficiency criterion that it is not possible to change the allocation of resources, increasing quantities of some goods and reducing quantities of others, without making someone (or some group) worse off than before. Thus, if it is possible to re-allocate resources so that some people are better off (in the sense that they prefer the second situation to the first) *without making anyone else worse off*, then the existing pattern of resource allocation is not economically efficient. If a particular allocation of resources meets this Pareto criterion of efficiency, it is said to be 'Pareto-optimal' [1978: 32n].

3 The taxonomy is a compilation from Elster's various arguments. The labels for each of the types of motivation are, more or less, original.

4 Broadly, the labour theory of value argues that the true or absolute value of a material product is dependent on the amount of labour time invested in it. The argument is held to be true because if each person produced for themselves every object they used, the amount of labour time they chose to invest would match the utility or value of the object to them. In a capitalistic system of commodity exchange, however, the value of products is determined by supply and demand so that 'exchange value' does not match the true 'labour value'. The difference between them, the 'surplus value', is appropriated by the capitalist who thus expropriates a significant proportion of the labour value which the worker has invested in the product.

The theory is widely criticized on a number of grounds. However, these centre on the issue of whether any object can have a 'true' value – they can only have a contingent value established by the social context of commodity exchange.

5 Although Elster draws parallels only with the economist's distinction between equilibrium and Pareto optimality, there are also clear parallels with the sociological distinction between social integration and system integration (see Lockwood 1976 and Habermas 1984, 1987).

4 Structure: secret patterns which determine experience

Many social scientists routinely use the term 'social structure' to describe patterns which they discover in their observations. In so doing they are usually implying the following: first, that the phenomenon under inspection can be analysed as a series of component units of a specified type (e.g. roles, classes, value-commitments, genders, societies); second, that these units are related to each other in quite definite ways; third, that the relationships between units connect together to give the phenomenon under observation a characteristic pattern which needs to be understood as a totality; and fourth, that the pattern of relationships is relatively stable and enduring over time.

In the 1950s and 1960s it became popular to describe the structure of the conjugal-nuclear family in just such a way. The units were the roles of father, mother, son, daughter, husband, wife, sister and brother. Relationships between roles could then be described – so, for example, the wife–husband relationship is conjugal involving mutual affection and exclusive sexuality, and the father–son relationship might be described as authoritarian and instrumental. The relationships were said to be connected in such a way as to constitute the conjugal-nuclear structural pattern, in other words, only sons and daughters can be siblings and only spouses can be parents. Finally, evidence would be adduced to demonstrate that the structure was widespread in its form either throughout industrial societies or across societies and historical periods more generally.

There are three possible routes by which such a notion of structure may enter into theory. The first, which comes from constructionist sociology, is the notion that structure is a human creation which is either intentional or unintentional. It is viewed as an emergent regularity which arises as a consequence of human agency. Thinking and acting subjects are understood to create structural arrangements and the constraints which inhere in them. Giddens' theory of structuration is an important example of such an approach to structure. Within this theory structure does indeed impinge upon and constrain each human individual and has the force of concrete reality, but its source and origin are within the sphere of human action – the whole structure has no greater reality than the sum of its constituent action components. Moreover, social structure is not fixed and immutable but flexible and susceptible to alteration.

A second approach to social structure is to regard it not as a real phenomenon which may or may not be constructed by human beings but as an observer category, a concept which appears in the mind of the sociologist. Under this regime, structure is a methodological or analytic category, a box in which all the regular and enduring aspects of relationships are placed while the unpredictable ones are placed outside it. Such an approach is recommended by the founding British social anthropologist Radcliffe-Brown (1952: 192–3). The concrete reality, says Radcliffe-Brown, is the set of actual social relationships between people. Structurally oriented social anthropologists are said to be concerned not with the particularity of a situation but with the possibility of generalizing across social situations. So the observer abstracts the general or normal form of a relationship, the common and repeated aspects, from the variations of particular instances. This abstracted general structural form has relative permanence and may be revisited but it also has limited susceptibility to change either as a long-term gradual process or under the cataclysmic effects of revolution or military conquest.

A third approach to structure is the main concern of this chapter. This is what may be termed a 'realist' or 'essentialist' approach, and it is, more or less exclusively, a continental European tradition. Here structure is held to be the determining factor which underlies surface appearances. Everyday social experience and the beliefs which sustain it are held to be a gloss which masks a genuine but hidden reality which lies beneath the level of consciousness. This hidden reality is described as a structure and the task of the sociologist is to theorize that essence, both its enduring form and the way it mutates, according to its own internal logic. In this view, action is contingent. A further task of the theorist is to elucidate the connection between action and structure in such a way as to render action as the transparent product of structure.

Keat and Urry (1975: 124–5) make a useful list of the possible components of 'hard' structuralist analysis of this kind, a version of which is set out here:

1   Social phenomena need to be understood as organized systems of relationships. Units can only be understood in terms of their relationships with other units.
2   As is indicated above, the analyst's task is to reveal the hidden secret reality which lies behind everyday awareness. This reality consists of a series of invariant relationships which are specified as rules or laws. In linguistic structuralism this reality consists of a set of unwritten grammatical rules (*langue*) which underpins or structures everyday utterances (*parole*); in Marxist analysis it consists in the laws of dialectical materialism which structure an epiphenomenal reality.
3   Structures are mechanisms of the mind subject to biological transmission. These mechanisms are unconscious and universal.
4   Structural analysis is typically semiological, it involves an analysis of signs. Signs, which include both utterances and discourse on one hand,

and other cultural products on the other, are to be understood as a code which, once broken, can reveal structural determinants.

5   The relationships which are thus identified are frequently specified as examples of binary opposition, which is the fundamental organizing principle for structures.

6   A conscious distinction is made between historically universal or synchronous elements of systems and historically particular or diachronous elements. This tends to lead in the direction of periodization in which developmental stages of structural processes are identified.

7   Structuralists seek to discover isomorphism or homology (identical regularities) between the various planes of social life, between for example the economic, the political, and the ideological planes. They also examine the connections between these planes as rules of transformation.

The rest of this chapter mainly examines the work of leading social theorists whose work follows all or most of these principles. The first section examines founding arguments: Freud's structural theory of the mind, Lévi-Strauss's structural anthropology, and Marx's dialectical materialism. The second examines and compares three contemporary and developed sociological accounts of social structure: Giddens' theory of structuration, Parsons' structural-functionalism, and Althusser's structuralist Marxism. Finally, we examine some examples of recent French structuralist and poststructuralist thought.

Founding arguments

The idea of structure has very widespread currency extending through linguistics, anthropology, psychoanalysis, political economy and literary theory as well as sociology. In this section we examine the three most influential statements of a 'hard' structuralist position, the sort of position which argues that structure is both real and determinative.

Freud: compelling thoughts

We begin with one of the most familiar but least sociologically influential structuralist arguments, Freud's structural theory of the mind. Freud's key discovery is the influence of the unconscious mind on perception and behaviour. This discovery was made principally in clinical settings, as he grappled to make sense of behaviour that could not possibly be interpreted as consciously motivated because it was self-destructive. As he came to understand that abnormal behaviour was compelled by mental processes that were beneath the level of awareness, Freud was obliged to generalize to a position in which all behaviour was understood to be thus compelled.

As is well known, Freud identifies three component units of the mental

---

Sigmund Freud (1856–1939)

Freud is one of the most important and influential figures in the analysis of human behaviour. Although he was not a sociologist, he was a major influence on structural-functionalism through Parsons, and on structuralist Marxism through Althusser. He was born of Jewish parents in Freiberg in what is now the Czech Republic but was then part of the Austro-Hungarian Empire. He studied medicine in Vienna and specialized in his practice in the treatment of nervous disorders. He created a fundamental shift in modern thought when he showed that such disorders had psychological rather than physiological origins. He was able to treat disorders using the therapy of psychoanalysis which sought to reveal subconscious compulsions to the patient. He insisted on continuing to work in Vienna after the Nazis took over in 1933 but was ransomed out by the American Government in 1938. He died in London.

Sources: *Penguin Dictionary of Sociology* (1984: *s.v.* Freud, Sigmund); Ritzer (1992: 32)

---

structure, the id, the ego and the superego. The id is the most primitive, original and unconscious component consisting of biologically based urges, needs and drives. These instincts merely demand gratification in the form of pleasurable responses from the outside world. The gratification-demand is unconstrained and the id energizes action in securing gratification even where demands are unrealizeable or contradictory. Indeed one of the characteristic structural patterns of the id is a binary opposition between instincts. As Wollheim (1971: 179–86) shows, in the early part of Freud's work he draws a distinction between sex-instincts and instincts of self-preservation. These stand opposed to each other because the former provides for an emotional attachment to other people while the latter provides for such an attachment to self – the maximum gratification of one instinct involves repression of the other. In the later work this opposition is retheorized into an opposition between a reproductive/love instinct (Eros) and an aggressive, self-destructive/hate instinct (Thanatos).

The ego functions to connect the id with the external world. The ego is a secondary and gradual development which emerges as the id seeks to have its demands gratified. It manages the person in such a way as to maximize satisfaction. It is thus demanding and assertive, seeking out food, comfort, warmth, sexuality, and so on, in order to feed the rapacious id. Whereas the id is wholly unconscious, the ego is only partly so. It has perceptual components which represent the external world to the id, indicating possible sources of and blockages to gratification. It also presents the id to the world, seeking to manipulate and modify the external in order to maximize sources of demand satisfaction. Not all demands can be met, inevitably, so where they are contradictory, an important, unconscious function of the ego is to repress the id, denying or delaying the principle of pleasure-seeking which drives it. Ego and id thus have a contradictory relationship: 'in its relation to the id [the ego] is like a man on horseback, who has to hold in check the superior strength of the horse' but 'a rider, if he is not to be parted from his horse, is obliged to guide it where it wants to go' (Freud 1965: 733).

However, the ego cannot range free in society, foraging for the items which will satisfy the id which carries and energizes it. Sooner or later it bumps up against other egos each also seeking to maximize pleasure for its id. The most immediate of such resistances are met in the parents. Frustrated in its demands, the ego projects aggression on to the parents but, to the extent that it proves ineffective, the aggression is, as Freud describes it, introjected, that is reversed and directed internally to become part of the mind. Thus parental resistances, what sociologists might understand as normative constraints, become internalized within the personality as the superego. The superego, rather than external society, now becomes the source of repressions. In sum, within the unconscious mind the repressions of the superego do battle with the compulsions of the id and this contradiction must be reconciled by a mediating and reasoning ego.

Abnormal behaviour occurs where the ego is unable to effect a reconciliation between the id and the superego, either because the elements are extreme or because of a preponderance of either compulsions or repressions. Two of Freud's most famous cases of abnormality are discussed by Wollheim (1971: 92–3, 130–2). One of the many abnormal behaviours experienced by a young woman Freud calls 'Dora' is a psychosomatic attack of appendicitis. Freud equates this with an hysterical pregnancy, an outward manifestation of Dora's repressed love for 'K', the husband of her father's mistress. The superego denies such a possibility, but the denial of pleasure to her demanding id leads to a self-destructive response. A contrasting case is that of the 'rat-man', an army officer experiencing unwanted fantasies in which he tortures his lover. He is so named because one such injury, which he imagines giving to his lover, is a Chinese form of torture in which a bucket containing rats is fixed to the buttocks, and the rats then gnaw their way into the anus. The rat-man was, within this theory, 'punishing' his lover on behalf of his (internalized) father who had never approved of her. Such an abnormality might be explained, then, by an excessively developed superego which represses normal pleasure-seeking.

There are two particular aspects of Freud's thought which place him firmly in the structuralist camp as defined by the seven principles set out above. Like other structuralists he is presented with a problem of examining that which is not apparent by an analysis of that which is. Many structuralists are therefore semioticists, they seek to analyse and decode signs. The signs which Freud seeks to decode are discovered in four expressions: dreams, slips, jokes, and physical symptoms. Of all these, dreams are the most revealing because they are the most symbolic expression of the contents of the unconscious mind. Decoding involves the reconstruction of three processes which occur in dreaming: condensation, the experienced dream has fewer contents than the underlying mental conjunction; displacement, certain events in a dream substitute for other real events to which they are connected by a chain of association; and representation, the rendering of abstract thoughts as pictorial imagery (Wollheim 1971: 69–70). The analyst seeks to return pictorial images back to words which the dreamer can understand.

The second important structuralist aspect of Freud's work is the construction of stages of human development. For example, the onset of sucking behaviour by an infant, even where no nipple is available, marks the initial development of the ego as it starts to seek food to satisfy its demanding id. It is designated by Freud as the oral stage. More important and controversial is the Oedipal stage which marks the internalization of the superego. Pre-Oedipally, the (male) child has developed a profound libidinal attachment to the mother and is ambivalent towards his father with whom he identifies but who is a rival for the mother's affections. The Oedipal stage involves a renunciation of the libidinal attachment to the mother and the introjection of the father. This involves the internalization of norms of appropriate erotic objects (i.e. mothers are not in this category) and therefore of a sexual identity. At the same time, as the son identifies with the father, he assumes control of his own emotions and situation.

This argument was originally controversial because it spoke for universal infantile sexuality, and even for incestuous infantile sexuality. It is currently controversial because it asserts that the formative experiences of boys are fundamentally different from the formative experiences of girls. This issue is prominent in a sociological application of the Freudian theory of the Oedipus complex in Parsons and Bales (1955; see pp. 109–15). Here boys and girls are said to internalize not only 'appropriate' sexual orientations but also more general role definitions, so that boys learn to be instrumental (task-oriented) and authoritative while girls learn to be expressive (emotional) and submissive. If it were to be accepted that such differences were determined by underlying structures of the mind then it would also have to be accepted that they were immutable.

Lévi-Strauss: primitive thoughts

Freud argues, then, that human behaviour has universal characteristics which stem from the common structure of the human mind. It is this thread which links Freud's work to the structuralist anthropology of Lévi-Strauss. Lévi-Strauss continuously stresses the invariance of human nature, the common link between so-called primitive peoples and so-called civilized ones. The unconscious activity of the mind imposes form on content, the forms are thus fundamentally the same for all societies. Therefore it is only necessary to understand the unconscious structure underlying particular institutions and customs to obtain a valid interpretation for all (Lévi-Strauss 1977: 21).

Claude Lévi-Strauss (b. 1908)

Lévi-Strauss was born in Belgium of a Jewish family and studied philosophy in Paris. At first it did not appear as if he would have an academic career but he had an opportunity to go to Brazil in 1934 to teach and work with indigenous people. The knowledge he gained from them sparked a life-long interest in anthropology. He spent the 1940s in the USA teaching at the New School for Social Research in New York City and working as a diplomat. He returned to France in 1950 and became a professor at the Collège de France in 1958. He continues to be a distinguished and public intellectual in that country.

Source: Beilharz (1991: 160)

Lévi-Strauss's first attempt to reveal structure was a study of marriage rules and their relationship to the incest taboo (1969). He was particularly interested in rules of exogamy, those specifying that marriage should occur outside the kinship group into which one is born. The structure which underlies the practice is not, says Lévi-Strauss, to do either with the avoidance of genetic inbreeding or with psychological confusion. Rather it is constituted as a principle of exchange which provides a significant functional contribution to social life. If there was continuous consanguineous marriage, society would progressively fragment into tiny and separate parts, the biological families of which it is composed. The exchange of partners provides for negotiation between families and ultimately to a set of norms which governs these exchanges. Without rules of exogamy there is no exchange and without exchange there is no society. So: 'Incest is socially absurd before it is morally culpable' (1969: 485). The problem is that the average participant in society knows nothing of this if asked. So the structure has to be carried unconsciously and to be transmitted genetically.

In a later reflection (1977) Lévi-Strauss argues that structure has four characteristics. First, it has systematic qualities, that is, it is made up of a number of elements, none of which can be changed without affecting all the others. Second, the relations between the elements are capable of 'transformation' so that they can be seen to be repeated in several different domains (e.g. kinship, economics, politics, myth). Third, the relations between elements are determinate, which means that one can predict how the structure will react if one of the elements changes. Fourth, the existence of a structure means that all the elements of social life are in principle intelligible (1977: 289–90).[1]

The central element in Lévi-Strauss's work is the revelation of structure by an analysis of myths, which he defines simply as the stories people tell about themselves. He first asserts that, although myth is linguistic in character, it must be analysed at a level above that employed in structuralist linguistics because the object is to discover not the latent structure of language but the latent structure of society. The units of myth are not phonemes or morphemes but mythemes, sentences which express relationships. Having broken down a myth, or the versions of a myth, into mythemes, these must then be sorted into categories. The juxtaposition of the mythemes in a logical relationship, as opposed to their 'order of telling', should reveal a structure. The process is similar to rehearsing the structure of a deck of cards on the basis of watching several card games, without having prior knowledge of the deck.

Lévi-Strauss demonstrates the process by analysing the Oedipus myth. The myth is broken down into such mythemes as 'Oedipus kills his father', 'Oedipus kills the dragon', 'Oedipus marries his mother' and so on. The mythemes are arranged in four columns representing, respectively: an over-emphasis on blood relations; a denial of blood relations; men killing monsters; and references to difficulty in walking upright. Column 1 emphasizes consanguinity and thus the conjugal origin of humanity; column 2 denies this; column 3 asserts the supriority of men over monsters and thus that, unlike monsters, they do not come from the earth; column 4 says that humans come from the earth because an association of this characteristic with lameness is commonly found in many cultures. There is, thus, homology between 1 and 3 and between 2 and 4; and there is opposition between 1 and 2 and between 3 and 4. The analysis therefore shows that: 'The myth has to do with the inability, for a culture which holds that mankind is autochthonous [not earthly], to find a satisfactory transition between this theory and the knowledge that human beings are actually born from the union of man and woman' (1977: 216). Lévi-Strauss is saying that there is a universal opposition between religion and biology and that human beings express this unresolvable contradiction in the stories which they tell to one another. However, their knowledge of the contradiction is unconscious and may only be revealed by structural analysis.

Binary opposition, of the sort found in the Oedipus myth, is for Lévi-Strauss a central characteristic of such representations of structure as mythic and symbolic systems. Frequently, he will intersect two sets of binary oppositions to produce a triangular system of possibilities. The most famous of these is the basic culinary triangle which classifies possible states in which food may be found. Here the two oppositions are normal–transformed and culture–nature. Normal, untransformed food is 'raw' in either culture or nature and thus forms the apex of the triangle. It may be transformed in either of two directions, culturally to become 'cooked' or naturally to become 'rotten' – 'cooked' and 'rotten' form the base points of the triangle. The three points in the triangle exhaustively cover all the possible states in which food may be found and are mutually exclusive.

Moreover, they are structural universals, found in all cultures. The categories by which human beings organize and understand the world are therefore said to be structurally determined.

Marx: contradictory thoughts

At first glance, Marx's theory of social change might not appear readily to fall into the same category as the theories of Freud and Lévi-Strauss. Whereas they stress that structures are carried in the unconscious areas of the mind, Marx's emphasis is on the material structures of production. However, the connection between the three does not lie in the realm of where the structures are carried but rather in the fact that they operate without reference to consciousness.

Karl Marx (1818–83)

Marx was born in Trier, in Prussia, which transverses what is now the Eastern border of Poland. The family was Jewish but had converted to Christianity. He took a doctorate at Berlin where he became associated with a group of radical philosophers called 'the Young Hegelians' and much of his life's work was to be a debate with the great philosopher whose name they took. He moved to Paris to try to find a job in 1843 and there met Friedrich Engels, who was to become his life-long benefactor, collaborator and friend. Marx was expelled from France in 1845 because of his revolutionary writings and moved to Brussels. But few European Governments were friendly to socialists at that time and he finally settled in London in 1849. Here he lived, wrote, politicized, and died in poverty.

Sources: *Penguin Dictionary of Sociology* (1984: s.v. Marx, Karl); Ritzer (1992: 46–7)

The grounds on which Marx is able to regard production relations as the fundamental organizing principle for human society are certain assumptions about human nature. The main assumption is that creative work is central to human existence – it is this characteristic which makes humans different from other animals. By work he means any sort of activity by which humans express themselves in the physical world. Humans are creative by nature, and their natural activity is to transform the social and physical world so that it reflects their intervention. The products of work are part of human nature because they are the form of human expression. However, it is possible for people to lose control of these acts of creation and of the things thus produced and thus to suppress or deny human nature.

The most direct statement of Marx's structuralist approach is in the preface to an appetizer, which appeared in 1859, about eight years before

Capital (1970: 20–22). First, Marx says that in constructing their social existence human beings everywhere enter into social relationships which are 'independent of their will'. These are the relationships which surround the production process and which will vary according to the particular historical stage of development of the system of production. These relations of production are the foundation of society, its economic base. On this economic base is built a political and legal superstructure so that production relations ('material life') condition general social relations, political relations and intellectual life. Thus, to quote a famous phrase: 'It is not the consciousness of men that determines their existence, but their social existence that determines their consciousness' (1970: 21).

Here Marx isolates two structural dimensions of the economic base. These are: the material *forces of production*, the particular arrangement of technology, raw materials, skills, technical possibilities and so on, and the control of these arrangements; and the *social relations of production*, especially relations surrounding ownership of the means of production. At a certain point of development these two dimensions come into conflict, typically the social relations of production will restrict the development of the material productive forces, and human beings will thus be impelled to challenge those social relations in a revolution. Such a change in the economic base will lead to a transformation of the entire superstructure.

The conflict between material forces and social relations is Marx's most important example of a structural contradiction. Structural contradiction is a key theoretical category because it provides an explanation for social change. For this reason Marx is often referred to as a 'dialectical materialist'. The term 'dialectical' means that he is interested in binary opposition and contradiction between structural elements, while the term 'materialist' means that he is interested in conflict in structures of production rather than say in ideas, or language, or kinship. So he insists that, for example, a revolutionary consciousness on the part of some individuals must be explained by the structural contradictions of material life. Thus no social order changes unless its material base has matured to an appropriate degree.

Marx sketches four stages through which the material base passes as it progresses from a primordial state of primitive communism, in which human beings individually control their own production, to Utopian communism, in which they collectively do so. These are the Asiatic, the ancient, the feudal, and the modern bourgeois or capitalist modes of production. The three precapitalist modes of production are the least of Marx's interests. However, they may briefly be characterized as follows:

- *The Asiatic mode* The forces of production within the Asiatic mode focus on the necessity for large-scale public works. The system is fundamentally agricultural but, as in the mass production of rice, requires massive irrigation schemes. The social relations of production which apply consist in public or communal ownership of these means of production. However, this communal ownership is necessarily focused on a religiously legitimated despotic leader. This is because the despot forcibly raises mass levies of workers to construct the great pieces of civil engineering required, and conscripts a standing army to enforce these contributions of labour power.

- *The ancient mode*   Here Marx focuses on the instance of Rome. The key means of production is land and the forces of production focus on labour-intensive agriculture. The land is owned by a city-based, patrician ruling class which must use slave labour to produce crops. The ruling class has a principal orientation to conspicuous consumption. It seeks to extend land ownership by forming a professional army to conquer neighbouring territories. As conquest of land occurs so its inhabitants are enslaved in agricultural labour.

- *The feudal mode*   The key difference between the fuedal and ancient modes of production is that under feudalism the landowning ruling class is rurally based. Feudalism is, therefore, very much a local social system in which central, societal institutions are under constant threat from 'robber barons'. The relations of production can therefore be based on peasant agriculture in which the serf controls a considerable amount of the land he works. However, he has a 'service relationship' with the local ruler in which he contributes a proportion of his labour time to growing the lord's produce.
(Marx and Engels 1979: 84–136)

By contrast with these three precapitalist modes, the principal features of the capitalist mode of production are as follows. First, the means of production distribution and exchange (capital) are owned privately by individuals for their own benefit – this benefit is material and is constructed as the surplus of revenues over costs. Second, because it is based on technologies which call for large-scale equipment, ownership tends to be concentrated in relatively few hands. Third, products are not held to be the intrinsic property of those who create them but rather can be bought and sold on a market as commodities. Fourth, nonowners of the means of production may be engaged in the production process, but as contracted wage workers who contribute a specific amount of labour power in exchange for a specific monetary return. Fifth, price competition and profit maximization compel the ruling class to engage in a 'labour process'. This means that they will seek to specialize and standardize tasks, so that workers become deskilled and thus vulnerable to lower wages, and so that supervision and surveillance of workers becomes simpler.

One of the important consequences for the worker is 'alienation'. It will be remembered that Marx regards production as fundamental to human nature. The products of human labour are an objective expression of the self. Wage labour and commodification under capitalism separate human beings from their very nature. Their products are torn away from them to be bought and sold in the market; the conditions under which they work are regulated and controlled by other people; and they are turned against one another in a pattern of individual competitive materialism, what Marx calls 'commodity fetishism'. However, although the term alienation speaks to the condition of the individual, it is a structural concept. In parallel with Freud and Lévi-Strauss, alienation is viewed as an unconscious process. Indeed the greater the level of alienation the less likely are workers to recognize its existence. Instead of trying to restore the natural state of life, workers resort to the pursuit of material gain and naïvely accept that capitalism is the best system possible.

The source of alienation is the necessarily exploitative relationship between capital and labour. The pattern of exploitation under the capitalist mode of production is as follows. Workers face certain costs. They must feed, clothe and house themselves and their families and they must have skills and education. Without these provisions there would be no labour force, and so they are known as the costs of the reproduction of labour power. However, the worker only needs to work a certain amount of time each week to meet these costs. If a capitalist can force workers to work for longer than this but pay them at a rate sufficient only to meet costs, the commodities produced can be exchanged so as to realize a 'surplus value'. This surplus value can then be used to increase the value of capital, thus increasing the power of the capitalist over the worker. So the capitalist progressively appropriates part of the worker's labour and thus alienates him from it. Moreover, the gulf between capitalist and worker progressively widens.

Thus the capitalist mode of production gives rise to a particular form of class system in which society is divided into a capitalist 'bourgeoisie', which owns the means of production, and a worker 'proletariat', defined by its need to sell its labour power in order to survive. The bourgeoisie is a transformative and energetic force which creates the enormous economic and engineering feats of modern society, even if it is a naked exploiter. Meanwhile, the proletariat is a mass class organized like an army by the bourgeois class and the bourgeois state – it is enslaved by machinery and bureaucratic supervision. This constitutes the underlying abstract structure of capitalist class society. The apparent pattern of class relations at any given point in time might be more complex and fluid but it is ultimately determined by this underlying reality of two great historic classes.

This abstract class structure has the following characteristics. It is: dichotomous – it involves a binary opposition between two great, mutually dependent classes; antagonistic – the classes have opposed material interests about whether the capitalist system should be maintained or not, and they have these interests whether they are aware of them or not; objective – the system exists independently of the will or the intentions of its participants; and dynamic – there is a constant struggle going on between the classes which determines the general direction of social change.

This is the fundamental contradiction on which Marx's theory of modern society is based, the contradiction of the structural relationship between classes which are mutually dependent yet antagonistic. So the bourgeoisie must control and exploit labour but not to the point at which it will refuse to work; and the proletariat is created by the bourgeoisie and yet must struggle against it. Marx's diachronic analysis turns on this dialectic. Ultimately, so severe does the contradiction become that the alienation of the proletariat is raised unwittingly to consciousness and workers do not merely struggle against the bourgeoisie but actively seek to depose it. In so doing the proletariat undermines the basis for its own existence, thus heralding the rise of a classless society. As it deposes the bourgeoisie it erases all class structures.

Contemporary theories of social structure

As is indicated in the introduction to this chapter there are, in principle, three different ways in which the concept of structure enters sociological theory: as a property of social relationships which emerges from human agency; as a set of analytic categories which can capture the patterned characteristics of social life; or as a real and underlying set of relationships which determines the appearances of social life. In the terms introduced in chapter 1 these can be regarded respectively as constructionist, functionalist, and critical structuralist approaches. In the founding arguments section we have examined arguments which are cognate with the critical structuralist approach, but we can now examine, specifically, sociological developments which will allow us to compare critical structuralism with other traditions. Constructionism is represented by Giddens' theory of structuration; functionalism by Parsons' scheme of functional imperatives; and critical structuralism by Althusser's rereading of Marx.

Giddens: the constructionist version

The details of Giddens' theory of agency are discussed in chapter 2. We can now examine the core concepts of structuration theory: 'structure', 'system', and 'duality of structure' (1984: 16). Giddens' (1984: 16–22) notion of structure is very different from that examined in most of the rest of this chapter. Structure is formally defined, somewhat obscurely, as: 'the structuring properties allowing the "binding" of time-space in social systems, the properties which make it possible for discernibly similar social practices to exist across varying spans of time and space and lend them "systemic" form' (1984: 17). These properties consist of rules and resources which actors draw upon when performing activities. By a rule, Giddens means something like a formula or procedure, a piece of taken-for-granted knowledge of how to act, which is expressed in practical consciousness. Social arrangements will be reproduced in similar ways at different times and places because the fundamental rules are known in common, or at least overlap considerably, between all the members of a social situation. He is less forthcoming on what he means by resources, referring to them only as the 'media by which power is employed' (1982: 39). However, it is clear that he does not mean external, physical resources but rather established patterns of autonomy and dependence. Although structure is internal to actors, Giddens also wants to say that structure is objective, that is independent and constraining relative to agents, and that structure is 'virtual', existing only when instantiated in particular actions. So, in these terms, there can be no class structure except when, say, a person in greasy jeans and a sweatshirt is excluded from an expensive restaurant, even though in that act of exclusion there is certainly constraint. However, this constraint comes from within the practical consciousness of the actors concerned that is, as 'memory traces', and is not determined externally.

Let us now see how Giddens conceptualizes large-scale and enduring social phenomena. These are the outcomes of processes of structuration. As numerous actors, tacitly drawing on their practical consciousness, produce and reproduce structures over time they create 'social systems' (1982: 34–5). Social systems are structures which have actually been reproduced. They consist of real and concrete activities of human subjects; they involve relationships of interdependence between individual actors and between collectivities; and they consist of a connected flow of events through time. They need to be distinguished from 'institutions' which are simply the enduring *aspects* of social phenomena, those which are most deeply layered in practical consciousness.

Systems vary in their degree of 'systemness', that is in the extent to which interdependence and endurance are reproduced in them. An integrated system is one in which there is an established reciprocity of practices between actors and/or collectivities such that relations of autonomy and dependence between them are regularized. There are two types of integration: social integration which means reciprocity of understanding between actors; and system integration which means reciprocity of exchanges between collectivities.[2] The former is accomplished by reflexive self-monitoring and the latter by the feedback loop indicated in figure 2.2.

Agents and structures, Giddens insists, are a 'duality', that is they are two aspects of a single phenomenon. They are not a 'dualism', that is two independent phenomena which might have causal relations between them. As is indicated above at various points, structure is internal to actors and it is both enabling and constraining. It is both medium and outcome, that is as actors draw upon structures in order to provide guidance for their own actions they reproduce them.

In summary, the analytic differences between structure, system and structuration are as follows:

- structure consists of rules and resources which provide the formulae and the means for action;

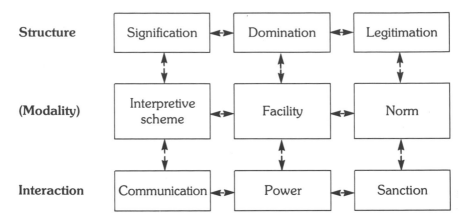

Figure 4.1 *Giddens' dimensions of the duality of structure*
(Giddens 1984: 29)

- systems are the accomplished relationships between actors/collectivities which are organized, regular, and relatively enduring; and
- structuration consists of the conditions and the media by which structures are transformed into systems.
(Giddens 1984: 25)

Structuration consists of three 'modalities' (typical channels or vectors) which connect aspects of structure with parallel aspects of interaction (see figure 4.1). As actors draw upon each modality of structuration to constitute their action so they reproduce the parallel aspect of structure. When actors communicate they draw on interpretive schemes, typifications in the stock of knowledge located in practical consciousness. In so doing they reproduce the rules of signification which connect signs with phenomena and with each other. Likewise, when actors control others or accept control by others they draw on resource facilities and thus reproduce structures of domination and subordination. Lastly, when they sanction (accept or reject) the behaviour of others they draw upon norms (rules of appropriate behaviour) and in so doing reproduce structures of legitimation.

Giddens is now able to 'explain' institutions (1984: 33–4). In different contexts actors will engage in interaction which places differential emphasis on each of the modalities such that the institutions reproduced take on a particular character. In so doing he transforms his tripartite analysis into a quadripartite form by distinguishing between two types of resource which are employed in the reproduction of domination. Allocative resources refer to an ability to command material objects, that is, to property; authoritative resources refer to an ability to command people, that is, to physical constraint, personal influence, and organizational position. Making this distinction allows the construction of four orders of priority of the modalities of structuration (see figure 4.2). So, for example, where

S-D-L   Symbolic orders/modes of discourse

D(auth)-S-L   Political institutions

D(alloc)-S-L   Economic institutions

L-D-S   Legal institutions

where S = signification, D = domination, L = legitimation

Figure 4.2   *Giddens' classification of institutional orders*
(Giddens 1984: 33)

actors draw primarily on authoritative facilities (D(auth)), secondarily on
interpretive schemes (S), and lastly on norms (L) they act to reproduce
political institutions, although Giddens does not tell us what the difference
might be between, for example, D(auth)–S–L and D(auth)–L–S. In any
event, human society is argued to be characterized by four institutional
aspects: symbolic and discursive (cultural) institutions; political institutions; economic institutions; and legal and sanctioning institutions. He is
quick to point out that these are aspects of human practice that will always
be present but that they will not necessarily be substantively differentiated
into an economy, a legal system, etc.[3]

As a last step, Giddens (1984: 34–6) wants to locate the duality of
structure in time, that 'most enigmatic feature of human experience' (1984:
34). He identifies the interactional round of everyday life as a *durée*, a
repetitive reversible routine linked to the passing of days and seasons.
These *durées* are connected together in the individual life-span which is
nonrepetitive and irreversible. But life-spans intersect with institutions
which are experienced as a *longue durée*, a long-term and reversible cycling
of generations. Thus, in an elegant construction, the life-span is the
structurating medium for the duality between the day-to-day cycle and the
institutional cycle.

Parsons: the functionalist version

We deal with Parsons elsewhere in this book, in the chapters on agency,
differentiation, and in particular, system. Here we cover solely the aspects
of his work which focus on social structure. This section provides the link
between the voluntarism of the pattern variables (see pp. 41–2) and the
systemic domination of the culture (pp. 146–9).

The first structuralist phase: permutating the pattern variables

We encountered some of the things Parsons has to say about social
structure in the above chapter on agency. It will be remembered that
Parsons discusses action situations as patterned by a series of alternative

courses of action called the pattern variables. There are two sorts of pattern variable: those that refer to possibilities about the actors' orientation to objects (affectivity–neutrality; diffuseness–specificity); and those that refer to what objects are themselves conceived to be (particularism–universalism; quality–performance).[4]

It must be stressed that Parsons initially conceives of the pattern variables quite literally as 'main dilemmas of choice in situations' (Parsons et al. 1953: 66) – he is at this point still viewing social life as a matter of agency. But note that the choice is not absolute and that there are already structural limitations contained within the scheme. First, actors' choices are not entirely open – they can choose to be oriented towards objects in one of only two ways and they can decide that objects take one of only two forms. Second, an actor can resolve each of the dilemmas in only a single direction – if she decides, for example, that a given other person is to be judged in terms of his performances then he cannot also be judged in terms of his qualities.

There are two structuralist phases in Parsons' work. In the first, he uses the pattern variables to show the way in which structural imperatives pattern actual societies in terms of concrete social arrangements. He is thus able to specify the different substantive possibilities for the organization of social and cultural systems. These various possibilities are described in terms of value-patterns set up by cross-classifying the pattern variables: '*every* concrete need-disposition of personality, or every role-expectation of social structure, involves a combination of values of the five pattern variables' (Parsons et al. 1951: 93, original italics). Parsons sets out two important ways in which the pattern variables tend to cluster: structural arrangements found universally in all societies; and empirical types of society (defined as a completely self-sufficient social system).

He offers four examples of structural arrangements which will be found in all or almost all societies (1991: 153–67). The universality of each structure is explained by reference to the functions it performs for the social system or for systems in the environment of the social system (e.g. culture, personality). The universal structures are as follows:

- *Kinship* comprises social groups which are defined by biological relatedness (families); roles are always diffuse and collectivity oriented. Kinship systems are universal because of the functional constraints imposed by the human organism, e.g. long periods of gestation and infant dependency.
- *Stratification* comprises social groups defined by the allocation of rewards to differentiated instrumental activities (especially as institutionalized in occupations, classes, status groups); the tendency is to roles which are universalistic, specific and affectively neutral. Its universality is explained by functional requirements of efficiency and effectiveness in which rewards go to the most hardworking and talented.

- *The state* comprises groups which are defined by the integration of the power system around territoriality and coercion (governments, political organizations, military organizations) [no pattern variable description of roles offered]. Its universality is explained by the double contingency that societies cannot survive if the use of force is unconstrained and widely available (*vide* parts of the contemporary USA); nor can they survive without some employment of force to prevent undesired action and external aggression.
- *Religion* comprises social groups organized around value integration between the individual personality and the cultural system (churches, social movements); [no pattern variable description offered]. Its universality is explained by the uncertainties and consequent anxieties imposed by the environment, as in Malinowski (see chapter 5), and the 'inevitable' unevenness, at the level of meaning, between the individual and cultural patterns. Religion functions to reduce anxiety and to mediate meanings.

The use of the pattern variables is rather more explicit in taking the second step of establishing patterns of substantive variation between societies. It must be remembered that all societies will encompass each of the four universal structures but the particular cultural pattern in the society, as specified in terms of the pattern variables, will determine which of these structures dominates and is most developed. The pattern variable pairs which appear best to allow such discrimination are particularism–universalism and quality–performance (ascription–achievement). By cross-classifying these we are able to identify the four principal types of societal social structure given in figure 4.3. Here the particularism-quality type has been re-exemplified in order to eliminate some inconsistencies in Parsons' analysis.

The second structuralist phase: theorizing with agility

The argument described so far is still a relatively soft form of structuralism in which structure is viewed as limiting the way actors choose but not determining their choices for them. Parsons' theory was transformed in a 'hard' structuralist direction when he encountered a Harvard social psychologist, and small groups theorist, named Bales. Bales had conceptualized four activities in which all small groups must engage if they are to maintain their characteristics as groups. Parsons takes these four activities, develops and abstracts them, and calls them the dimensions of action space. In so doing, he integrates them conceptually with the pattern variables. He thus moves towards a structuralist position in which the dimensions of action space define the behaviour of individual actors located in relation to them. Actors no longer move through action space as a matter of choice but rather there must be a significant group of actors in each of the spaces defined and their behaviour is no longer a matter of choice.

	Particularism	Universalism
Quality	Religion (dominant, e.g., in Arunta, traditional India)	State (dominant, e.g., in Nazi Germany, Soviet Union, feudal Europe)
Performance	Kinship (dominant, e.g., in ancient China)	Occupational stratification (dominant, e.g., in contemporary EC, Japan, USA)

Figure 4.3 *Parsons' analysis of the principal types of social structure*

Parsonsian structuralism is known as and indeed is a structural *functionalism*. Action is conceived to be organized as a series of living systems, the instance of greatest interest being the social system. These systems are said to operate in terms of survival and are imperatively driven in that direction. There are functions which must be performed if the: 'equilibrium and/or continuing existence of the system is to be maintained' (Parsons and Smelser 1956: 16). These functional 'imperatives' or 'exigencies' or 'problems' in turn constrain certain social arrangements to match each of them. In sum, social arrangements are determined by the functions that they perform in relation to the needs of the system of which they are a part.

Parsons orders functional imperatives in terms of two dichotomies: whether they are to do with the provision of means for system survival, in which case they are said to be instrumental, or to do with the selection of ends or goal-states, in which case they are said to be consummatory; and whether these needs must be secured internally within the system or externally. By cross-cutting these binary distinctions Parsons achieves a fourfold typology of functional imperatives. They are as follows:

- *Latent pattern-maintenance and tension-management* (internal/instrumental)   Here the problem is to maintain the overall blueprint of the system through time, despite periods of inactivity. There must be some latent memory of how the system works even when it is not actually working and there must also be provision for the remembered elements to be raised to the level of activity.
- *Integration* (consummatory/internal)   Here the imperative is to maintain solidarity between the units of a system (the subsystems), to make

sure that the exchanges between them are smooth and orderly and not obstructive and conflictual.

- *Goal-attainment* (instrumental/internal)   A goal is defined as a change of direction which brings the needs of the system more into line with the conditions of its environment. So goal-attainment can involve establishing a goal either to modify the environment or to modify internal arrangements. This imperative also includes a requirement that complex goals must be ordered in a hierarchy of priorities and that resources must be allocated so that goals may be realized.

- *Adaptation* (instrumental/external)   A system must also ensure the availability of disposable facilities and resources which are procured from an environment. Where a system has a single goal, adaptation is an unproblematic and undifferentiated consequence of goal-attainment. However, where there are complex and multiple goals, the facilities procured must be flexibly disposable, otherwise the process of goal-setting will become constrained by resource availability.

However, the pattern variables have not disappeared entirely. Parsons shows how this scheme can conceptually be conflated with the pattern variables scheme (Parsons et al. 1953: 179–90). First, he notices affinities between certain attitudinal (a) and certain object-oriented (o) pattern variable alternatives. For example, there is an affinity between affectivity (a) and particularism (o) – one tends, for example, to love other people whom one also considers to be 'special' – and between specificity (a) and universalism (o) – when others are evaluated according to general standards one's relationship to them is defined in narrow terms. By examining such affinities four clusters of pattern variables can be discovered:

Specificity (a)-Neutrality(a)-Universalism(o)-Performance(o)
Affectivity (a)-Specificity(a)-Particularism(o)-Performance(o)
Diffuseness(a)-Affectivity(a)-Particularism(o)-Quality(o)
Neutrality(a)-Diffuseness(a)-Quality(o)-Universalism(o)
(Parsons et al. 1953: 180)

These clusters can then describe the four dimensions of action space, as discussed above. For example, adaptation is defined in pattern variable terms as SNUPe, latency as NDQU.

The scheme of functional imperatives is conventionally known as the AGIL scheme, after its initials. It is also conventional to arrange them as a pattern of four boxes, as in figure 4.4. To obtain such a figure: 'we visualize the pattern variable clusters within each cell, give the cell an appropriate name, and move the pattern variable designation to the sides of the table' (Parsons et al. 1953: 180).

	Universalism Neutrality	Affectivity Particularism
Specificity Performance	Adaptation (A)	Goal-attainment (G)
Quality Diffuseness	Latent pattern-maintenance and tension-management (L)	Integration (I)

Figure 4.4 *The pattern variables and the AGIL scheme*
(Menzies 1977: 68, adapted)

The AGIL scheme now becomes the basis for the specification of structures relative to the system of interest. If one is interested in a societal social system it is imperative that it should have the four subsystem structures specified in figure 4.5, that is:

- A set of social arrangements focusing on socialization, expressive behaviour, recreation, and the internalization of value-commitments including religious, familial, educational, artistic and sporting social structures. These perform what in Marxist terminology might be called the function of social reproduction, or what is called social integration in the work of Habermas (see chapter 5). Parsons starts with the view that a social system always involves the institutionalization (the putting into regular social practice) of a cultural system of values. It must ensure that its social practices match general value-orientations, either by the construction and reconstruction of value-orientations, or by the effective translation of changes in value-orientations into new practices. So there must be social processes which articulate social system with culture, those which are normally called religious and ideological social processes. The system must also deal with threats to the stability of the cultural pattern which come from individual personalities, what Parsons calls 'motivational tensions'. Processes of socialization have an important role to play here, as do ritual and recreational processes.
- A societal community which consists in arrangements for the establishment and application of a set of shared regulative norms. In accomplishing this, legal institutions and systems of social control are critical but so also are such generalized institutions as citizenship and civil rights, and so are such distributional systems and media as markets, private property, contract and money.[5]
- A polity, which is a structure of leadership, setting goals for the society and mobilizing individuals and resources in relation to their realization.
- An economy, which secures facilities from the physical environment

A   G

Economy	Polity
Cultural-motivational system (Latent pattern-maintenance and TM subsystem)	Integrative subsystem

L   I

Figure 4.5 *Parsons' analysis of the subsystems of society (1956 version) (Parsons and Smelser 1984: 53, adapted)*

and, by a process of production, transforms them into flexibly useable objects.

The scheme allows elaboration in two directions, 'upward' and 'downward'. The four structural responses to the functional imperatives of a societal social system are themselves (sub) systems each with its own set of imperatives and each with its own structural responses. Downward specification is exemplified in figure 4.6 which shows the structural subsystems of economic and political structures respectively. Economies must have four structures: they must get resources from the social environment via capitalization (A); they must process resources in a production system (G); they must ensure that activities are organized and coordinated (I); and they must ensure that participants remain active (L). Equally, political systems must have taxation and revenue (A), executive (G), administrative and legal (I), and legislative, constitutional and ideological (L) structures.

Macroscopic or upward elaboration is indicated in figure 4.7. The social system performs the integration function for the more general system which Parsons calls the action system. The other structural elements of the action system are: the (physical) behavioural system (A) which provides it with material energy; the personality structure (G) which organizes means in relation to goals; and culture (L) which provides pattern and meaning to action. The action system is equally one of the four more general structures of what Parsons (1978) calls the human condition. It performs the function of integrating the human condition. The environment of the action system consists of: the physico-chemical system (A) which is the ultimate source of resources used by human beings; the human organic system (G) which sets physical goals; and the telic system (L), the supernatural 'reality' (1978: 356) within which ultimate issues are settled. Parsons proceeds to elaborate the subsystems of each of the components of the human condition.

Having located the structures of social and other systems in relation to one another, Parsons can now specify the pattern of relationships between

Economy (A)   Polity (G)

a	g	a	g
Capitalization	Production including sales and marketing	Taxation and revenue	Executive
Economic commitments: physical, cultural and motivational resources	Organizational subsystem (entrepreneurial function)	Legislative, constitutional and ideological	Administrative and legal
l	i	l	i

Figure 4.6 *Parsons' analysis of the subsystems of the economy and polity (Economy from Parsons and Smelser 1956: 44)*

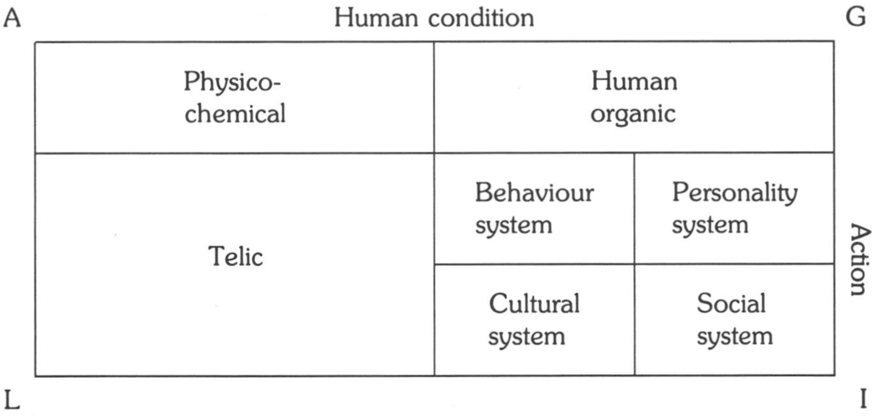

A   Human condition   G

Physico-chemical	Human organic	
Telic	Behaviour system	Personality system
	Cultural system	Social system

L   I

Figure 4.7 *Parsons' macroscopic elaboration of the AGIL scheme: the subsystems of action and of the human condition (Parsons 1978 passim)*

the structural elements and, in so doing, specify the directions in which systems change (Parsons et al. 1953: 182–90). Each of the four dimensions represents a different orientational and motivational cluster of action. Action in the A dimension, for example, is oriented to the manipulation of physical objects in terms of their instrumental capacity; in the I dimension it is oriented to the manipulation of signs indicating reciprocity of expectations. An important structural constraint is that not all of them can be manipulated at the same time – instrumentality (A), for example, precludes reciprocity (I) (e.g. manipulating others contradicts being generous to them), and performance and gratification (G) preclude mutuality (L) (e.g. pursuing individual success contradicts the establishment of good relations with others). Therefore, at any particular time one or another of the phases must be emphasized or dominant. The dominance of a particular phase is determinately related to the phase dominance which preceded it. This is because a period of dominance in a particular phase will produce deficits in another dimension.

Parsons et al. speculate about various possible relations of phase dominance. However, the best approximation they can establish is the (diagramatically clockwise) process A→G→I→L→A→ . . . etc. In everyday social terms: once things are acquired (A) some decisions need to be made about what to do with them (G), which then requires that people doing different things sort out how to work together (I), and they can only do this if they can learn and understand what the whole situation is about (L), which then informs about what sort of things to acquire (A).[6]

We are covering, in this section, the most structuralist aspects of Parsons' work, those which stress the effects of unseen imperatives on the actions of individuals. Elsewhere we examine other aspects of Parsons' work, particularly the emergence of social systems from human interaction and the processes of differentiation which pervade social systems. It remains to be said that despite these structuralist orientations, Parsons is utterly unlike Lévi-Strauss or the next theorist we examine, Althusser, in terms of the denial of the subject.

As will have been gathered, Parsons confounds his readers by producing a bewildering array of categories for analysing action, and it is also true to say that when he actually employs them to analyse the real-life appearances of action the analysis often appears as a futile and trivial exercise in jargon mongering. However, one suspects that substantive analysis is neither his purpose not his motivation. He is actually building a conceptual scaffolding which will link human agents with an ideal realm of ultimate values. It seeks to reconcile voluntaristic choice with the overarching and determining universes of meaning. Although AGIL appears to reconstitute the choices enshrined in the pattern variables as structural imperatives, Parsons thereafter virtually refuses to use the scheme to explain action and uses it only for classification. The explanations lie, as we have said, in the relationship between the actor's choices and abstracted, idealized meanings and values.

Althusser: the structuralist version

Just as Parsons' structural-functionalism might be found at the end of modernist conservatism, so Althusser's structuralist Marxism might be described as part of the denouement of modernist radicalism (Crook 1991). In the late 1960s a revolution occurred in Marxist thought which might be described as its final intellectual flowering, although it remains to be seen whether there will be further developments. The key wrtings in this reinterpretation come from Althusser.

Louis Althusser (1918–90)

Althusser was born in Algeria and studied at the École Normale Supérieure, in Paris, where he eventually became Professor of Philosophy. Althusser was a leading ideologue of the Communist Party of France and his arguments were a response to multiple threats to the ideological foundations of that socialist project. These included both the threat from an empiricism which was beginning to invade academic Marxist sociology and economics, and a threat from humanistic and democratic socialist orientations which were beginning to corrode the ideological purity of European Communist Parties hungry for electoral success. Interestingly, although Althusser is widely regarded as the most convincingly structuralist of Marxists, he himself denied any link with 'structuralist ideology'. His work was extremely fashionable in the 1970s but his notoriety was confirmed by the fact that, in 1980, he strangled his wife to death and was subsequently confined to a mental hospital for four years.

Sources: *Penguin Dictionary of Sociology* (1984: *s.v.* Althusser, Louis); Ritzer (1991: 297)

Hi Marx!

Althusser's approach is philological – he reads Marx's texts seeking to extract from them the true and fundamental concepts. In so doing he identifies a principal rupture in Marx's thought between an earlier phase and a later phase.[7] The earlier elements are idealistic and humanistic, deriving from the philosophy of Hegel. They are constituted in the anthropological statements about work and human nature and the consequent discussion of alienation. These idealistic concepts of human nature are, Althusser argues, abandoned when Marx begins to collaborate with Engels on the production of *The German Ideology* and the new position is stated in embryonic form in the 'Preface' analysed above. Here Marx invents a new science, the science of dialectical materialism, which is elucidated in its most complete form in the general discussion of political economy in *Capital*.[8]

Marx's analysis proceeds, Althusser says, not by offering presuppositions about the nature of humanity but by outlining the basic concepts of economic phenomena. The central concept is 'mode of production'. The concept must be defined in its general complexity, its 'global' structure,

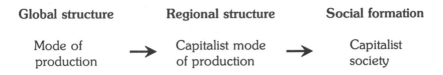

Global structure		Regional structure		Social formation
Mode of production	→	Capitalist mode of production	→	Capitalist society

Figure 4.8 *Mode of production and social formation in Althusser's theory*

and also in terms of its historical moments, its 'regional' structure. The global structure, production in general, determines the development of regional structures, for example, the capitalist mode of production (CMP), which in turn determines apparent phenomena, what have become known as the 'social formation', capitalism (Althusser and Balibar 1972: 240–3). This might be expressed as in figure 4.8.

The global structure of the mode of production consists of a unified relationship between three elements: the direct labourer applying energy (labour power) to the production process; the means of production, that is the land, tools, plant and other technical facilities; and the nonlabourer who appropriates surplus product. There are two connecting relationships between these, the by now familiar 'forces of production' (FP) (control of labour in the production process) and the 'social relations of production' (SRP) (ownership/nonownership of capital property) (Craib 1984: 135; Glucksmann 1974: 237).

Craib (1984: 135–6) summarizes Althusser and Balibar's characterizations of specific arrangements of these elements as four regional modes of production: the feudal mode of production; a transitional domestic outwork mode of production which lies between feudalism and capitalism; the capitalist mode of production, and the socialist mode of production. These reflect the possible combinations between labourer and nonlabourer allowed by the intersection of the FP with the SRP, as given in figure 4.9. Under feudalism, while the nonlabourer lord owns the land, the peasant labourer makes decisions about how it is to be used. In domestic outwork, the labourer owns the machinery, a textile loom for example, but the capitalist middleman, the nonlabourer, determines what is to be produced on it. The CMP and socialism represent the extreme possibilities of subordination and emancipation of the labourer respectively. Interestingly, this scheme finds room for neither the ancient nor the Asiatic modes of production.

Base determinism

Althusser insists that any social formation constitutes a 'complex unity' and is not to be understood in terms of its mode of material production alone. This complex unity is discovered in relationships between practices. A practice is 'any process of *transformation* of a determinate given raw material into a determinate *product*, a transformation effected by determi-

Social relations of production

Nonlabourer owns   Labourer owns
means of production means of production

	Nonlabourer owns means of production	Labourer owns means of production
Forces of production — Nonlabourer controls production process	Capitalist	Domestic outwork
Labourer controls production process	Feudal	Socialist

Figure 4.9 *Althusser and Balibar's implicit classification of modes of production*

nate human labour, using determinate means (of 'production')' (Althusser 1977a: 166, original italics). Each practice receives its characteristic pattern neither from the raw material nor from the product but from the moment of transformation which combines 'men, means and a technical method of utilizing the means' (1977a: 167).

The critical practices in any mode of production are, unsurprisingly, practices of production. The nature of these determines the mode of production (but only in 'the last instance' as is discussed below). Production practices are material in character, transforming natural substances into useful products by the methodical application of systematically organized means of production. But other practices are also contained within a given mode of production and are critical in the determination of variations in the social formation. These include: political practices, which transform one set of social relations into a new set of social relations; ideological practices, which include the religious, political, moral, legal or artistic transformation of consciousness; and, finally, theoretical or scientific practices, which transform representations, concepts and facts into theories (1977a: 167). An interesting by-product of this formulation is that Althusser is suggesting that Marxist ideologues are also productive workers by arguing that the structure of the transformation in which they engage is homologous with material production, that the production of theories corresponds with the production of commodities.

This specification of different kinds of practice leads to an argument about structural arrangements in any social formation. Any such formation has two structural components, the infrastructure or economic base which combines FP with SRP, and the superstructure which itself has two 'levels' or 'instances'. These are the politico-legal structure, which includes law and the state, and the ideological structure comprised of religious, ethical, legal and political orientations (see figure 4.10). This arrangement, says Althusser, may be considered as analogous to a three-storey building in

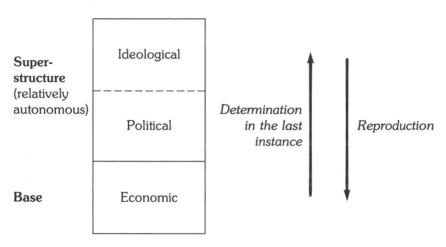

Figure 4.10 *Althusser's base–superstructure theory*

which the economic base is the ground floor, with political and ideological levels built upon the base. The analogy suggests: 'that the upper floors could not "stay up" (in the air) alone, if they did not rest precisely on their base' (1977b: 129). Althusser stresses that the relationship between base and superstructure is a precise fit.

However, Althusser also insists that the relationship between base and superstructure is not one of simple economic determinism in a vulgar sense. He does not wish to argue, as Engels did for example, that the cabinet of ministers is a mere committee of the ruling economic class (1977a: 111). Rather he argues for a new structural analysis of the relationship between base and superstructure. This relationship takes two directions. Going up, the base has the quality of 'determination in the last instance', a phrase which Althusser does borrow from Engels. This does not mean that the economic base has the final say in a historical sense, but that it is the economic level which determines just how much autonomy might be found in the superstructure. To use another of his famous phrases, the economic structure is always the 'structure in dominance', it defines the general pattern of relationships between the various levels of structure. Again, in his own conceptual terms, it imposes a 'complex unity' upon the 'totality'.

Relationships of determination also apply in a downward direction in the structural edifice. First, the political and ideological levels are argued to exist in a state of 'relative autonomy'. For example, in a capitalist society, it is possible for there to be an antibourgeois political opposition, even a communist opposition. Similarly, it is possible for such academics as Althusser himself to develop critiques of capitalism. These are said to be forms of autonomy which are in some sense 'allowed' by the economic base. They offer an illusion of freedom in the superstructure thus allowing the secret constraints of the economic arena to survive unchallenged. Their autonomy is therefore 'relative' to the structure in dominance. Second, the superstructure is said to engage in 'reciprocal action' towards the base. Here the state and ideological arrangements operate to keep the capitalist system going. They reproduce labour power (FP) and they reproduce the SRP. Citing Marx, he writes: 'every child knows that a social formation which did not reproduce the conditions of production at the same time as it produced would not last a year' (1977b: 123). The formation must ensure its own future by making sure that its members know what they have to do and are committed to doing it. It is the superstructure which accomplishes this outcome.

In the last instance the subject is dead

Althusser accepts from Marx a view of the state as the object of political class struggle. Within this analysis the state has certain agencies (e.g. the police, courts, prisons, the military) which ensure the orderly operation of capitalism. These are the 'repressive state apparatuses' (RSAs) and the object of the political struggle is to maintain or to gain control of them in order to further one's own class interests (1977b: 134–5). Thus, for example, the RSAs are used by the capitalist class to repress industrial strikes and protest movements. Althusser argues that the capitalist state is also much more complex than this, accomplishing reproduction not merely by the use of force but also by the manipulation of ideas.

Alongside the RSAs there is therefore said to develop a plurality of 'ideological state apparatuses' (ISAs) but which traverse the boundary between the state and civil society. They include churches, schools, families, political parties, trade unions, the mass media, and cultural and recreational institutions. These institutions operate to establish an imaginary view, in the minds of individuals, of the conditions of their existence, for example: that there is no alternative to capitalism; or that democracy is a genuine power-sharing arrangement; or that individuals make real choices about the direction of their own lives. They imagine these things to be true when the reality lies elsewhere. Althusser is convinced that the key ISA in accomplishing this under contemporary conditions is the school: 'although hardly anyone lends an ear to its music: it is so silent!' (1977b: 146). No other ISA is as effective because the school has the obligatory attention of every member of society for eight hours a day, five days a week, 200 days a year, for ten years.[9]

If this were the entire sum of Althusser's argument he would be presented with a problem. The exact fit between base and superstructure, in which the base determines the level of autonomy of the superstructure and the superstructure reproduces the base, would ensure that there would be no possibility of change, when change is the precise object of Marxist theory. He finds his solution in the notion of contradiction. In Marx this contradiction occurs simply at the level of economic production (between FP and SRP as expressed in the contradiction between antagonistic classes). But under normal circumstances, suggests Althusser, the contradiction is displaced into the relatively autonomous components of the superstructure. People can work out their antagonisms in political or ideological arenas rather than struggling over ownership of the means of production. Another way of saying this is that social formations are characterized by uneven development, the different levels of structure do not correspond. For a significant change to occur the contradictions in each of the structural levels must line up. There must be an accumulation of circumstances and social currents which fuse into a 'ruptural unity' (1977a: 99) in which contradictory forces condense in a single temporal and spatial location. Displacement and condensation are phenomena of what Althusser calls 'overdetermination'.[10] Here:

> [T]he 'contradiction' is inseparable from the total structure of the social body . . ., from the formal *conditions* of existence, and even from the *instances* it governs; it is radically *affected by them*, determining, but also determined in one and the same movement, and determined by the various *levels* and *instances* of the social formation it animates. [1977a: 101, original italics]

So the notion of 'overdetermination' extends the idea of contradiction beyond the base to the superstructure, thus providing a legitimacy to Marxist political and ideological action as well as to direct industrial action.

All of these arguments apply independently of the personal will of the participants. Even where there is a revolutionary rupture, participants may have a wide variety of political commitments, to environmentalism or peace for example, but they are still the representatives of the class struggle. Althusser thus 'solves' the problem of action by removing agency from the picture altogether. He becomes responsible for what has become known as the 'death of the subject'. Just how radical and antihumanistic a position this is can be gauged from the following quotation:

> The structure of the relations of production determines the *places* and *functions* occupied and adopted by the agents of production, who are never anything more than the occupants of these places, insofar as they are the 'supports' (*Träger*) of these functions. The true 'subjects' (in the sense of constitutive subjects of the process) are therefore not these occupants or functionaries, are not, despite all appearances, the 'obviousnesses' of the 'given' of naive anthropology, 'concrete individuals', 'real men' – but *the definition and distribution of these places and functions. The true 'subjects' are these definers and distributors: the relations of production* (and political and ideological social relations). But since these are 'relations' they cannot be thought of within the category *subject*. [Althusser and Balibar 1970: 180, original italics]

More colourfully, it is not Goffman alone who submits to dramaturgical analogy. The machinery of capitalism might be thought of as a

> theatre which is simultaneously its own stage, its own script, its own actors, the theatre whose spectators can, on occasion, be spectators only because they are

all forced to be its actors, caught by the constraints of a script and parts whose authors cannot be, since it is in essence an *authorless theatre*. [Althusser and Balibar 1972: 254, original italics]

Recent French structuralism and poststructuralism

We opened this chapter with a consideration of three founding positions in the debate about structure. We can now move to the end of the debate. The high point of structuralist thinking is represented in Althusser's reinterpretation of Marx and in Lacan's contemporary reinterpretation of Freud, to be discussed next. However, these structuralist edifices were to fall in the 1980s to a radical poststructuralist attack. The leading figure in this attack is the literary theorist Derrida, whose argument is traced briefly at the end of the present chapter. However, it might be argued that the most sociologically influential poststructuralist is Foucault, but his poststructuralism is so radical that it moves into the realm of substantive rather than formal theory. It is therefore considered in chapter 7, on power.

Lacan: French Freud[11]

Two key points of sociological theory emerge from the earlier discussion of Freud. First, human action is governed by structured and unconscious processes which incorporate the constraints of the external social world. Second, the part of the mind called the ego is the significant location of autonomous behaviour which, if normally mature, can tame the grasping and rebellious id and resist the authoritarianism of the superego. Lacan (1968) so completely rejects this second point that he virtually turns Freud upon his head. In Lacan the conscious element of the ego is an introjection of the external world and thus an alienative denial of the autonomy of the subject. The genuine location of selfhood is the unconscious part of the mind. The unconscious is real, in the sense of original, the ego only imaginary or epiphenomenal.

Jacques Lacan (1901–81)

Lacan spent most of his life as a practising psychoanalyst in France. His earliest work appeared in 1936 with the theory of the mirror stage, but his argument that psychoanalysis should be reconstructed as a linguistic theory did not appear until the 1950s. Because he rejects the standard assumption of psychoanalysis that its objective is to promote a happy adjustment on the part of the patient, Lacan has always been a controversial figure in his own discipline. He was, for example, at one stage, expelled from the International Psychoanalytic Association.

Sources: *Penguin Dictionary of Sociology* (1984: *s.v.* Lacan, Jacques); Beilharz (1991: 154–5)

Like Freud, Lacan traces the development of the individual through a series of phases. However, what makes him so 'French' is that he draws on the national tradition of structural linguistics to analyse this development. In Freud, the interpretation of the unconscious, through the pictorial symbolizations of dreams and the linguistic ones of slips and jokes, reveals that the unconscious is indeed a symbolic order. Lacan's breakthrough is to show that the unconscious is structured like a language and that it is through an analysis of language that it can be revealed. Lacan's developmental phases are symbolic or linguistic. They are also cumulative – individuals do not move out of one phase and into another but rather pile on onion-skin layers of experience which persist throughout the biography.

The source of human development is libido or desire. The originating desire is the relationship to the mother in which the child desires to be the total object of desire, to be the direct extension and completion of the mother. Its relationship to the mother is entirely subordinate and alienated – it has no selfhood. The beginning of a move out of this relationship occurs within what Lacan calles the 'mirror phase' that occurs between the ages of six and eighteen months. This is when the child notices its own reflection and makes the discovery that it is not simply an incoherent and dependent extension of others but a whole, discrete and conceivably autonomous individual. Thereafter the individual will always pursue the chimera of an imaginary ideal of perfect self-formation as glimpsed in the mirror.

Lacan can now reinterpret Freud's Oedipal transition in linguistic terms, that is as a metaphorical shift. As the father enters the scene, the desire for the mother is repressed (into the unconscious) and repositioned in a new and linguistified relationship. The father enters the subject in a symbolic form, neither as real nor imagined, but as a word. In a startling wordplay, of the type for which he has become famous, Lacan argues that the individual now starts to act 'In the name of the Father'. The wordplay is not only religious, assimilating the parent to an authoritative God, but proscriptive, by virtue of the phonetic similarity between the French word for name (*nom*) with that for no (*non*). The linguistification of the relationship to the parent lends not only authority but mediation and distance. The shift leaves the subject with an ambivalent relationship towards self and the Other: the self is both desirable and sinful (*Eros* and *Thanatos* in Freud); the Other must be both dominated and obeyed. And it also sets up a conduit for the channelling of externalities into the internal self via the extended use of linguistic signifiers (sounds). Thus Lacan constructs a highly sociologized version of Freud in which the structure of society and the structure of the personality are homologized in the structure of language.

The Oedipal transition marks a shift between orders of signification, from the imaginary to the symbolic. These two are elements in a trinity of orders, Imaginary–Symbolic–Real, which form a touchstone for Lacanian thought. The imaginary order originates in the mirror phase, when the child imagines its own ego, but extends to any context in which the subject (falsely) identifies itself directly with itself or with others in an unmediated way. The symbolic order, that in which relationships are mediated through signs, is paradoxically less sure in its associations. Linguistic signs always involve metaphor, in which meanings are infinitely condensed, and metonymy, in which they are displaced. By the use of these devices, the symbolic order always seeks to encroach on, organize and make sense of the imaginary order. Lacan is therefore a true structuralist in that subjective being is socially (linguistically) determined, the signifier (the sound) is privileged over the signified (the thought), while the agency of the imagined ego is alienative and false. The third order, the Real, is both contextual and inaccessible. It is the realm of facticity which the symbolic seeks to classify but which can never be known directly because all that a human being can know is language.

We can therefore view Lacanian theory as a psychoanalysis of frustration. It regards human subjects, if we can mimic his wordplay technique, as knights errant (stumblers in the dark) in pursuit of an unattainable holy grail of self-realization: they cannot become one with the mother; they cannot go through the looking-glass and become their own ego-ideal, but can only see the self as the Other; they cannot directly identify with a father they only know through the sound of his name; and they cannot obtain direct apprehension of physical reality. They can only play endlessly and unsatisfyingly with symbols. While he may provide a challenging theory of social motivation, Lacan therefore offers a philosophy only of damnation and despair. He has put an iron treadmill in Nietzsche's 'prison-house of language'.

Derrida: the last poststructuralist[12]

Derrida speaks directly to French linguistic theoretical traditions. He particularly takes issue with the association specified by Saussure between the signifier (the sound) and the signified (the thought evoked by the sound). This argues Derrida lends privilege to speech as against writing. All such linguistic theory is based on an analysis of speech, and writing is typically understood as a subtype of speech. Speech thus implies 'presence' (or immediate existence) on the part of an object which is signified. This suggests a philosophical logocentricism in which it is assumed that the universe consists of a present and knowable whole which can eventually be apprehended by transcending fragmentary and individual experience. Furthermore, it assumes that each signifier is neologistic and has no relationship to a history of classifications.

Derrida proposes instead a *grammatology* or science of writing which will disprivilege speech and show that language is conventional rather than realistic. Language works as a system of classification – it establishes differences or bipolar oppositions of present/absent. However, written language involves not only this *différence* (differentiation) but also *différance*

Jacques Derrida (b. 1930)

Like Simmel, Derrida is a Sephardic Jew, and like Althusser, he was born in Algeria, North Africa. He studied at the École Normale Supérieure at Ulm and he is now Professor of Philosophy at the École des Hautes Études en Sciences Sociales in Paris. He has also spent a considerable amount of time in the USA, on extended visits to Harvard, Irvine, and Cornell. He is responsible for the introduction of the word 'deconstruction' into the language. His most controversial moment must have been in 1992 when a public debate erupted at Cambridge University on the question of whether he should be awarded an honorary degree.

Source: Beilharz (1991: 54–5)

(deferment). By the latter he means that differences or classifications found in language are the products of prior events. So a written word is the product of some prior speech act, but speech is not the reality which writing represents because speech is itself the product of a prior act of classification. The written word, cat, for example, depends on someone having spoken that word, but this in turn depends on others having recognized that certain carniverous, domesticable, nonfood, quadruped mammals with retractable claws were different from other objects.

Derrida's analysis of writing seeks to show that every sign, including the spoken ones, contains 'traces' or memories of previous acts of classification – speech becomes a form of proto-writing (*archi-écriture*). These traces connect not only to present objects but absent ones – to write 'cat' is to invite a contrast with 'dog'. If this is true then the meaning of a piece of writing never involves a direct linkage to a present object. In fact writing can never have a determinate meaning. Rather meaning is contextualized to the relationship between the text and its reader. Writing does not reproduce reality, it creates and recreates it and is thus always full of political importance (Hawkes 1977: 149). Culler sums up this general orientation to language as follows:

> [O]ne might think of language as a play of differences, a proliferation of traces and repetitions which under conditions that can be described but never exhaustively specified, give rise to effects of meaning. [1979: 171–2]

It is in this sense that Derrida is a poststructuralist. The meanings of signs become entirely arbitrary and are not founded on some reality which can be assumed to be orderly and determinative.

Derrida seeks to demonstrate this by a process of deconstruction of texts. Any text will have a readable subtext which contradicts and supplements its own position:

[D]econstruction is the vigilant seeking out of those 'aporias', blindspots or moments of self-contradiction where a text involuntarily betrays the tension between rhetoric and logic, between what it manifestly *means to say* and what it is nonetheless *constrained to mean*. To 'deconstruct' a piece of writing is therefore to operate a kind of strategic reversal, seizing precisely those unregarded details (casual metaphors, footnotes, incidental turns of argument) which are always, and necessarily, passed over by interpreters of a more orthodox persuasion. [Norris 1987: 19, original italics]

Deconstruction is an attempt to uncover the genealogies of the ways of thinking which have gone to make up a text. Derrida's chief target is the claim of various philosophical texts to having uncovered a truth or reality, but, in effect, he also stands opposed to any foundationalist sociology which insists on a monothematic explanation in terms of culture or rationalization or materialism or functional imperatives. The alternative he offers is that of a playful, linguistic sociality.

Conclusion

Summary

1 In a structuralist argument, structure is a hidden reality which determines surface appearances. The three most important structuralists are Freud, Marx and Lévi-Strauss. Freud analyses the unconscious structure of the mind; Marx analyses the material structures which underlie history; and Lévi-Strauss analyses the structure of myth.

2 Giddens offers an account of social structure which stands radically opposed to this structuralist position. Society is said to be 'structurated' by the actions of human agents. In acting out established rules using available resources actors give structure continuity through time.

3 For Parsons, by contrast, the structure of society is determined by the overall needs of the system. Certain social arrangements need to be made if the system is to survive.

4 The most developed structuralist theory in sociology is offered by Althusser, drawing on Marx. Althusser insists on the insignificance of subjectivity and concentrates on the effectivity of structural contradictions in accomplishing historical change.

5 The debate about structure has been at its most intense in contemporary French intellectual life. Lacan has sought to integrate Freudian ideas with linguistic structuralism but the entire position has come under attack from the poststructuralists, Derrida and Foucault.

Critique

Structuralist sociological thought is heroic in character. In one sense it might be considered the perfect form of general theory because it seeks to explain everything by reference to a single set of general determinants. It is a simple act of intellectual courage for Althusser to propose that the material forces of production determine social life, or for Freud to propose that human behaviour can be explained by reference to the way in which tensions are resolved between the id, ego and superego.

We can concentrate our critique on Althusser because his is the most sociologically developed version of structuralism (and because Giddens and Parsons are criticized elsewhere). His contribution was to take the vulgar economic determinism out of structuralist Marxism and, in so doing, to provide for explanatory possibilities for both the maintenance of capitalism and for its downfall which had not previously been available. His account is also a relatively complete one, in the great tradition of grand theory, which encompasses not only economic structures but also political and ideological ones. The theory generated an enormous debate within both Marxist thought and sociology during the 1970s. The attack from within Marxism came from the historian Thomson, and his epigones, who insisted on a Marxist humanism: that human beings were not the mere puppets of structure; that classes were not structures but events formed in struggle and conflict; and that in order to understand history one needed to understand developments in human consciousness.[13] A parallel attack came from the British sociologists, Hindess and Hirst (see e.g. Cutler et al. 1977: 270–3) who argue that theories of structural determination fail because they cannot account for specific differences between individuals but can only offer accounts of shared positions.

Most critics agree that Althusser failed to kill the subject off and merely left it undertheorized. This might best be understood by questioning his account of ideological state apparatuses. These are needed, he says, to ensure the reproduction of the system. But he also says that the contents of consciousness are determined by structural location. If the latter is true, why should there need to be specific apparatuses to school potentially rebellious or apathetic agents – from where does their rebellion or apathy come? The complexities of social life and the variety of responses to it need to be addressed, it might be argued, at the level of conscious decision. Indeed, this has proved to be the general social scientific consensus. Althusserianism proved to be a mysterious theoretical detour of the 1970s which, because of its one-sidedness, brought about just that which it sought to avoid, the demise of a Marxist structuralism.

Despite its heroic nature, structuralist theory must be considered a failure. It fails because it is trapped in a circularity of simplicity and complexity. It is insistently reductionist, claiming to conflate all the myriad complexities of behaviour to a single, general set of principles. But then it finds that the details of human action simply will not be reduced. The subject refuses to lie down and die and engages in behaviour not predicted by the theory. To accommodate this detail the theory becomes subjected to auto-critique and distortion. It elaborates to allow for complexity and thus denies its own foundations. Finally the auto-critique becomes so severe that the structure is denied, as in Derrida and Foucault (see chapters 4 and 7), and we are presented with the spectre of theorists who are neither structuralists nor anti-structuralists but post-structuralists. Such theorists deny the premises of structuralism but speak its language. Because it is so radical, structuralism demands a radical and destructive critique, with the result that it has failed to provide the theoretical progress which its practitioners promised.

Further reading

For a general introduction see Bottomore and Nisbet, 'Structuralism' (1979). To get the feel of Freud read 'The Ego and the Superego' (1965) or his layperson's introduction to his theory, *A General Introduction to Psychoanalysis* (1952). Wollheim's *Freud* (1971) is an excellent secondary source. Marx's 'Preface' can be found in a number of collections, e.g. *Selected Writings* (1977). Lévi-Strauss's material is difficult but try some of the general chapters in *Structural Anthropology* (1977; 1978) and also the chapter entitled 'The Story of Asdiwal' as a superb example of his analytic technique. A good introduction is Leach's *Lévi-Strauss* (1974).

Readings from Giddens are suggested at the end of chapter 2, but see especially, *The Constitution of Society* (1984).

The most straightforward introduction to Parsons' AGIL scheme is in Parsons and Smelser, *Economy and Society* (1956). The scheme is elaborated in his *Action Theory and the Human Condition* (1978) and in the appendix to Parsons and Platt, *The American University* (1973). By far the best introductions are Rocher, *Talcott Parsons and American Sociology* (1974) and Menzies, *Talcott Parsons and the Social Image of Man* (1977).

Althusser's material is difficult. His book *For Marx* (1977a) is the starting point but the essays in *Lenin and Philosophy* (1977b) offer more digestible portions. A brief and excellent introduction is Geras, 'Althusser's Marxism' (1972). To locate Althusser in the Marxist tradition see Anderson, *Considerations on Western Marxism* (1976).

There are two very good general collections on structuralism which canvas the main debates. They are De George and De George (eds), *The Structuralists: From Marx to Lévi-Strauss* (1972) and Sturrock (ed.), *Structuralism and Since* (1979).

Notes

1 Lévi-Strauss uses the term 'model' in setting out these characteristics. This has been interpreted by some (e.g. Bottomore and Nisbet 1979) as a confirmation of Lévi-Strauss's nominalist position. However, it is clear that by model he means the pattern in the mind not a construction by an observer. Throughout all the rest of his writings he remains steadfast in his commitment to a realist interpretation of structure.

2 This distinction is generally held to be implicit in the work of Parsons. However, the main responsibility for bringing the distinction to the attention of the sociological community lies in

a seminal paper by Lockwood (1976). Giddens does not acknowledge Lockwood's contribution.

3 The move from a tripartite to a quadripartite analysis means that the parallels with Parsons' AGIL scheme are difficult to miss. However, nowhere does Giddens appear to acknowledge the similarity.

4 There was originally also a fifth pattern variable, i.e. 'collectivity orientation–self orientation', of which Parsons is generally dismissive and which he says can be assigned either to actor's orientation to the object or to the status of the object. From this point forward we shall assume that the collectivity–self pattern variable takes no significant part in Parsonsian theorizing and is absorbed into the other four pattern variables.

5 Following Lockwood, it has become common to refer to *Latency* as 'social integration' the: 'orderly and conflictual relationships between the *actors*'; and to *Integration* as 'system integration': 'the orderly and conflictual relations between the *parts*, of a social system' (1976: 371). In a radical departure from this convention, Habermas (1984; 1987) combines *Latency* and *Integration* as 'social integration' and *Adaptation* and *Goal-attainment* as 'system integration'.

6 At one point Parsons et al. speculate about alternating phase dominace along the diagrammatic diagonals, saying, for example, that the most likely accummulation of deficits for adaptation will occur in integration. As we shall see in chapter 5, this appears to be the most appropriate formulation for analysing the long-term evolution of societies on the grand scale. The formulation of phase dominance discussed in the present chapter is based on empirical research on small groups.

7 These two are occluded in the above discussion of Marx's approach to structure.

8 Althusser proceeds by attacking vigorously alternative interpretations of Marx and then by deep textual analysis of Marx's writings. Here we concentrate only on the bare bones of the sociological aspects of Althusser's argument.

9 For further development of this argument, see chapter 6.

10 Althusser is clearly uncertain about the use of this term but can find no satisfactory alternative. It connotes determination 'from above' rather than 'too much determination'. Note also the use of the Freudian terms, 'condensation' and 'displacement'.

11 This section relies on Lacan (1968) and also owes much to the appended commentary by Wilden, to Bowie (1979) and to Turkle (1979: 47–68). Turkle is also the source of the pun in the subtitle.

12 This section relies on Culler (1979), Hawkes (1977: 145–50), Jameson (1972: 172–88) and Norris (1987). This time the ghastly pun is an original sin.

13 For a review of Thomson's debate with Anderson, who is Althusser's defender, see Giddens (1987: 203–24).

5 System: an overarching order

It is an everyday commonplace to conceive of society as a system, especially when we are thinking about assertions of our own individualism. We sometimes speak of an individual as 'being up against the system' or as being 'oppressed by the system'. We can even admire those who are able to 'buck the system'. These references to systems can have two types of meaning, although in everyday discourse these are often blurred. In the first, society is understood to be divided into privileged and disprivileged parts. The 'system' is held to be a set of power arrangements which are put in place by the privileged in order to preserve and maintain their position. Here the system which is doing the oppressing is a particular kind of system, perhaps the capitalist system, or the patriarchal system, or the Communist system. Those who are oppressed, or who are in opposition, are located in the disprivileged part of society, but they have the comfort of interests shared, and possible alliances, with others in a similar position. The second type of meaning presents the system as a more all-pervasive entity, something which stands above and is opposed to each and every person, no matter what their level of privilege. Each individual is held to fight a lonely battle against the constraints of society. Rather curiously, within such a conception, society or the system is held not to be the responsibility of any particular individual or group of individuals. It hangs over us, like a dark cloud, directing our moves and our thoughts. It has no particular character so it cannot be replaced by something else. That something else will only be another system. So resistance to the constraints of the system often takes the form of withdrawal rather than rebellion.

This chapter considers theories which more or less take the latter view of system. Theories which address structures of privilege are addressed in chapters 4, 7 and 9. The contrast which most effectively identifies system theories is that with agency and rationality theories, discussed in chapters 2 and 3. Agency and rationality theories understand society to be the outcome of the actions of individuals. Individuals are held intentionally to construct social institutions, either because these institutions give meaning to their lives, or because they contribute to the realization of their material interests. These theories are individually reductionist, that is they seek to 'explain away' social structures as the mental predispositions of individual actors. System theories, by contrast, do not seek to explain the existence of society at all. Just as the majority of biologists accept the reality of the organic world as a given, sociologists, it is argued, can accept the reality of the social world as a given. This view is ostensively supported, argue system theories, by the difficulties which individualistic reductionists face in explaining away the scale, complexity and variety of the social world. A great religion, such as Hinduism, cannot be explained away simply as providing meaning or as supporting the pursuit of interests. Rather, people are born into it without choice and participate in it without question. It is not their construction but, on the contrary, appears to order their thoughts and their lives. They are the consequence of the social institution. So system theories are often sociologically reductionist – they 'explain away' the psychological processes of actors as the consequences of their location in social institutions. Society or the system is held to be greater than the sum of the individual actions which make it up.

The use of the term 'system' to describe society carries with it a notion of 'systemness'. This means that the elements of the whole system are connected together in determinate ways. If there is a change in one part of society, then this will have flow-on consequences for other parts of society. More importantly, it means that society has a logic or direction of its own which is independent of the will or intention of its members. Indeed, critics often accuse system theories of attributing will or intention either to society itself or to its constituent social institutions.

An important theoretical consequence of this idea of a directional logic is that change in the parts of the system cannot occur independently. Indeed, if a particular social unit were to challenge the logic of the system, it would be pulled back into line. This means that the structure and form which the constituent units of society take is explained by their relationship to the system as a whole. This type of explanation is known as a functionalist explanation – the particular form and substance of a social unit is explained by the way that it functions within the system, by the contribution it makes to the system and the development of its logic. For instance, in a capitalist, industrial society, the structure of the family is nuclear, it has been argued, because this allows for the maximum mobility of human labour and talent. For this reason, theories which stress the logic of the system are often called functionalist theories and we shall give some attention in various parts of this chapter to patterns of functionalist explanation.

A point-form summary of the main characteristics of system theories can be set out as follows:

1 Society exists in its own right and is a proper topic for investigation. While it is recognized that human beings are, at one level, competent thinking and acting subjects, they are best analyzed from a sociological point of view as the nonaware consequences of social institutions and processes.
2 Individuals confront the system as if it is a social reality and not as if it is an intentional construction. Society imposes itself on individuals through processes of social learning (socialization) and of social

control. Motives and interests are received within socialization processes.

3   Society imposes an overall logic or character not only on the individuals which make it up but also on the social units or subsystems which make it up. The system must be analyzed as if it has a capacity for autodirection or as if it operates in terms of a single governing principle. The system has the capacity to ensure that elements which diverge from the governing principle are controlled, reintegrated or re-equilibriated. Any failure by the system to re-establish the pattern will result in disintegration.

4   The elements of the system are more or less specialized in the activities which they perform. They are therefore interdependent with one another and thus interconnected.

5   The predominant form of explanation is functionalist in character. The structure of social units is the consequence of the contribution which they make to the overarching system.

6   The system as a whole cannot be reduced to the sum of its parts, and particularly to the actions of individual members. System theories emphasize methodological holism as opposed to methodological individualism – they assert that social systems must be apprehended in their structural completeness. If broken down to individual actions many of their essential qualities would be lost.

7   This means that system theories concentrate on the structure of such large-scale social phenomena as national societies, religions, political systems, and complex organizations, rather than on interpersonal interaction and small-group behaviour.

The founding arguments for systems theory come from Durkheim's almost imperialistic assertion of the reality of the social as against the reality of the individual. We concentrate especially on his analysis of religion as an overarching force which has the function of providing social cohesion. In Durkheim, the logic of the system is contained in the tension between cohesion and differentiation. Durkheim's ideas have reached us by two routes: debates between psychological and sociological functionalism in British social anthropology in the early twentieth century; and Parsons' mammoth study of the foundational sources for contemporary sociology in general (1937). So basic is the former that we deal with it in our section on founding arguments. However, Parsons has become the central figure in the construction of modern system theory and so receives extensive and special treatment in the central part of the chapter. In the last part of the chapter we focus on two recent revivals of Parsonsian system-theoretic statements. The most committed of these is the development of neofunctionalism which is associated with Alexander; while a more convincing argument, which links Parsonsian concepts of system with critical structural and constructionist themes, is to be found in the recent work of Habermas. So the chapter focuses on the sources, the substance, and the revival of Parsonsian thought on social systems. This singular concentration is defensible in terms of a widely shared view that Parsons is the leading sociological theorist of the twentieth century.

Founding arguments: Durkheimian functionalism

The central problematic in system-theoretic arguments is the issue of how a society survives in a coherent and internally integrated way. The answer, typically, takes the form of a statement that the component parts of society contribute to its integration and maintenance. These fundamentals emerged from a comparison between traditional forager and tribal societies on one hand, and modern industrial societies on the other. This was initiated by Durkheim, based on a reading of Spencer and Gillen's account of the social structure of indigenous Australians, and also by responses to and developments of Durkheim by the British social anthropologists Malinowski and Radcliffe-Brown. The central point made in these arguments is that religion is a crucial integrating element.

Durkheim: facts and functions

Durkheim was intensely motivated by a perceived need to establish sociology both intellectually and institutionally. For him, it was critically important to establish both a subject matter and a form of explanation differentiated from other behavioural disciplines, especially psychology. Durkheim is therefore the most explicit and assertive theorist of the reality of social institutions and processes and of their distinctiveness relative to organic and psychological phenomena.

Durkheim (1964) begins by asking the reader to reflect on their

---

Émile Durkheim (1858–1917)

Durkheim was born in Épinal in Lorraine, a border province of France which was the subject of a dispute with Germany. He came from a Jewish Rabbinical family, although he was himself an atheist. He studied in Paris, taught high school for a few years, and held academic posts at Bordeaux and the Sorbonne. However, his chair at the Sorbonne was originally in pedagogy rather than sociology and he, in fact, devoted much of his life to accomplishing the acceptance of sociology as an academic discipline. He was a serious, committed, and hard-working, if somewhat dry and humourless scholar, and an intense patriot.

Sources: *Penguin Dictionary of Sociology* (1984: s.v. Durkheim, Émile); Ritzer (1991: 82–3)

experience of the social world. It is experienced not as something which is merely inside the head, nor even as something which is intentionally created. Rather it is experienced as something pregiven, which is difficult if not impossible to change, and which imposes itself upon the individual. Laws and customs prescribe what one is to do: one does not choose or construct the appropriate way to purchase goods in a shop, or how to vote in an election, or how to establish a relationship with a sexual partner. Society is experienced as an objective reality which produces and repro-duces itself. It is a *sui generis* (self-generating) reality. Moreover, this reality is an indivisible unity. Once it exists it has a facticity which resides exclusively in society and not in the individual members who go to make it up (Durkheim 1972: 69).

The contents of social reality are social facts, defined as follows:

> A social fact is every way of acting, fixed or not, capable of exercising on the individual an external constraint; or again, every way of acting which is general throughout a given society, while at the same time existing in its own right independent of its individual manifestations. [1966: 13, italics deleted]

This definition encompasses three elements (Lukes 1975: 11). A social fact may be recognized, first, because it is external to the individual. By this Durkheim means that the causes for their existence lie outside ourselves. Certainly, they are beqeathed to us by previous generations, but the more important sense in which they can be argued to be external is that the causes for their existence cannot be discovered by introspection. Rather, the causes of social facts can only be established by means of a scientific or empirical investigation. Second, social facts are real because they exercise constraint upon individuals. This can at least in part be established by the presence of sanctions. Typically, if a person seeks to deny the reality of a social fact, then that person will encounter coercive or persuasive practices which indeed establish its reality. The constraining consequences of denying the reality of the state by not paying taxes, for example, will indeed become apparent. However, constraint can also be indirect, in the sense that society presents itself as an absence of alternative. One usually knows exactly how to act because there is only one way of acting. Third, social facts are independent of the actions of any single individual and general throughout a social group or society. This does not mean that all the members of a society or group must participate in it for it to be real. Rather, it means that the phenomenon must be an element in the social arrangements in which all the members of a group participate. For example, for a government to be real it is not necessary that all the members of a society should be cabinet ministers, but only that there should be a recognizable connection between all the members of society and the government.

Durkheim insists that explanations for social facts must remain at the level of the social. When human beings form groups they express themselves collectively in 'collective representations' which include: 'religion . . . law, morals, customs, political institutions, pedagogical practices, etc., in a word to all forms of collective life' (1951: 313). The critical test for their separate social existence is that they would not have occurred had individual persons not combined and interacted with one another. So: 'The determining cause of a social fact should be sought among the social facts preceding it and not among the states of the individual consciousness' (1964: 110). Such explanations should have two components: the efficient cause, a set of antecedent conditions which are necessary and sufficient to produce it; and the final cause or function, a future end state, which the social fact produces.

Efficient causes are to be found in the internal constitution of the group, what Durkheim calls the social milieu. Two aspects of the milieu are identified as having a high level of causal efficacy: the number of social units which make up a society, its size; and the degree of concentration of the group, that is the extent to which ties between its members are intense and deep, its 'dynamic density' (1964: 113). However, the notion of function tells us more about Durkheim's conception of the social system than does the efficient cause and we shall concentrate on that aspect of his claims about sociological explanation.

Durkheim says: 'The function of a social fact ought always to be sought in its relation to some social end' (1964: 110–11, italics deleted). In this injunction the word 'social' is of the greatest importance. Durkheim specifically proscribes teleogical explanations, that is explanations in terms of individual purposes or desires. Rather, to ask what the function of a social fact might be is to ask about 'the need which it supplies' (1933: 49). The relation between social facts and system needs is analogous to the relationship between the operations of the parts of an organism and the organism as a whole. Just as the function of respiration is to oxygenate tissue, the function of education might be to supply trained capacity to specialized social roles. In summary, to indicate the function of a social fact is to identify the system need which it meets. Indeed, Durkheim occasionally writes of the social system as the social organism.

Durkheim: the solid society

The critical system need, in which Durkheim is interested, is social solidarity or cohesion, the ties which bind the members of society together. His intellectual project is to identify the social facts which meet this need under varying conditions in the social milieu. So he poses the question of what produces social solidarity when the scale and dynamic density of society change from low to high. When they are low the society is segmented into isolated and relatively small groups (tribes, clans, or villages), within which the members share common traditions and experiences, so that individual consciousnesses bear a high degree of resemblance. In this context: 'Individual minds, forming groups by mingling and fusing, give birth to a being, psychological if you will, but constituting a psychic individuality of a new sort' (1964: 103). This new being is moral, rather than merely normative in character, imposing not merely a set of customs or laws but commitments to a community. Durkheim describes it thus: 'The totality of beliefs and sentiments common to average citizens of a society forms a determinate system which has its own life; one may call it the collective or common conscience' (Durkheim 1933: 79, italics deleted).[1]

This *conscience collective*, then, stands outside individual conscious-nesses but at the same time imposes itself on and pervades them. When its precepts are transgressed, individual members of society feel a pronounced sense of moral outrage – the transgressor must be repressed by punishment or expulsion. Such repressive practices also have the function of reinforc-ing collective sentiments and thus solidarity. Durkheim calls the type of solidarity produced by a dominating *conscience collective*, *mechanical solidarity*, because it is similar to the relationships between the molecules of inorganic materials.

We shall examine, in chapter 9, the central process of social change identified by Durkheim. In brief, however, the fundamental change in the social milieu is an increase both in the scale of society and in its moral density – so economic, political and other links are established between previously isolated segments. The society becomes more unified but also the degree of specialization of social units increases with the possibility of trade and exchange between them. This increase in the division of labour means that there is now far less resemblance between the individual members of society and thus a much reduced possibility for the emergence of a solidarity-maintaining *conscience collective*. However, society does not fall apart. Rather the very process which disrupted the *conscience collective* now functions to meet the need. The form of solidarity provided is, however, not at all the same. It is an *organic solidarity* in which the various social units cohere because they depend on each other for the continuing existence of the entire system. The corporate manager maintains solidarity with the consumer, the government regulator, the employee, the supplier, and so on, because they share a need to keep the system running, even though bilateral relations may be competitive and even conflictual.

Nowhere is Durkheim's functionalism as apparent as when he approaches the issue of religion. The above analysis of the forms of social solidarity is drawn from his early theoretical work. A later analysis (1915) focuses on the idea that an advanced division of labour cannot wholly replace the *conscience collective* in the functional provision of social solidarity. Rather there must remain an overarching religious system which provides a focus of identification for the disparate elements of society.

In order to examine the contribution which religion makes to the system, he takes as his case the most basic or elementary form of religious behaviour which he can identify, that of the indigenous Arunta of central Australia. He first locates the emergence of religion within a social milieu in order to demonstrate its social facticity. Religious feelings appear to be at their most apparent when people assemble together to engage in ceremony. The existence of ceremony lifts experience out of the ordinary and serves to convince people that there exists, alongside the everyday world, a world of the sacred. Indeed, argues Durkheim, the temporal and spatial coincidence of assembly with religious expression is compelling evidence in support of this conclusion.

The question now becomes that of the focus of religious behaviour – the issue of what it is that people worship during religious practices. The Arunta worship a totemic ancestor, an animal or plant being, which continues to inhabit the sacred realm, the dreamworld. The corresponding animal or plant in the physical world is the vehicle for veneration of the totemic ancestor. It is hunted and consumed only under the most deeply religious and restricted conditions and is otherwise proscribed. Each clan group within the Arunta people has its own totem and is indeed named for that totem. So Durkheim's fundamental conclusion is that, as each clan worships the totem it venerates, it establishes itself as a living entity in the minds of the individual worshippers. An emotional homology is established in which the totemic ancestor, the physical plant or animal, and the clan, are together identified as sacred. Under contemporary conditions, the association between God, religious symbols, and society is similarly established in state and religious ceremonies.

Durkheim: society ritualized

Durkheim goes on to specify this functional relationship in detail in relation to religious ritual (1915). He distinguishes three styles of religious ritual: negative rites, positive rites, and piacular rites.

Negative rites are proscriptions on behaviour, which might include interdictions on the utterance of sacred names or on the consumption of certain foods at certain times, or which might include complete abstinence from food or sex or speech. The social function of such practices is that they insist that the individual should be subordinated to the collectivity, that the individual should engage in self-denial for the benefit of the group.

Piacular rites have an even more explicit social function. The main examples are mourning and confessional rites. The former are significant in bringing the group together and re-allocating status after the physical demise of one of its members. Confessional and penitentiary rites identify norm-breakers and sanction them, thus re-establishing the reality and force of norms.

However, Durkheim saves most of his attention for positive rites. The positive rites which have the greatest importance are rites of sacrifice because these have the greatest potential in establishing the relationship between the ordinary world of human beings and the supernatural realm. Arunta sacrificial rites conclude with the consumption of a small piece of the flesh of the totemic animal, an act which establishes the unity of the individual with the totem, and of individuals with each other – they are thus of the same flesh. The notion of communion in sacrifice is also well known within the Christian religion. Imitative and commemorative rites operate in a similar way. In imitative rites people mimic the totem by behaving as it would behave. Again this establishes their identity with the totem and their communion with one another, given that they are all doing it and that other clans imitate different totems. Commemorative rites establish shared traditions and histories and, more importantly, common origins. Christmas and Easter are commemorative rites which have this function in contemporary society.

In summary, 'By the mere fact that their apparent function is to strengthen the bonds attaching the believer to his god, [rituals] at the same time really strengthen the bonds attaching the individual to the society of which he is a member, since the god is only the figurative expression of the society' (1915: 226). Religion simultaneously expresses the unity of society by expressing society as a collective representation and by specifying the limits of acceptable conduct within society. In both of these ways individual consciousness is subordinated to the collective will.

Malinowski: society psychologized

The stress which Durkheim placed on religion as a system-unifier meant that many of the debates about systems and their functions have focused on the functions of religion. The corner of that debate on which we focus here is between the founding British social anthropologists, Malinowski and Radcliffe-Brown (discussed in detail in the next subsection). While each describes himself explicitly as a functionalist, they are radically opposed in terms of the system on which explanation is focused.

Bronisław Malinowski (1884–1942)

Although born in Krakow, Poland to an academic family, Malinowski spent most of his academic career at the London School of Economics. An anthropologist, his most famous piece of fieldwork is the period he spent in then German New Guinea in 1915–18. He died while a visiting professor at Yale.

Sources: *Penguin Dictionary of Sociology* (1984: s.v. Malinowski, Bronisław); Raison (1969: 188–9)

If we examine the abiding example of religion we find incommensurable accounts. Malinowski observes that religious practices take place at those times and places at which uncertainty is at a maximum. For the Trobriand islanders of Northern New Guinea, whose lives depend on fishing, religious rituals occur both during the building of canoes, and when the canoes put to sea each morning. People seek the assistance of the gods in providing clement weather, canoes which can withstand storms, and accessible shoals of fish. Religion thus has the function of reducing psychological anxiety which has been induced by the uncertain material conditions of human existence.[2]

Malinowski's fundamental explanatory scheme (1939: 942) is that needs (i.e. conditions indispensable to personal welfare and the physical continuation of the group) give rise to responses. Ultimately, needs are always psychological or organic in character and thus focused on the individual, but responses are always collective in character. Thus, individual needs give rise to social organization. However, as basic needs are met, the responses give rise to elaborate patterns of other, secondary needs, which must also be met.

The basic thread of Malinowski's argument is summed up in figure 5.1 and might best be explicated by considering the concrete example on the right of that figure rather than the abstract proposal on the left. Here it is shown that there is a basic organic need for reproduction expressed in sexual and parental urges. This gives rise to the human relationships of marriage and family. But the existence of such relationships produces a secondary need – the issues of, for example, who marries whom and who is responsible for children need to be regulated. The need for regulation is met by a system of social control which includes a set of norms or rules and some sanctions which will allow them to be enforced. A third set of needs arises from these, the need to manage personal desires, hopes and fears in relation to such regulation, and here religion provides such meaning and legitimation.

Thus Malinowski claims to be able to reduce all social arrangements and cultural patterns to psychological dispositions: 'The individual, with his physiological needs and psychological processes, is the ultimate source and aim of all tradition, activities, and organized behavior' (1939: 962). The interesting thing about psychological and physiological needs is that they are universal, which might leave one wondering how Malinowski can explain the wide variety and complexity of social organization and cultural patterns. However, it does allow him to specify certain universal institutions: the family, an economy, political organization, a legal system, education, religion, and so on, and thus to make a realistic claim to offering a general theory. As the subsequent section on Parsons shows, a key contribution of Malinowski is to specify three levels of systemic organization, the psychological, the collective-institutional (social) and the symbolic and integrative (cultural). These become enduring elements in modern theories, even if the psychological functionalism disappears.

Radcliffe-Brown: society reified

In Malinowski then, the system of focus, the system need which explains the existence of the social phenomenon, is the individual consciousness or

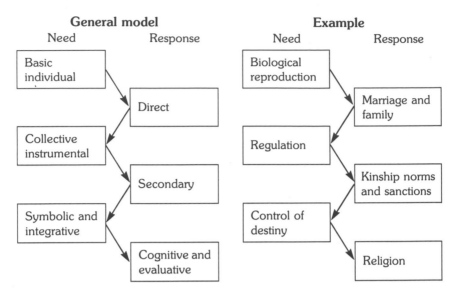

Figure 5.1 *Malinowski's functional scheme – arrows indicate causality (Malinowski 1939 passim)*

psyche. It is this which sets Malinowski against Radcliffe-Brown. Radcliffe-Brown is virtually a pure Durkheimian, except that he admits that the direct relationship between religion and society found in totemistic religions cannot be generalized to all societies. For him the functions of religion are unintended and the system focus of religion is society. Religion binds human beings together in society by inducing in them a double sense of dependence. It tells them, first, that they can be confident of the material and social support of those with whom they have relationships, and, second, that they must, in return, submit themselves to the constraints of these relationships (Radcliffe-Brown 1952: 176). The function of religion is to induce general social commitment, rather than to meet psychological needs or to induce commitment to a particular social group.

Radcliffe-Brown (1952: 178–87) fully accepts Durkheim's sociological reductionism and indeed his organismic analogy. However, in speaking of an organism, he argues, we can avoid the teleological (goal-oriented) implications of the term 'needs' by substituting for it the term 'necessary conditions for existence'. The function of a recurrent physiological process is a correspondence between it and the necessary conditions of existence of the organism, the organism being the system of relevance. The various processes are arranged in a particular way so that the organismic system may be said to exhibit a particular structure (e.g. the structure of a fish is different from the structure of a bird but there are functions which are common to each).

> ## A.R. Radcliffe-Brown (1881–1955)
>
> He was born Arthur Reginald Brown in Birmingham, England, adding his mother's family name later. He studied at Cambridge (where he was known as 'Anarchy' Brown for his unpredictable behaviour and lively conversation) and did fieldwork in Australia, Tonga, and the Andaman islands in the Indian Ocean. He held Chairs of Anthropology successively at Cape Town, Sydney, Chicago and Oxford, before the Second World War, and taught at Alexandria, London, Manchester and Grahamstown (South Africa) thereafter.
>
> Source: Raison (1969: 178–9)

In turning to social life, Radcliffe-Brown specifies the system state, in relation to which social processes function, as the continuity of structure (for a summary of his view of structure see chapter 4):

> The concept of function . . . involves the notion of a structure consisting of a *set of relations* amongst *unit entities*, the *continuity* of the structure being maintained by a *life-process* made up of the *activities* of the constituent units. [1952: 180, original italics]

To clarify: the activities of social units function so as to ensure the continuity of social structure, for example the punishment of a crime ensures the continuity of norms.

Radcliffe-Brown adds several general qualifications to this position, as follows:

- Unlike organic systems, social systems cannot actually be observed as wholes but must be extrapolated from the functioning elements.
- Unlike organic systems, the structure of social systems can change without discontinuation of structure.
- Social systems have a functional unity: 'a condition in which all parts of the social system work together with a sufficient degree of harmony or internal consistency' (1952: 181).
- Social systems change by virtue of change in the functioning of their constituent units.
- Not all the elements of social life necessarily have a function.
- Similar units may have different functions in different societies.

Although Radcliffe-Brown's analysis is neither rigorous nor systematic, even by comparison with Malinowski, it performs the important service of maintaining the possibility of purely sociological explanations of social phenomena. As the next section shows, it is Parsons who comes closest to succeeding in establishing a functional theory without having to assign causal privilege to one system or another.

Parsonsian structural-functionalism: systems within systems

Parsons' work is the opposite of Radcliffe-Brown's in terms of its level of rigour, elaboration and symmetry. It is unquestionably the most developed and complete sociological theory of the twentieth century, yet it is also vilified because of its explicit functionalist roots. There are several phases in Parsons' work which make it difficult to simplify. Some elements in these phases are examined in chapters 2 and 4. However, there is a unifying theme which runs throughout Parsons' work, a concern with the system of action. The concept of action solves the problems of reductionism by incorporating individual and social systems in a single interrelated pattern.

The system of action

The notion of an action system (Parsons 1991: 3–6) is, in its fundamentals, derived from Weber (see chapter 2). An action system is composed of one or more actors located in a situation which includes other actors, physical things, and such cultural objects as symbols, ideas and beliefs. The individual acts towards these elements of the situation in particular ways, treating them as means and conditions in the realization of goals and, in so doing, establishes stable relationships with them. Action itself is any behaviour which has an effect on the gratifications and deprivations which the actor experiences, that is any behaviour which is motivated.

Unlike agency and rationality theory, Parsons' scheme is explicitly systemic, that is, the actor does not orient to the situation in an ad hoc way but in terms of regular and stable patterns of expectations. These expectations come to be shared mutually between actors so that the expected response of the other individual must be taken into account in gratifying oneself. Further, some of these expectations become generalized and abstracted into signs and symbols which enable communication and shared understanding to occur between individuals. In summary, the minimum conditions for an action system are: actors oriented to a situation in terms of motivation; a stable set of mutual expectations between actors; and a shared set of meanings about what is going on.

All of the above is definitional, rather than theoretical, in that it specifies the subject matter of social science rather than explaining anything about it. While we are in definitional mode, let us examine what Parsons means by a system (Parsons et al. 1951: 107–9). A system is a set of parts or elements which have the following characteristics:

Talcott Parsons (1902–79)

Although Parsons is now discredited as an abstractive and conservative thinker, he was often regarded by many, and is still regarded by some, as the leading sociological theorist of the twentieth century. Certainly, his theorizing can continue to be regarded as the epitome of the grand theory tradition and the chief object for most of its detractors.

He was born in Colorado, USA, the son of a professor at a small theological college. He took his first degree at Amherst, a small liberal arts college in Massachusetts, in 1924, and then moved to Europe, where he did graduate work at the London School of Economics, with Malinowski and Hobhouse, and at Heidelberg, where Max Weber had last taught. His doctoral thesis was a comparison of Weber's and Sombart's explanations of the rise of capitalism.

His first academic positions, at Amherst and Harvard, were in economics but he introduced sociology at Harvard in 1931. His early career was not auspicious but after the publication of *The Structure of Social Action*, in 1937, he rose rapidly to prominence. His singular institutional achievement was to establish a Department of Social Relations at Harvard, in 1946, which included anthropologists and psychologists as well as sociologists. The Department was unified around a shared theory of human behaviour specified in *Toward a General Theory of Action*, published in 1951. Parsons was a prolific author, publishing some 270 items, and he was also influential through his numerous and prominent graduate students.

Sources: *Penguin Dictionary of Sociology* (1984: *s.v.* Parsons, Talcott); Beilharz (1969: 181–2); Raison (1969: 214–16); Ritzer (1991: 240–1)

- The parts are interdependent with one another so that variation in one has consequences for the others.
- Controversially, this interdependence is orderly, that is its general tendency must be towards the self-maintenance of the system as a whole. This is called a tendency towards equilibrium. Equilibrium may, however, be dynamic in character, that is, it may change in an orderly way over time. Certain events will be incompatible with system equilibrium and should they occur, processes will be set in train within the system in order to re-establish equilibrium.
- However, such equilibrium need not be indefinite and will only occur within a set of boundaries. So, where there is variability in the environment of the system, effective internal processes will operate to protect system equilibrium from this variability. Such processes might consist of the exclusion of disruptive elements or their modification to conform with internal conditions.

The subsystems: the holistic trinity

The environment of the action system includes, at a higher level of generality, the system of ultimate values, the (supernatural) arena in which 'ought' questions are decided, and at a lower level of generality, the system of the physical world. However, we must concentrate here on the internal structure of the action system rather than on its relationships with these environing systems (for a description of these relationships see chapter 4). In most of Parsons' work, the parts of the action system are held to be three subordinate systems: the personality system, the social system, and the cultural system. In the subsequent discussion of these the reader might be advised to follow the diagram given in figure 5.2. The main focus here is the social system because it is on this system that Parsons does most of his analysis, but in order to undertake such an examination we must first review the basic structures of personality and culture.

In identifying the elements of the three subsystems of action Parsons employs a master scheme, a 'fundamental paradigm' of action: 'Every concrete act . . . involves cognitive, cathectic and evaluative elements organized together' (Parsons et al. 1951: 162).

- Cognitive elements are to do with knowledge, what can be known about objects in the situation and how they are differentiated from one another in categories.
- Cathectic elements are to do with emotional, what Parsons calls affective, responses to objects.
- Evaluative elements are to do with the way in which objects are judged and ranked against each other.
  (Parsons et al. 1951: 162)

The *personality system* refers to a bounded and equilibriated set of need-dispositions. A need-disposition is a relatively stable inclination to a particular pattern of gratification. It incorporates two elements: a motivational orientation (a structure of wants) and a value-orientation (a set of standards or patterns according to which wants are realized). The motivational orientation has three aspects:

- a definition of the situation (cognitive) in which the actor discriminates between objects in the world;
- a set of wants (cathexis) in which objects are invested with varying levels of positive and negative emotion; and
- evaluative selection among these wants in which certain objects will be given preference.

These orientations are 'governed' by value commitments which are guidelines for the choices made within each of the modes of motivational orientation. In parallel then:

- Cognitive value-orientations provide the standards of validity for judgements of fact.

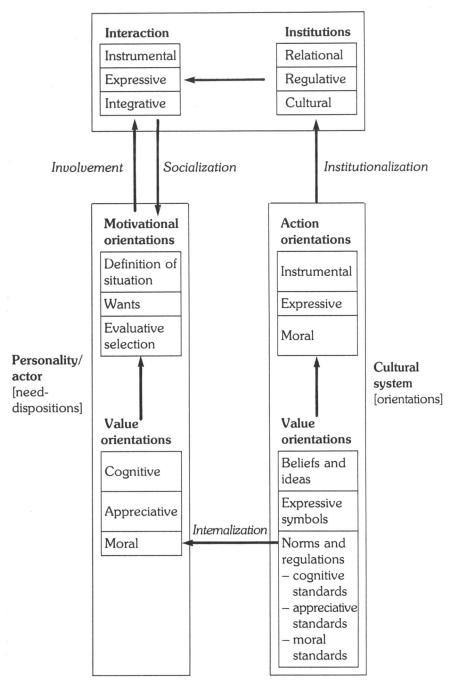

Figure 5.2 *Parsons' theory of the system of action*

- Appreciative orientations provide standards of taste and appetite.
- Moral orientations provide standards of the appropriateness of a course of action.

Within the personality, then, the actor seeks to gratify but is constantly checking gratification against value-commitments received from the environment. This is the Freudian aspect of Parsons' thought: the motivational orientation corresponds with the id, value-commitment with the superego (see chapter 4).

Internalized value-commitments enter the personality from the *cultural system*. Culture is made up of: '"ways of orienting and acting," these ways being "embodied in" meaningful symbols' (1951: 159). The elements of culture are value-orientations and action-orientations. Employing the master scheme, there are sets of symbols for three types of value-orientation:

- Beliefs and ideas symbolize cognition.
- Expressive symbols (e.g. flags, logos, music, art) communicate emotion.
- Normative and regulatory standards are ways of evaluating.

Normative standards find a central place in the theory and accordingly are further subclassified according to the master scheme:

- Cognitive standards are different from actual beliefs – they offer sets of norms about how ideas and beliefs can be evaluated, e.g. criteria of truth or validity.
- Appreciative standards do the same for expressive symbols, e.g. criteria of taste or beauty or sexuality.
- Moral standards refer all such normative ideas to criteria which establish their consequences for the entire action system, e.g. justice, fairness, righteousness, propriety, divinity or collective destiny.

Lastly, action-orientations which give primacy to one or other of the three categories of value-orientation are classified as:
- instrumental, where the main object is the efficient realization of goals;
- expressive, in which goals are set; and
- moral, in which it is decided whether particular patterns of goal-setting and goal-seeking are the right thing to do.

Normative standards are critical, Parsons supposes, because, by virtue of their externality, they allow actors to make judgements of their own behaviour as well as of the value-status of objects. For this reason, in a controversial formulation, he argues that: 'Value-orientations elaborated into cultural patterns possess . . . the potentiality of becoming the common values of the members of a collectivity' (1951: 165). This potentiality arises from the fact that such normative patterns overwhelmingly influence social interaction and that actors must seek to render their expectations of each other's behaviour consistent. In so doing, they will construct and refine a single set of value-orientations.

In one sense, the cultural and personality systems might be said to encounter and grapple with each other in the *social system*. This is the arena in which an individual, seeking to gratify itself by the realization of wants, will confront and negotiate with other actors also seeking self-gratification. This produces, in the social system, a tendency which Parsons repeatedly refers to as a strain towards consistency. Within this view, actors are continuously oriented to order and predictability – they will seek to share understandings with others because this stabilizes the situation by establishing a mutuality of expectations. The vehicle for the establishment of such understandings is interaction. However, within the social system this interaction is to be understood as taking place not between person-alities but between roles. A role is the intersection of the personality with a particular social system. For example, the intersection of the actor, Luciano Pavarotti, with the social system, television industry, is the role, opera singer – the role is but a part of the personality, sitting alongside such other parts as son, car driver, citizen, etc. As interaction patterns stabilize between a set of roles, so that a set of goals comes to be shared between the role-members of a social system and boundaries are established around them, the social system can itself be regarded as a collectivity or collective actor. Collectivities can thus equally be regarded as entering into inter-action with one another.

Again, employing the master scheme, it is possible to specify three sets of problems in the social system to which interaction may be oriented and thus to specify three types of role content (Parsons et al. 1951: 208–21). There are:

- instrumental problems, those of securing, processing and allocating material resources and rewards, which are met by economic roles, e.g. manager, factory hand, artisan;
- expressive problems, those of establishing emotional relations, which give rise to expressive roles, e.g. lover, mother, entertainer; and
- integrative problems, those to do with the solidarity of the social system which give rise to leadership roles, e.g. politician, priest, teacher.

However, such patterns of interaction are not given free reign but are channelled and limited by institutionalized value-orientations. Institutions are role-patterns in which the constituent roles are congruent – examples include monogamous marriage and private property (1991: 39–40). Again there are three types:

- relational institutions, which define roles and their patterns (contract, consanguinity, friendship, employment);

- regulative institutions, which ensure the pursuit of interests is a collective endeavour (profit, authority, community); and
- cultural institutions, which generate the contents of culture (religion, science, education).

Religion as culture and culture as religion

In examining the diagram in figure 5.2, care must be taken not to assume a simple correspondence between each of the sets of three types and thus a static equilibrium between them. This is, first, because where there is a connection between systems there is multiple interaction between the categories. For example, in engaging in instrumental interaction the actor must have selected personal goals from a 'list' of wants and defined the situation. Second, these are in an important sense, as so far discussed, categories without content. For example, no particular belief or idea is specified within culture, and no particular form of instrumental action (e.g. capitalistic, socialistic, feudal) is specified within the social system. This content is provided, as we shall see, by the pattern variables (see chapter 2).

More importantly, the 'traffic' between the three systems is not one way – only four interchanges are specified. The most critical has already been mentioned – normative standards located in the cultural system are internalized in the personality as value-orientations. There is also a further indirect link between culture and personality. As interaction between roles occurs within the social system, elements of the cultural system become fixed as enduring and expectable patterns or relationship between roles. This is the process of institutionalization, the process by which action-orientations are transformed into institutions. Institutions themselves become the content of socialization, the process by which the personality learns about role patterns. The remaining interchange is the process of involvement, in which the personality energizes roles in order to seek gratification.

This pattern of interchange has been the focus of much of the criticism of Parsons' theory. Despite his continuous caveats that he does not assume symmetry between the three systems, it is difficult to escape the view that culture, especially the normative components of culture, determine everything else. Although he protests that culture lies alongside motivation in the personality, he gives us no vehicle to allow the personality to influence culture – the traffic is all one way. If there is theorized to be a strain towards consistency and equilibrium in the system, then the commonalities of culture are privileged and the individual differences of personality are subordinated. As Parsons says: 'The integration of a set of common value patterns with the internalized need-disposition structure of the constituent personalities is the core phenomenon of the dynamics of social systems' (1991: 42).

The reason why Parsons' cultural system looks rather like Durkheim's *conscience collective* is that he conceptualizes it differently from the other systems. The personality and social systems are active and dynamic, charged with the energy that comes from actors' motivations but the cultural system has no capacity to accept energy inputs: 'A cultural system does not "function" except as part of a concrete action system, it just "is" ' (1991: 17). In so far as individual motivations are argued to find no outlet, agency is being suppressed by system, humanity is 'oversocialized' (see Wrong 1976).

The cybernetic hierarchy: more information

The above represents the theoretical orientation to systems developed in the middle period of Parsons' career, the period just after the Second World War. This might be regarded as the high point of Parsons' theorizing and is certainly the focus for much of the criticism levelled at him. However, as is discussed in chapter 4, just after the publication of this material Parsons encountered a small-group theorist called Bales, and his work took on an altogether more structuralist character. A trivial aspect of this change in intellectual orientation, but one which appears to be of interest to many, is that Parsons ceases to think in threes (the systems of action, the modes of orientation to objects) or fives (the pattern variables) and instead standardizes on quadripartite classifications (the functional imperatives). As is mentioned in chapter 4, one consequence is that Parsons adds the behavioural organism to the subsystems of action. Another is that the elaboration of systems within systems becomes a preoccupation, so much so that recent interpreters (e.g. Rocher 1974; Craib 1984) have often over-emphasized this phase of Parsons' work.

Bales' work on small groups provided Parsons with a new master scheme of four functional imperatives known by the letters AGIL. Figure 5.3 shows how Parsons now comes to conceptualize the system of action in general. Note the general change in which the evaluative mode has been broken down into integration and latency components. Note also that the subsystems of the social system are respecified. In particular, the I box comes firmly to be occupied by the societal community, which had always been challenged by the legal system for squatter's rights in that box. Note also that the 'latent pattern-maintenance and tension management' sub-system becomes the fiduciary subsystem, that which holds the society 'in trust'. This respecification fits nicely with Parsons' keen commitment to establishing the importance of the place of the university in social life (see especially Parsons and Platt 1973). Another important development is that the cultural system is no longer closed to the influence of the other three subsystems. Rather, each generates its own medium of exchange (in AGIL order, intelligence, performance capacity, affect, and definition of the situation) which allow each subsystem to affect the others.

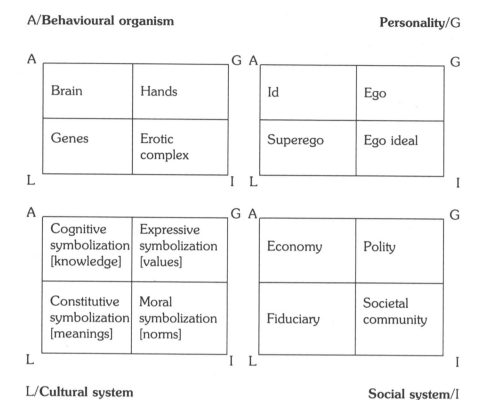

A/Behavioural organism **Personality/G**

A ⎡ Brain | Hands ⎤ G   A ⎡ Id | Ego ⎤ G

| Genes | Erotic complex | | Superego | Ego ideal |

L ⎣ ⎦ I   L ⎣ ⎦ I

A ⎡ Cognitive symbolization [knowledge] | Expressive symbolization [values] ⎤ G   A ⎡ Economy | Polity ⎤ G

| Constitutive symbolization [meanings] | Moral symbolization [norms] | | Fiduciary | Societal community |

L ⎣ ⎦ I   L ⎣ ⎦ I

L/Cultural system **Social system/I**

Figure 5.3 *The subsystems of the action system (Parsons and Platt 1973: 436, adapted)*

Figure 5.4 shows the new organization of the component subsystems of the social system. In particular, it shows the detail of the societal community and the fiduciary subsystems, which had not been worked when Parsons and Smelser first proposed the AGIL scheme. Although the terms used in the diagram are not Parsons' own, the new scheme for the fiduciary system reveals a sensible ordering of the apparently haphazard collection of structural arrangements which had been grouped under its previous manifestation. Just as the action system is interconnected through the vehicles of generalized media, so also are there such media which interconnect the elements of the social system. In AGIL order, these are money, power, influence and commitment.

At first blush, it might appear as if Parsons has escaped from the 'religious' or cultural determinism of the postwar period but this is not so. Figures 5.3 and 5.4 only show the 'horizontal' arrangement of systems and subsystems, but they also have a 'vertical' arrangement. This arrangement is conventionally known as the 'cybernetic' hierarchy (Parsons 1966: 28–9). The hierarchy is organized from the top down in reverse AGIL order. The

A/**Economy**   **Polity**/G

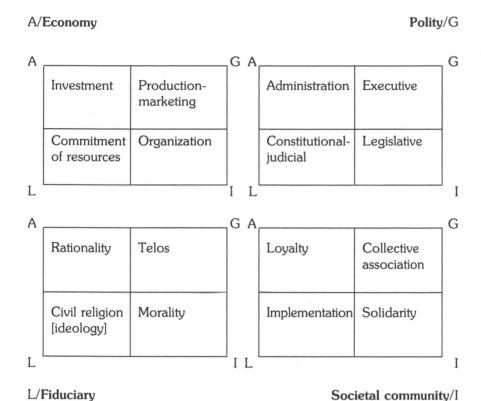

Figure 5.4   *The sybsystems of the social system*
(Parsons and Platt 1973: 428, adapted)

higher a system is the greater its information content, the lower it is the greater its energy content. Speaking roughly, higher-order systems put to use the energy generated in lower-order systems but can only do so in so far as that energy is available. So lower-order systems limit the possibilities of upper-order systems, but upper-order systems direct and control the lower-order ones. This means that, within the social system, the governing system is the fiduciary; while, in the general system of action, the governing system is the cultural. It also follows that, within the general system of living things, action is subordinate to 'supernatural' or 'ultimate reality'. Religious determination would thus appear to be assured. Indeed, Parsons concludes his lifetime's work on system theory with an explicit statement in this direction:

> In the sense . . . of emphasizing the importance of the cybernetically highest elements in patterning action systems, I am a cultural determinist rather than a social determinist. Similarly, I believe that, within the social system, the normative elements are more important for social change than the "material interests" of constitutive units. [1966: 113]

Neofunctionalism: paradise regained

Parsons' theory stands out in the modern period as the most successful attempt to provide a general and substantive theory of the social, challenged only by Schütz (see chapter 2) and Althusser (see chapter 4). The postmodern theoretical phase is marked by an absence of a similar level of courage, within which the work of Habermas (see the subsequent section below and chapter 9) stands out like a beacon. In the postmodern phase much sociological theorizing either retreats into historicism (e.g. Foucault, Mann and Wallerstein (see chapter 7) or is metatheoretical in character. The primary example of the latter type of thought, in which one develops a theory of theory rather than a theory of society, is the revivalist school called neofunctionalism, of which the leading exponent is Alexander (1982a; 1982b; 1983; 1984; 1988). Neofunctionalism is the vehicle for a revival of Parsonsian thought. Whatever criticism we may direct at Alexander for taking a metatheoretical position, we must at least congratulate him for lifting American sociology, in particular, out of an intellectual desert of empiricist claims and returning it to the central tradition of theoretical debate which is its foundation.

Jeffrey C. Alexander

An American, Alexander was an undergraduate at Harvard and a graduate student at the Berkeley campus of the the University of California. Although at this stage he identified with New Left Marxism his theoretical and political orientation shifted in the 1970s towards pluralism and functionalism. Now Professor of Sociology at the University of California, Los Angeles, he is the founder of the school of sociological thought known as neofunctionalism, and one of a handful of leading contemporary theorists.

Source: Ritzer (1991: 600–1)

Presupposing theory

Alexander begins by seeking to re-establish a traditional view of science. Science encompasses the continuum of activity shown in figure 5.5. Some activities are closer to the empirical observation of the world, while others are more metaphysical in character and are often classed as 'theoretical'. While the various positions on the continuum are interdependent they are also partly autonomous. Following the rejection of Parsons, (American) sociology entered the grip of a positivistic orientation which postulated a radical break between the left and the right of the continuum, in which the left was regarded as a nonscientific and, therefore, inappropriate activity in

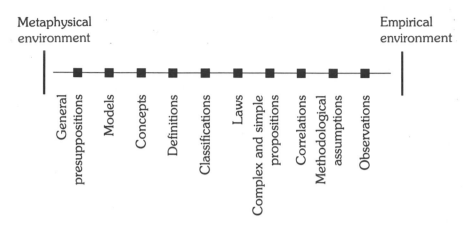

Figure 5.5 *Alexander's scientific continuum (Alexander 1982a: 3)*

sociology. So entrenched has this positivistic argument become that it is often argued that theory needs to be deduced from empirical observation. Alexander makes the alternative claim that science proceeds by both empirical and theoretical logic, and that serious attention now needs to be paid to the latter, especially to defining the general presuppositions of sociological thought.

Alexander argues that there have always been two nodal points in debates about the epistemology of social science. These are: first, whether the observation of human behaviour is to be approached subjectively or objectively, whether or not consciousness, intentionality, etc. can explain human behaviour; second, the problem of free will and determinism, whether action is voluntary or externally constrained. These two points of debate tend to be occluded: if one holds to the position that behaviour is a product of human consciousness, one will also hold to the view that it is voluntary; similarly, objectivism is linked with determinism. However, in sociology, as a particular form of knowledge, these two presuppositional positions are applied at two levels of analysis, what Alexander calls modulations, the individual and the collectivity. At the level of the individual, one must make presuppostions about action and, in particular, about the relationship for the actor between means and ends; at the level of the collectivity, one must make presuppositions about order, that is about the way actors are related to one another. The various presuppositional orientations produced by the intersection of these dichotomies is set out in figure 5.6. We now consider them in detail.

The central issue in action theory is whether action is conceived to be rational or not. Here Alexander gives the particular meaning to rationality, that it is instrumental in character, that is, where: 'action is guided by ends of pure efficiency . . .[and] goals are calculated to achieve broader normative purposes in the most efficient manner possible, given constrain-

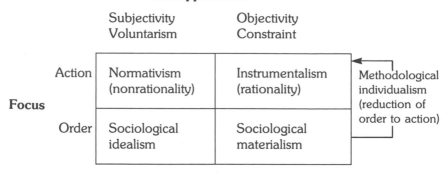

Figure 5.6   *Alexander's presuppositional scheme*

ing external conditions' (1982a: 72). Such instrumentalist presuppositions assume that actors continuously calculate and economize, and are guided only by technical rather than moral considerations.[3] Actors do not set goals for themselves but merely adapt to external material conditions. Alternatively, when sociologists presuppose that action is nonrational they are viewing it as: 'produced not only by the nature of [extant] conditions but by the substantive ideal content of the norms themselves' (1982a: 76). Theorists taking such a position constantly draw attention to the ways in which action is guided by norms which are not technically rational. Under such a regime, action remains voluntary because the guiding norms are selected and the subjective content of selection must accordingly be explored.

Against claims of the spuriousness of the problem of order, Alexander wishes to accord it a privileged position, alongside action, as generic to all social theory. Certainly, in the terms in which Alexander defines order, the argument is difficult to deny: 'The problem of order is the problem of how individual units, of whatever motivation, are arranged in nonrandom social patterns' (1982a: 92). Some presuppositions about order treat it as a residual category, as reducible to the actions of individuals, and one can identify normativist (Schütz, Garfinkel, Giddens, see chapter 2) and instrumentalist (Homans, Coleman, Elster, see chapter 3) suborientations within this position. However, far more important are presuppositions of collectivist, that is, holist and non-negotiated forms of order. Here order is imposed by a detached and powerful segment of society. Ends are reduced to material interests in maintaining or deposing the power structure. Within such an orientation, which is chiefly associated with Marxist thought, nonrational action and normativity are dismissed as the errors of ideology or 'false consciousness'. The alternative position, sociological idealism (e.g. Durkheim, Parsons), internalizes order within the subjective consciousness. Here, order is the product of the commitment of the individual to collective norms, rather than such norms being imposed.

Alexander finds each of these positions to be inadequate:

> If a materialist orientation dominates theory, internal order will appear to be no order at all, and the order that is constructed will eliminate voluntarism altogether. If a reified conception of the individual dominates theory, the possibility for reconciling voluntarism and order will be denied in principle. . . . The internal collective 'solution' can take the form of sociological idealism . . . Actual theoretical attention is [here] devoted, however, exclusively to the normative, internal aspects of collective order. The conflict between internal and external dimensions of social life is effectively eliminated. [1982a: 110]

However, Alexander's theory finds a proper place in this chapter because he wishes to privilege two aspects of his analysis: voluntarism and the collectivity. In his own words he wants to preserve the notion of a 'voluntary striving for ideals' (1982a: 124), a notion which puts him firmly in the Parsonsian camp. However, he claims to want to do more than a Parsons, let alone a Durkheim. The failures of sociological theory stem from the selection of one presuppositional pole and the rejection or reduction of the other. If one rejects individualism as the basis of a truly sociological theory, one must seek a 'multidimensional' approach which embraces all of the positions specified in figure 5.6, and in particular both materialist and idealist presuppositions about order. Armed with this criterion, Alexander now proceeds to a reading of the sociological classics, Durkheim, Marx, Weber and Parsons, to establish the extent to which they match up to it and what remains to be done.

Reading the scriptures

The high priests of sociological materialism and sociological idealism are, respectively, Marx and Durkheim. Alexander (1982b) now addresses these as the prime examples of what he holds to be inadequate and unstable, unidimensional theories. He notes, first, in Marx's early work on alienation, a significant commitment to normativity at the level of action. The individual is indeed freedom-seeking and thus feels alienated. However, the collectivity is ordered by the constraints of class, and so Marx faces a contradiction. Alexander agrees with Althusser's view (see chapter 4) that Marx responds to this contradiction between natural freedom and actual constraint by moving in the direction of the latter. The strands of this orientation are familiar: capitalism develops according to inexorable laws; the revolution comes not from the transformation of human consciousness but emerges from structural contradictions; the consciousness of individuals is 'false' and is the reflection of a manufactured ideology; bourgeois society is characterized by the instrumental pursuit of commodities; human workers are constituted by the capitalist system as reproduced labour power; social being does not determine consciousness but is determined by it; and the eradication of alienation, which had been the means to the establishment of a new community, now is transformed into an end in itself, the eradication of class society.

In undertaking this transition, Marx commits what for Alexander is the cardinal sin of the conflation of action with order. In more familiar, if equally technical terms, Marx commits a holistic or sociological reduction. He explains the actions of individuals, which Alexander has argued to be voluntaristic, by reference to the structure of society. This sets up instabilities – Marx can only crack the capitalist system by specifying a voluntaristic vanguard of the proletariat which foments revolution, for example.

Alexander claims that a similar transition occurs in Durkheim's work although in the opposite direction.[4] In his early work on the division of labour, Durkheim faces a series of presuppositional tensions: between (material) causes and (ideal) functions; between individual liberty and collective solidarity; between instrumental contract and its normative precontractual elements; and between the voluntarism of organic solidarity and the constraints of the forced division of labour and anomie. As we have seen, he resolves these tensions in terms of an idealistic collectivism focused on religion. Here, Durkheim shows that the voluntary, non-rational associations which are called ritual allow an abstract symbolization of shared beliefs. This symbol, the totem, in turn provides a basis for ordering society. Moreover, once this breakthrough has occurred, Durkheim can view all human associations, not merely the religious ones, as nonrational bases for the emergence of collective representations based on shared sentiments.

Durkheim's view though is, in Alexander's estimation, as one-sided as that of Marx. In Durkheim, all the institutions of society are more or less religious or, at least, moral in character. They are created representations of the collectivity rather than constraints upon it. There is no longer: 'any instrumental interest at all in occupational groups, any coercive power or "artificial identity" in the state, any rationalizing purpose in the law, any ideology in education' (1982b: 288). In moving in such a direction, like Marx, Durkheim commits Alexander's cardinal sin, he conflates action with order. As we have seen in the early part of this chapter, Durkheim denies individualism in favour of a cultural hegemony which virtually consigns the material constraints of the economy to the sphere of irrelevance. Such constraints, says Alexander, force their way into the theoretical vision and provide as much instability to Durkheim's unidimensional view as they do to Marx's.

If Marx and Durkheim can be regarded as qualified failures at producing unidimensional theories, Weber and Parsons represent qualified failures in attempts to produce multidimensional ones. The formal representation of Weber's multidimensional presuppositional approach (1983) is to be found in the typology of action (see chapter 2). This is not merely a classification but a list of alternatives: in instrumentally rational action, actors allow calculations of means and conditions to overcome norms and ends; in value-rational action, the reverse occurs; in affectual action, the individual resists collective order; while in habitual action, the collectivity has supremacy. Alexander insists that these are not merely empirical types but mark the boundaries of a multidimensional, presuppositional space in which the actor bounces around and in which means, ends, norms, conditions, the psyche, and the collectivity must all be reconciled. In other words, Weber (almost) meets Alexander's criterion of multidimensionality, that is, he treats the various presuppositions as analytic aspects of action and order which are simultaneously present in concrete instances. This multidimensionality is demonstrated in a series of empirical studies: in the Protestant Ethic argument (see chapter 9), religious ideals give rise to economic rationalization; conversely, the development of world religion is viewed as a search for rational religious principles; in the analysis of stratification (see chapter 9), class is viewed both as a pregiven structure and as a social community; and in the analysis of urban revolution Weber addresses the intersection between the instrumental interests of urban strata and new egalitarian ideas.

Yet not even Weber was immune from original sin. The seeds of the problem were sown in his sociology of religion. Here, he explained the Chinese patrimonial system as a response to the material need to tame geography by the construction of large-scale public works and the consequent need to administer that construction. But then he follows this with an explanation in terms of Confucian values which is quite opposed and separate. So the presuppositional structure is here dualistic rather than multidimensional.

This fall from grace becomes complete in the political writings. Here there is a movement from 'types of legitimation' to 'types of domination', from charisma to its routinization, from tradition to bureaucracy, from transcendental legal values to the compromises of interest found in common (conventional) law, and from status to property and occupation. In sum, Weber argues for a rationalization process in which there is a radical break between contemporary and traditional society. Contemporary society, he supposes, can only be understood to be organized on an instrumental basis, and contemporary action can only be utilitarian.

However, if Alexander's view of Durkheim, Marx and Weber is one-sided, his view of Parsons is particularly so. Alexander (1984) argues that the characterization of Parsons as a functionalist, a systems theorist, or conservative ideologue is true at the level of appearance, but the genuine and underlying presuppositional orientation is multidimensional. Parsons sets out his multidimensional agenda in the early work on the unit act (see chapter 2). Here, action is conceived as voluntary effort to accomplish goals by the manipulation of various constraining and limiting means and conditions, with the relationship between the three being established by norms. Parsons' insistence that action involves both normative and conditional elements represents, for Alexander, his strength. This statement about action is carried through to the analysis of order in the cybernetic hierarchy, in which order emerges from the tension between the environment of values and the physical-organic environment.

However, the key elements of Parsons' multidimensional theory are to be found in the so-called middle period which we examine above. These comprise: the three-system model which establishes the analytic separation and interdependence of society, culture and personality; the specification of allocation (material) and integration (normative) as the main problems of the social system; and the relationship between inadequate socialization and social control. This multidimensional approach is elaborated in the later work which focuses on interchange between AGIL systems.

At this point Alexander becomes less sure that Parsons is meeting his own criteria of multidimensionality. Parsons, he says, includes the following presuppositional errors:

- the reduction of order to action in the early work on voluntarism – there is no statement of order other than that it emerges from interaction;
- an insistence in the middle period that participation in social life is predominantly voluntary – the core phenomenon of action is the integration of common values with need dispositions;
- the bracketing of material constraints as irrelevant in the analysis of deviance and socialization;
- the presentation of economic and political institutions as facilitating rather than as constraining the realization of norms and values;
- a corresponding overemphasis on the societal community and pattern-maintenance subsystems;
- the assignment of priority to cultural elements in the cybernetic hierarchy;
- the treatment of the university as a crucial social institution;
- the stress on value-implementation at the expense of value-generation; and
- the characterization of modern society as the voluntary society in which material position is consequent upon individual intention in the fields of education and stratification.

All of this constitutes for Alexander a drift towards unidimensional sociological idealism. For others, this is not so much a drift as a confirmation. Certainly there was no treatment of Marx to compare with the treatment of Durkheim, Weber, Marshall and Pareto in Parsons' early work. If he does incorporate instrumentalism he does so from weaker or partial exponents. And while conditions are mentioned in the unit act, they are never consistently explored but stand outside the central focus of analysis. Money and power are transformed from control relationships into mediators of values. Alexander's claim about error and drift in Parsons must therefore be held to be misplaced. Parsons knew what his position was and he argued it consistently.

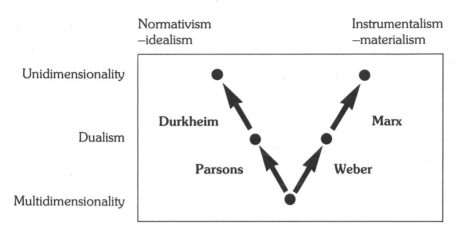

Figure 5.7 *Alexander's proposal of presuppositional drift in classical theory*

Functionalism redeemed

We have said that Alexander's theory is a metatheory, a theory of theory, but it is also something more. In providing a set of criteria against which classical theory can be evaluated, he is making a statement of what theory should 'really' be, and in doing this he is also making a statement of the way the world 'really' is. So it is a substantive theory as well as a metatheory. Alexander is telling us insistently that the world is multi-dimensional, that it has normative and instrumental aspects, and that both action and order involve balance and reconciliation between these aspects. The evidence for supposing that this is the case is that the greatest sociological thinkers have concentrated on precisely these elements. The question is whether we should be convinced by his evidence.

The evidence is summarized in figure 5.7. Here it is shown that Durkheim and Marx shift their presuppositional position from dualism to idealism and materialism respectively. Both Weber and Parsons start mutidimensionally but shift towards somewhat dualistic positions, emphasizing one presuppostional orientation or the other. If these are indeed the greatest theoretical minds, this should tell us that any attempt to combine the two orientations specified is unstable because they are radically and logically opposed – they are not mutually sustainable. Indeed, Alexander's claims notwithstanding, only Weber manages to sustain them consistently. What we should rather suppose is that Alexander's presuppositional dualism is itself problematic, that we should perhaps look for a theoretical breakthrough which establishes a unified presuppositional structure, and that we might best accomplish this if we tried to write theory as well as reading it.

Although we may take Alexander's analysis to be flawed we must nevertheless accept its tremendous influence in reviving theoretical interest, especially in the work of Parsons. In drawing on his analysis of the classics, Alexander (1985) specifies the essential characteristics of neofunctionalism as follows:

- a focus on the system as a totality of interrelated parts whose activities have consequences for each other;
- a concern with both action and structure – expressivity and ends are as much of a concern as are conditionality and means;
- an interpretation of integration as a possibility which can only occur in the face of deviance and systems of control – integration implies a conception of equilibrium as an observer category, although not as an actor's category;
- the view that culture is an autonomous field and that socialization is a critical process;
- an argument that differentation is the main process of social change; and
- a focus on theorizing as an activity which is independent from empirical research and observation.

Alexander (1988: 301–33) seeks to put these principles into practice in developing his own, rather brief, theory of society considered at the micro-level. Here he retains his fundamental distinctions between the normative and the instrumental and between action and order, beginning with the action but concentrating on order.

Human action has two dimensions: interpretation and strategization. Interpretation in turn involves two sub-processes: typification and invention. Typification is drawn from Schütz (see chapter 2) and means the process by which we come to understand our own actions, and the actions of others, by classifying them, seeing them as an instance of a wider set of events. The process of typification is, however, not merely passive but involves social interaction within which new 'types' of event are invented. By contrast, strategization involves identifying one's interests, setting objectives and seeking to transform the world so that these objectives can be realized. Strategization involves calculations of time, energy and knowledge. The last indicates that strategization is itself contingent upon interpretation – it must take place within available knowledge.

The systemic element in Alexander's theory becomes apparent when he considers the order dimension. First, he seeks to put some distance between himself and Parsons. Parsons identified three (later four) sub-systems of action: culture, social system, and personality (plus, later, the behavioural organism). Alexander (1988: 316) asserts that these three are not conceptualizations of action itself but rather are conceptualizations of the environments of action. Moreover, these environing systems 'simultaneously inspire and confine' action.

The social system affects action by the following means:

- by providing objects and settings – the division of labour and institutions of political authority are critical arenas;

- by the influence of social solidarities which define communities of interest; and
- by channelling participation through social roles.

Similarly, the cultural system affects action by the following means:

- by providing the symbols by which actions can be invented and typified (classification);
- by indicating what is meaningful or significant (sacralization);
- by generating patterns of preference which can be applied widely and concretely i.e. values (valuation); and
- by identifying system-threatening actions and isolating them (purification).

Lastly, the personality affects action in the following ways:

- by cathecting (setting up emotional ties) with objects; and
- by setting up defences and repressions which allow differential participation in action.

Throughout his analysis Alexander insists that the causal relationship between action and its system environments is bidirectional: 'If I have conceptualized action correctly, these environments will be seen as its products; if I can conceptualize the environments correctly, action will be seen as their result' (1988: 316). However, the treatment of the environments is far more extensive than the treatment of action; he is far more able to discuss the ways in which the evironments structure action than the ways in which actions construct environments. The dualism between action and order remains unstable and continues to invite conflationary drift.

Habermas' communicationism: steering theory straight

The debilitating lacuna in Parsonsian system theory, according to neofunctionalists and others, is its drift away from an engagement with the material conditions of life and the instrumental action by which they are managed. However, in a recent survey of the accomplishments of and prospects for neofunctionalism, Alexander and Colomy (1990a: 38–9) applaud a newly translated contribution by Habermas (1984; 1987) which, in caricature, seeks to introduce Marx to Parsons. This contribution represents a singular development in Habermas' thought. In chapter 6 we consider the early phase of Habermas in which, while breaking with the Frankfurt School, he nevertheless retains a concern to analyse transformations in the pattern of legitimation at the level of culture as the source of social change. By contrast, in the publications of the 1980s, considered here, he encounters Parsons and seeks to integrate Parsons' ideas with those with which he has long been familiar. In so doing, he transforms himself into a fully-fledged system-theorist, while maintaining a critical orientation. In seeking to

---

Jürgen Habermas (b. 1929)

Habermas was born in Düsseldorf, in the industrial heartland of Western Germany. He was deeply influenced by his early experience of the excesses of Nazism and has, as a consequence, been closely associated with the Frankfurt School, having been Adorno's assistant from 1956 to 1959. In 1964 he became Professor of Philosophy at the Johann Wolfgang von Goethe University in Frankfurt, a position he continues to hold, although during the ten years from 1971 he was Director of the Max Planck Institute. He has also held a number of visiting appointments in philosophy in the USA. Habermas is a humane and deeply committed theorist who can find no boundary between facts and values, and thus none between philosophy and sociology.

Sources: *Penguin Dictionary of Sociology* (1984: s.v. Habermas, Jürgen); Beilharz (1969: 133)

---

situate himself between functionalism, interpretivism and critical structuralism, Habermas is the closest to meeting Alexander's criterion of multidimensionality since Weber.

Like Parsons in the early period (see chapter 2), and like Alexander, Habermas begins with a reading of the classics. They are a slightly different set of classics, however. Marx, Weber and Durkheim are there and so, as we have said, is Parsons but so too are the humanistic Marxists, Lukács, Horkheimer and Adorno (see chapter 6) and, significantly, the agency theorists, Mead and Schütz (see chapter 2). Habermas' intention is not merely to encompass the instrumental and the normative but to seek to connect interpersonal interaction with collective life. However, in reviewing the classics, and in reviewing reviews of the classics, we run the risk of an excess of ancestor worship. In examining Habermas, we therefore concentrate on the novel aspects of his theorizing. McCarthy tells us that there are three such aspects:

> (1) to develop a concept of rationality that is no longer tied to, and limited by . . . subjectivistic and individualistic premises . . .; (2) to construct a two-level concept of society that integrates the lifeworld and system paradigms; and, finally, (3) to sketch out . . . a critical theory of modernity . . . [Habermas 1984: vi]

The first is considered in chapter 2, the third in chapter 6. Here we consider Habermas' systems theory.

Lifeworld and system

As is noted in chapter 2, Habermas begins with a sociology of action and moves to a sociology of order. He identifies one of Durkheim's problems in analysing integration under conditions of the advanced division of labour, as a failure to distinguish between: mechanisms which harmonize actors' orientations on one hand; and mechanisms which ensure that the unintended consequences of their actions fit together in a functional sense on the other. The latter, system integration, does indeed occur as the natural, happy consequence of interdependence and exchange between social units, but the former, social integration, requires a respecification of the moral contents of the *conscience collective*. Habermas argues that this distinction requires a dualized conception of society: 'society is conceived from the perspective of acting subjects as the *lifeworld of a social group* . . . from the observer's perspective . . . as a *system of actions* such that each action has a functional significance according to its contribution to the maintenance of the system' (1987: 117, original italics). The lifeworld is socially integrated by consensus, while the system is integrated by 'the nonnormative steering of individual decisions not subjectively coordinated' (1987: 150).

In a primitive society, lifeworld and system are broadly coextensive. However, societal evolution subjects each to a primary process of transformation: the lifeworld becomes more complex, differentiating into regions of culture, society and personality (i.e. increasingly these are areas of life that are understood by actors not to be identical); and the system becomes rationalized, that is steering capacity is increased by the emergence of autonomous organizations focused on political administration and on economics which specialize in steering. This gives rise to a second-order transformation in which the system is decoupled from the lifeworld. Systemic interconnections are established by steering organizations using only the delinguistified media of money and power. They are foci neither of normative regulation nor identity formation. These latter retreat instead to a privatized lifeworld sphere which is communicatively mediated and which stands in opposition to the system.

Habermas now proceeds to integrate his own arguments about communicative action with Parsonsian system theory. First, he argues that Parsons' 'systems within systems' elaboration is not much more than a semantic exercise. Action is not an environment for society but its content – culture, personality and social interaction are the substance of the lifeworld. Moreover, such constructs as the 'telic system' and 'ultimate values' are abstractions from lifeworld activity. The only 'real' systems are the structural responses to the AGIL imperatives originally proposed by Parsons and Smelser – economy, polity, societal community, and fiduciary. These are now reinterpreted in the terms of the system/lifeworld couplet introduced in chapter 2 (see figure 5.8). The economy and the polity are steering agencies, focused on system integration and organized along the lines of strategic action. Societal community and fiduciary are the public and private sectors of the lifeworld, focused on social integration and characterized by communicative action. Note that in undertaking this reinterpretation, Habermas moves system integration to A/G from I and renders I/L the shared location for social integration.

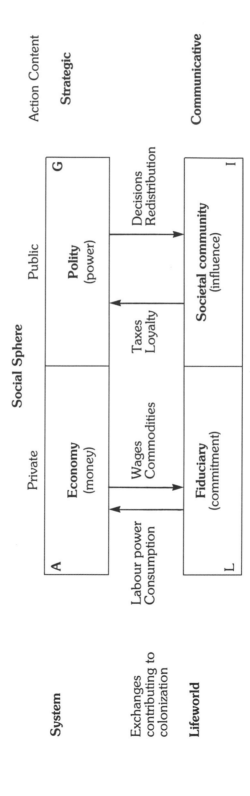

Figure 5.8 *Habermas' reinterpretation of Parsons' theory of the social system*

Internal colonization

Habermas now turns to media of interchange. Each of the AGIL sub-systems generates such a medium, respectively, money, power, influence and commitment. An assumption is made that because the private and public spheres are not decoupled, the critical interchanges are made across the system/lifeworld divide. However, such interchanges are not equivalent in their effect. Money and power can be institutionalized and accumulated so that they can be fixed in place and can grow in the forms of property and hierarchies of offices. The parallel institutionalizations of influence and commitment, prestige and moral authority, are fragile and, because they are constituted of communicative action, contestable. So, for example, there is no institutionalized public sphere of social integration in which the influence of academics, journalists, artists, intellectuals and so on can resist, let alone, overcome the encroachments of money and power (1987: 275). Only the waning institutions of science and the church remain.

Thus relations between system and lifeworld become 'mediatized', that is, they are established as a pattern of exchange in which individuals approach organizations not in their lifeworld-generated identities, not as human beings, but in the guise of the differentiated roles of employee, consumer, taxpayer, and client. The system thus becomes reified, it becomes the 'real' form of social membership. Further, the processes of monetarization and juridification, which Habermas describes, gives rise to a situation in which system and lifeworld are recoupled within a pattern which he calls internal colonization. Not only system–lifeworld exchanges, but also exchanges within the lifeworld itself, become strategic in character, and participation only occurs where there is a trade-off mediated by money or power. So, for example: marriage becomes contractualized; family members take each other to court in civil and criminal cases; education increasingly becomes employment oriented; retirement is governmentally organized and regulated; universities are subjected to managerialist dictates; professional practice becomes subject to legal and administrative regulation; science re-orients to national goals and technological advancement; elite taste gives way to mass-mediated appetites; labour unions become instrumentalist rather than solidaristic; and political debate gives way to images and slogans generated by campaign donations. Each of these, and many other examples, indicates that money and power are penetrating the lifeworld and reproducing it in the image of the system.

The crisis in systems theory

Habermas' theory remains critical in that it regards the reification of the system as a pathological deformation of communicative interaction in the lifeworld (1987: 375). In an earlier formulation (1976: 5) he had specified three rather than four systems – prior to the encounter with Parsons, the fiduciary and societal community systems were treated as a single socio-cultural system. In this earlier scheme the political-administrative system stands between the economic system and the socio-cultural system which are themselves only indirectly connected. The political-administrative system exchanges steering performances for taxes with the economic system, and social welfare performances for mass loyalty with the socio-cultural system. Here the systems theory provides the stage for a reprise of the Marxian theory of crisis. Crisis and breakdown will provide Habermas with a route back to a postcapitalist or even postmodern society based on communicative action (1976: 17).

These crises originate in the economic system and are progressively displaced to higher levels of generality until they can no longer be resolved. It is noteworthy that already Habermas was thinking in terms of system crises at four levels rather than three, and that these correspond with the systems formulation in figure 5.8. A crisis can be defined as a situation in which a system fails to generate sufficient exchangeable resources to meet the expectations or demands of other systems. The four crisis-types, their origins, and modes of displacement, are as follows:

- *Economic crisis*   Here Habermas accepts general Marxist economic predictions about the long-run decline in the rate of profit and about boom-and-bust cycles. In order to preserve capitalist economic relations the state accepts increasing responsibility for regulation, protection, infrastructural provision, and public sector production. Crisis is thus displaced to the political-administrative system.
- *Rationality crisis*   The outcome of this displacement is, as Habermas puts it, that: 'The Government budget is burdened with the common costs of a more-and-more-socialized production' (1976: 61). Rationality crisis takes the form of a paradox between the need to intervene in the economy and the fact that to intervene is to deny the normal social relations of capitalism. The alternative is to subsidize capitalism freely and without imposing responsibility, but this displaces the crisis to the lifeworld arenas. The state fumbles and stumbles between planning and *laissez-faire*, and thus appears 'irrational'.
- *Legitimation crisis*   When the state subsidizes production and redistribution through welfare transfers, it reveals itself as the servant of capitalism. Mass loyalty is withdrawn and the state can no longer appeal to national sentiment. Loyalty can only be 'purchased' by transfer payments but where the demand for such payments outstrips available resources a withdrawal of legitimation will occur.
- *Motivation crisis*   A legitimation crisis provokes a disintegration of the societal community and a withdrawal to a highly privatized domesticity, to what Habermas calls 'familial-vocational privatism'. This consists of a predominant orientation to consumption rather than contribution. This, we may suppose, will in turn lead to renewed crisis tendencies in the economic system.

In his later and more complete thesis (1984; 1987) Habermas is able to offer little hope of a way out of pathology via system crisis. Here the process of internal colonization is able successfully to reconstitute life-worlds in the image of the steering systems. He offers only the most forlorn hope for their autonomous re-establishment via the mass media and the 'new' social movements. First, he shows that the mass communications media have an ambivalent potential. On one hand they have served to destroy a previous bourgeois public sphere of interpersonal debate but, on the other, they can draw a mass public into that debate. Although at the time of writing he was able to dismiss 'video pluralism' and 'television democracy' as mere 'anarchist visions' they are now much closer to realization (1987: 391). Second, Habermas sees emancipatory potential in the protests of the new social movements which are precisely directed at the seam of the system/lifeworld divide in that they seek to impose normativity on monetarized and juridified exchanges. Some of these (e.g. environmentalists, peaceniks, East European democrats) resist colonization while others (e.g. counterculturists, new religious movements) withdraw from the system and seek to offer new foci for the reconstruction of the lifeworld.[5] However, the weight of antipathological developments in general would appear to be slight.

Conclusion

Summary

1 Durkheim conceives of society as a religiously ordered system. In forager societies this integrative pattern is quite explicit in the beliefs and practices of totemic religion. However, in a complex society the integrating idea system is an abstracted collective consciousness.

2 The most elaborate description of the system comes from Parsons. For him the system is elaborated into a series of subsystems, each of which performs a function for the larger system of which it is an element. His main focus of interest is the action system, the components of which are culture, the social system, personality, and the behavioural organism. However, these systems are not of equivalent status but are arranged in a hierarchy in which culture determines the shape of the other subsystems of action.

3 Alexander, while claiming a commitment to multidimensionality, broadly endorses Parsonian systems theory. Action is subordinated to the influences of the cultural, social and personality systems.

4 Habermas seeks to reconcile constructionism with critical structuralism and functionalism. Society is fundamentally divided between system and lifeworld. The system colonizes the lifeworld by juridification and monetarization, and contemporary society is therefore argued to be system dominated. However, the system is riven by crises which will

allow a re-establishment of the communicative practices of the life-world at a future time.

Critique

Everywhere system theory is riven by dualisms: the pattern variables; communicative and teleological action; normativity and instrumentalism; idealism and materialism; social integration and system integration; life-world and system; organic and mechanical solidarity, and so on. These dualisms are an expression of its failure adequately to theorize its subject matter – any solution it proposes seems to need to be counterbalanced by an 'on the other hand'. Analytic occlusions in the form of 'multidimension-ality' or 'unconscious distortion' or even *conscience collective* notwith-standing, the most critical dualism is between action (the individual) and system (order, the collectivity). Trapped by its own conceptualization, system theory must elect between the Scylla of theorizing that systems are constructed out of the actions of individuals and the Charybdis of the nonrelevance of human intentions.

Genuine system theory occupies the second of these two positions but it is a relatively rare species which is arguably doomed to extinction. This tendency can be found in Durkheim, in Radcliffe-Brown and in Parsons' later work on the cybernetic hierarchy. Here the system imposes require-ments on social action in a pervasive and complete way so that individual purposes and intentions are virtually eliminated from the formula. In Durkheim, individuals participate in religious ceremonies not because it is in their individual interest to do so or because they are feeling some degree of psychological anxiety, but only because they are socialized to be committed to group solidarity. In Parsons, social control mechanisms operate against deviance because deviants threaten system equilibrium or patterning and not because they threaten the individual material interests or even the individual definitions of normality of those who control policing and juridical arrangements.

This type of grand system theorizing faces a number of difficulties:

1 It misplaces teleology, transferring purposiveness from the individual to the system. This is most apparent in Durkheim's *conscience collective* which, not surprisingly, allowed him to be dismissed as a näive group-mind theorist for much of the twentieth century in Anglo-Saxon sociology. It is also apparent in the cybernetic hierarchy, where Parsons proposes that direction for the action system is located in a sphere of ultimate reality (which some have mischievously posited as Parsons' version of heaven) which is entirely separated from action.
2 It proposes a functionalist explanation which defies widely shared understandings of causal logic. Functionalist explanations account for the existence of social phenomena by reference to a future goal-state of the system, for example, families might be argued to perform socializa-tion in order to accomplish the goal-state of pattern maintenance.

However, the goal-state occurs later in time than the event which it is supposed to be causing. Effect cannot precede cause.

3 It confers the status of necessity on all social phenomena. All items (presumably including such 'useful' phenomena as racial discrimination, patriarchy, poverty and prostitution) exist because they are necessary for system survival. Indeed, they make positive contributions to the maintenance of the system. So system functionalism is beset by a pervasive conservatism.

4 It fails to tell us which among a series of possible alternative phenomena can make the most positive functional contribution.

There is also a standard range of particular criticisms of Parsons' work, and since Parsons is the most important system theorist, these too must be mentioned:

1 The most trivial of such criticisms is that Parsons is not theorizing at all. Theory, it might be argued, focuses on the explanation of substantive processes whereas Parsons' statements about systems merely offer lists of categories which can be endlessly elaborated and subdivided. Even the pattern variables fail to provide content because he is unable to specify the conditions under which one side or the other of the pattern variables will be institutionalized or internalized. The so-called theory is merely a very general and abstract set of conceptual categories.

2 There is a very real problem about the asymmetry of the relationship between culture and the individual actor. Although Parsons accepts from Freud the notion that the individual is motivated by the optimization of gratification, the moment that Parsons' actor is allowed out into the world, the energy-charged contents of motivation are repressed by the constraints of the functional requirement of consensus with other actors. Even if Parsons wishes to retain consensus as a system requirement, he must not conflate it with the wants of the individual actor. If the actor is selfish then the relationship everywhere between individual and society must be fraught with tension and conflict. Parsons' own solution to this problem is, of course, the internalization of value-orientations but this begs many questions, not the least of which is how the normative content of culture comes to be constituted.

3 Although Parsons initially conceives the degree of commonality of values as an empirical question, a matter to be established between interacting individuals, it is clear that once he starts discussing societies he cannot avoid assuming that values are widely shared. Indeed, the very definition of a social system makes reference to a shared pattern of values and understandings. This is, at the very least, an overstatement of the situation. The value systems of any but the most simply organized of societies (e.g. two-person interaction systems) are imperfectly integrated, that is, characterized by misunderstanding,

oppression, ignorance, falsehood, conceit, cheating, contradiction, and conflict, as well as a host of other minor and major 'pathologies'.

4 In glossing these system malintegrations, Parsons provides his theory with serious disability in the area of social change. The sources of change are almost invariably specified as exogenous, that is, as the consequence of disturbances in environing systems which feed through the various exchange media. Otherwise the cultural constitution of the personality, taken with the nonenergetic and internally integrated character of culture itself, implies that internal possibilities for change are eliminated. As is discussed in chapter 9, Parsons does indeed have a theory of change which is far more developed than that offered by any of his critics, but it is a theory which suggests the orderly development of a moving equilibrium rather than the ruptures of revolution.

5 Parsons' idealist emphasis on the determining character of the contents of culture seriously understresses certain aspects of social life which are the concern of Marxist and, to some extent, Weberian thought in particular. These surround the tendency of actors, individually and collectively, to seek to realize their material interests. It is by a consideration of these elements that one might seek to explain the constitution of culture, or the conflicts which produce and accompany social change, or the application of coercion and force.

6 Parsons therefore constructs society as an idealized utopia which closely corresponds with the set of value-commitments institutionalized in the USA in the middle of the twentieth century which are known as the 'American dream'. This is a society characterized by the fusion of material interests so that they all focus on: consumption and libertarianism at the level of interpersonal material relations; domination at the level of culture to manufacture value-consensus; and exchange by means of the market.

Such a view could only be maintained in so far as value-consensus was apparent. With the emergence of serious divisions and conflicts in American society in the 1960s and 1970s the above critique was provided with empirical support. Parsons' theory, despite having established the fundamental conceptual pattern for sociological thought in the Anglophone world, ceased to be the received wisdom and indeed ceased to be a focus for theoretical debate. Only in the 1980s has there been a serious revival of Parsonsian thought.

There have been two main attempts to rescue functional analysis from these general and particular problems. Nagel (1961: 401–28), for example, proposes a reconstruction of the causal relationship to solve the problems of logic and teleology. So instead of addressing the social phenomenon as effect and the systemic goal-state as cause, the findings of system theoretical sociology can be transposed so that, for example, 'the family causes pattern maintenance'. The problem here is that the focus of our interest is probably in explaining the phenomenon rather than the system state. More importantly, it removes from the system its privileged, governing status over action.

Merton's solution (1968: 73–138) equally challenges the governing role of the system. It takes the form of a series of responses to the general critique set out above. He seeks to resolve the issue of teleology by making a distinction between manifest functions, those which are intended and recognized, and latent functions which are not. This demonstrates a sensitivity to the action/system duality but does not resolve it because system-level teleology remains for latent functions.

He also makes several suggestions to solve the problem of conservativism: a reminder that Radcliffe-Brown makes a distinction between positive eufunctions and negative dysfunctions; an assumption that a social phenomenon persists by virtue of a net balance of positive and negative functional consequences; the notion that social phenomena can have multiple functions; and the parallel notion that functions can be performed by what he calls functional alternatives, but might better be called alternative structures. However, none of these lifelines succeeds – they either reduce system theory to an aimless search for consequences or they leave system teleology intact. We can still only 'explain' structures which have a latent, positive net balance of consequences and which have not been displaced by alternatives in terms of system needs.

The intransigent theoretical failures which inhere in the specification of system have generally forced a retreat in the direction of action. In the case of Parsons, the so-called systems theory has an actional foundation. The theoretical prototype of the system, the unit act (see chapter 2), precisely specifies a voluntaristic orientation in which purposes are located at the level of the individual. In his middle period (the three-system model) the conditions which constrain such voluntarism disappear from the formula and the governing system, culture, is an analytic abstraction from the concrete orientations of individuals. The pattern variables remain as a classification of human intentions. Only in the later, cybernetic phase does individual intention disappear from the social system entirely, but only, as Habermas expertly shows, by artificially placing intentions in the cultural environment. Alexander's sympathies with Parsons' middle period indicate a similar orientation in his theoretical approach, assertions to the contrary notwithstanding.

This brings us to Habermas himself. His arguments about the mediatization and colonization of the lifeworld would tend to suggest a materialistic orientation in which system dominates action. However, the distinction between lifeworld and system is founded on distinctions at the level of action between strategic and communicative practices. The formation of autonomous steering organizations and the transformation of linguistic human relationships into juridified and monetarized forms is not the consequence of ineluctable system requirements. These are merely vehicles for the strategic intentions of individuals. Habermas' fundamental concern is less to do with the rise of the system than with the progressive eclipse of communicative action by strategic action.

Further reading

Durkheim's writing about the system can be found in *The Division of Labour in Society* (1933) and *The Elementary Forms of Religious Life* (1915). For introductions to his work, see Giddens, *Durkheim* (1978) or Thompson, *Émile Durkheim* (1982), but by far the best secondary source is Lukes, *Émile Durkheim: His Life and Work* (1975). Malinowski's functionalist position is set out in 'The Group and the Individual in Functional Analysis' (1939), and Radcliffe-Browne's is in *Structure and Function in Primitive Society* (1952).

Parsons' writings are relatively impenetrable. The basic statement of systems can be found in the coauthored volume *Toward a General Theory of Action* (1951) and in *The Social System* (1991). For a shorter, synthetic version, see 'An outline of the social system' (1965). The cybernetic hierarchy is outlined in the relatively accessible first chapter of *Societies* (1966). Summary and commentary are available in Rocher, *Talcott Parsons and American Sociology* (1974) and Menzies, *Talcott Parsons and the Social Image of Man* (1977).

Alexander and Habermas are also voluminous authors. Possibly the best route into Alexander's work is via the collection of essays, *Action and its Environments* (1988) which contains the most original elements of his theory. Habermas' major statement is *The Theory of Communicative Action* (1984; 1987). The best introduction to Habermas is Pusey, *Jürgen Habermas* (1987). An excellent set of debates about Habermas is *Habermas and Modernity* (1985) edited by Bernstein.

Notes

1 Elsewhere Durkheim discusses the way in which the sociological averaging process can neutralize individual differences so that this average: 'expresses a certain state of the group mind' (1933: 8). Many early critics seized on this expression to argue that Durkheim's theory could be dismissed as naïve. Certainly, expressions such as this one about a group mind would give them reasonable grounds for so doing.

2 Malinowski is at least as much interested in the secondary anxieties which are produced by such practices. These are such anxieties as whether the ritual has been performed properly and whether the gods will listen. Primary anxieties only produce patterns of magic; secondary anxieties produce the elaborate and integrated pattern of ritual and cosmology which is known as religion. For the sake of simplicity, magic and religion are treated as coterminous in the text here.

3 For a review of theories which offer extreme versions of this position, see chapter 3.

4 It will be remembered that no such transition is specified in the remarks on Durkheim in the early part of this chapter. I take the specific view that Durkheim always focused resolutely on the functional constraints of the system (whose principal need is specified as solidarity) and always reduced action to order.

5 A proposal for a further focus for communicative action in the collegial structures established by professional groups is suggested by the neofunctionalist, Sciulli (1986). The argument has been contested from a neoWeberian point of view by Waters (1989b).

6 Culture and ideology

We have now completed our survey of the main conceptual themes which have emerged from the four great traditions of sociological theorizing identified in chapter 1. From constructionism we receive the concept of agency; from utilitarianism, that of rationality; from critical structuralism that of structure; and from functionalism that of system. These four concepts can be viewed as the raw material of theory. We can now move on to examine the ways in which they are used to explain four substantive facets of human social life. These are the main arenas of theoretical debate as currently specified in the discipline: culture, power, gender, and differentiation and stratification. We shall here discover the ways in which these four main concepts interweave, complement and conflict with one another, as sociologists seek to make sense of and to explain the social world around them.

In one sense the concept of culture has been dealt with extensively in the previous chapter on system. Here we analysed the ways in which functionalists regard the cultural system as determinative of all other aspects of social life. However this is only one of two principal meanings of the term 'culture' (Arato and Gebhardt 1978). The functionalist version conforms with a formal definition of 'culture' as the totality of meanings, values, customs, norms, ideas and symbols relative to a society. In this chapter, by contrast, we examine arguments which correspond with an everyday definition of 'culture' as activities with an elevated intellectual or spiritual content. These include principally the performing and expressive arts (e.g. literature, drama, painting, opera) and also the natural sciences and the liberal arts (humanities and social sciences).

The differences between these two conceptions of culture are often expressed in the hierarchical figures of high or elite culture on one hand and popular or mass culture on the other. The former is the province of the cognoscenti, the select group which, either by its own or by more general definitions, is in touch with the highest standards of cultural expression. High culture is regarded as accessible only to those adequately socialized to understand it. Such an opportunity can come either from ascriptive privilege or merit, but in either case the acquisition of high culture normally involves a claim to privilege in judgements of what is true or beautiful or righteous. Under modern conditions high culture is elaborate and complex; it is intellectually challenging rather than entertaining; it is often nonrepresentative or abstract; it focuses on style or form rather than content; and it often claims to be avant-garde (ahead of its time). By contrast, popular culture is the taste of the mass: its messages are simple and undemanding; its content is direct and accessible and makes no pretence to style or genre; it speaks to the immediate experience of the audience; and its object is to amuse or to thrill rather than to stimulate. Popular culture relies for its legitimation on immediate standards of gratification rather than on standards presumed to be transcendental or foundational.

As well as being subject to hierarchization, modern culture is susceptible to processes of horizontal differentiation by function. The starting point for such a view is the assumed unity of medieval and earlier cultures which were integrated around religious themes which offered an ultimate and immutable standard for action. For many sociological analysts of culture, Kant's taxonomy of philosophical realms (the critiques of pure reason, practical reason, and judgement) can identify the three differentiated and autonomous provinces of culture which emerge from these universal religious values (Crook et al. 1992: 47–9). These are: science which is organized around the value of truth and the pursuit of knowledge; law and associated secular morality, which are organized around the value of goodness and the pursuit of justice; and art, which is organized around the value of beauty and the pursuit of aesthetic expression. Once in train, cultural differentiation involves a continuous elaboration through branching and splitting as new and autonomous cultural realms become established.

Because the meaning of the term culture is so diffuse, and its relationship to theory therefore so pervasive, we investigate a particular cultural problematic in this chapter, that of how culture, especially modern culture, might be explained. Such explanations are predominantly functional in character, although paradoxically, they emerge from theories which are resolutely anti-functionalist. These are critical structuralist and radical constructionist theories in which culture has an ideological function, that is, it persuades or constrains people to accept situations which are fundamentally against their natural or class interests. Here, culture is an epiphenomenon, reducible to the class and state structures of capitalism. Such a view enables theory to take a critical orientation in relation to modern culture. However, in so doing such theory derogates actors, especially working-class actors, as dupes who cannot really fathom the realities of their situation. By contrast the structural-functionalists, whose analysis of cultural determinism we examine in chapter 8, treat culture as a systemic reality which can explain social structure and individual behaviour, but they equally treat actors as passive recipients of ideas.

Theories of culture as ideology have the following characteristics:

1 Culture principally consists of ideas. These ideas vary from reality in two ways: they assert that cultural products have a (positive or negative) value which is independent of the context in which they are produced; and they assert that social structure is objective and un-

changeable. The main contents of culture may therefore be described as ideological.

2   Culture consists of a unified and integrated whole which is all-pervasive. Alternative idea systems tend to be marginalized by exclusion or vilification.

3   Ideologies are produced by cultural specialists. In feudalism and early capitalism these specialists were located in religious contexts. Under contemporary conditions culture is the specific realm of schools and the mass media.

4   The ideologies which are produced have a specific relationship to class and power interests. They serve dominating groups by diverting the attention of subordinate groups away from the realities of exploitation. And they may go as far as serving dominant groups by legitimating radical differences in power.

5   Such theories model actors, especially subordinate actors, as passive receptors of cultural information. Actors can easily be trained to focus on immediate, material gratifications and deprivations. Culture thus dominates over agency.

6   Culture serves as the vehicle for the reproduction of social structure in its current form. In so far as actors receive ideas only from the dominating culture, alternative directions in social structure are impossible.

The founding arguments in this area, like so many others, come from Marx and Weber. Marx proposes the ideological character of culture, and both he and Weber specify its direction of development. The most direct inheritors of the Marxist position are the early twentieth-century communist ideologues, Gramsci and Lukács, and we examine their ideas of cultural hegemony and reification. The Frankfurt School and its contemporary heir, Habermas, pay equal attention to Marx and Weber – we review their critiques of the dominating unity of modern culture, as well as the differing but nevertheless critical positions taken by Elias and Bourdieu. Bourdieu, in particular, views culture as class differentiated but just as effective in reproducing patterns of domination and exploitation. We then move on to examine two neoWeberian critiques of Marxist ideology theory: Abercrombie, Hill and Turner contest the Marxist claim that ideologies dominate all classes; and Archer argues that culture has determinate status and is not merely epiphenomenal. Finally, we investigate the question of whether, under contemporary processes of postmodernization, we can continue to speak of an autonomous cultural realm separate from social structure and from action in any meaningful sense.

Founding arguments

The fundamental positions in the debate about culture are set out by Marx and Weber. Marx takes a structuralist and materialist position in which cultural ideas are viewed as the product of economic relationships. Weber takes up an explicitly constructionist position, in his analysis of the relationship between religion and the rise of capitalism, in which economic structures are viewed as the consequence of human ideas. Weber also argues that cultural systems have their own logic of evolution which is independent of other developments.

Marx: false consciousness

The originating statement for the analysis of social reproduction is the famous one made by Marx in relation to human consciousness, in which he argues that consciousness must be understood in relation to the material conditions of its formation.

> In the social production of their existence, men inevitably enter into definite relations, which are independent of their will, namely relations of production appropriate to a given stage in the development of their material forces of production. The totality of these relations of production constitutes the economic structure of society, the real foundation, on which arises a legal and political superstructure and to which correspond definite forms of social consciousness. The mode of production of material life conditions the general processes of social, political and intellectual life. It is not the consciousness of men that determines their existence, but their social existence that determines their consciousness. [Marx 1982: 37]

Interpreted in the most vulgar fashion, this statement means that because the only knowledge and commitments which people have are determined by the form of their existence, they can have no conception of alternative arrangements. The reproduction of current arrangements is assured because they are the only arrangements to which commitment can be offered: 'Upon the different forms of property, upon the social conditions of existence, rises an entire superstructure of distinct and peculiarly formed sentiments, illusions, modes of thought and views of life' (Marx 1982: 37).

Marx and Engels were not, of course, quite as vulgarly deterministic as these selected quotations might suggest. Although the material base determines the ideational superstructure, it does not determine it in a direct and isomorphic way, that is, the proletariat does not necessarily believe that there is a two-class system and that the ruling class is right to rule. Rather, the relations of production generate a set of ideas whose consequence is the preservation of the status quo. This set of ideas is an *ideology* explicitly, though not necessarily intentionally, generated by the ruling class in order to legitimate the persistence of the status quo:

> The ideas of the ruling class are in every epoch the ruling ideas, i.e. the class which is the ruling *material* force of society, is at the same time the ruling *intellectual* force. The class which has the means of material production at its

disposal, has control at the same time over the means of mental production . . . The ruling ideas are nothing more than the ideal expression of the dominant material relationships. [Marx and Engels 1970: 64, original italics]

Ideologies operate indirectly – they deceive and divide. Rather than advertising the virtues of capitalism they encourage acceptance and taken-for-grantedness. Religious ideas, for example, divert attention from miseries of the material world so that its form becomes acceptable:

Religious suffering is at the same time an expression of real suffering and a protest against real suffering. Religion is the sigh of the oppressed creature, the feeling of a heartless world, and the soul of soulless circumstances. It is the opium of the people. [1977: 64]

In Marx's thought then, commitment to religion develops out of the real torments of material existence but it encourages believers to seek amelioration of these conditions in a fantasy world populated by imaginary beings. Real conditions of oppression are left unaddressed by those who suffer from them.

The transformation of consciousness is a key element in Marx's theory of social change. This involves a move from a situation in which the contents of consciousness are a product of the dominant ideology to one in which there is a commitment to the radical alteration of social arrangements. This is the famous *Sprung in die Freiheit* (leap into freedom) in which the proletariat is constituted not merely as a class *an sich* (in itself) but as one which acts *für sich* (for itself). This transformation is not accidental but is the inevitable consequence of processes operating within the capitalism.

In the development of productive forces there comes a stage when productive forces and means of intercourse are brought into being, which, under the existing relationships, only cause mischief, and are no longer productive but destructive forces (machinery and money); and connected with this a class is called forth, which has to bear all the burdens of society without enjoying its advantages, which, ousted from society, is forced into the most decided antagonism to all other classes; a class which forms the majority of all members of society, and from which emanates the consciousness of the necessity of a fundamental revolution, the communist consciousness. [Marx and Engels 1970: 94]

The inevitable material processes operating within capitalism are the tendency of the rate of profit to decline in the long term and the consequent immiseration of workers because of downward pressure on wages.[1] There is thus a contradiction between the forms of intercourse, that is ideological statements about the social relations of capitalism, and existing social and material relationships. The inevitability of the transformation of consciousness and the struggles which surround it lie in this transformation of material life 'which can be determined with the precision of natural science' (Marx 1982: 38).

The precise form of worker organization is given in the material transformations which occur within capitalism:

> Large-scale industry concentrates in one place a crowd of people unknown to one another. Competition divides their interests. But the maintenance of wages, this common interest which they have against their boss, unites them in a common thought of resistance – *combination*. Thus combination always has a double aim, that of stopping competition among the workers, so that they can carry on general competition with the capitalist. If the first aim of resistance was merely the maintenance of wages, combinations, at first isolated, constitute themselves into groups as the capitalists in their turn unite for the purpose of repression, and in the face of always united capital, the maintenance of the association becomes more necessary to them than that of wages. . . . Once it has reached this point, association takes on a political character. [Marx 1982: 35–6, original italics]

Workers' organizations, trade unions and leftist political parties, are then a step in the constitution of class consciousness. They are initially a response to material developments in capitalism which depress wages, but they eventually promote a struggle about the legitimacy of their own existence. It is this struggle which promotes the emergence of revolutionary class consciousness: 'In the struggle . . . this mass becomes united, and constitutes itself as a class for itself. The interests it defends become class interests' (1982: 36).

However, by some means, consciousness tends to remain resolutely false and ideologically governed. This is the product of a particular cultural development which Marx identifies as the emergence of the commodity, a: '. . .very queer thing, abounding in metaphysical subtleties and theological niceties' (1954: 76). The commodity form has a special ability to transform 'use values' into 'exchange values', the medium of this transformation being money. So the diverse products of human labour are transformed into commodities when they bought and sold for money at a price established in a market. The metaphysical significance of the commodity lies in the fact that it externalizes the products of human labour from the labourer; it is 'queer' because it is 'unnatural', it stands in contrast with a primordial state in which products were used by their own producers. Marx elaborates on this peculiarity in terms of the 'commodification' of human labour itself: commodity production is possible only where 'labour power' is bought and sold for a wage (Crook et al. 1992: 7).

Culture then moves in the direction of *commodification* so that an increasing proportion of social objects are brought within the ambit of exchange relations, by being bought and sold for money in a market. As they thus become objects external to the self commodities receive a significance previously given only to religious objects, they are treated with awe and reverence. Modern culture is thus, according to Marx, afflicted by commodity fetishism. Two related processes contribute to the development of commodity fetishism: the creation of new commodities and the colonization of previously noncommodified cultural products. Within the former process advertising and the mass media create demand by the manipulation of material preferences. In colonization, the commodity form is extended to areas of cultural and personal life previously considered to be 'qualitatively' insulated from commercialization. Family life simply becomes a process of mass-consumption; beauty becomes prostituted in the art market; science is transformed into technology; and justice can be bought for the price of a good lawyer (Crook et al. 1992: 7).

Weber: affinities for ideas

Weber's analysis of the rise of industrial capitalism (1976) is in many ways a response to that of Marx. Weber wanted to show that ideas have an independent role in history, that changes in material relationships can be attributed to changes in idea systems. He begins by examining two apparently anomalous facts: that the countries in which capitalism was most advanced, Britain and Germany, were also mainly Protestant countries, whereas mainly Catholic countries such as Italy and Spain experienced relatively low levels of capitalist development; and that people in senior business positions in countries like Britain and Germany were rarely Catholic. Weber asks whether there might be any association between the religious belief-system of Protestantism and the initial emergence of industrial capitalism in the world.

Weber commences his analysis by examining certain religious theologies prevalent in industrial Europe, principally Catholicism, Lutheranism, and Calvinism. He was looking for some motivational basis for people to commit themselves to a life in pursuit of individual material wealth, a goal which seems unsurprising to people who live in capitalist societies, but which was absolutely unusual in feudal society.

Weber's analysis of Catholicism focuses on monasticism as the model form of religious experience. Catholics are asked to imitate Christ, and those who imitate Christ most closely are members of religious orders. Fundamentally, a Catholic demonstrates faith by following rules, rules of ritual behaviour and rules of everyday behaviour. The most pious Catholic is the person who conforms with the rules most closely. Those who thus reach a state of grace find their reward in the other world of paradise. Catholicism therefore motivates in the direction of conformity to an established order.

While Catholicism is highly social in its orientation, Lutheranism is by contrast highly individualistic in its orientation. In Lutheranism the key to salvation is an individual relationship to God based on personal faith. Faith is entirely internal and emotional and does not need to be demonstrated to others. It too is other-worldly, focusing on a spiritual relationship and not on relationships with other people in this world. Neither Catholicism nor Lutheranism provides the motivational impetus that Weber seeks.

Weber finds the necessary motivational spur in the Protestant theology of Calvinism which was the prevailing idea system of the 'Reformed' churches of North-West Europe, Scottish Presbyterianism, and the English puritan denominations, Methodism and Congregationalism. In Calvinism, God is tremendously awesome. He is all-powerful (omnipotent) and all-knowing (omniscient). He created the world and knows its future. God is also transcendent, never interfering in or revealing himself to the world. He is therefore unknowable.

This theology has three behavioural implications for the faithful. First, because God is omnipotent and omniscient, he has decided who is to be saved and who is to be damned and he knows the future. Salvation is therefore a matter of predestination by God, and since God is bound to be selective about admission to paradise, there will only be a small group, known as the elect, who can meet the required standard. Second, because God created the world, we must expend labour and effort in this world only for the greater glory of God and for no other purpose. Third, the only knowledge the faithful can have of God is through the presence of his son Jesus on the earth. As in Catholicism and Lutheranism, Calvinists must imitate Christ in his piety and his asceticism (willingness to forego the pleasures of the flesh). The last injunction prevents lives of mindless hedonism as a response to predestination.

These theological precepts have certain motivational consequences. The Calvinist must focus attention on this world, foreswearing both mysticism and self-indulgence. More importantly the precepts create anxiety in the minds of the faithful about salvation. God knows who is to be saved but will not divulge the secret, so how can membership in the elect be demonstrated? The answer lies in the biblical phrase, 'By their works ye shall know them.' God would not allow the elect to live lives of poverty and failure, so the faithful must work in this world to demonstrate election. They are said to have a calling, to be called by God to perform a particular vocation. God's chosen are those who are materially successful. This-worldly success has two important characteristics: first, it must be individual success since only individuals and not families or other groups are members of the elect; and, second, it must be achieved systematically because the merest hint of moral failure is a sure sign of damnation.

Weber calls this orientation the *Protestant Ethic*: systematic, this-worldly activity in the pursuit of salvation. It is at this point in the argument that Weber makes an explanatory breakthrough. He describes the central elements of what he calls the *Spirit of Capitalism*, the overall guiding principles of capitalism. These are: first, acquisitiveness, an orientation in which persons seek continuously to possess more material things; second, reinvestment, a commitment continuously to use profits to increase capital rather than to consume them; and, third, systematic accounting practices of which the earliest example is double-entry book-keeping. Weber argues that there is an *elective affinity* between the Protestant Ethic and the Spirit of Capitalism. By this he means that persons choosing one will tend to choose the other because they are similar orientations. They are both ascetic rather than indulgent, rational rather than traditional, and material-istic rather than spiritual.

However, Weber regards Protestant theology as a causal factor only in the initial emergence of capitalism. Once under power, secular capitalism has a self-sustaining, treadmill-like character and its material success provides an attractive model to societies which have not experienced it. Unlike Marx, Weber sees almost no virtue in capitalism, especially at the spiritual level.

Weber therefore identifies the process of cultural modernization as an increasing formal *rationalization* of social action (Crook et al. 1992: 8–9). Formal rationality displaces tradition and progressively erodes any ethical basis of commitment to general or substantive values. In modern societies, the 'ethical rationality' of consistent moral principle is increasingly margin-alized by an 'instrumental rationality' which imposes a calculus of cost and benefit on all social action. Worth, or value, thereby becomes increasingly instrumentalized, so that the value of work is assessed according to the measurable criterion of a wage, rather than the imponderable of creativity. Similarly, education generates credentials rather than learning, while art, literature and music become mere instruments of relaxation and leisure. In sum, rationalization involves: 'the depersonalization of social relation-ships, the refinement of techniques of calculation, the enhancement of the social importance of specialized knowledge, and the extension of techni-cally rational control over both natural and social processes' (Brubaker 1984: 2).

Brubaker identifies three main unifying themes in Weber's analysis of societal rationalization. The first of these is knowledge: to act rationally is to act on the basis of knowledge (1984: 30–2). In modern society the growth of positivistic scientific and technological knowledge systems inflates the importance of knowledge as a basis for action almost to the level of sanctification. Such forms of knowledge displace religious know-ledge systems and in so doing intellectualize and demystify the world.

The second unifying theme is impersonality (Brubaker 1984: 32–3). Traditional, personal expressions of power are displaced by abstract sources of authority in the economic and political realms. Economic power is understood to be the consequence of market forces, that 'hidden hand' which dictates the actions of both capitalist and worker. It controls them by the twin threats of bankruptcy and unemployment which are defined as no person's fault but simply that of the 'system'. In the political realm, the governing system is constituted as a set of legal rules administered by ranks of ethically neutral bureaucrats.

Last, rationalization involves extensions of control over natural and social objects (Brubaker 1984: 33–5). Here the central focus is the technical rationalization of social relationships, their reduction to aspects of scientific, industrial or administrative processes. Much as in Marx's formulation of the commodification of labour, human beings may be seen as being disciplined to conform with the instrumental needs of centrally organized industrial and administrative systems. Success in establishing control depends on calculability and specifically on the measurement and empirical analysis of the consequences of individual human action.

NeoMarxian critical theory

In the analyses of the work of Marx which have been made so far in this book, we have read Marx as an Althusserian (see chapter 4). However, there an alternative, humanistic version of Marx available in his early work, in which he views human beings as relentless seekers of self-realization and creativity, who will eventually rebel against the material constraints of alienative capitalist work conditions. Indeed, the social transformation through revolution which is envisaged by Marx always involves the cultural transmission of emancipatory ideas. There can therefore be said to be a tension in Marx's theory which might be expressed as an opposition between structure and culture. We here examine the work of twentieth-century Marxists who emphasized the humanistic and cultural side of Marx.

Gramsci: idealizing the class struggle

No other neoMarxist theorist so completely attacks the possibility of a materialist direction in Marxist thought as does Gramsci (1977a; 1977b; 1985; Davidson 1977; 1991; Jones et al. 1977; Kolakowski 1981). His objective is to restore to Marxist thought the Hegelian or humanistic vision which Marx espoused prior to the *Contribution* of 1859 (see above). The materialistic orientation had always focused on domination within the relations of production. Gramsci attempts to shift our attention away from production and towards politics because it is in politics that power resides, and the working class must grasp power through politics if it is to transform its condition.

Antonio Gramsci (1891–1937)

Gramsci was born in Turin, Italy. After leaving school he worked as a journalist and then as an active leader of the Italian Communist Party. He was arrested by the Italian fascist regime in 1927 and spent the rest of his life in prison or under guard in a clinic. His most influential writings were those he composed while incarcerated.

Sources: *Penguin Dictionary of Sociology* (1984: *s.v.* Gramsci, Antonio); Joll (1977)

The central focus of Marxist politics must be, then, control of the state. In Gramsci the modern state consists not only the governmental apparatus but also of the intersection between 'political society', which consists of the governmental means for accomplishing compliance on the part of the masses, and 'civil society', which includes such 'private' organizations as the Church, the unions, schools, and the mass media. The state is therefore: 'the entire complex of practical and theoretical activities with which the ruling class not only justifies and maintains its dominance but manages to win the active consent of those over whom it rules' (in Jones et al. 1977: 151). Civil society is critical in the latter enterprise and the emergence of the modern state consists precisely in the progressive extension of the influence of the state from the sphere of political society to the sphere of civil society. Formerly autonomous communities and economies are eliminated or integrated so that state and society become indistinguishable.

Throughout Gramsci stresses that state domination is accomplished not only by means of coercion but by persuasion and the accomplishment of consensus: the state is a Janus-faced combination of *dominio* (coercive domination) with *direzione* (legitimated authority). The central concept in this analysis is *hegemony*: 'control of the intellectual life of society by purely cultural means' (Kolakowski 1981: 242); it is the establishment of hegemony which allows *direzione* without *dominio*. Hegemony is an accomplishment of social groups or classes which can penetrate and control 'private organizations' so that knowledge, values and standards can be manipulated in their own favour.

However, Gramsci here is faced by a chicken-and-egg problem. He wants to say that, within capitalism, the bourgeoisie uses the springboard of capitalist enterprise to take control of the state and from there penetrates the institutions of civil society. But he also wants to take a stand against Lenin's view that control of the instruments of power in society (state and economy) have priority.[2] Working-class political action, argues Gramsci, must give priority to the dissemination of ideas about alternatives to oppression, and thus the establishment of alliances with other sympathetic classes. Socialist activists must work to rekindle latent communitarian sentiment, repressed by the bourgeoisie, and funnel it in the direction of change.

A key target in this emancipation of consciousness is the church. Gramsci identifies it as a critical mobilizer of the idea-systems which support bourgeois control. It can take this role because it provides an intellectual link between the ruling class and the masses – the clergy is privileged by the ruling class but revered by the masses. As the clergy articulates between the two groups, theology can alter to accommodate changes in the material relations between the classes. The particular example which captured Gramsci's interest was the shift in Catholic thought in nineteenth-century Italy in the direction of a liberal modernism. This had the effect of detaching religious intellectuals from their support of traditional, feudal-peasant classes, and placing them in alliance with a rising nationalist bourgeoisie. The proletariat, isolated and leaderless, failed to develop an autonomous culture of opposition.

The concept of hegemony has particular relevance in terms of gaining control of the state. The ruling class obtains control of the state, and thereby control of the means of violence, by providing intellectual and moral leadership, although hegemony is always 'armoured by coercion'. This intellectual and moral leadership must take the form of an alliance between differentiated interests, the 'historic bloc'. In particular, a hegemonic class must often ally itself with nationalistic or patriotic interests or with democratic interests. Such an alliance is termed a national-popular strategy or orientation, one in which differentiated interests are combined in a concept of one-nation, within which there is conceived to be equality of treatment for members and resistance to foreign domination. The possible components of an historic bloc are the industrial bourgeoisie, the industrial proletariat, the premodern middle class and petty bourgeoisie, and the peasantry.

Gramsci specifies two main examples of such historic developments, the Fascist (and/or Stalinist) state and the welfare state:

- In the Fascist state the main alliance is between the premodern middle class and the bourgeoisie. The middle class tolerates the persistence of capitalism in return for exclusive control of the state apparatus. The working classes are rigorously subordinated. Gramsci was convinced that such an outcome could only occur when the two industrial classes had been fundamentally weakened by long and continuous struggle. Indeed the Italian and German Fascist states and the Russian Stalinist state did emerge from the ravages of the First World War.
- In the welfare state, national-popular consciousness is accomplished by a compromise alliance between the industrial bourgeoisie and sections of the proletariat. The welfare state is an instance of what Gramsci calls a passive revolution, a reorganization of the state from above by the bourgeoisie which has the consequence of defusing discontent and disorganizing the opposition. Its strategies are, the democratic co-option of possible sources of opposition, especially the opposition of socialist or otherwise 'progressive' intellectuals, and the provision of welfare security to the industrial proletariat.

Throughout, Gramsci stresses that it is intellectuals who provide an ideological articulation between allied classes. Only through a shared ideology can mutually opposed interests be reconciled. It must be stressed that Gramsci's version of ideology is not simply an 'opiate of the masses' argument nor does he reduce ideological activity to mere epiphenomenal status, as might be said to be done in the later work of Althusser (see chapter 4). Rather, ideology is itself the context of the class struggle – a new social order can only emerge if it is qualitatively affirmed within the cultural life of the proletariat and of society in general.

Lukács: grasping cultural reality

As in the case of Gramsci, the analysis of culture provided by Lukács is a revision of Marx's materialist conception of history.[3] Lukács wants to stress the importance of ideas and consciousness, taking a humanistic or spiritualist view of culture, similar to that of the philosopher Hegel, who was Marx's intellectual antecedent, and also to Weber. His principal inspiration is Marx's early work in which Marx traces the effects of the progress of productive forces in diminishing the true nature of humanity. Lukács is interested in the way in which culture becomes disjointed or separated from this essential humanity and then turns back on it to repress it.

György (later Georg) Lukács (1885–1971)

Lukács was born in Budapest, now in modern Hungary, to a Jewish banking family. He studied at Berlin with Simmel, Rickert and Windelband, and at Heidelberg, where he became part of Max Weber's intellectual circle. He gravitated towards Communism during the First World War and published his own, heretical interpretation of Marx in 1924. The work proved shocking to the Marxist community because it implied not only that capitalist culture provided a false view of reality but that historical materialism was a component of bourgeois culture, at least in its most positivistic variants. After a swingeing critique by the Soviet ideologue, Zinoviev, at the Third International in 1924, Lukács went into retreat, re-embracing Leninist arguments and contributing, on an ideological level, to the Stalinist hegemony which he formerly appeared to despise.

Sources: *Penguin Dictionary of Sociology* (1984: *s.v.* Lukács, Georg); Lichtheim (1970)

Lukács (1968) locates his argument in relation to Marx's analysis of commodity fetishism. Commodity exchange takes place prior to capitalism, but it is only under capitalism that it becomes a 'universal structuring principle'. Here the commodity form pervades the totality of society to such an extent that it remoulds society in its own image. All relationships, all values, all labour become determined by the commodity form. Human relationships are transformed from patterns of mutual commitment to contractual engagements in which specific services are exchanged and these contracts can be administered by the state and even litigated; the worth or value of any object, including artistic objects which might previously have had a special significance, are specified in terms of exchange (the significance of Van Gogh's *Irises*, for example, now lies not in its aesthetic quality but in the price at which it is exchanged from time to time between bourgeois owners). These exchange values are governed, not by human intention and creativity, but by impersonal laws and forces which are mainly held to be 'economic' in character (supply and demand, boom and slump, growth and decline). Exchange values also apply equally to human labour – since the commodity form allows qualitatively different objects to be exchanged via the medium of money, it allows these different objects to be equated, so that, in so far as wage-labour allows labour power to be exchanged for goods, it equates labour power with ordinary goods and labour power becomes an ordinary commodity. Since labour power is the essence of humanity, human beings themselves thereby become commodified.

Lukács sums up this process in the term *reification*. He means by this a process in which things which are abstracted from human beings and from their activities and relationships – labour power, goods and services, artistic products, laws of economics, unemployment rates – are increasingly treated as if they are real and separate from the people who produced them. He says: 'a relationship between people takes on a "phantom objectivity", an autonomy that seems so strictly rational and all-embracing as to conceal every trace of its fundamental nature' (1968: 83). He theorizes that the social world is transformed from a spiritual arena of ideas and values into a material arena in which all the contents, human and cultural, have the character of things or objects.

Lukács stresses that the phenomena of reification spread out and became divorced from their economic origins. For capitalist production to succeed it must progressively dominate all other areas of society and, as it spreads, commodification and reification travel with it. Lukács illustrates this argument by quoting at length from Weber's analysis of the rationalization of the modern state. He stresses the parallels which Weber draws between the organization of the state bureaucracy and the organization of business. All matters become standardized and calculable and all human choice and intention come to be understood as elements in chains of cause and effect. Consciousness becomes defined as the illusion, an exact reversal of the truth.

> Bureaucracy implies the adjustment of one's way of life, mode of work and hence of consciousness, to the general socio-economic premises of the capitalist economy, similar to that . . . of the worker in particular business concerns. The formal standardisation of justice, the state, the civil service, etc., signifies objectively and factually a comparable reduction of all social functions to their elements, a comparable search for the rational formal laws of these carefully segregated partial systems. [1968: 98]

Lukács is now able to link this concept of reification to the traditional Marxist category of false consciousness. True knowledge, genuine cultural expression, must rely on a perception of the totality – one must be able to comprehend the entire pattern of capitalism in its completeness. However, so long as human beings live divided and specialized lives they will experience a divided and partial consciousness and the totality will be beyond their grasp. This divided consciousness occurs where the conditions of existence, as specified in capitalist production systems or modern bureaucracies, are radically opposed to innate commitments to emancipation. The reality of this contradiction is graspable only in so far as it is raised to the level of awareness. The agency for such awareness is the Marxist political party which seeks to connect the immiserated and contradictory experiences of workers with the Marxist theoretical programme. This activity, known as *praxis*, produces that grasp of the totality known as class consciousness and enables a radical cultural transformation.

Meanwhile, under capitalism, bourgeois culture remains resolutely reified. However, it is not merely proletarian culture which is 'false' – bourgeois culture also separates subjective experience from objective conditions and thus prevents transformation of those conditions. The following are examples of some of the contents of false bourgeois culture which are discussed by Lukács:

- empiricist philosophy, because of its demand that all phenomena should be subjected to an abstract and formal rationalism;
- economics, because it redefines the exploitative action of the bourgeoisie as the conseqence of impersonal laws and forces held to be beyond human control;
- natural science, because it abstracts and fragments knowledge and diverts attention from the conditions of existence and experience;
- sociology, because it seeks to treat social phenomena objectively, to divorce them from the context of human agency and to absolve the observer from the necessity of praxis ['To treat the world of human behaviour and historical processes as a reality no less "given" and "objective" than stones and stars is to permit one's consciousness to become "reified" ' (Kolakowski 1981: 277)]; and
- modern art and literature, because they selectively abstract from reality rather than truly reflecting its totality – it follows that the only true art and literature occur in the form known as 'socialist realism' which depicts the exploited but heroic nature of the working class and its capacity to liberate all of humanity.

As might be expected, the only true culture which does indeed grasp reality is the totalizing knowledge system of Marxism, which systematically links the individual subject to the objective conditions of existence.

The Frankfurt School: in with the outcrowd

The Frankfurt School sociologists approach culture on the basis of a claim to privileged knowledge. They identify a reference point that allows them to take the position of the free-floating intellectual, to stand apart from the contexts of their own biographies and thus to be able to offer a generalized critique of cultural developments. This standpoint is founded in the concept of 'reason', the application of rational standards to the conduct of human affairs. The rationality implied is a substantive rationality, comparable with Weber's *Wertrationalität* (see chapter 2), which focuses on the ultimate ends of human existence and the values which must be institutionalized if these ends are to be realized. The central assumption which underpins reason is that the ultimate end of human existence is human autonomy. Therefore, the central project in any humane society is emancipation. Cultural developments which threaten human freedom can therefore be subjected to critique.

The Frankfurt School (founded 1923)

The Institut für Sozialforschung (Institute for Social Research) was founded by the Austro-Marxist, Grünberg. However, the unique philosophical and theoretical orientation, known as the Frankfurt School of sociology, only began to emerge with the appointment of Max Horkheimer to the Directorship of the Institute in 1930. Horkheimer managed to attract or retain a galaxy of the leading, mainly Jewish, intellectuals in Germany at the Institute, including Adorno, Benjamin, Fromm, Kirkheimer, Lowenthal, Marcuse, Neumann, and Pollack. With the rise of the anti-semitic and anti-liberal Nazi regime the Institute moved first to Geneva in 1933 and then to New York in 1935. Horkheimer and Theodor Adorno re-established the Institute in Frankfurt in 1955 but many of its leading members remained in the USA, most notably Herbert Marcuse who became the doyen of the American New Left from his California base. The School has always extended its interests beyond sociology to encompass political science, philosophy, and aesthetic theory.

Note that the Frankfurt School theorists thus eschew any notion of objectivity or value-freedom in the social sciences. Their sociology is directly value-relevant. Indeed objective or value-free theoretical orientations precisely deny the possibility of emancipation, they fail to expose institutions to the 'critical tribunal' of reason.

The critique which Frankfurt School theory directs against liberal capitalism closely parallels Weber's argument about rationalization. Just as Weber argues that *Wertrationalität* (value-rationality) is progressively displaced by *Zweckrationalität* (instrumental rationality), they argue that critical reason is becoming displaced by instrumental reason. Instrumental reason is linked to efficiency, involving: 'the optimum adaption of means to ends, thinking as an energy conserving operation. It is a pragmatic instrument oriented to expediency' (Horkheimer 1978a: 28). Even dictators can appeal to this sort of reason, says Horkheimer, but what they mean is that they have the most tanks and that others should yield to them.

Instrumental reason leads to a culture of means rather than a culture of ends – the way that an outcome is accomplished becomes more valued than the outcome itself. Nowhere is this more apparent than in the relationship between technology and economic production (Frankfurt 1973: 94–5). The success of technology as a means has led to an overproduction of commodities which then need to be consumed in order to maintain and develop the technology. So technologized production represents a double threat to human freedom: freedom in the material sense is lost in the workplace as the production system controls and stifles human creativity; and it is lost in a spiritual sense as human beings become slaves to consumption. Human beings are motivated not by dreams of truth, or civilization, or peace, or freedom from hunger, but by: 'the dream of stepping up to the next level of automobile or the next better "gadget" ' (Frankfurt 1973: 95). Indeed, critical sociologists save much of their venom for the economic insanity of these malevolent and 'monstrous chariots which periodically change their color' (1973: 95).

During the 1930s and 1940s these general orientations were mobilized in a critique not only of the Fascist states of Germany and Italy, which is altogether unsurprising, but also of the Communist state of the Soviet Union. All authoritarian state dictatorships represent instrumental reason, the culture of means, in its most extreme form. Pollock (1978) and Horkheimer (1978b) identify this authoritarian form as state capitalism, the ultimate stage of capitalist development. Pollock (1978: 72–8) specifies six ways in which state capitalism differs from liberal or private capitalism:

- Government displaces the market in coordinating the production and distribution of commodities – it does so by means of plans which specify economic ends and means over given periods.
- Prices are regulated by the state in relation to this plan.
- An interest in making profit disappears as the main economic motivator – the state decides who will and who will not make profit.
- The production process is governed by the principles of scientific management, so that workers are not involved in decision-making but merely execute the plan in the most cost-efficient manner possible.
- Planning is enforced by state command and coercion.
- The state becomes the instrument of a unified political elite comprising senior managers, the upper levels of the government bureaucracy and the military, and party leaders and apparatchiks.[4]

State capitalism is always accompanied by the manifestations of propaganda as the main element of culture (Adorno 1978). Ordinary liberal or monopoly capitalism has already provided a standardized mass culture focused on instrumental reason. By the use of propaganda, state capitalism refocuses this orientation. It lays a repetitious stress on the cult of leadership, on scapegoating and on external threat. It thus integrates the masses around simplified conceptions of common national interest. Simultaneously, state capitalism systematically represses and excludes critical reason.

With the defeat of European Fascism in 1945, the members of the Frankfurt School turned their attention to their host society, the USA. They identified this particular social formation as an instance of the democratic form of state capitalism as specified by Pollock (see note 4). The term 'neocapitalism' has occasionally been deployed by some members of the School to distinguish this democratic type from the totalitarian form of state capitalism.

The most trenchant critique of neocapitalism is offered by Marcuse (1964; Held 1980: 70–6; MacIntyre 1970: 62–73). Marcuse addresses what might be thought of as the fundamental theoretical contradiction in Marxist and subsequent critical theory. This is the contradiction between the idea that capitalism carries the seeds of its own destruction, and the idea that capitalism manages to find ways to prevent revolutionary transformation. Marcuse is, on the whole, pessimistic, sensing a general trend towards the successful institutionalization of capitalism as manifested in: the increasing concentration of capital and the advance of mechanization; the expansion of the state especially in the arenas of military development and support for the globalization of capitalism; the progressive homogenization of classes into a single mass; and the permanent threat of nuclear conflict which prevented the exploration of alternative national trajectories.

The chief vehicle for these developments is a highly technologized culture. It promotes the continuation of capitalism in several ways:

- It creates affluence, thus removing many of the grounds for dissent, and diverting attention from a true interest in liberation.
- It focuses attention on consumption patterns which are common to all classes in society and blurs the distinctions between them.
- It softens working conditions as factories are automated and as the labour force shifts into white-collar occupations, thus reducing a sense of opposition.
- It allows the development of a welfare state in which people's lives are dominated by bureaucratic imperatives.
- It markets increased leisure that offers an illusion of freedom without offering access to critical reason.
- It provides for sexual permissiveness within a surface gloss of advertising and mass-mediated entertainment that also offers an illusion of freedom from sexual repression.

Marcuse does recognize that there is a possibility of opposition and critique under neocapitalism – after all, his own oppositional writings were banned in Nazi Germany. However, opposition social movements are ephemeral and disorganized protest manifestations rather than an effectively organized radical Left, and this he bewails.

Under neocapitalism, culture goes through a particular transformation and takes on a particularly important role. The transformation is specified by Benjamin as 'the disintegration of aesthetic aura' (Arato and Gebhardt 1978: 193ff; Held 1980: 89–109). Precapitalist artistic productions, he argues, were embedded in mystical knowledge systems and ritual practices, in a word, in religion. They were thus invested with a special charismatic or sacred quality, an evocation of the supernatural or spiritual. This is an 'aura'. The capitalist revolution liberated art from its religious foundations. However, apparently autonomous art retained its auratic quality as a series of unique or special products which transcended everyday existence, linking humanity into a realm of ultimacy.

This happy state has been disrupted by technological development. Technologized mass media allow artistic products to be reproduced in multiple copies and to be transmitted instantly. Cultural products cease to be unique and no longer demand to be exhibited in public and collective settings. Rather, they become mundane and standardized and able to be consumed in private. In a word, they become nonauratic.

Benjamin was not entirely pessimistic about cultural developments. He was aware of the consciousness-raising possibilities of the transmission of critical and revolutionary ideas through the technologized media to the masses. However, other members of the School, especially Adorno and Horkheimer (1979), were entirely without optimism. For them, the harnessing of cultural production to economic and political objectives via the technologized mass media represents the development of a *culture industry*. The main characteristics of industrialized culture (Held 1980: 91) are:

* standardization and pseudo-individualization – the adoption of a series of packaged images or styles (e.g. Westerns, cops-and-robbers, domestic sitcoms) which are flat in terms of quality or general significance.
* the rationalization of promotion and distribution techniques which attack the autonomy of classical artistic forms by challenging their validity and cost-effectiveness.

The culture industry becomes the instrument of the dominant commercial and state administrative systems of neocapitalism. The culture industry manages conformity, impedes critical judgement, promotes adjustment and obedience, and displaces dissent. Its actions are the planned and deliberate intentions of the managers of mass media organizations who seek to create enthusiastic consumers, compliant workers and placid citizens. The culture of neocapitalism is truly a mass culture, imposed from above, and not an indigenous popular culture.

Contemporary constructionist theories of culture

Although the ideas of Gramsci and Lukács were suppressed under the aegis of the structuralist ideology of Marxism–Leninism, their critique was highly effective. Lukács, in particular, showed that a Marxist theory of ideology required the leavening of a Weberian theory of an independent culture. Here we review three attempts to combine constructionism with critical structuralism: Habermas' theory of societal rationalization; Elias' theory of societal civilization; and Bourdieu's statement of the relationship between class position and cultural reproduction.

Habermas: rationalizing culture

In addressing the work of such a comprehensive thinker as Habermas, identifying seminal influences is inevitably hazardous. His critique of modern culture owes much to Marx, Lukács, Horkheimer and Adorno, but he finally settles on a reworking of the Weberian theme of rationalization in the light of Marxist thought. The argument has two phases: an earlier, more philosophical and Marxist phase in which there is an attempt to provide a foundation for a critique of contemporary culture on the basis of certain interests held to be central to human nature; and a more sociological, neoWeberian phase which follows the 'linguistic turn' described in chapter 2. As we shall see, even in this later sociological phase, Habermas wants still to find an absolute standard for cultural critique and to open it to the force of reason, much in the fashion of the Frankfurt School.

In the first phase, Habermas conceives of knowledge as the foundation of culture (1972). The human species has at its disposal three possible means by which social organization can be established: human beings labour, they communicate, and they can exercise freedom of thought. They thus have technical, practical and emancipatory interests. In so far as human beings are social, they can and will seek to realize one or more of these possibilities. Their interests, as a species, therefore lie in expanding this realization through the media of work, language and power respectively. The interests in turn define three categories of possible knowledge: 'information that expands our powers of technical control; interpretations that make possible the orientation of action within common traditions; and analyses that frees consciousness from its dependence on hypostatized powers' (1972: 313). At their most scientific levels these three forms of knowledge are represented by:

- the natural sciences, which operate within a methodological framework of empiricism and analysis and which enable technical control over objectified processes;
- the historical-hermeneutic sciences (e.g. history, philosophy), which operate within a methodological framework of the interpretation of

common experience and are oriented to a maximum intersubjectivity of mutual understanding; and

- the critical social sciences (e.g. economics, sociology, political science), which may begin within an empirical–analytic framework but also can move beyond it to transform and liberate the consciousness and allow actors to free themselves from constraints that would otherwise seem natural.

(Habermas 1972: 308–11)

There can be little doubt which of these three categories of science is favoured by Habermas. He is most critical of the natural sciences which promote the illusion of the possibility of a pure theory which is divorced from human interests. This is what allows natural science to be put to work in the service of any political regime, no matter what its consequences are for human freedom. These nomological or positivistic sciences[5] can thus lend 'countenance to the substitution of technology for enlightened action' (1972: 316). Meanwhile, hermeneutic science objectifies tradition as a reference point: 'It defends sterilized knowledge against the reflected appropriation of active traditions and locks history up in a museum' (1972: 316). Each must be at least leavened and complemented by a value-relevant, emancipatory social science which makes no pretence to objectivity.

Science (i.e. natural science) assumes a special function in the rationalization of modern societies. In so far as it is able to produce a form of knowledge which is apparently pure and value free, it can be mobilized as superior to the practical and emancipatory sciences, because it is held to be independent of particular interests. It therefore displaces communicative and practical orientations in politics. Politics is no longer oriented to the establishment of common goals and their accomplishment, but to the resolution of social problems as if they are purely technical issues. Politics confines itself to the smooth process of the economy or to providing rewards for privatized needs. Science thus operates as an ideology by 'disethicizing' political issues. The links with Weber and Lukács are thus reforged:

> The reified models of the sciences migrate into the sociocultural life-world and gain objective power over the latter's self-understanding. The ideological nucleus of this consciousness is the elimination of the distinction between the practical and the technical. It reflects . . . the new constellation of a disempowered institutional framework and systems of purposive-rational action that have taken on a life of their own. [1971: 113, italics deleted]

Habermas reserves his greatest sense of loss for the consequent repression and dissolution of a practically oriented 'public sphere', a world of public discussion and argument which can influence political directions. This had been institutionalized in the early phases of liberal capitalism as a *bürgerliche Gesellschaft* (i.e. middle-class society) (1989). Contemporary culture, by contrast, is characterized by an increased orientation to the control of human thought and behaviour rather than a commitment to stimulating it.

The development of Habermas' thought is characterized by an open-minded exposure to public debate and rigorous self-criticism. The key criticism which persuaded him to shift his position, to take the linguistic turn, is the accusation of transcendentalism (Bernstein 1985). If there are transcendent human interests in material control, communication and emancipation which are a priori then these must always emerge. If they are foundational elements which are structurally built into human nature then they cannot be repressed. If so, the natural sciences cannot dominate the emancipatory sciences and Habermas' critique fails.

In *The Theory of Communicative Action* (1984; 1987) he sociologizes the theory, locating the reference point for a critical orientation not at the level of foundational interests but at the level of social relationships. As discussed in chapter 2, such relationships are open to alternative patterns of mediation: they can be mediated by linguistic utterances (speech) and be oriented to reaching consensus on the basis of mutual understanding – communicative interaction; or they can be mediated by delinguistified money and power and be instrumentally oriented to achieving material ends – strategic interaction. A culture can be characterized as tending towards a predominance of either of these orientations.

These cultural tendencies are represented as two possible patterns of rationalization which more or less correspond with Weber's *Zweck-* and *Wertrationalität*:

- *purposive rationalization*, an increasing tendency to select means according to their efficiency and to make decisions according to their consistency with established practice;
- *communicative rationalization*, an increasing tendency to relax constraints on argumentation and consensus-building by posing counter-factuals to the systematically distorted communications of ideology.

This distinction now allows Habermas to move towards a reconstruction of Weber's theory of societal rationalization. The emergence of modern society represents an advance in both forms of rationalization. Weber identifies three fundamental shifts, characterized by Habermas as positive:

- the emergence of the Protestant Ethic which provides a practical and ethical connection between a methodical and orderly pattern of everyday life (purposive rationality) and the ultimate ends of salvation (communicative rationality);
- the differentiation and autonomization of the value-spheres of culture (science, morality, and art) which liberates them from tradition,

religion and each other, and thus allows for independent consensus formation in each arena; and

- the formalization of law, which liberates it from traditional and religious influences.
  (Habermas 1984: 143–272; Pusey 1987: 48–52)

For Habermas these developments promoted the emergence of a liberal bourgeois public lifeworld in early capitalist society which had been freed from the constraints of tradition and religion. It could, through its coffee-house conversations, its pamphleteering and its independent news sheets, enter a genuine communicative discourse (1989). This autonomous public lifeworld was short-lived however. For Weber, its disappearance is the product of a simple process of secularization and formalization, but Habermas finds this view 'unconvincing'.

Rather, for Habermas, the success of purposive rationalization, the emergence of what Weber called the 'iron cage' of a rationalized culture without ethics and meaning, is the consequence of two processes. The first is bureaucratization, the reorganization of the state into formal domains of action that are no longer connected with the normativity of the lifeworld – bureaucracies are machine-like and inhuman, cut off from everyday concerns. The second is commodification, as identified by Marx, in which capitalist enterprises progressively monetarize relationships and human values – culturally shared values and individual commitments equally become obstructive nuisances which the enterprise must repress or control.

The transformation of modern culture therefore takes place in a series of steps or stages (which are described in further detail below). First, system and lifeworld are decoupled – the state and private enterprise are separated from the domains of domesticity and community. Second, relationships between system and lifeworld are mediatized – they cease to be matters which are uttered but rather they are exchanged within monetary or rule-compliance patterns. Third, the constituent organizations of the system invade and colonize the lifeworld and turn it into the image of themselves. The public lifeworld is populated by commercialized mass-media organizations, the private one by objectified worker-consumer-voter-clients rather than by positively communicating subjects. We have a purposively rational modern culture which is disethicized and meaningless, without goals or values.

On this reading, Habermas appears to be located precisely between constructionism and critical structuralism. He wants to say simultaneously that: (a) human beings are naturally communicative; (b) they can choose between purposive rationalization and communicative rationalization; (c) that they have selected the former; (d) that this selection nevertheless has a causal logic; and (e) that they can still choose to do something else. The multiple contradictions between these positions indicate that a basis for a critical theory of modern culture may remain as much a romantic illusion for Habermas as it was for Marx or Weber.

Elias: a civilized theory

Elias addresses himself to long-term changes in personality or psychological predisposition (1978; 1982). However, because he writes of personality orientations as if they are common across all the members of society, we can consider the argument to be about culture, as it is conventionally conceived in contemporary sociology. The argument is broadly similar to Weber's argument about societal rationalization, except that Elias specifies that the evolutionary logic of culture lies in the direction of an increasing level of civilization.

Mennell, who is Elias' main interpreter and epigone, defines civilization in the following way:

> To be civilized is to be polite and good mannered and considerate towards others; clean and decent and hygienic in personal habits; humane and gentle and kind; restrained and self-controlled and even-tempered; reluctant to use violence against others save in exceptional circumstances. To be a civilized person is to have learned a great deal since childhood; after all, infants cannot even control their anal sphincters, and cannot brook the slightest delay in their feed without throwing a fearful tantrum. Well into childhood it is difficult not to lurch between aggression or tears one moment and affection the next. Above all, though, to be civilized is to live with others in an orderly, well organized, just, predictable and calculable society. [1992: 29]

Weberian notions of rationalization (calculability, predictability, organization) are here then, but so too are Freudian notions of repression of the id (self-control, even temperament). Indeed, Freud also wrote about civilization as the external expression of patterns of internal repression.

The civilizing process has a particular directionality. Elias uses the middle ages as a convenient point of departure. Here people ate with bare hands, shared utensils, defecated and urinated in public, and made little effort to disguise sexual interest or activity. Today, by contrast, there are wall-like barriers between individuals, an: 'invisible wall of affects' which arises 'at the mere sight of bodily functions of others, and often, at their mere mention, or as a feeling of shame when one's own functions are exposed to the gaze of others, and by no means only then' (1978: 69–70). This directionality, or curve as Mennell (1992: 38–42) calls it, is traced through several arenas of activity:

- *Table manners* Medievals shared a common dish of food and ate mainly with the hands; by the sixteenth century, each person used their own spoon; by the seventeenth century they used their own bowl; by the nineteenth a range of personal utensils was common.
- *Toilet behaviour* Medievals could perform, and certainly speak about, their bodily functions openly with other people; by the nineteenth century they were performed in private and only spoken of with embarrassment.

- *Blowing the nose* Medievals used their fingers, although one's clothing was a possibility; by the eighteenth century, handkerchiefs were used by the upper class; by the late twentieth century paper tissues were used by everyone.
- *Spitting* Medievals regarded it as a necessary, common and frequent evacuation; by the sixteenth century the product had to be ground in with the foot; by the seventeenth one used a handkerchief, in polite circles; by the nineteenth spitoons were a common item of furniture; they disappeared in the twentieth century and were replaced by 'no spitting' signs; today, no-one spits, and even the signs have disappeared.
- *Sleeping and sex* Medievals shared beds and baths and they slept naked; by the eighteenth century, sharing a bed was regarded as unacceptable in the upper class; sleeping apparel was introduced; sex was progressively confined to the bedroom; sex became shameful and could not be discussed openly.
- *Violence* There is a progressive reduction in the extent of public displays of cruelty and aggression.

However, this culture of civilization is not autonomous. It is the consequence of changes in social structure. These changes centre on processes of the formation of the state. As the state formalizes and seeks to extend its control over society, it increasingly specifies the norms of individual behaviour both by enforcement and by example. There are three successive mechanisms by which state power increases:

- *The monopoly mechanism* Competition between social powers will inevitably lead to the victory of some over the others; the predominant groups will tend to monopolize the means of subsistence and production and constitute themselves as a royal group.
- *The royal mechanism* The power of the royal group becomes absolute (and thus focused on state-building) when there is a structural balance in the society between its various functional groups (church, nobility, merchants, military, etc.).
- *The transformation from private to public monopolies* The increasing complexity of society undermines the private rule of the royal lineage and a progressive differentiation occurs between the property and income of rulers and the property and income of the state.
(Mennell 1992: 66–79)

The particular cultural effect of these processes is 'courtization', the establishment of a courtly elite which transforms warriors into courtiers. A society with a royal court is a society with specialists in modelling and controlling social conduct. Notions of manners, etiquette, and elite taste originated in royal courts. As royals pacified warriors by inducing the internal controls of repression and self-restraint, so courtiers became public servants who were to have the same success in accomplishing cultural control in the society-at-large.

Bourdieu: capitalizing on culture

Bourdieu's theory of culture has three principal characteristics (Branson and Miller 1991; Garnham and Williams 1980; Harker et al. 1990). First, it is a theory of social practices. While culture stands outside of us and constrains us it is nevertheless constructed as the collective product of individual human agencies. Human beings are conceived as motivated by interests which they seek both to protect and enhance. As actors mobilize material resources and ideas in this endeavour they contribute to the reproduction of a collective pattern of preferences and values across time. Indeed this reproduction does not merely consist of the simple replication of culture across generations. Rather, social process consists of material and ideational struggles which alter cultural patterns – the process of reproduction involves extension or expansion (see Stewart et al. 1980: 277–8 for a discussion of types of reproduction).

Second, it is a materialistic theory. It treats the contents of culture as objects which can be produced, consumed, accumulated, transmitted, inherited, bartered, marketed, and transformed, much in the way that material objects can be so manipulated – his is a 'science of the economy of human practices'. In particular, cultural items are regarded as a form of symbolic capital which are used in the struggle to realize interests and which can allow some individuals to dominate others.

Third, it is a theory of cultural differentiation. Bourdieu's view of culture differs from those offered in the arguments of Lukács, Gramsci and the Frankfurt School. They speak of culture as an ideology which invades and dominates the consciousness of all the members of society. The figures that underlie Bourdieu's analysis are those of high and low culture. High and low, or elite and popular cultures, are phenomena of class. They allow classes to be reproduced by their members by providing symbolic markers of membership. Just as in the more explicitly Marxist formulations then, culture has a functional relationship with the maintenance (reproduction) of structured material inequality. However, the differentiated contents of culture stand radically opposed and separated.

Bourdieu first demonstrates that culture is capital by showing that such practices as theatre and museum attendance, concert attendance, newspaper readership, and so on, are distributed variably across the population according to class. This distribution can be reduced to a relationship between educational attainment and cultural practice – the capacity to engage in cultural practices is received in educational experience. It is as if given cultural practices are coded, and therefore only accessible to those who have the key to the code, with the key being awarded through education. The educational key is differentially distributed according to social origin. Bourdieu says that only persons in cultured families, families with taste, have access to the key.

He identifies three zones of taste (organized cultural preference):

- *Legitimate taste* This is the key to membership in the fraction of the dominant class with the highest level of education (examples include preferences for obscure Bach keyboard works, Breughel or Goya paintings, and avant-garde jazz and art-film).
- *Middle-brow taste* This is common in the middle classes (examples include preferences for such accessible classics as *Rhapsody in Blue*, such popular painters as Utrillo and Buffet, and balladic or 'standard' popular music.
- *Popular taste* This is common in the working class but is inversely related to educational capital, so it is also relatively prevalent in the nonintellectual fractions of the dominant class (examples include such popular or light classics as *The Blue Danube* and popular music which has no artistic pretension).
(Bourdieu 1984: 14–18)

This would be profoundly unenlightening if Bourdieu was making only a Weberian observation that the members of different classes have different lifestyles, and practise closure in relation to them. His particular contribution is to identify a link between cultural reproduction and social reproduction. The fact that a dominant economic class is able to demonstrate its superiority in terms of its access to high culture, legitimates its position of superordination. Persons who are members of subordinate classes are not merely materially constrained, they are also culturally, that is evaluatively, inferior. The facts of a system of social inequality are thus legitimated.

It must be stressed that Bourdieu recognizes the relative autonomy of education, that there is no organized conspiracy on the part of any class to control it. Indeed, the inheritance of economic capital is a far more solid guarantee of social reproduction than is inheritance of cultural capital. However, where such unequal inheritance is called into question, for example where there is separation of ownership and control in business corporations, the individual members of a dominant class will progressively capture the means of cultural reproduction, thus ensuring social reproduction. For example, where university qualifications in business administration are regarded as indispensable in management, the children of managers will disproportionately enter university courses in that area. The reproduction functions of the educational system can be summarized as follows:

[T]he educational system, with the ideologies and effects which its relative autonomy engenders, is for bourgeois society in its present phase what other forms of legitimation of the social order and of hereditary transmission of privileges were for [other] social formations . . . [T]he inheritor of bourgeois privileges must today appeal to academic certification which attests at once his gifts and his merits. . . . This privileged instrument of the bourgeois sociodicy which confers on the privileged the supreme privilege of not seeing themselves as privileged manages the more easily to convince the disinherited that they owe their scholastic and social destiny to their lack of gifts or merits, because in matters of culture absolute dispossession excludes awareness of being dispossessed. [Bourdieu and Passeron 1977: 210]

We are now in a position to examine the formal components of Bourdieu's cultural theory. The social world is conceived of as a space which is constituted from past human practices and provides an arena for present and future ones. The shape or dimensions of the space are defined as a series of superimposed 'fields' – the metaphor for which might be found in physics (e.g. force field, magnetic field) rather than pastoralism. The fields are dimensions of a struggle for the realization of interests and the acquisition of resources – they include, for example, the fields of economic production, of intellectual life, of educational attainment, of art, and of political power. The fields are organized hierarchically by the struggles within them. They intersect and serve to reproduce one another. The register for the translation of hierarchies between fields is class.

The principal dimensions of class in effect in the contemporary formation are, as is illustrated in figure 6.1, cultural capital and economic capital. The intersection of these dimensions produces a series of social positions. Agents can practise two sorts of struggle in relation to them. They can seek to effect trajectories of individual mobility. Such trajectories can be hierarchical (upwards or downwards within fields) or transverse (shifting across fields). Alternatively, they can struggle to shift the entire position of a group either hierarchically or transversely. The *nouveaux riches* can aspire, for example, to a shift of field by providing appropriate education in subsequent generations. Each of these personal or positional trajectories alters the shape of the space in future generations, that is reproduces it in an expanded form.

However, the possibilities for such trajectories are limited not merely by the inheritance or acquisition of economic capital but of cultural capital. The position in social space defines a *habitus* or living-space. The habitus is a set of established dispositions to act in certain ways which arises from the adjustment of the individual to the social position. It constitutes the individual's conceptual map of the social world and of the norms of individual behaviour. It parallels the symbolic interactionist concept of the 'generalized other', the structural-functionalist one of 'need-dispositions', or the Weberian notion of lifestyle. The habitus is, by and large, unconscious, specifying such action-patterns as forms of discourse, body language, social distance, appropriate relationships, aspirations, and so on. Each habitus is coherent and is unified by its own internal logic of practice which renders such actions consistent with one another and replicable in new situations.

Bourdieu is now able to close the disconnection left by Weber between

Amount of capital

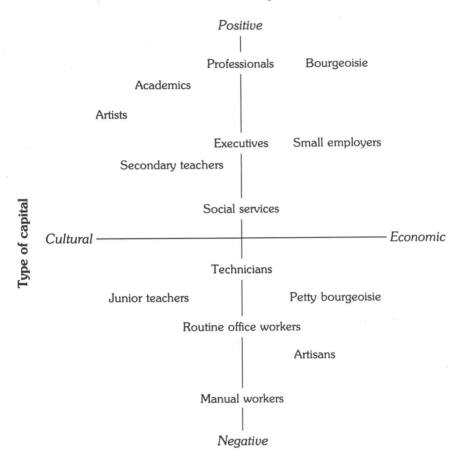

Figure 6.1   *Bourdieu's view of the space of social positions (based on Bourdieu 1984: 128–9)*

life chances and lifestyles. Position in social space conditions the habitus (1984: 171). The primary basis for this conditioning is early childhood experience in which the practices of parents regulate their interaction with the child, but it is also confirmed in the education system. The habitus is constructed as a parental compromise between what might conceivably be aspired to and the material conditions of existence. In so far as these conditions do not change, the habitus of the child replicates the habitus of the parents. The habitus thus becomes a way-of-doing-things common to all those in a particular position. Its relationship to 'taste' is that it generates the schemes by which cultural objects are classified and differentiated (high/low, rich/poor, tasteful/vulgar, respectable/common, light/heavy, etc.) and the standards of appreciation and evaluation which allow an individual to express preferences. The intersection of habituses thus classifies all human practices and cultural objects into a series of distinctive lifestyles or 'tastes' in the cultural arena.

Bourdieu is able to map lifestyles across the positional space specified in figure 6.1 and thus demonstrate homology. For example, he maps (French) taste in food – the bourgeoisie tends to strong-tasting main courses and rich desserts; professionals prefer delicate, lean and light foods; artists tend to the recherché and exotic; while manual workers opt for large, long-simmered, salty and fatty dishes – but also in sport, music, representational art, etc. Thus, he argues:

> [T]he spaces defined by preferences in food, clothing or cosmetics are organized according to the same fundamental structure, that of the social space determined by the volume and composition of capital. Fully to construct the space of life-styles within which cultural practices are defined, one would have to establish, for each class and class-fraction, that is, for each of the configurations of capital, the generative formula of the habitus which retranslates the necessities and facilities characteristic of that class of (relatively) homogeneous conditions of existence into a particular life-style. One would then have to determine how the dispositions of the habitus are specified, for each of the major areas of practice, by implementing one of the stylistic possibilities in each field (the field of sport, or music, or food, decoration, politics, language etc.). By superimposing these homologous spaces one would obtain a rigorous representation of the space of life-styles . . . [1984: 208]

By this means he closes a circle: the relationship, position → habitus → lifestyle, becomes reversible. Differences of class become 'inscribed in people's minds' as distinctions of taste, the capacity to differentiate and appreciate. Taste specifies: whether people are included or excluded; who one's allies are; who one's opponents are; who one marries; how one is likely to perform in school or work, etc. Social differences specify cultural distinctions and these convey a 'a sense of one's place', a feeling for one's own possibilities and limitations. Objective constraints are thus reinforced by perceptions.

The neoWeberian critique of ideology theory

For many Weberians none of the above attempts to reconcile Weber with Marx can succeed. Each of them is seen as insisting on the reduction of culture to social structure: in Habermas, societal rationalization is the consequence of the domination of the state and the economy; in Elias, civilization is the consequence of state centralization; and in Bourdieu, habitus is the reproductive drone of class. Here we review two critiques which seek to liberate the Weberian notion of culture from the structuralist grasp.

Abercrombie, Hill and Turner: bourgeois ideology

Each of the above arguments suggests that culture consists in a unified, or at least consistently integrated, set of ideas which captures and dominates the minds of human beings. Culture thus has the effect of reproducing social structure. It tells people what is possible, what is right, and what their place is in the social scheme, and it thus carries the mould of society across the generations. Abercrombie, Hill and Turner (1980; Abercrombie and Turner 1982) argue that there are some very clear parallels between this 'dominant ideology' thesis and structural-functionalist theories of common value systems (see chapter 5). In the latter the culture does not dominate in the sense of an imposed power but rather represents an emergent consensus of normative guidance shared throughout the society. Nevertheless, culture in this type of analysis performs the equivalent functions of excluding or controlling dissent and deviance and making latent provision for the continuation of the system through time.

For Abercrombie, Hill and Turner, the two arguments are equally susceptible to criticism, but they focus their attention most particularly on Marxist ideas. The fundamental flaw identified in Marx and Engels is that they have two concepts of ideology. As noted in the 'founding arguments' section of this chapter, on one hand, Marx and Engels claim that the ruling ideas in a society are the ideas of the ruling class while, on the other, Marx theorizes that social being determines consciousness. Abercrombie, Hill and Turner argue that these two views are contradictory: the working class cannot, simultaneously, be dominated by the ideas of the ruling class, and experience a specifically working-class consciousness.[6] Indeed, these authors argue that not merely capitalist societies, but many types of society, are characterized by differentiated, unintegrated or nondominating cultures.

Abercrombie, Hill and Turner see (British) culture as developing through three stages:

- *Feudalist culture* Here they challenge the conventional view that feudal society was unified by universal commitments to Christian belief. In fact, Christianity was only genuinely effective in the noble ruling class. Here it unified diverse noble interests and also, by means of its support for monogamy and family duty, provided legitimation for the inheritance of property. The peasantry remained culturally separate and also internally divided in their isolated villages. In these small communities, the monopoly of the nobility over the organized means of violence and over land tenancy gave it control of the peasants and they had no need to rely on religion.
- *Liberal capitalist culture* Early bourgeois culture developed from an opposition to traditional noble domination. It stressed materialism, individual utility and accumulation of wealth, best expressed in the Protestant Ethic. As the bourgeoisie indeed became dominant, it developed this ethic into a culture of respectability focused on family

and domestic morality and on economic self-reliance. The ideology served to legitimate and protect the small-scale, family, capitalist firm characteristic of the period. However, the working class was not nearly as unified in its ideological orientations. Some sections of the working class absorbed some modified elements of bourgeois culture, others carried forward a peasant traditionalism, while still others engaged in reformist and revolutionary opposition to the ruling class.

- *Organized capitalist culture*   In the twentieth century, the figure of a dominant ideology appears less substantial than ever. Where it exists, it takes the form of a stress on accumulation, managerialism, state neutrality and welfare, but it is disparate and incoherent and it has no personal component. This is partly because the dominating institutions of late capitalism are not a class of persons but a group of organizations in the state and private sectors, whose facelessness obviates legitimation. Working-class ideology appears even more incoherent, involving a dualistic commitment both to a continuation of liberal democracy with its welfare benefits and to opposition in the service of reform.[7]

Abercrombie, Hill and Turner conclude that:

[A]lthough in previous modes of production the dominant ideology is relatively coherent, in late capitalism it is losing definition. In feudalism and early capitalism the dominant class, *not* the subordinate class, is incorporated by the dominant ideology . . . However, in late capitalism the dominant ideology is relatively attenuated because there is no economic requirement for it. [1980: 185, original italics]

They argue that there can therefore be no general theory of the functions of ideology relative to the reproduction of social structure. Rather ideology is mobilized in the service of particular class groups seeking to defend or to advance their position. Culture, as a whole, is an ideological mosaic.

Archer: two cultures

Archer takes a more abstract route to a critique of Marxist and structural-functionalist positions (1988). She begins by identifying two levels of analysis, the Cultural System (CS) and Socio-Cultural interaction (S-C). CS is: 'the propositional register of society at any given time' (1988: xvi). It consists of all those items of beliefs and ideas which assert truth or falsity and which are therefore open to possible contradiction. S-C consists of: 'All those other non-propositional things to which we assent or from which we dissent – such as tastes and preferences, likes and dislikes, affinities and animosities, patriotism and prejudice . . .' (1988: xvii).

She then identifies two channels of theoretical conflation between these levels. In downward conflation, the CS maps directly onto and determines S-C by means of regulation and socialization. This is the form of argument found in functionalist analysis described in chapter 5. By contrast, many of the neoMarxist arguments discussed in the current chapter might be categorized as forms of upward conflation, in which S-C 'swallows up' the CS by means of domination and manipulation. Archer finds neither of these conflations to be acceptable because each treats only one of the levels of analysis as real while the other is epiphenomenal (i.e. it has no existence of its own). Both levels, asserts Archer, are active and real and, indeed, an acceptance of the motive capacity of each level is necessary if one is to analyse the dynamic processes of culture. Archer also analyses attempts at 'central conflation' in which the two levels are held to be mutually interactive but in these too the degree of linkage established between the two levels is so concretized as to rule out the possibility of cultural disorder and the dynamics which it can engender.

Archer wants to rule out conflationism altogether and instead to substitute an 'analytical dualism' in which CS and S-C are analytic aspects of culture which mutually interact with and influence one another. Archer (1988: 275) breaks into this chicken-and-egg cycle at the CS level, developing a series of four propositions about cultural dynamics:

(i) There are logical relationships between the components of the CS. [Here she means that the component propositions are not causally contingent on one another but that they have a relationship in which it is possible for them to contradict one another or to complement one another.]

(ii) There are causal influences exerted by the CS on the S-C level. [Contradictions represent problems which actors must solve and in so doing constrain each other; complementarities allow freedom.]

(iii) There are causal relationships between groups and individuals at the S-C level. [There will be groups with differing interests and differential capacity to realize them. Such groups will seek to dominate each other. In so doing they will use cultural power by mobilizing aspects of the CS which support their positions, as ideology. They will also seek to respecify the CS in ways which legitimate their interests.]

(iv) There is elaboration of the CS due to the S-C level modifying current logical relationships and introducing new ones. [Where groups present competing idea-systems actors will be presented with choice; where they offer independent or complementary idea-systems there is freedom to elaborate the CS.]

This now allows her to indicate a general tendency in cultural development. This is captured in the figure:

Cultural Conditioning → Socio-Cultural Interaction →
Cultural Elaboration

Cultures become more differentiated and varietized because the antecendent cultural conditions present and indeed force choices, and because individuals and groups seeking to make such choices will exploit cultural opportunities.

Postmodernism: culture triumphant

The most recent theoretical debate about culture centres on the issue of whether culture has taken a new turn, entered a new phase, at the end of the twentieth century. The cultural registers analysed by the neoMarxist and neoWeberian scholars, whose work is reviewed above, are essentially modern in character. These authors can successfully explore the issue of whether culture is a stabilizing ideology precisely because modern society itself appeared to be fixed by axial principles, either materialistic or rationalistic or both. If society appears to be dominated by a single set of ideas then Gramsci or the Frankfurt School can investigate how these ideas are manufactured; if society is divided by materialism into a small and fixed number of classes, then Bourdieu or Abercrombie, Hill and Turner can investigate whether culture exhibits similar internal differentiation.

There is widespread agreement among cultural theorists that this view is no longer sustainable. First, there are signs that culture has elaborated to a point at which it offers such a wide range of alternative choices that any 'taste' or 'opinion' or 'lifestyle' is legitimate. Value-preferences appear no longer to need to be subordinated to a single set of standards. Second, this elaboration has proceeded to the point at which class-cultural categories can no longer successfully be reproduced because they can no longer be recognized as class-specific. The boundaries between elite and popular culture appear to have collapsed into a generalized mass. So, the argument goes, we may no longer be living under the aegis of an industrial or capitalist culture which can tell us what is true, right and beautiful, and also what our place is in the grand scheme, but under a chaotic, mass-mediated, individual-preference-based culture of postmodernism.

Speaking broadly, there are two main theoretical positions which can be taken on this development. In the first, postmodernism is held to be an extension of previous arrangements, that is, as an ideological handmaiden to 'late capitalism' or in some variants as a development which occurs in a differentiated cultural realm. In the second, postmodernism is the form of an emerging society which represents a radical phase-shift relative to modernity. There are varieties in this position too but each of them points to an era in which culture and society fuse and interpenetrate, and in which it would be impossible to conceive of culture having ideological functions.

Here we review the main influences on each side of the debate – Jameson for the Marxists, and Lyotard and Baudrillard for the postmodernists, together with some of their more derivative epigones.

Postmodern culture as ideology

Jameson: what you see is what you get   The hardest Marxist version of the first position comes from Jameson (1984). Jameson accepts that cultural change is in train but interprets it as the 'cultural logic of late capitalism'.

He proposes a threefold periodization of capitalism (1984: 78, 88), which comes originally from Mandel:

- market capitalism, which involved the integration of markets within nation-states;
- imperial or monopoly capitalism, in which the capitalist states established colonies so that they could capture both suppliers of raw materials and international markets; and
- multinational or consumer capitalism, which establishes a new integrated global space for capitalist expansion and within that expands markets by expanding individual acquisitiveness.

This explosion of capitalism into the global arena is paralleled by a global expansion of culture which liberates it from particular social contexts. There is: 'a prodigious expansion of culture throughout the social realm, to the point at which everything in our social life – from economic value and state power and practices to the very structure of the psyche itself – can be said to have become 'cultural' in some original and as yet untheorized sense' (1984: 87).

The postmodern culture which focuses the mind on the centrality of this global space, and dislocates individuals from the realities of their own situations, has four characteristics:

- It is 'depthless' (i.e. 'what you see is what you get'). Cultural products have no intensity and no emotion behind them because they are decentred from the people who produce them. They are merely consumable images.
- It is ahistorical and immediate. It provides no reference back to previous human suffering and struggle. Traditions can be 'mixed and matched' in pastiche rather than drawn upon or resisted.
- It is timeless. It focuses on the organization of fragments of cultural meaning in space. The time-relationship of these fragments is not signified externally but has to be reconstituted internally by the individual actor.
- It conceives of the world as a technological entity rather than as a natural one, as a computer network rather than an ecological balance.

Harvey: flexible ideas　Harvey (1989) locates the emergence of post-modernist culture even more precisely in the logic of capitalist development. The key development in what Jameson calls the monopoly capitalist period is Fordist accumulation of capital, named after the American industrialist who organized the first mechanized assembly lines. The key to Fordist accumulation is standardization – the standardization of tasks, of products, and of consumption (all captured neatly in Ford's reported phrase: 'you can have any color, so long as it's black'). By these means, one can pump out vast numbers of identical products and sell them widely. Capital is accumulated by mass production for mass markets.

In about 1970 Fordist accumulation met with the sort of crisis Marx had predicted for it. Markets became saturated; governments became overburdened by welfare debt; the working class resisted labour economies; profits fell; and the money supply was expanded setting inflation in train. The rigidities of the economic system prevented the development of new markets, new manufacturing methods and new labour contracts. The shock of a rapid escalation in the price of oil in 1973 provoked a particular crisis which opened a space for a new form of capital accumulation, 'flexible accumulation'. Here capitalists do the following:

- They employ some workers on the basis of their capacity flexibly to perform a range of tasks.
- They employ others on flexible contracts.
- They use technology and production systems which will allow them rapidly to repattern products.
- They stimulate demand by encouraging through advertising a taste for apparently new and different products.

At the level of production and distribution they have thus compressed time – in terms both of production turnover and of the 'life' of each product type.

Harvey now wants to connect the transformation of culture directly to these long-run tendencies in capitalism. The pattern of flexible accumulation has imparted, he argues, a new temporariness to commodities, and especially to the commodified cultural forms of the electronic mass media. Two developments are important: the generalization of fashion from elite to mass markets to create lifestyle fads; and an increased marketing of services, especially entertainment services, which are ephemeral in character. Taken together these solutions to accumulation problems have led to a new postmodern sensibility, or consciousness, in which time and space are compressed and in which the chief contents are those most ephemeral of products, referent-free images, which have now come to take precedence over narratives. In formal terms, this is often called a compression of time and space.

An autonomous and effective postmodern culture

Lyotard: language games

If we can count Jameson and Harvey along with Bell (1979; see chapter 9) and Habermas (1981) as critics of postmodernism, then among its best friends must be Lyotard (1984) and Baudrillard (1988). Lyotard's focus is entirely cultural, he is interested in the development of knowledge, and most particularly scientific knowledge. However, the move from modern to postmodern knowledge parallels social developments: 'the status of knowledge is altered as societies enter what is known as the postindustrial age and culture enters what is known as the postmodern age' (1984: 3). Modern knowledge comprises all those sciences which legitimate themselves by reference to grand or meta-narratives: 'such as the dialectics of the Spirit, the hermeneutics of meaning, the emancipation of the rational or working subject, or the creation of wealth' (1984: xxiii). These overarching myths are losing their credibility, according to Lyotard:

> In contemporary society and culture . . . the question of the legitimation of knowledge is formulated in different terms. The grand narrative has lost its credibility, regardless of what mode of unification it uses, regardless of whether it is a speculative narrative or a narrative of emancipation. [1984: 37]

Postindustrial developments see the computerization and commodification of knowledge. Increasingly, 'performativity', the capacity to deliver outputs at the lowest cost, replaces truth as the yardstick of knowledge. Cultural production dissolves into a series of localized and flexible networks of language games and, since the cultural is the source of legitimation for the social, general social structures (nation-states, parties, professions, institutions and historical traditions) correspondingly lose their capacity to attract commitment.

Baudrillard: signing off modernity
Baudrillard's work derives from an intensive French linguistic tradition which treats language and its contents, rather than, say, material relationships, as the stuff of social life. Drawing on this tradition he develops a periodization of the way in which signs (symbols) relate to their referents. He describes this relationship as simulation, the pattern of representation. Three orders of simulation have succeeded one another since the Renaissance:

- The Renaissance is the period of the 'emancipated sign'. It ends the link which medieval culture had fixed between signs and their referents. In the Renaissance signs could be used to counterfeit new orders and possibilities, to think about alternatives. Here signs are rich in meaning and possibility – they are art.
- The industrial revolution sees the emergence of signs of value-equivalence. This is the era of production in which a series of exact copies can be reproduced in an endless stream. All commodities are translatable into all others by exchange. Here signs are flattened and dull – they are commodities.
- The contemporary simulation era sees signs become the reality. All signs (all information) are reduced to binary oppositions, described as 'the code'. Reality is (computer) modelled or mass-mediated out of such oppositions and these models become reality. Here signs are devoid of all meaning – they are digitized 'bits'.
(Baudrillard 1988: 135–47)

The above is an inevitable oversimplification of Baudrillard's scatologi-
cal and invective language. Consider the following description of 'the
code':

> From the tiniest disjunctive unities (the question/answer particle) to the
> macroscopic level of systems of alternation that preside over the economy,
> politics and global coexistence, the matrix does not vary: it is always 0/1, the
> binary scansion that affirms itself as the metastable or homeostatic form of
> contemporary systems. It is the processual node of the simulations that dominate
> us. They can be organized as an unstable play of variation, or in polyvalent or
> tautological modes, without endangering this central principle of bipolarity:
> digitality is, indeed, the divine form of simulation . . .
>   Why does the World Trade Center in New York City have *two towers* . . .?
> [1988: 143, original italics]

The apparent reasons are that its architects were hypersimulating the
binary code they continuously received through the mass media, and
because such binary codings are the only items which can be interpreted by
the mass in a postmodern world.

In postmodern society, the producing and consuming subject is
decentred by the power of signs, and so relations of production and power
no longer have force. The effectivity of culture is so increased that only the
(binary) relations between its 'signs' have force. The postmodern experience consists in 'hypersimulation', a double counter-reflection in which life
simulates the simulated contents of the mass media. The social thus does
not reference or mediate the signs, that is they have neither labour-value
nor use-value, but merely consumption-value. Social reality is not produced by the signs but merely absorbed by them, so that society disappears
and the signs become a 'hyperreality'. What we could once describe as 'the
social', radically dedifferentiates or implodes into a mass, a shapeless void.
In describing this development Baudrillard indicates an affection for
physicalist metaphor:

> The social void is scattered with interstitial objects and crystalline clusters which
> spin around and coalesce in a cerebral chiaroscuro. So is the mass, an *in vacuo*
> aggregation of individual particles, refuse of the social and of media impulses: an
> opaque nebula whose growing density absorbs all the surrounding energy and
> light rays, to collapse finally under its own weight. A black hole which engulfs
> the social. [1983: 3–4]

Society dedifferentiates so completely that it is a mere mass, no longer
composed of individuals or groups or social classes capable of meaningful
or rational social action, but only capable of consuming spectacular
arrangements of simulacra.

Lash: culture unchained

Both Jameson and Harvey attempt to retain the analytic and normative
salience of cultural modernity within a Marxist perspective. A similar

comment might be made about Lash (1990; Lash and Urry 1987) except that he seeks to retain the Weberian theme of the autonomy of ideas, insisting that postmodernism should be: 'confined to the realm of culture' (1990: 4, italics deleted). Just as Weber sees an elective affinity between Calvinistic Protestantism and capitalist acquisitiveness, Lash argues that postmodernism stands in a relationship of 'compatibility' with the post-industrial capitalist economy. Drawing on the work of the Frankfurt School's most prominent theorist of culture, Benjamin, he identifies the following components of postmodernist culture:

- The three main cultural spheres (art, science, and morality-law) lose their autonomy and interpenetrate one another.
- Cultural objects no longer have an auratic quality as the boundary between high and popular culture disappears. [Note that, for Benjamin, art has already lost its auratic quality in the statist Europe of the interwar period and in the postwar, materialistic USA.]
- The cultural economy becomes dedifferentiated – producer, product and audience merge into a single spectacle.
- Signs (cultural symbols) no longer represent reality but become reality. (Lash 1990: 11–12)

In the last of these points Lash betrays some difficulty in confining his argument to the realm of culture. If signs become reality then they exercise a takeover of social structure and culture engulfs society. A similar betrayal is given in Lash's explanation for the emergence of postmodernity. It emerges because there is an elective affinity between bourgeois identity and postmodernist culture. By bourgeoisie, Lash appears to mean the rising professional classes of the mid-twentieth century. Because this class has its origins in, and indeed shares important class characteristics with, the working masses, it seeks to legitimize itself by delegitimating traditional bourgeois culture. So it elevates elements of popular culture to elite status and simultaneously widens and massifies the audience for high culture. It therefore demands an acceptance of cultural heterogeneity. If this is true, that postmodern culture is only Bourdieuvian cultural capital: 'a set of symbols and legitimations which promote the ideal interests of this new, "Yuppified" post-industrial bourgeoisie' (1990: 21) then Lash must accept Bourdieu's argument for an intrinsic link between the cultural and the social.

Crook, Pakulski and Waters: postculture
In a conventionally sociological initiative, Crook, Pakulski and Waters (1992: 47–78) draw on themes originally identified by the Frankfurt School and others to show that postmodernizing trends in culture are the consequence of a hyperextension and hyperintensification of modernizing developments. However, the radical extension of these trends promotes reversals which indicate the emergence of a postculture, a condition in which culture no longer appears as a differentiated sphere. In postculture,

culture merges with society and personality to form a seamless and undifferentiated whole. The key developments which produce this outcome are already present in modern culture. They are as follows:

• Modern culture is highly differentiated but a postculture moves towards hyperdifferentiation. By this they mean that each cultural component becomes a unique product, dislocated from all traditions. The process releases cultural fragments of intense symbolic power which can transgress traditional boundaries, as for example between the arts and sciences. Postmodern culture can be conceived as a dazzling variety of styles which can be mixed and matched in various packages. The most obvious example of hyperdifferentiation is the blurring of the distinction between high and popular cultures.

• Modern culture is a highly rationalized pattern of technical cultural expertise located either in tradition or its transcendence by claims to being avant-garde. Postculture is so hyper-rationalized that there can no longer be any claim to expertise nor any development of tradition. Cultural forms are dictated by their consumption in the market rather than the conditions of their production. Cultural items no longer conform to rationalities of purpose or value. A postmodernized style is an absence of style – each product is an, apparently irrational, one-off which often embodies playfulness and pastiche. Postmodernist architecture, with its random mixture of styles and functions, its absence of dimension in internal spaces, and its 'toytown' columns and gables, exemplifies this inversion of rationality.

• Modern culture is highly commodified. Postculture is so hypercommodified that material commodities are subsumed by the signs which represent them. Packaged styles are consumed promiscuously within a context of hypercommodified meanings in which the only standard is consumption itself. Under such conditions, for example, one attends opera not because one is cogniscent of a tradition and its meanings but because it signifies a particular social membership – it is a lifestyle choice rather than an intellectual commitment.

In summary:

Postculture [exhibits] that semiotic promiscuity and preference for pastiche and parody which commentators widely associate with postmodernism. A television commercial sells cat food by setting the sales pitch to the music of a Mozart aria, Andrew Lloyd Webber writes a hugely successful pastiche of a late Romantic Requiem, the Kronos string quartet plays Hendrix. [Crook et al. 1992: 37]

Conclusion

Summary

1   The originating positions in the sociological debate about cultural forms are given by Marx and Weber. For Marx, the material condition

determines consciousness, while for Weber culture and society exist in a more complex relationship in which elements of one arena can be determinative in the other. Weber sets the parameters of a theory of modern culture by suggesting that it has an ineluctable logic of rationalization.

2   Constructionist cracks appear in Marx's structuralist position under the weight of arguments from Gramsci, Lukács and the Frankfurt School. Gramsci insists that bourgeois society is held together not only by material constraint but by hegemonic cultural control. Emancipation must be accomplished by cultural means. Lukács adopts a broadly Weberian position in his theory of the reification of culture. The Frankfurt School is even more constructionist in suggesting a conspiratorial attempt to manufacture a culture of acquiescence.

3   Among more explicitly Weberian theorists, culture stands at the disposal not merely of an economic ruling class but of any group seeking to monopolize power. The common thread which underlies the theories of Habermas, Elias, and Bourdieu is that culture can be turned into a tool of exclusion and control by any social group which can establish its power over others. However, there remains a tendency to view culture as a dominating and exclusive ideology established by ruling groups, and which cannot admit alternatives.

4   Each of these arguments can be criticized on the grounds that power does not need to be armed by culture. NeoWeberian theorists (Abercrombie, Hill and Turner; Archer) tend to argue that cultures are relatively unintegrated and internally contradictory, offering a range of possible world-views rather than a single ideology. These world-views become resources in the competition and conflict which occurs between social groups.

5   The two fundamental positions – that culture is a unified and determined ideology and that culture consists of a range of human constructions – are represented in the debate about the emergence of a postmodern culture. For Marxists, postmodern culture is the legitimating ideology for a new phase of capitalism, while for postmodernists, culture breaks free from, and then turns back on, society to achieve a new level of autonomy and effectivity.

Critique

The general argument that is canvassed in this chapter is that culture is a reflection of material relationships which has the consequence of reproducing them. The argument might be expressed in the figure:

$$\text{structure} \rightarrow \text{culture} \rightarrow \text{agency}$$

Even the most recent statements of an autonomous and effective postmodern culture implicitly or explicitly accept this premise. Marxist theories, most obviously, see postmodern culture simply as a reflection of the material relationships of late capitalism. More subtly, those who argue that postmodernization turns the society–culture relationship 'on its head' are implicitly accepting that modern culture was indeed materially or socially determined. The contribution of this general argument is significant. It shows that culture does not stand in an autonomous and determining relationship to society as is argued in functionalist theory (see chapter 5). Rather, culture needs to be understood as standing in complex causal relationship with social agency and social structure.

However, as in the case of many of the arguments examined in this book, the view is flawed by being too one-sided. Just as functionalism needs the corrective of the notion of the material determination of culture, so critical-structural theories of culture may require a constructionist corrective. The grounds for such a corrective might be as follows:

1   The argument which connects structure, agency and culture is functionalist in character and is therefore vulnerable to general critiques of functionalist argument. Critical structuralists argue that culture reflects, directly or indirectly, material structures because these structures would not survive if actors were really aware about the patterns of exploitation and disadvantage which they contain. So culture redirects potentially disruptive action towards support for the determining structure. Its function is to help reproduce that structure. Such an argument must fail because it is neither possible for an event (e.g. materialist individualism) to be caused by another which succeeds it in time (e.g. reproduction of capitalism) nor for cultures be attributed with purposes.[8]

2   It claims that there are several sorts of actor in the world. On one hand, there are those who produce culture. These are viewed either as conspirators with, or lackeys of the bourgeoisie, and they set out to deceive the rest of the population with a tissue of lies about the right, the true and the beautiful. On the other hand, the consumers of popular culture are conceptualized as unresponsive sponges who merely soak up the outpourings of the culture industry, believing every utterance. Between them sit the privileged social scientific observers who can expose the true purposes of cultural production. Such a differentiated model of the actor is unacceptable. While there may indeed be different levels of cultural knowledge and different standards of appreciation, there can surely be no foundational or absolute standard which permanently ascribes truth status to the beliefs of some actors and constructs other beliefs as false.

3   If culture is claimed to react back on to social relationships in a process of reproduction, then culture cannot simply be epiphenomenal. Assuming a separate reality of the material and cultural realms, what must be occurring is causal interaction between them. This is especially apparent in the Marxist account of the emergence of class consciousness

which appears in various guises in the theoretical positions reviewed in this chapter. The development of class consciousness requires the praxis of Marxist intellectuals, which is surely an ideological or cultural activity with material consequences. So culture cannot simply be conflated to material relationships.

4　As Archer is quick to point out, all such theories are dualistic as well as conflationary. (It must also be said that she is somewhat slower to recognize dualism in her own analysis.) The issue of theoretical dualism is explored in detail by Holmwood and Stewart (1991) and there is a brief review of their work in the concluding chapter of this book. However, it might be said in brief here that an attachment to dualism implies theoretical failure. Critical theorists explore the issue of culture so extensively precisely because it is problematic for them. Culture presents a threat to a materialist conception of human history and it must be conflated if that argument is to survive apparently disconfirming evidence and the contradictory experiences of those whose behaviour it seeks to explain.

Further reading

For the founding positions see Marx, 'Preface to a Contribution to a Critique of Political Economy' (in *Selected Writings* 1977) and Marx and Engels, *The German Ideology* (1970), and Weber, *The Protestant Ethic and the Spirit of Capitalism* (1976).

The most important original source for Gramsci is *Selections from the Prison Notebooks* (1985) but for commentaries see *Gramsci* (1977) by Joll or the more extensive *Antonio Gramsci* (1977) by Davidson. Lukács' most important work is *History and Class Consciousness* (1971) for which Lichtheim's *Lukács* (1970) is a useful introduction. The best collection of original writings from the Frankfurt School is Arato and Gebhardt (eds), *The Essential Frankfurt School Reader* (1978) but an accessible introduction can be found in Held, *Introduction to Critical Theory* (1980).

Habermas is difficult to read. The most complete statement is in *The Theory of Communicative Action* (1984; 1987) but more accessible are *Toward a Rational Society* (1971) and *Legitimation Crisis* (1976). A good route into Habermas is Bernstein's introduction to *Habermas and Modernity* (1985) but the most complete and helpful introduction is Pusey's *Jürgen Habermas* (1987). Elias can be read in the original in *The Civilizing Process* (1978; 1982) but reading Mennell's *Norbert Elias* (1992) can be almost as effective. Bourdieu's theory of culture is best read in *Distinction* (1984).

Abercrombie, Hill and Turner's argument can be read in *The Dominant Ideology Thesis* (1980) or in the earlier journal article of the same title (1978). Archer's book is called *Culture and Agency* (1988).

The two basic positions on postmodern culture can be found in Jameson 'Postmodernism' (1984) and Baudrillard *Selected Writings* (1988). More synthetic statements which canvas the issues are Lash, *The Sociology of Postmodernism* (1990) and Crook et al., *Postmodernization* (1992).

Notes

1 This tendency is explained in terms of the labour theory of value.

2 Lenin would doubtless have endorsed the opinions of the Chinese leader Mao-Tze Dong who believed that: 'Power grows out of the barrel of a gun' and US President Lyndon B. Johnson who is reputed to have said: 'When you have them by the balls their hearts and minds will follow.'

3 This section concentrates on the early and most influential part of Lukács' work, the Hegelian phase culminating in *History and Class Consciousness* (1968), first published in 1923.

4 Pollack also identifies a democratic form of state capitalism in which the bureaucracy is prevented from undertaking administrative action purely on its own behalf.

5 'Nomological' means, commitment to a knowledge of natural laws; 'positivistic' means, commitment to knowledge based on observation.

6 In fact the arguments are complementary rather than contradictory. The view that it is 'natural' for the working class to be without property, power, etc. can sit quite happily in ruling-class and working-class cultures simultaneously.

7 Mann (1982) agrees that normative harmony is necessary among ruling groups and also that there is an absence of normative harmony among the working class. However, he argues, it is precisely this absence of normative harmony which helps to keep the working class compliant. The absence of common working-class consciousness of either the dominant or oppositional kind is explained by him as a mixture of the pragmatic acceptance of economic compulsions, voluntary deference, nationalistic sentiment, and reformist-democratic sentiment, and all of this in terms of the increasing incorporation of the working class into the central institutions of advanced capitalism (1982: 391).

8 For an extended critique of functionalist arguments see the conclusion to chapter 5.

7 Power and the state

One of the notorious debates in sociological theory during the 1960s and 1970s focused on social integration or social order.[1] On one side were ranged theorists who believed that society was held together by agreement between its members on shared norms – these were known as consensus theorists. On the other were those who believed that society was riven by intractable cleavages and had to be held together by coercion – these were so-called conflict theorists. The previous two chapters address the theoretical status of normative agreements: in chapter 5, we examined functionalist theories which argue that normative agreements are indeed held to be shared; while in chapter 6, on culture, we examined critical structuralist and critical constructionist theories which consider the possibility that shared norms are imposed as an ideology. In this chapter we examine the alternative positions in what might be considered the other side of this debate – the status of power and coercion in sociological theory.

'Power' is a term which is often used routinely and unreflectively, without fear of the dangers of unresolved complexity, both in everyday life and in the more casual practices of social science. In common parlance, we may speak of 'union power' or 'the power behind the throne' or 'the capacity of absolute power to corrupt absolutely' or 'a powerful speech' understanding what we mean when we use the word. However, it proves to be full of tricks and hazards when we try to locate it precisely within sociological theory. Consider some of the questions the term 'power' raises in the mind of the political philosopher, Lukes:

Is power a property or a relationship? Is it potential or actual, a capacity or the exercise of a capacity? By whom, or what, is it possessed or exercised: by agents (individual or collective?) or structures or systems? Over whom or upon what is it exercised: agents (individual or collective?) or structures or systems? Is it, by definition, intentional, or can its exercise be partly intended or unintended? Must it be (wholly or partly) effective? What *kinds* of outcome does it produce: does it modify interests, options, preferences, policies, or behavior? Is it a relation which is reflexive or irreflexive, transitive or intransitive, complete or incomplete? Is it asymmetrial? Does exercising power by some reduce the power of others? (Is it a zero-sum concept?) Or can its exercise maintain or increase the total of power? Is it demonic or benign? Must it rest on or employ force or coercion, or the threat of sanctions or deprivations? (And, if so, what balance of costs and rewards must there be between the parties for power to exist?) Does the concept only apply where there is conflict of some kind, or resistance? If so, must the conflict be manifest, or may it be latent: must it be between revealed preferences or can it involve real interests (however defined)? Is it a behavioral concept, and, if so, in what sense? Is it a causal concept? [1978: 633–4, original italics]

Lukes is able to go on to ask a similar set of questions about the parallel concept of 'authority' and a further set of questions about the relationship betweeen the two.

This tells us several things about the way in which power is theorized in sociology:

- power is a fundamental item on the theoretical agenda – no theorist of any stature can avoid the issue;
- there is widespread disagreement about the meaning of power and its sources;
- as Lukes (1978: 633) indicates, this is at least partly because when we theorize about power we are making statements about the way that the social world operates – we are stating a world view; and
- many theories of power are, in fact, conceptual expositions on the meaning of the term rather than substantive theories of its causes and effects.

In summary, the theorizing of power has been constituted virtually as a century-long debate about the meaning of one word. The topic of power therefore makes a negative contribution to the reputation of sociological theory because it adds to the appearance of an inability to find agreement on the most basic of issues.

As we have said, however, theories of power are not merely conceptual definitions but also substantive arguments. These arguments address the following points:

1 Power implies that certain social entities (individual actors, collective actors or structures) have particular consequences ('effectivity') for other, similar entities. This effectivity may imply a capacity or ability to put things into effect or change things, to alter the physical and social environment (known as 'power to'). It may also imply that one social entity can control the actions of another (known as 'power over'). Although the claim might be made that 'power over' and 'power to' represent alternative theoretical positions, the difference is merely one of emphasis, because each implies the other.

2 Power stands in a specific relationship to the distribution of resources in society. For many theorists, power is reducible to (i.e. it can be explained by) the distributions of such other resources as property or status. For many others, power is a resource which stands in its own right and can contest or control the use of other resources.

3 Power exhibits a specific degree of concentration. For some theorists, power is inevitably concentrated and centralized in modern society, in a

monolithic way, while others view it as widely distributed and continuously contested, in a pluralistic way.

4   Power enters into all or most human relationships. It can be argued either to be an analytic aspect of all relationships in a definitional sense or to be an alienable and exchangeable resource which is transferred between the parties to relationships.

5   Power bears a specific relationship to human intentionality or teleology. The issue thus reruns what many consider to be the fundamental cleavage in sociological theory, that between agency and structure. It can be regarded as a matter of intention or as an unconscious pattern of organization.

6   The use and application of power tends towards primary specialization within a social institution called the state or the polity. The state or polity is characterized by a specific level of autonomy and differentiation relative to other social units.

There are three sources for the founding arguments in sociological theories of power: Marx's critical structuralism; Weber's constructionism; and classical elite theory which promotes both functionalist and utilitarian themes. Modern theories of power coalesce into three basic positions, and these provide the fundamental organization for the chapter. The first is the neoMarxist or critical structuralist position that society is dominated by a ruling economic class which determines the shape of the state. The second draws on functionalist and constructionist themes to argue that society is managed by a political elite which rules with the consent of the governed. The third is broadly utiliarian in its orientation, arguing that power structures emerge from the conflicts and compromises achieved by individuals seeking to realize their individual interests.

Founding arguments

The founding arguments lay out three basic positions, respectively, of critical structuralism, constructionism and functionalism. Marx's critical structuralist version of power sees it as an aspect of the economic relationships which fundamentally determine the shape of society. Weber draws distinctions between different types of power on the basis of the extent to which they are held to be legitimate. Classical elite theory claims that power is an independent resource generated in organizations, especially the organizations of government, and is necessary for the operation of society.

Marx: power, power everywhere

In a trivial sense Marx never wrote about power; in an important one he wrote about nothing else. The history of human societies is, he theorizes, so suffused by power differences and power struggles that a separate specification of power is unnecessary.

Human history is conceived by Marx as a struggle over material resources. The relationship of material resources to the acquisition of power is circular: the more material resources one has the more one can control others, and the more one can control others the more material resources one can acquire. This relationship appears to be definitional – a monopoly of scarce material resources can induce obedience among those who need and do not have them, and this implies that the primary locations for the effects of, and struggles over, power are within firms and business enterprises. However, Marx also tries to show that the material and power differences generated in economic units shape the pattern of power relationships in political and ideological arenas. Within this general orientation, power is applied and experienced not by specific individuals but by classes and groups.

The most extreme level of power differentiation is experienced in capitalist societies. In the capitalist mode of production, property is entirely alienable and privatized and labour is entirely contractualized. Possibilities for the accumulation of property and for the exploitation of labour are theoretically limitless. However, in spelling out the consequences of these processes in his work on labour and surplus value, Marx shows that power tends to become highly concentrated.

The fundamental premise in this argument is the labour theory of value. This theory argues that commodities are entirely the consequence of the expenditure of labour power, they are objectified labour power, and thus that the value of any commodity is the sum of of all the quanta of labour power that have gone into its production. In what is known as simple commodity production, a hypothetical system in which each worker entirely produces and has the right of disposal over the product, everyone knows the labour value of a product and will refuse to barter or exchange products for anything other than the true labour value. Workers will not exchange products for less than the value of the labour which they have put into them.

In the capitalist mode of production, commodities are bought and sold for money in a market. By contrast with simple commodity production, here the wage-worker receives less than the labour-value of the product. The system of exchange which establishes this principle, argues Marx, operates as follows. The cost to the labourer of producing a commodity is the sum of: the cost of feeding, clothing and housing worker and family; plus the cost of skill acquisition and of education. This total is called the cost of the reproduction of labour power. However, the labourer needs only to work a certain amount of time to meet this cost. So if a capitalist can force workers to labour for longer than this amount of time, but pay them at a rate sufficient only to meet the cost of the reproduction of labour power, a sale of the commodities at a higher value can provide a surplus which can be retained by the capitalist.

[B]y paying the daily or weekly value of the . . . labouring power, the capitalist has acquired the right of using that labouring power during the whole day or week. . . . Over and above the . . . hours required to replace his wages, or the value of his labouring power, [the worker] will, therefore, have to work . . . hours of surplus labour, which surplus labour will realise itself in a surplus value and a surplus produce.

The rate of surplus value, all other circumstances remaining the same, will depend on the proportion between that part of the working day necessary to reproduce the value of labouring power and the surplus time or surplus labour performed for the capitalist. It will, therefore, depend on the ratio in which the working day is prolonged over and above that extent, by working which the working man would only reproduce the value of his labouring power, or replace his wages. [Marx 1982: 35, italics deleted]

The practice of paying wages less than the exchange value received for commodities has the consequence of valorizing (adding value to) capital by the continuous accrual of surplus value in the form of profit. Ownership of the means of production as private property therefore becomes increasingly pronounced and concentrated. To the extent that ownership becomes concentrated, power becomes concentrated.

In order to ensure that wage workers continue to maximize surplus value there must be a continuous effort to control the labour process, that is, a continuous reconstruction of work in the direction of longer hours, greater specialization, the declining application of skill, and an increasing application of technology. Workers are thus reduced to a homogeneous mass of individuated and controlled objects in the system of production, unable to resist capitalist exploitation.

There are logical difficulties with respect to the labour theory of value, most particularly in terms of Marx's equation of labour value with exchange value (price). Clearly there is nothing essential about the price of a product – it merely depends on supply and demand.[2] There must also be very real doubts, in the face of skill differentials, about Marx's assumption that all labour is of equal value under any technological regime – technology can multiply the productivity of labour. However, it would be difficult to disagree with the view that material resources can be a source of power differences.

Marx's analysis of the relationship between economic class power and state power is much more problematic. As Jessop (1982: 9–20) points out, even Marx and Engels themselves were far from single-minded on the issue. The orienting proposal is a 'base–superstructure' model in which developments in the economic base are paralleled by changes in the political superstructure. The party-political struggles which appear in the state are illusions which deflect attention away from genuine class antagonisms: 'It is always the direct relationship of the owners of the conditions of production to the direct producers [which is] the hidden basis of the entire social structure, and with it the political form of the relation of sovereignty and dependence, in short, the corresponding specific form of the state' (Marx 1982: 37).

In general, however, this view is an abstract and guiding structural principle in Marx and Engels rather than a statement of actual practices. Nowhere do they assert that there is a perfect epiphenomenal correpondence between economy and state. Rather this connecting thread is 'split and frazzled', their position being that: 'different forms of the state and state intervention are required by different modes of production and that the nature of state power is determined by the changing needs of the economy and/or by the changing balance of class forces at the economic level' (Jessop 1982: 10).

Weber: authoritative theory

As in the case of most topics, Weber takes up a position on power which is explicitly opposed to that of Marx. For Marx, power is epiphenomenal but, for Weber, it is a fundamental concept and he gives it a much more detailed and explicit specification.[3] As might be expected, Weber understands power always to be a consequence of intentional human action. It is an aspect of the way in which human beings relate to one another. He defines power as: 'the probability that one actor will be able to carry out his own will despite resistance, regardless of the basis on which this probability rests' (1978: 53).[4] He thus views the concept of power to be sociologically amorphous, to embrace: 'all conceivable qualities of persons and all conceivable combinations of circumstances' which gives one person control over others. This single, theoretical generality allows Weber to develop a conceptual hierarchy of increasing specificity to describe the types and subtypes of power. This hierarchy of power terms is described in figure 7.1.

Weber's principal interest lies in the forms of power which appear to be grounded in the consent of the governed, so he commences his analysis by specifying power of this type. This is *domination (Herrschaft)*[5] and is defined as: 'the probability that a command with a specific content will be obeyed by a given group of persons' (1978: 53). The principal effect of the specification is to separate power based on command, whether accidental

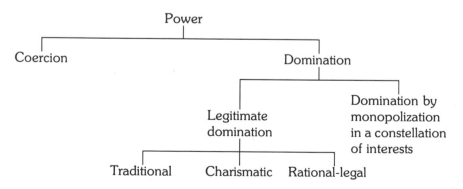

Figure 7.1 *Weber's hierarchy of power concepts*

and occasional or formally organized, from power based on direct coercion.

However, the definition of domination is still too imprecise for Weber's purposes. He therefore makes a further distinction between: 'domination by virtue of a constellation of interests (in particular: by virtue of a position of monopoly)' and, 'domination by virtue of authority, i.e., power to command and duty to obey' (1978: 943). He thus distinguishes, quite carefully, between nonlegitimate and legitimate domination and, in so doing, recognizes that power can come from the control of resources. However, he is more interested in legitimate domination which is defined as:

> [T]he situation in which the manifested will (*command*) of the *ruler* or rulers is meant to influence the conduct of one or more others (*the ruled*), and actually does influence it in such a way that their conduct to a socially relevant degree occurs as if the ruled had made the content of the command the maxim of their conduct for its very own sake. [1978: 946, original italics]

The ruled may accept command from a variety of possible motives including: a sense of duty, fear, 'dull' custom, personal advantage, attachment to the ruler's values, or emotional or ideal motives of solidarity (1978: 946–7). A system of domination will not be stable over time, however, unless the ruled accept that when the ruler claims the right to command the claim is a legitimate one, that is, that it takes place in the context of values. In Weber's words, the command must come to be accepted as 'a "valid" norm' (1978: 946) which is shared between the rulers and the ruled.

Weber's argument now proceeds theoretically rather than merely typologically. The kind of legitimacy which is claimed influences a series of other social practices, principally: the way in which domination is exercised; the form of obedience it receives; and the structure of any administrative staff set up to guarantee it. Weber therefore sets out his now famous typology of legitimate domination. The central discriminating dimension is the basis on which legitimacy may be claimed. Weber (1978: 215) constructs three such possible bases:

- *Traditional* domination primarily occurs in status-stratified societies. Persons in authority inherit a particular status at birth which ascribes to them the right to make decisions. Subordinates likewise inherit a form of status loyalty by ascription. The commands of the superior are accepted because the relationship between the two statuses is 'as it has always been'. However, the authority of the superior is not unlimited. It must conform with established customary rights and any deviation from such custom will threaten the legitimacy of the relationship.
- *Charismatic* domination is rendered legitimate in terms of particular personal powers or gifts which set the leader apart.

- *Rational-legal* domination draws its legitimacy from two components: the 'legal' component implies rules or laws which are accepted by subordinates who expect that superiors will operate within them; and the 'rational' component which implies that rules are effective and efficient in accomplishing specific and immediate objectives.

Weber then goes on to discuss the forms of power *structure* which emerge when each of these claims are made. The best known of these is the pure type of rational-legal authority that gives rise to a bureaucratic administrative staff, which has the following characteristics:

- Its activities are governed by rules.
- It has a specific sphere of competence.
- It is organized hierarchically.
- Its members are specifically trained for their occupations.
- Its officers do not own the means of production.
- They do not own their jobs, but can be dismissed from them.
- Its actions are recorded in files.
  (Weber 1978: 218–20)

The bureaucratic administrative staff emphasizes the abstraction and impersonality of the legal norms by which the exercise of power is legitimated and the specificity of its application.

By contrast, traditional domination gives rise to one of four organizational structures: patriarchalism, patrimonialism, sultanism, or feudalism. Weber's main interest lies in patrimonial bureaucracy, the type which most immediately precedes modernity. Patrimonial bureaucracy is a system in which rulership is absolute and undivided and in which power is exercised through a coterie of notables. Their loyalty is ensured by the granting of benefices, which are rights to 'own' offices, and to which significant material rewards are attached. Equally, the theoretical significance of charisma lies only in its capacity to disrupt established claims to authority on one hand, and its instability and consequent capacity to provide a context for the establishment of new claims to authority on the other.

Weber warns that the typology of legitimate domination is only an ideal-type construct and also that no pure instance of it could survive with any measure of stability. Empirical instances always include impure mixtures of the types of domination. However, Weber is less interested in a taxonomic list of organizations than in the transformation of Western society from power structures based on claims to tradition, principally patrimonialism, to the form based on claims to rationality. Power structures based on claims to charismatic personal qualities are only interesting because they operate to effect the transition.

Classical elitism: conspiracies of power

There is a long tradition which argues for an entirely independent and dominant system of political stratification. Within this tradition, two main strata are identified: the elite and the non-elite or *mass*. An elite is a social group with a disproportionate power to command. Meisel's (1962) 'three Cs' specify the essential elements of an elite. The three Cs are:

- group *consciousness* – the elite members must be aware of the existence of the elite and of their own membership in it;
- *coherence* – the individual members must act in concert in pursuit of group interests; and
- *conspiracy* – there must be an exchange of information between members and the evolution of common strategies for furthering group interests.

An elite is therefore an intentional construction. The earliest elite theorists were Pareto (see chapter 3), Mosca and Michels (Parry 1969: 30–54; Bottomore 1966).

Pareto (1966) bases his theory of elites on an interesting but now discredited theory of social behaviour (outlined in detail above in chapter 3). Human behaviour is the outcome of two elements: *derivations* which are ideas which rationalize and try to legitimate conduct, the veneer or gloss which makes social life possible; and *residues* the basic instincts or motives of the actor which genuinely determine conduct. There are two, contradictory types of residue relevant to power formations and these are constant throughout history. The first is the 'instinct of combinations', the inclination to create new objects and new social groupings. The second is 'the instinct of the persistence of aggregates', the inclination to preserve what has already been established. Each person has a predominance of either the first or the second type of residue.

People who emphasize the first residue are speculators (equivalent to those Machiavelli had earlier described as 'foxes') who are insightful and cunning and who have the ability to persuade others to follow. Those emphasizing the second are rentiers ('lions') and they are conservative and unimaginative. The non-elite is composed almost entirely of lions, but the elite is composed of both foxes and lions and, indeed, needs to have both. The character of governing practices is determined by which group predominates in the struggle between the innovating, demagogic, persuasive foxes, and the conservative, repressive and violent lions. This struggle leads to a process circulation, or mobility between the elite and the non-elite, but Pareto's evidence for this argument is little more than speculative.

A less colourful but rather more useful account of elites is given by Mosca (1939). Like Pareto, Mosca argues that all societies are inevitably ruled by a small group of persons. This assumption relies on the view that a small group can more readily organize itself than a large one and that, if it is to control the masses, it must act coherently and strategically to maintain its power. There are two types of elite structure: the autocratic-aristocratic type in which authority flows downward and the elite is self-recruiting; and the liberal-democratic type in which the rulers are authorized to govern by the non-elite and there is circulation of individuals between the elite and the non-elite. Mosca is more circumspect about the circulation of elites than Pareto, suggesting it as a possibility rather than as a general tendency. However, he does indicate that this type of mobility is increasing in Western societies.

Weber's student Michels (1958; Parry 1969: 30–54; Bottomore 1966) takes issue with the proposal about elite circulation made by Pareto and Mosca. He proposes instead an 'iron law of oligarchy'. Elite membership rests on an ability to control organizations, so that in effect there is an elite–mass differentiation not only of society as a whole but also of the organizations which go to make up society. These organizations – trade unions, companies, political parties, etc. – often have goals which are technically difficult to realize and they also have internal coordination problems which are immense. To manage these things requires expertise, and expertise can only be gained through experience of leadership. In turn, leadership experience is available only to a few. Consequently, asserts Michels, 'Who says organization, says oligarchy', that is oligarchy will always develop in so-called democratic organizations, the rank-and-file will surrender control to a minority, and the minority will consolidate and maintain its position by the monopolization of organizational expertise.

Critical structuralism: power from the possession of property

The first group of modern theorists we examine take their major cues from Marx in seeking to explain power in terms of the possession of material structures. The argument has two moments: it first suggests that the only real form of power involves a struggle between economic classes over ownership; it then suggests that such apparent complexes of power as the state or politics can be reduced (i.e. more or less totally explained by) this class struggle. The first set of theories, comprising contributions from American critical theories of the 1940s and 1950s, concentrates on the second of these moments.

The American radical left: military-industrial complexities

Burnham's *The Managerial Revolution* (1941) is an early attempt to combine elite theory with Marxism. In classical Marxist theory society is governed by the owners of the means of production, the *ruling class*. This theory has become outmoded, Burnham argues, by the development of corporate capitalism in which shareholding owners are distributed through-out the population. It is therefore very difficult to speak of a small-scale, bourgeois ruling class. Burnham resolves the problem by arguing that legal ownership of the means of production is insignificant by comparison with the issue of who controls them, and this control has been taken over by managers. Similarly, within the state, politicians have surrendered control of political processes to expert bureaucratic managers. An alliance between these public and private sector managers will see the eventual demise of the traditional bourgeoisie. Society will be ruled by a managerial elite of skilled technical experts in both the private and the state sectors.

A similar position is taken by Mills (1959; 1970). Like Michels, he views power as an aspect of organizations or, in his own terms, of institutions. The interesting suggestion that he makes is that these institutions are not independent of one another and that their elites interpenetrate. In short, contemporary society is said to be ruled by a single, integrated, and unified elite, a *power elite*.

C. Wright Mills (1916–62)

Mills was an unconventional man who had a conventional career. He was born in Waco, Texas, USA, took a Bachelor's and Master's at the University of Texas, a PhD at Wisconsin, and spent most of his relatively short life as Professor of Sociology at Columbia University in New York. A feisty and combative man, he attacked all the icons of sociology and of American society. He had the courage to be a left-radical when that was not at all fashionable.

Sources: *Penguin Dictionary of Sociology* (1984: s.v. Mills, C. Wright); Ritzer (1992: 211)

His claim that there is a power elite in society is based on an analysis of the post-Second World War USA. The evidence is: first, that politics no longer consists of the public rehearsal of coherent alternative policies but is rather a squabble between corporate interest groups anxious to feed at the public trough; second, that there has been an enlargement and enhancement of military organizations oriented to the maintenance of the state against real or assumed enemies; and third, that the corporate economy is therefore geared heavily towards military production.[6] The power elite is a unified ruling group with shared interests focused on the maintenance of the state's military position:

> [T]he power elite has been shaped by the coincidence of interest between those who control the major means of production and those who control the newly emerged means of violence; from the decline of the professional politician and the rise to explicit political command of the corporate chieftains and the professional warlords; from the absence of any genuine civil service of skill and integrity, independent of vested interests. [1970: 246]

In this analysis, power is reduced to control of economic resources specifically oriented to the prosecution of wars, cold and hot. The theory is particularly applicable to such societies as the USA, China, and the former USSR, which practise superpower adventurism of various kinds, but becomes rather more dubious if expressed as a generalization to all societies.

Poulantzas: power at work

Whereas Burnham and Mills seek to link Marxist thought with the elitist tradition Poulantzas' theory of power (1973: 104–14; 1978: 146–53; 1986) draws more directly and explicitly on the structuralist and materialist aspects of Marx's thought. His theory is therefore directly related to that of Althusser (see chapter 4). Poulantzas begins by defining power as: 'the capacity of a social class to realize its specific interests' (1986: 144). The amount of power which a class has can be defined precisely by its relative success in the class struggle. Classes are placed in a position either of positive power (domination) or negative power (subordination) by their location in the system of relations between classes. Power, he insists, is 'strictly relational' because it springs from 'a relational system of material places occupied by particular agents' (1978: 147).

Nicos Poulantzas (1936–79)

Poulantzas was born in Athens, Greece, where he took a law degree in 1957. He moved to Paris in 1960, taking a doctorate at the Sorbonne in 1964. Thereafter he gravitated towards Communism and became a leading figure in the development of Marxist thought. He wrote in the language of his adopted country. Poulantzas died by his own hand.

Source: Ritzer (1992: 301)

A key conceptual vulnerability in Poulantzas' conception of power is the notion of class interests. Classes are independent of individual human wants and desires and therefore class interests cannot be located at the level of agency, rationality or psychology. The interests of any class consist in an extension of its capacity as a social force, of the effect which it has on society. Put another way, objective class interests lie in pushing back the limits placed on it by other classes. Poulantzas thus seems to be arguing tautologically that: power is the capacity of a social class to extend its power. In his own words: 'The capacity of a class to realize its objective interests, and so its class power, depends on the capacity, and so on the power, of its opponent' (1986: 151).

Classes exercise power in three fields: the economic, the political and the ideological. The economic field constitutes and shapes the other two fields, but the particular power capacity of a class in the economic field does not directly determine its particular power capacity in either of the other two. It can therefore be perfectly normal to have a formation in which, say, the bourgeoisie dominates the economy, the working class dominates the state through a social democratic party, and a professional middle-class fraction dominates in the ideological realm. This gives the state a special relationship to the economy in Poulantzas' theory, it is 'relatively autonomous'. It is not an independent source of power nor is it the simple instrument of the bourgeoisie. Rather it is an arena within which capacities derived from the economic arena are brought to bear in a struggle. One way in which the state reflects material power struggles, for example, is that wage-workers have no capacity to influence the police, judiciary, or state administrative systems. But it is also possible and necessary for such wage-workers not to surrender the state to the bourgeoisie. Indeed, the first revolutionary step which the working class takes must be to capture the state.

The relative autonomy of the state

The issue of state autonomy was a major focus of debate in Marxist analysis during the 1970s. The position which opposes Poulantzas' structuralism is called 'instrumentalism'. It is itself based on an interpretation of Marx and Engels. Jessop describes it as follows: 'In its least developed form the instrumentalist approach merely involves the claim that the state is not an independent and sovereign political subject but is an instrument of coercion and administration which can be used for various purposes by whatever interests manage to appropriate it' (1982: 12). The state is thus conceived as an empty shell whose existence pre-dates the capitalist mode of production and which is a site for the struggle between classes and class fractions. However, under capitalism, the bourgeoisie holds the whip-hand in such struggles. Here, the cabinet is, for example, conceived of by Marx and Engels as a committee for managing the affairs of the bourgeoisie (Jessop 1982: 12).

The main proponent of the instrumentalist position in the modern period is Miliband (1969; 1983) who argues that: 'an accurate and realistic "model" of the relationship between the dominant class in advanced capitalist societies and the state is one of partnership between two different, separate forces, linked to each other by many threads, yet each having its own separate sphere of concerns' (1983: 72). Miliband's project is to trace each of these connecting threads, mainly the ones between business leaders and political leaders. He establishes the connections in numerous ways, including establishing that:

- Business leaders colonize both political leadership roles and the upper levels of the state bureaucracy.
- They share common values with political leaders by virtue of common socialization experiences.
- They share membership of corporatist boards and commissions with political leaders.

- They 'consult' each other.
- They share memberships in recreational associations and clubs.
- The families of business leaders intermarry with the families of political leaders.
- They provide financial support for political parties.
- They provide taxation support for the state as a whole.

The interests of business leaders therefore become paramount in the operations of the state as a direct consequence of their actions.

Foucault: speaking of power

The above are paradigmatic structuralist arguments in so far as they argue that power is reducible to material structures. However, we noted towards the end of chapter 4 that structuralism was progressively dismantled in favour of a poststructuralist orientation in which the task of the observer is to deconstruct appearances and to establish the historical origins of meaning structures. Although, at that point, we focused on the work of Derrida, the poststructuralist who has had most influence in sociological theory is Foucault. He takes as his principle task, however, not the deconstruction of linguistic structures, but the deconstruction of power structures.

Michel Foucault (1926–84)

Foucault was born in Poitiers, France, the son of a Catholic medical practitioner. He studied at the École Normale Supérieure and the Sorbonne in Paris, at the latter with Hippolyte and Althusser, among others. He became a Communist but left the party in 1951. He taught in Sweden, Poland and Germany before heading the Philosophy Department at the University of Clermont-Ferrand. By the 1960s he had become famous enough to return to Paris where he eventually became Professor of the History of Systems of Thought at the prestigious Collège de France. Foucault would have denied being a sociologist, in his own words he was a 'historian of the present'. He was a leading public intellectual, editing the leftist weekly, *Libération*, and speaking out on penal reform and gay rights. Foucault died of AIDS-related causes.

Source: Merquior (1985)

In fact, no theorist since Marx has radicalized the discussion of power quite as intensively as has Foucault. He is so committed to the point of view of the subjugated that when he addresses the actions of the powerful he does so with distaste and with reluctance. He refuses to view subjugation as the consequence of any disembodied system or of the exchange of power as an alienable resource. He thus refuses absolution to those responsible for subjugation. Power is always something which some people do intentionally to other people and most people will do it at some time in some context.

People control other people largely by means of language, by discursive action which defines the other and restricts the conceptualization of alternative possibilities. However, they also do it by control of the other's body, by specifying its actions in time and space in rules and regulations. Power is therefore diffused throughout society and continuous in its effects.

[P]ower is not to be taken to be a phenomenon of one individual's consolidated and homogeneous domination over others, or that of one group or class over others. . . . Power must by analysed as something which circulates, or rather as something which only functions in the form of a chain. It is never localised here or there, never in anybody's hands, never appropriated as a commodity or piece of wealth. Power is employed and exercised through a net-like organisation. And not only do individuals circulate between its threads; they are always in the position of simultaneously undergoing and exercising this power. . . . In other words, individuals are the vehicles of power, not its points of application [1980: 98]

[P]ower is a total structure of actions brought to bear upon possible actions; it incites, it induces, it seduces, it makes easier or more difficult; in the extreme it constrains or forbids absolutely; it is nevertheless always a way of acting upon an acting subject or acting subjects by virtue of their acting or being capable of action. A set of actions upon other actions. [1982: 220]

This type of power is particularly characteristic of modern, rationalized societies. Its prototype is the prison (1979). Until about the turn of the nineteenth century criminal deviance, so defined, was controlled by public attacks on the offender's body. In extreme cases this might include ripping the body apart by drawing and quartering and indeed the spectacle of public execution was relatively common. For lesser crimes, amputation, branding, or the pillory might be the appropriate means. Foucault identifies such punishments as political rituals. In the society of the eighteenth century and earlier, power was exercised by a sovereign state, from the top down. Crime was an offence against sovereign power and public punishment was a visible expression of that power which would reinforce public belief in it.

In a complete historical turnaround, these public and spectacular punishments disappeared during the course of the first few decades of the nineteenth century. Punishment became secretive and it became kinder. The shift is associated with what is commonly called the modernizing or bourgeois revolution which saw the development of a new and more effective technology of control. Previously only the most public offences against the sovereign were punished and this protected the monarch's 'super-power' status. Now there was a class society in which the key issue was universal compliance with the social order. The solution was incarceration, a system in which offenders were excluded from 'normal' society, rigidly disciplined rather than punished, and observed incessantly so that no transgression was possible. This was 'the birth of the prison'.

Foucault identifies three critical power techniques: discipline, training, and surveillance:

- *Discipline* involves shutting people off, separating them from each other, organizing their time, regimenting their bodily movements in minute detail, keeping them busy, breaking experience up into time-segments, and generally treating the body as if it is a cog in a machine.
- *Training* involves the continuous supervision of activities through a hierarchy of authority, introducing universalistic standards of performance which allow judgements to be 'normalized', and the use of formal examinations to establish whether norms have been met.
- *Surveillance* involves continuous inspection, maximum visibility and, if possible, 'panoptical' architecture (an architecture in which all inmates are continuously but individually visible from a central viewpoint).

So successful was the prison and its associated activities that the technique was extended to provide a generalized pattern of incarceration for a wide range of deviants and possible deviants: the poor were confined to workhouses, lunatics to asylums, the sick to hospitals, children to schools, and workers to factories. The early nineteenth century saw a great 'walling-in' of large segments of the population.

This pattern Foucault calls the 'discipline-blockade' (1979: 209), the establishment of a closed institution which has the negative function of controlling deviance. However, the technology was so effective that it became generalized to become a 'discipline-mechanism', the organization of the entire social fabric on the basis of generalized surveillance so that it becomes 'the disciplinary society'. This development is characterized by three processes:

- the inversion of disciplinary orientations so that discipline is no longer a negative punishment but a positive accomplishment of the good citizen and worker;
- the differentiation of disciplinary techniques into small and flexible packages (e.g. open-plan offices; self-evaluation; professional counsellors; quality circles) which can be exported from one context to another;
- the central organization of discipline by the state, specifically through the police.

A primary example of this, the 'great invention of bourgeois society'

(1980: 105), is the normalization of sexuality (1981). In its prebourgeois manifestations, sex was associated with alliances between kinship groups and so thoroughly embedded as to be a human relationship which was inaccessible to sovereign power. The bourgeois revolution 'liberated' sex from kinship and redefined it as 'sexuality', that is individual, personal, sexual expression. This liberation was, for Foucault, a false representation. The association of sex with sexuality opened it up to disciplinary control and, ultimately, it became a further vehicle for that control. Four strategies were employed:

- *The medicalization of women's bodies* Foucault describes this as 'hysterization', linking women's entire organic and psychological being to the womb, thus defining them by sex and opening them up to expert medical control.
- *The sexualization of children* Experts began to define children's sexuality as normal but unnatural and thus opened up childhood and family life to expert interference.
- *The control of population* The social functions of procreation in relation to population size and environmental effects were recognized, which opens procreative sex to state and expert management.
- *The psychiatric specification of perversion* Distinctions were made between normal and pathological sex and interfering correctives applied to the latter.
  (Foucault 1981: 104–5)

Once decoupled from kinship alliances, sex in its new form of sexuality can carry with it discourses of control. Sexuality becomes one of Foucault's chains of power in which the participants carry with them the knowledge of its truth as that which is defined by medical, psychiatric and social scientific expertise.

> [Sex was] at the pivot of two axes along which developed the entire technology of life. On the one hand it was tied to the disciplines of the body . . . On the other hand, it was applied to the regulation of populations . . . It [gave] rise to infinitesimal surveillances, permanent controls, extremely meticulous orderings of space, indeterminate medical or psychological examinations, to an entire micro-power concerned with the body. . . . Broadly speaking, at the juncture of the 'body' and the 'population', sex became a crucial target of a power organized around the management of life rather than the menace of death. [1981: 145–6]

We can conclude by summarizing the set of general propositions about power that Foucault (1981: 94–5) derives from an examination of these specific complexes of power:

- Power is an aspect of mobile and inegalitarian relationships.

- It is an aspect of all relationships, including nonpolitical ones.
- Major societal dominations are rooted in everyday relationships.
- Power relations are intentional and subjective.
- Resistance is part of any power relationship.

Habermas: the communicationist alternative

Foucault's theory of power presents a major problem to critical theorists. He argues both that it suffuses all relationships through speech and that it increases inevitably. There is no place in Foucault from which a privileged cognoscenti can stand as a critic of society because to speak is to exercise power, especially if one claims to make an authoritative statement. There is, therefore, no possibility or prospect of emancipation in Foucault. Habermas therefore theorizes, in opposition to Foucault, that two types of speech are possible – an ideal, communicative speech in which no control is implied because actors are deliberately seeking to reach understanding, and systematically distorted speech in which one actor seeks to control another by deception.

Habermas' formulation of power draws upon an argument developed by the political philosopher, Arendt, which locates the exercise of power firmly in the context of the consent of the governed. Habermas accepts Arendt's argument that the consent of the governed is an ideal standard for the exercise of power but insists on the possibility that actual social arrangements may fall short of the ideal. We can begin with a brief review of Arendt's view and then move on to address Habermas' revised position.

Arendt's interpretation (1986) is reminiscent of Weber. She draws on ancient conceptions of power which identify it with the rule of law to insist that the concept of power must be restricted to instances of legitimate domination. The exercise of power, whether by a monarch or by a faceless bureaucracy, must always depend on the support of the governed. Power must therefore be distinguished from violence or coercion, in which instruments of force are used to achieve compliance. In a curious formulation she argues that tyranny is 'therefore the most violent and least powerful' form of government: 'The extreme form of power is All against One, the extreme form of violence is One against All' (1986: 63).[7]

Her formal definition of power corresponds with the Parsonsian notion of mobilization of the collectivity in the pursuit of collective goals (see below) but without the rigours of 'binding obligations'.

> Power corresponds to the human ability not just to act but to act in concert. Power is never the property of an individual; it belongs to a group and remains in existence only so long as the group keeps together. When we say of somebody that he is 'in power' we actually refer to his being empowered by a certain number of people to act in their name. The moment the group, from which the power originated to begin with (*potestas in populo*, without a people or group there is no power), disappears, 'his power' also vanishes. [1986: 64, italics deleted]

Arendt's conception is communicationist because of its insistence that power emerges from the establishment of a political community: 'Power springs up whenever people get together and act in concert' (1986: 68). Habermas (1986) endorses this view that power can be defined as: 'the formation of a *common* will in a communication directed to reaching agreement' (1986: 76) but only as a normative standard. It is, however, an absurd and unrealistic view of practical politics. He has two reasons for so arguing: first, Arendt's analysis might indeed successfully be applied to the origins and to the overall legitimacy of political institutions, but it cannot be applied to the acquisition of power within institutions by individuals and groups – powerful position is accomplished not by communicative inter-action but by acting strategically (see chapter 2); second, it is not the case that each individual political decision requires the consent of the governed, rather such decisions are frequently accomplished by the manipulation or persuasion of opinion or simply by overwhelming established practical domination.

Political institutions accomplish this level of domination by building in what Habermas calls structural violence or impositions which manifest themselves as blockages to communication rather than as force.

[I]nconspicuously working communication blocks can explain, perhaps, the formation of ideologies; with [this concept] one can give a plausible account of how convictions are formed in which subjects deceive themselves about themselves and their situation. . . . In systematically restricted communications, those involved form convictions subjectively free from constraint, convictions which are, however, illusionary. They therefore communicatively generate a power which, as soon as it becomes institutionalized, can also be used against them. [1986: 88]

This allows Habermas to maintain a critical stance in relation to contemporary politics while remaining true to a communicationist position. While it is certainly more realistic than Arendt, the argument is contradictory. Habermas simultaneously wants to argue that subjects are fundamentally oriented to truth-value communication and yet are also capable of systematically deceiving themselves. In the final analysis then, Habermas must retreat to a cultural theory of power which derogates actors by constructing them as ideological dupes.

Functionalism and constructionism: power as politics

In this section we consider approaches to power which regard it as an independent and substantive capacity. Here power cannot be reduced to economic ownership, nor is it viewed as an aspect of relationships. Rather, power is viewed as a virtual substance which can be exchanged, accumulated, distributed and concentrated. Individuals have greater or lesser amounts of power by virtue of their location in organizations which generate it. Government or the state or politics is often viewed as the primary organizational site within which power becomes available. Here, power theorists owe much to classical elite theory as the source of their arguments, principally in view of that theory's claim that there must be some concentration of power in society if decisions are to be reached and activities to be coordinated at all. They also draw on Weber's constructionist theme that power is often exercised within the context of a normative agreement about the legitimacy of power differentiation. We begin with that paradigmatic functionalist, Parsons (see chapter 5).

Parsons: a classical economy of power

Parsons (1970; 1986; also see Giddens 1977) establishes the distinctiveness of his approach by setting himself against Marxist analyses, particularly that of Mills. For him, the particular problem in the Marxist 'relational' view of power is that power is viewed as a 'zero-sum' concept – the degree of domination which one class has is exactly balanced by an equal degree of subordination for the other which when added together totals zero. Instead, Parsons proposes that we can conceive of power as an infinitely expandable resource, similar to an economic resource. The basis for this view is the observation that, as societies become more complex, there is a clear increase in the level of transformative capacity, the ability to alter the physical and social world. Parsons, then, understands power as transformative capacity ('power to') rather than control ('power over').

The site for this transformative capacity is the *polity*, a term he prefers to 'the state'. By this Parsons does not mean a concrete, substantive, social system, such as the government, but rather: 'the ways in which the relevant components of the total system are organized with reference to . . . effective collective action in the attainment of the goals of collectivities' (1986: 96). However, because the government organizes collective action in the pursuit of the goals of the society as a whole, it is the primary site of power. In an important statement, Parsons discusses power as the medium by means of which the polity operates: 'I conceive power as . . . a generalized medium in a sense directly parallel in logical structure, though very different substantively, to money as the generalized medium of the economic process.' (1986: 97). Indeed, as is discussed in chapter 8, Parsons identifies four such generalized media of exchange: money, power, influence and commitment. Just as the economy uses money to combine the factors of production (land, labour, capital) to increase the level of economic resources, the polity uses power to combine decision-making factors (contributions, demands and legitimating values) to increase transformative capacity.

The possibility for such an increase in transformative capacity lies in the fact that power can be aggregated, accumulated and invested much like money can. The act of voting in an election, for example, is conceived to be analagous with choosing where to bank your money. Each elector is understood to have a small amount of power which is transferred at election time to political leaders, and then passed back, presumably in a valorized form, when a subsequent election is called. In giving up their power, each elector confers on political leaders the right to impose disadvantages, including coercive disadvantages, on those who do not comply with political directives. The act of voting confers legitimacy on political power.

This notion of legitimation locates Parsons' conception of power as coterminous with Weber's conception of authority. Parsons is arguing that the greater the extent to which power is authorized the more power there will be.[8]

Parsons' general orientation to power is summarized in the following definition:

> Power is the generalized capacity to secure the performance of binding obligations by units in a system of collective organization when the obligations are legitimized with reference to their bearing on collective goals and where in case of recalcitrance there is a presumption of enforcement by negative situational sanctions – whatever the actual agency of that enforcement. [1986: 103]

Mann: four sources of power

One of the most cited and celebrated arguments about power in the 1980s is Mann's attempt to offer a history of power. Because it is a major investigation of historical developments in the distribution and application of power throughout human history Mann (1986: 6) specifically foreswears any theoretical or conceptual analysis. Yet the theoretical origins of his approach are explicit. Power, he argues, emerges constantly in human history because: 'Power is, to use Talcott Parsons' expression, a "generalized means" for attaining whatever goals one wants to achieve' ; or slightly more precisely, it is: 'the ability to pursue and attain goals through mastery of one's [social] environment' (1986: 6). Mann appears to set himself against Parsons in claiming that power is dualistic – it is, he claims, both 'distributive' (Marxist) and 'collective' (Parsonsian) (1986: 6) or in other terms 'authoritative' and 'diffused' (1986: 7–8). However, this claim is a conceit, because he always stresses the Parsonsian pole of the argument. For Mann, power is indeed a resource rather than an aspect of relationships and it is a resource generated in organizations.

Mann (1986: 22–8) identifies four such organizational sources of power:

- *Ideological* power derives from the fact that human beings want to operate in terms of meanings, norms and rituals and it is ideologies which meet these wants. Ideological power can be 'transcendent', that is standing apart from society in a sacred way (religion and certain political ideologies are examples), or 'immanent', that is diffused throughout society as the group cohesion which derives from a sense of shared membership.

- *Economic* power derives from production, distribution, exchange and consumption. It is expressed through a class structure and consists in 'circuits of praxis', everyday patterns of labour.
- *Military* power derives from competition for physical survival and aggrandizement. It produces direct control within a concentrated centre and indirectly coerces surrounding areas.
- *Political* power derives from the control of territory and its populations by centrally administered regulation and sanction. It is concentrated in the state. It has two sociospatial aspects: territorial centralization and geopolitical diplomacy.

Power networks, sets of institutionalized relationships, formate on one or another of these sources to varying degrees, sometimes overlapping and sometimes competing. In the closest he comes to a theory of the direction of power development, Mann indicates a quasi-dialectical process in which:

the most powerful of the networks become(s) institutionalized as dominant
→ other networks are partially merged into them
→ some entire networks and parts of dominant networks remain 'interstitial'
→ interaction between these interstitial elements eventually will produce an emergent more powerful network.

The most powerful development in human history which follows this pattern is, for Mann, the development of Western civilization, although he is unwilling (or unable) to provide theoretical grounds for that success: 'it just happened that way' (1986: 31).

Although Mann might appear to be a theoretical accidentalist, we must remember that his own claim is merely to undertake a historical sociology. The reasons that his work finds an important place in any general account of power are that he widens the context beyond capitalism and liberal democracy and that he offers an extended treatment of military sources of power unavailable elsewhere in sociology.

Field and Higley: the power of a common position

For Field and Higley (1973; 1980) the issue of whether power is exercised communicatively is empirical but they are in no doubt that it is generated strategically. In their revivalist treatment of elite theory, elites are defined precisely by the occupancy of strategic positions in bureaucratic organizations because it is here that power, defined as: 'the ability to make offers and threats that are likely to alter the motivations of [other] persons', 'normally inheres' (1973: 8). They are most interested in national rather than local elites, so the organizations that matter are those: 'that are large or otherwise powerful enough to enable the persons who command them to influence the outcomes of national policies individually, regularly and seriously' (1980: 20).[9]

In so far as elites are linked to the emergence of bureaucratic organizations, they are a peculiarly modern phenomenon. But they are also claimed to be universal throughout modern societies for another, explicitly functionalist reason. The cultural understandings which unite societies are always rough and ambiguous. In particular, there is in large collectivities no possibility of a common commitment to the particular and detailed features of organization and policy. Complex societies 'need' persons to make authoritative and arbitrary decisions, in Habermas' terminology, to steer them, and elites fit the bill.

Beyond the existence of elites, Field and Higley make no claim to universality in terms of such features as opinion, integration, recruitment, etc. which they regard as contingent. However, there is some relationship between the level of development of a society and its elite structure. They specify four levels of economic development of modern society in terms of the sectoral distribution of the labour force and the political values adhered to by the mass:

1   workforce almost entirely primary production — *egalitarian mass*;
2   minority of workforce in industrial workshops, majority in agriculture; incipient bureaucracy of social control (police, etc.) — *egalitarian mass*;
3   about half of workforce in agricultural employment; growth of industry and administrative public service — *mass has mixed political orientations*;
4   plurality of workers non-manual; small minority in agriculture — *managerialist mass*.
    (Field and Higley 1980: 21–32)

Against these they juxtapose types of elite characterized by their form of integration:

• A *disunified* elite is characterized by multiple factionalism.
• An *imperfectly unified* elite consists of two main factions, egalitarian and anti-egalitarian.
• An *ideologically unified* elite is characterized by a common conception of how society ought to be.
• A *consensually unified* elite is characterized by differing ideological positions but agreement on power sharing between adherents to differing ideologies.

The possible distributions of elite patterns across the four levels of

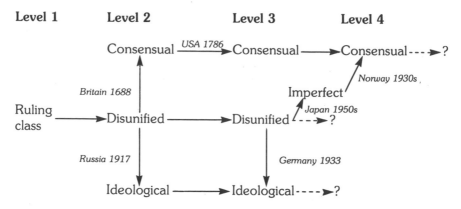

Figure 7.2   *Field and Higley's theory of elite development (Field and Higley 1980: 42, simplified)*

development is shown in figure 7.2. The implication is that elite structures must be compatible with the type of organization required at a given level of development and with the orientations and attitudes of the non-elite. As in all the theories in this section the value-implication is an apology for liberal democracy in so far as disproportionate power holding is claimed to be necessary and in so far as the 'consensual unified' form is claimed to be an evolved outcome with superior survival capacity.

Utilitarianism: power as individual performance

This set of theories accepts Parsons' view that power is potentially distributed widely throughout society and that it is not aggregated entirely into legitimated state authority. Thus there is continuous contest and struggle in society about domination and resistance which produces temporary alliances, working compromises, coalitions of convenience, and other deals. While power is argued to be present in all social relationships, the orientation is very different from that of Foucault. It is the work of American political scientists who are united by the view that power differences emerge within interaction from the intentions of agents persuing their individual interests.

Dahl: making decisions

The key focus for debate about power in political science appears to have been the issue of the concentration of power rather than its substance. The paradigm which has dominated this debate in the post-Second-World-War period has been a behaviourist and relational model. Its opening question,

'What does it mean to say that person A has power over person B?', draws on an assumption that power resides in individual persons and thus invites an analysis of A's action in relation to B. The question tends to be followed by two supplementaries: 'How do you measure power?' and 'What can you discover about its concentration when you do?' The object of the original two questions is to get to the third, but the assumptions of the originals predetermine the answers to the consequent questions. That is, if power is believed to be distributed to individuals and is characteristic of any relationship, the researcher will always discover a pluralistic distribution of power.

The starting point for the debate was a study of the distribution of power in Atlanta, Georgia by Hunter (1953). In an America seeking to convince itself of an ideology of individualized freedom, Hunter had the conviction to argue that Atlanta was run by a single, integrated elite of politicians and businessmen. However, his Achilles' heel was that he used a reputational methodology, asking prominent members of the community to identify who had power. Not surprisingly, they identified publicly prominent people much like themselves, often people that they knew personally.

This weakness was quickly pounced upon by Dahl (1961) in a study of the community power structure of New Haven, Connecticut. Here Dahl identified central issue areas on which one might expect power to be exercised, isolated the key decisions within those areas, and then discovered who was influencing the decisions. Here then, power exists not in so far as it is recognized but in so far as it is exercised. Since power is exercised intermittently, to the extent that an issue has relevance for a given individual or group, Dahl discovered a pluralistic power structure in which power was apparently divided between differentiated actors and groups.

Dahl used his study to mount a generalized attack on power elite models of the type proposed separately by Mills and Hunter. In so doing he developed a quite specific theoretical approach to power. In an early paper he spells out exactly what he 'understands' by the term power: 'A has power over B to the extent that he can get B to do something B would not otherwise do' (1957: 203). Note that this definition implies:

- *agency* – A has to act and B must respond;
- *relationship* – the action must be toward B; and
- *behaviourism* – there is no reference to subjective meaning, only to individual gratification.

The last characteristic is emphasized in so far as Dahl indicates that power is a subtype of causal relationship: 'For the assertion "[A] has power over [B]", one can substitute the assertion, "[A's] behavior causes [B's] behavior"' (1986: 46).[10] A's behaviour is conceived by Dahl as stimulus and B's as response. Dahl appears to be less interested in why B should respond in a particular way to A's stimulus.

In his later work, Dahl generalizes his discussion of power to what he calls the family of influence terms – control, influence, power, authority, domination, persuasion, inducement, coercion and force (1991). He now appears to want to substitute the term 'influence' for 'power' by defining influence as: 'a relation among actors such that the wants, desires, preferences or intentions of one or more actors affect the actions or predispositions to act of one or more other actors.' (1991: 32). 'Power' itself becomes a subtype of influence, that in which: 'compliance is obtained by creating the prospect of severe sanctions for non-compliance' (1991: 42). However, in the remainder of this exegesis we shall continue to use the term 'power' in the earlier, more general sense.

Power varies in several dimensions, including:

- *magnitude* – the amount of power an actor has;
- *distribution* – the number of actors across which power is dispersed or concentrated;
- *scope* – the extent to which power is restricted to specialized activities; and
- *domain* – the extent to which power is restricted to certain groups of subordinates.
  (Dahl 1986: 41–3; 1991: 21–6)

Dahl's main focus is the distribution of power – for example, we note above his interest in asserting the existence of a pluralistic distribution of power in mid-twentieth-century USA. The vehicle by which he examines this issue is the emergence of a new form of popular, representative government in the seventeenth and eighteenth centuries. The political system into which this form evolves is called 'polyarchy' which is defined in terms of seven characteristics:

- control over government decisions by elected officials;
- free, fair and unconstrained elections;
- the right of virtually all adults to vote;
- the universal right to run for public office;
- freedom of political expression;
- freedom of access to information; and
- freedom of political association.
  (Dahl 1991: 71–94)

In a polyarchy, differences in the magnitude of political power between individuals are reduced; the scope of power also tends to reduce; the domain extends; and power is distributed more widely. Polyarchies will emerge in 'modern, dynamic, pluralist societies', that is, where economic development is at a high level and growing, and where the level of societal differentiation is such as to generate a wide range of relatively independent interest groups. These characteristics will tend to disempower police and military organizations and thus reduce the possibility of a nonpolyarchal or authoritarian regime.

Bachrach and Baratz: not making decisions

Dahl's arguments themselves unleashed a furious debate in American political science. The main focus for opposition to Dahl was his insistence on behaviouristic agency, that for A to be powerful A must pro-act in relation to B. Dahl appeared to fail to take into account situations in which B acts in ways in which A would prefer without A having to provide the stimulus. Indeed, one of the processes identified in psychological behaviourism is stimulus generalization, in which individuals begin to find responses intrinsically rewarding and tend to enact them without stimulus. It might, in fact, be argued that any A is more powerful where B conforms without the necessity of applying a stimulus.

The main proponents of this alternative position are Bachrach and Baratz (1962; 1963; 1970). They argue that power has two faces:

> Of course power is exercised when A participates in the making of decisions that affect B. But power is also exercised when A devotes his energies to creating or reinforcing social and political values and institutional practices that limit the scope of the political process to public consideration of only those issues which are comparatively innocuous to A. To the extent that A succeeds in doing this, B is prevented, for all practical purposes, from bringing to the fore any issues that might in their resolution be seriously detrimental to A's set of preferences. [1962: 949]

This second face of power, nondecision-making, involves two processes: the mobilization of bias, making sure that issues which might be significant to some groups never enter the decision-making process; and 'organizing out', that is excluding opposing interest groups from the decision-making process.

Bachrach and Baratz agree that power is relational rather than resource-based. However, their definition differs from that of Dahl by taking nondecisions into account:

> A power relationship exists when (a) there is a conflict over values or courses of action between A and B; (b) B complies with A's wishes; and (c) B does so because he is fearful that A will deprive him of a value or values which he regards more highly than those which would have been achieved by noncompliance. [1970: 24]

Compliance can be accomplished either by decisions or nondecisions. Bachrach and Baratz's contribution is to identify the latter as a central component of power. They are processes by which demands for change can be stifled, excluded, hidden, killed-off, or emasculated before they can effectively be expressed (1970: 44). However, Bachrach and Baratz's orientation is fundamentally similar to Dahl's in that power remains at the level of subjective wants and desires rather than at the level of objective interests.

Polymorphic power

Lukes: three dimensions of power

Lukes (1974) argues that none of the above discussions of power is adequate because none covers all the aspects of power which one can identify. In particular, he criticizes the 'one-dimensional' view of Dahl and the 'two-dimensional' view of Bachrach and Baratz on the grounds that each is too individualistic and behaviouristic. Instead he argues, much in the fashion of Marx, Poulantzas and Foucault, that society is entirely suffused by power which not only affects the capacity of individuals to realize their wants and desires but actually constructs their wants and desires for them.

The three dimensions of power which Lukes identifies can be located in relation to the arguments of the American political scientists.

- The first is Dahl's single dimension: 'the making of decisions on issues over which there is an observable conflict of (subjective) interests' (Lukes 1974: 15, italics deleted).
- The second is Bachrach and Baratz's nondecisions: 'the ways in which decisions are prevented from being taken on potential issues over which there is an observable conflict of (subjective) interests' (1974: 20, italics deleted).
- The third is Lukes' own addition, although it is highly reminiscent of Poulantzas and Habermas. It consists of: 'the many ways in which potential issues are kept out of politics whether through the operation of social forces or individual decisions' under conditions of 'latent conflict which consists of a contradiction between the interests of those exercising power and the real interests of those they exclude' (1974: 24–5, italics deleted).

Lukes argues that an assertion of the first dimension is associated with a conservative value position, of the second with a commitment to reform, and of the third with a commitment to radical restructuring.

The fact that Lukes parenthesizes the word 'subjective' in each of the first two dimensions and then uses the adjective 'real' in the third, indicates that using interests in the definition of power is a tricky issue. His own definition is couched precisely in terms of interests: 'A exercises power over B when A affects B in a manner contrary to B's interests' (1974: 34). However, as he admits: 'In general, talk of interests provides a licence for the making of normative judgements of a moral and political character'

(1974: 34). The difficulties he faces are illustrated by his own definition of interests, given elsewhere, which suggests that they have two components, each of them clearly subjective. They are: 'a person's more ultimate goals and aspirations'; and his interests 'in the necessary means to his more ultimate goals, whatever the latter may be, or later may come to be' (1986: 6).

Lukes, like Poulantzas and Habermas, finds himself in a cleft stick: he must either accept that interests are goals and aspirations which can only subjectively be determined, or he must accept the responsibility of privileged knowledge of the true interests of others and thus for determining what is good for them. He clearly does not want to accept the latter, with its implicit foundationalism and necessary resort to the concept of 'false consciousness', but if he accepts the former, his third dimension will be subsumed by the second. The issue remains unresolved.

Clegg: going around in circuits of power

Clegg (1989) virtually takes Lukes' three dimensions of power and reifies them as circuits. Circuits are channels through which power relationships must pass. The model has three characteristics. First, it conceives of power as located in organizations. Second, it conceives of power as manifested as varying levels of 'strategic agency', an ability to take control of resource flows and to use them to realize one's own interests. Third, it conceives of power as at least partially contingent on patterns of agency.

> In the circuits framework, power is multifarious: it is episodic power; it is also the circuit of power through rules and domination, as well as the overall empirical articulation which configures the theoretical circuits in any application of the model. [1989: 215]

Clegg therefore describes the three circuits as follows:

- *Episodic agency power* (cf. Dahl) This is the circuit of enacted struggle in which agencies (individuals and organizational units) mobilize context and resources in order to affect outcomes which will realize their own interests and thwart those of others.
- *Dispositional power* (cf. Bachrach and Baratz) This is the circuit of relatively institutionalized power relations which comprises rules of meaning and membership and the specification of passage points through which resources are obliged to flow.
- *Facilitative power* This is the underlying circuit of the distribution of meanings (cf. Foucault) and resources (cf. Poulantzas).

The circuits articulate with one another in the fashion described in figure 7.3 and here a contradiction arises. There is a clockwise flow of influences which would tend to suggest equal and contingent effectivity for each of the

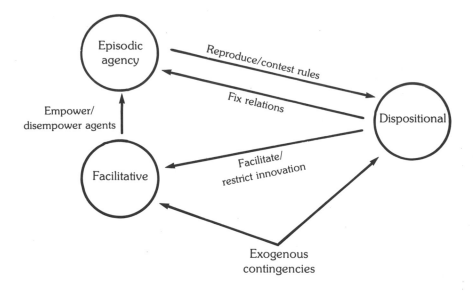

Figure 7.3   *Clegg's three circuits of power*

circuits. If anything, dispositional power appears the most effective because it influences the other two circuits while itself only being influenced by agency. Yet Clegg also argues that: 'The circuit of facilitative power is the major conduit of variation in the circuits of power' (1989: 233). If facilitating resources are the source of change then they must be determinative. Clegg's worthy theoretical instincts appear to render him unable to accept the uncertainties of contingency and so the argument collapses into a quasi-Marxist account which asserts that contradiction in the arena of the production of facilities is the main source of change in power systems.[11]

Conclusion

Summary

1   The founding theoretical arguments about power take one of two positions. In the first, exemplified by Marx, power is viewed as a fundamental structural relationship that is universally present, that is an aspect of groups rather than individuals, and that operates below the level of intention and recognition. In the second position, exemplified by Weber and the classical elite theorists, power is intentional and is sourced in the actions of individuals.

2   Critical structuralist theories of power draw their inspiration from

Marx. For them society is fundamentally organized in power terms. The typical neoMarxist formulation is that society is structured in terms of a ruling class and a subordinate class and that the formations of the state and politics are determined by these fundamental structures. In poststructuralist and communicationist versions, power is even more deeply embedded in the way members of society speak to one another.

3   The heirs to Weber and to classical elite theories view power as an enabling resource, similar to money. In the purely functionalist tradition, Parsons views the aggregation of power as a necessary condition for the organization of a large-scale and complex society. Within a more constructionist tradition of elitism, elite formation is equally regarded as a necessity, even if a slightly distasteful necessity. For each, concentrations of power are the consequence of widespread societal compromises and agreements.

4   There is also a radical utilitarian theory of power, available in American political science, that argues that power differences are the consequence of struggles between individuals seeking to realize their wants. Here power is the consequence of two types of behaviour: making decisions, and intentionally restricting access to decision-making.

5   There have been two attempts to synthesize these disparate arguments about power. For both Lukes and Clegg the key positions are critical structuralist and utilitarian theories. Ultimately, each gives the greatest weight to a critical structuralist position in which power differences are viewed as the consequence of a structural pattern of material resource distributions.

Critique

As Lukes says: 'in our ordinary unreflective judgements and comparisons of power, we normally know what we mean and have little difficulty in understanding one another, yet every attempt at a single general answer to the question has failed and seems likely to fail' (1986: 17). There would appear to be two types of failure. Most of the theories reviewed here might be described as 'what about?' failures. They claim that power is a unitary concept grounded in a single foundation of structure or agency. The problem is that critics can always find instances of the application of power which do not fit the proposed explanation. The following are examples:

• Poulantzas must grant 'relative autonomy' to a state which gives the appearance of making independent decisions.
• Miliband grants so much autonomy to the state that he has difficulty in demonstrating that the bourgeoisie can still control the state even if a working-class political party is in power.
• Foucault fails to recognize differential power concentrations and thus

the effects of grand structures of domination, the state and the business corporation; and, although he argues that resistance is present in all power relationships, he fails to demonstrate how, or even to allow that, it is in principle possible for resistance to result in emancipation.

- Arendt says that naked force is not power at all and misses the possibility that power does not have to be exercised to exist.
- Habermas equally can only find applications of power in distortion and self-deception and finds no place for its direct application.
- Parsons conflates power with authority and thus denies the possibility of naked force.
- Field and Higley see power as concentrated only in organizations and miss it as an aspect of everyday relationships.
- Dahl can see only the direct application of power by individuals.
- Bachrach and Baratz fail to recognize deep-seated and unintentional power differences.

The theories of Lukes and Clegg fail on slightly different grounds – they are 'house of cards' failures. They begin by claiming to do all things and then collapse into partial statements which focus on deep-seated structures.

Further reading

Key extracts from most of the theoretical statements covered here can be found in Steven Lukes (ed.), *Power* (1986). They are also summarized in his chapter 'Power and authority' (1978) and in Clegg's *Frameworks of Power* (1989). On classical elite theory see Parry, *Political Elites* (1969).

Poulantzas' key statements on power are in *Political Power and Social Classes* (1973) and *State, Power, Socialism* (1978) while Miliband's is in *The State in Capitalist Society* (1969). Their debate about the relative autonomy of the state can be found in Blackburn (ed.), *Ideology in Social Science* (1972) and is summarized by Jessop in *The Capitalist State* (1982). Foucault's arguments about power are in *Discipline and Punish* (1979) and *Power/Knowledge* (1980).

The best approach to Parsons' theory of power is via the chapter on the subject by Giddens in his *Studies in Social and Political Theory* (1977). A standard reading in this area is Mann's *The Sources of Social Power* (1986). The key readings for the remaining authors covered in this chapter are: Dahl *Who Governs?* (1961); Bachrach and Baratz *Power and Poverty* (1970); and Lukes *Power: A Radical View* (1974).

Notes

1 For an extended discussion of the conflict–consensus debate see Cohen (1968).
2 This is most apparent at the point at which labour inputs to products are reduced by the

application of inanimate sources of power via technology. So the value of a car built in a highly automated plant is no different from one built in a traditional assembly line plant with high labour inputs. Nor can it be shown, as is occasionally argued by Marxists, that the labour value of producing automatic machinery plus the labour value of producing the car in an automated fashion is equivalent to the labour value of producing a car on an assembly-line basis.

3 This analysis of Weber's conceptualization of power terms owes much to Lukes (1978).

4 There is a considerable debate about the translation of Weber's definition. The debate centres on whether the most commonly accepted translation, the one used here by Parsons and Henderson, represents a particularly interpretivist reading. After an exhaustive exploration of the issue, Walliman et al. provide the following, rather awkward translation: 'Within a social relationship, *power* means every chance (no matter whereon this chance is based) to carry through the own will (*even* against resistance)' (1980: 264, original italics).

5 *Herrschaft* is translated frequently as 'authority', a term which specifically implies not merely obedience by the governed but their active collaboration in the legitimation of its exercise. This translation is preferred by Parsons *inter alia*, allowing him to develop the conception of power described below. For Weber, *Herrschaft* can be either legitimate or nonlegitimate. The term 'authority' is best confined to legitimate domination.

6 The term, 'military-industrial complex', was actually coined by the right-wing Republican President of the USA and former general, Dwight D. Eisenhower, who must have known something about it.

7 As might be guessed, Arendt faces some difficulty in defining 'authority' as a separate concept. Authority, she says, is vested in persons (cf. Weber's charismatic domination) or offices (cf. rational-legal domination) and involves 'unquestioning recognition' by those asked to obey. However, the problem is that she has already defined power, as a whole, in terms of consent (1986: 62) which leaves little separate conceptual space for authority.

8 Such a conception would present some difficulty if one was to compare a totalitarian political regime with a democratic one.

9 Field and Higley's conceptualization is at odds, in one respect, with conventional semantics. In their analysis, elites are individual persons rather than parts or sections of societies or organizations.

10 This is, to say the least, an unusual use of the expression 'causal relationship'. Surely the cause of the B's behaviour is not A's behaviour but certain situational preconditions which place them in that relationship. Dahl is trivializing the notion of cause.

11 This is all the more surprising, given that in a work which is primarily exegetical there is no systematic treatment of either Marx or Poulantzas.

8   Gender and feminism

One of the most extraordinary characteristics of contemporary social theory is that, while it consistently attempts to make general statements about human society, it overlooks its most general and universal fact. This is the fact of universal gender difference and inequality. It is perhaps the most startling evidence of the effectiveness of patriarchal domination that the social science which specializes in questions to do with human differentiation and inequality has remained blind to, or possibly conspired in the concealment of, this fact. While every other aspect of society has been theorized at a social level, as the product of social or material structural constraints or of human construction, gender has traditionally been assumed to be a 'natural' phenomenon which did not need to be explained, which could be conceptualized as 'sex'.

Even under the current circumstances in which gender has assumed its rightful place as a topic for sociological theorizing, the origins of such theory lie largely outside the discipline. Social theories of gender arise largely from the practical concerns of women's movements rather than from attempts to complete theoretical projects in sociology – gender theory is largely feminist theory. There are two consequences. First, sociological theories of the gender dimension tend to be fragmentary and short – unlike the extensive philosophical feminist literature. This chapter is based on small pieces of theory, often only the length of an article, which have little coherent relationship to one another. Second, theorizing about gender is unintegrated relative to sociological theory in general. The authors covered here are not, in the main, covered in the other chapters of this book. They are excluded voices which are making only the first moves in the direction of a developed theoretical position.

For these reasons, identifying a theoretical orthodoxy is far more hazardous than in the cases of the other dimensions of social life which we address in this book. Nevertheless, if we were to attempt to identify the central elements of a contemporary sociological theory of gender, they would probably include the following, although there would not be universal agreement on all of them:

1   Differentiation by sex or gender is universal across societies.
2   This differentiation is pervasive throughout any individual society, extending to families, economic arrangements, political arrangements, religion, recreation, artistic production, etc.
3   A conceptual distinction must be maintained between 'sex' and

'gender'. Sex refers to biological characteristics which are bimodally distributed across any natural population and whose categories are female and male. Gender refers to social identities and expectations which are socially constructed often in relation to real or assumed sex characteristics. Its categories are feminine and masculine, or woman and man.

4 In recognizing this distinction, sociological theory has developed away from theories of gender which specify it in terms of sex-roles and towards a consideration of gendered social structures.

5 Gender inequality is also universal across societies. This gender inequality always takes the form of masculine domination. The term most frequently used for masculine domination is 'patriarchy.'

6 Theories of patriarchy often rely on a distinction between 'private' and 'public' spheres of social life. The former consists of domestic and familial activities, while the latter refers to nonfamilial economic and political activities in particular. The maintenance of the distinction and its association with the woman/man distinction often leads to a reification of social gender in which the public contributions of women and the domestic contributions of men remain unrecognized.

7 Patriarchy is supported and reproduced by religious, symbolic, linguistic and cultural systems which exclude or devalue femininity. In patriarchal societies, women are therefore made not only materially but morally inferior to men.

This chapter begins by examining theoretical statements by male sociologists on the topic of gender. Here it will be shown that sociological theory traditionally holds to the view that gender differentiation is inevitable and that there is no such thing as gender inequality, although it also discusses the exceptional contribution of Engels. We then move on to examine some mid-twentieth-century feminist arguments which lay the foundations for a challenge to these views, specifically those of de Beauvoir, Friedan and Millett.[1] Thereafter the chapter reviews contemporary contributions to the sociological theory of gender which fit broadly within critical structuralist and constructionist traditions. It closes with a brief discussion on some recent poststructuralist theories of gender difference which in many respects stand opposed to sociological arguments.

Malestream theory

Feminist sociologists often use the term 'malestream' to describe the dominating centre or mainstream of the discipline. In so doing they are suggesting either that it is either blind to gender or that it views gender differences and subordination as 'natural' and therefore as not needing a sociological explanation. This examination of malestream theory is divided into two sections. The first looks at the fragments of nineteenth-century theory which have anything to say about the topic. The second looks at contemporary developments.

Foundations

Here we examine three nineteenth-century founding arguments. The first two are broadly constructionist arguments from the English anthropologist Maine, and from Max Weber. Each of these takes a complacent and noncritical approach to gender. The third comes from Marx's friend and collaborator, Engels. Engels is less malestream than most because he is at least critical about the subordination of women in society. His work is therefore often incorporated into contemporary feminist thought. However, he is often regarded, nevertheless, as malestream because he subordinates the causes of gender differences to the operations of masculine structures of capitalism.

Maine: subordination by contract

One of the first treatments of gender domination comes in the work of Maine, a nineteenth-century anthroplogist. Maine's significance is that he introduces the term 'patriarchy' in his account of the evolution of legal systems (1963). The analysis falls well short of modern scientific standards of anthropological and sociological research. It shares with much nineteenth-century British social scientific thought the view that society was the culmination of centuries of evolutionary development. However, the conceptual treatment given to structural change is in fact sophisticated relative to the social context in which it was produced.

Maine argues that prior to the institutionalization of modern law, society was constituted by families which were universally patriarchal in character (1963: 118–19). On the basis of Biblical sources, he outlines the dimensions of patriarchal organization:

> The eldest male parent – the eldest ascendent – is absolutely supreme in his household. His dominion extends to life and death, and is as unqualified over his children and their houses as over his slaves; indeed the relations of sonship and serfdom appear to differ little beyond the capacity which the child in blood possesses of becoming one day the head of a family himself. [1963: 118]

Because patriarchal families were economic units, they were imperialistic, constantly seeking to increase their lands and their labour supply by conquest and by adoption. They could therefore grow into communities and even rudimentary states but the cohesive bond remained common obedience to the oldest living male ascendent.

Ancient Roman law is a characteristic initial development out of patriarchy. Here women became, in effect, 'daughters' to their husbands at marriage. They could be disciplined and governed by their husbands without the hindrance of legal or state protections. By contrast, in modern (i.e. nineteenth-century) law unmarried women are formally free and only married women were subjugated to the will of their husbands. In formal terms, by the nineteenth century, women were voluntarily submitting to the will of men by means a contractual arrangement between the individuals involved. Women thus no longer had the status of possessed objects. Maine interprets this change as part of a more general movement from the normative specification of relationships on the basis of *status* to specification based on *contract* (1963: 165).

Maine, with not a small measure of self-righteous satisfaction, relates that in nineteenth-century England, as elsewhere, the legacy of this conjugal arrangement was that:

> Ancient law subordinates the woman to her blood-relations, while a prime phenomenon of modern jurisprudence has been her subordination to her husband. . . . The status of the Female under tutelage, if the tutelage be understood of persons other than her husband has . . . ceased to exist; from her coming of age to her marriage all the relations she may form are relations of contract.[2] [Maine 1963: 149, 164]

Weber: patriarchalism

As the founding figure in constructionist social theory, Weber's interest in gender is restricted to its development as a system of organizational domination rather than as a general structure of power. For this reason, Weber uses the term 'patriarchal*ism*' rather than 'patriarchy'. He regards patriarchalism as the most elementary example of his category, traditional domination (see p. 223), the situation in which claims to domination are made on the basis of the customary establishment of rules and powers.

> 'Patriarchalism' is the situation where, within a group (household) which is usually organized on both an economic and a kinship basis, a particular individual governs who is designated by a particular rule of inheritance. Gerontocracy and patriarchalism are frequently found side by side. [1978: 231]

Patriarchalism is a strictly limited type of domination within a highly elaborated typology of organizational forms. It occurs only where the patriarch exercises authority solely within his own household. It may be contrasted with two other forms: 'gerontocracy', where a patriarch or a group of patriarchs rules outside the household; and 'patrimonial bureaucracy', where this extension of domination is achieved by the employment and maintenance of a personal staff tied to the ruler by benefices rather than by ties of kinship.

Under patriarchalism, the power of the patriarch is unconstrained. Within the household, women and children constitute property – women, Weber argues, are dependent: 'because of the normal superiority of the physical and intellectual energies of the male' (1978: 1007). Like Maine,

Weber views the status of related women and children under patriarchy as little different from the status of slave, capable of being bought, sold, rented, and mortgaged. He also appears to accept Maine's view of a gradual differentiation of these two statuses in ancient Rome and a progressive formal liberation of women and children from patriarchal domination.

Engels: owning women

By contrast with Weber's constructionist view, the orientation of critical structuralist thought on the issue of gender is the view that the oppression of women is an aspect of the class structure. Control of private property not only allows some men to control other men but also allows all men to control women. The confinement of women to the domestic sphere means that they toil to ensure the reproduction of the system – they breed, rear and educate new workers and they feed and emotionally sustain worker-husbands. In addition, women constitute a reserve army of labour which can be brought into the system in time of war or when production expands and then just as readily cast back into the domestic sphere. The existence of such a reserve army also serves the interests of the ruling class by diluting the bargaining power of male labour.

This male domination originates in the institution of property. Marx himself did not write extensively on women but his collaborator Engels did construct a primitive anthropology of the family which has become an important foundation for socialist feminist theory (1975). Engels accepts from Morgan, a contemporary anthropologist, the view that prehistory may be conceived as a series of stages. These are set out in figure 8.1.

The first stage, savagery, corresponds with 'primitive communism' or what would now be called 'forager' (hunter–gatherer) societies. Here, not only is property owned communally but conjugal relationships are conducted on a free and open basis. There is no means here by which one gender can dominate the other. Subordination emerges later alongside

Stage	Marriage form	Gender pattern
Savagery	Group marriage	Differentiated (men hunt, women gather) but equal
Barbarism	Pairing marriage/ concubinage/ polygyny	Women as property in the patriarchal family
Civilization	Monogamy	Conjugal female subordination

Figure 8.1 *Engels on stages in the development of conjugal relationships*

private property, within a second stage called 'barbarism'. Here the ownership of pastoral flocks and of agricultural land becomes a critical source of power. Men establish patriarchal families which can aggregate holdings of land, animals and slaves (Engels 1975: 121). Marriage consists of polygynous and concubinal pairing which is under the absolute control of men. In this stage: 'In order to make certain of the wife's fidelity and therefore the paternity of her children, she is delivered over unconditionally into the power of the husband; if he kills her, he is exercising his rights' (Engels 1975: 122).

Friedrich Engels (1820–95)

Engels was born in Barmen near Düsseldorf, Germany, to a prosperous business family which made its fortune in textiles. He studied philosophy in Berlin and joined a radical group there, known as the Young Hegelians, an earlier member of which had been Karl Marx. However, Engels did not meet Marx until later, when he wrote articles for *Neue Rheinische Zeitung*, the revolutionary newspaper of which Marx was the editor. He visited England in the 1840s where the condition of industrial workers affected him deeply. He then moved to Brussels where he developed a close association with Marx. He continued to run the family business, which interfered with his political activities, but at least allowed him to subsidize his lifelong collaborator.

Source: McLellan (1977)

The subordination of women reaches its lowest ebb within monogamy, under what Engels describes as the transfer of mother-right to father-right, that is the transfer of the right to control children. Monogamy arises, 'from the concentration of wealth in the hands of a single individual – a man – and from the need to bequeath this wealth to the children of that man and of no other' (1975: 138). In the previous era of collective property, barbarism, group marriage had prevented the reproduction of the institution of individual private property because it denied unambiguous individual heritability. The subjugation of women and their restriction to the domestic sphere in monogamy was therefore not an independent process but contingent on the development of a capitalist system of production.

In a formulation which has become highly influential in socialist feminist theory Engels insists that the relationship between the genders is a class relationship:

The first class-antagonism which appears in history coincides with the development of the antagonism between man and woman in monogamous marriage, and the first class oppression with that of the female sex by the male. [Monogamous marriage is] a relative regression in which the well-being and development of one group are attained by the misery and oppression of the other. [Engels 1975: 221]

Engels also wants to link subordination to the progressive repression and restriction of female sexuality. Women, but not men, are disadvantaged by the disappearance of group marriage. Men can continue the sexual practices of group marriage through adulterous affairs but for women sexual promiscuity is a sign of moral inferiority. The ultimate consequence is the commodification of women's sexuality in the institution of prostitution (Engels 1975: 138). This radical form of exploitation can only disappear if there is a general social revolution. But curiously, the socialist revolution will bring about not a restoration of group marriage but rather 'genuine' monogamy:

> [W]ith the transformation of the means of production into social property there will disappear also wage labor, the proletariat, and therefore the necessity for a certain – statistically calculable – number of women to surrender themselves for money. Prostitution disappears; monogamy, instead of collapsing, at last becomes a reality – also for men. [Engels 1975: 139]

Engels thus reveals himself as an unreconstructed romantic. Unconstrained sexual relations will be prevented by individual sex-love which will induce partner exclusivity.

Contemporary developments

Here we consider the two main contemporary malestream and antifeminist theories of gender, each of which seeks to reduce social gender to the biological inevitabilities of sex, Parsons' functionalist theory, and the narrow structuralism of sociobiology. We also examine the way in which such masculinist views have been incorporated into substantive theory and research on social stratification.

Parsons: instrumental man

For many years the principle sociological alternative to Engels was the functionalist theory of the differentiation of gender roles in the family developed by Parsons (in Parsons and Bales 1955). Families are differentiated on two dimensions: the relative power of the individuals; and the types of activity in which they engage. The first differentiates parents from children. The second is more controversial because it differentiates men from women and we can examine it in some detail.

Parsons suggests that all human groups require the performance of two types of activity. These are: first, task-performance or 'instrumental' activities; and second, activities aimed at the maintenance of solidarity by means of the expression of affectivity or emotion. The latter are called 'socio-emotional' activities in small-groups research, but Parsons calls them 'expressive'. Families, as examples of small groups, differentiate along these lines by gender, so that women perform expressive tasks and men instrumental tasks.

The fact of instrumental-expressive differentiation is, for Parsons, not problematic. However, there remains the difficulty of why, on his assumption, men should universally be the instrumental leaders and women the expressive leaders. His explanation is biological:

> [T]he bearing and early nursing of children establish a strong presumptive primacy of the relation of mother to the small child and this in turn establishes a presumption that the man, who is exempted from these biological functions, should specialize in the alternative instrumental direction. [Parsons and Bales 1955: 23]

However, Parsons is not content to let the matter rest at the level of biology. He moves on to analyse the socialization processes which reproduce gender differences. He draws on Freud's argument about the Oedipal stage in child development (see chapter 4). Parsons starts with the assumption that the father typically is absent during the early phases of socialization of boys. As the child moves out of the stage of oral dependency and gains some measure of autonomy through self-control (the 'anal phase') it can enter a relationship with its mother in which it is not merely loved but actively returns love. The pattern here is that the mother is both instrumental and superior while the son is expressive and inferior.

The Oedipal stage occurs between the ages of three and six and here the father must prise the boy away from the affections of his mother. As Parsons puts it: 'the father is, symbolically at least, the primary source of the new "demands" for conformity and autonomous performance. The mother . . . remains the primary source of "security" or "acceptance" in the love-relationship' (Parsons and Bales 1955: 80). The father establishes his significance to the son then by the use of discipline. The son reacts to the deprivation of motherly love and becomes aggressive. Daughters, by comparison, do not need to separated from their mothers and brought under paternal discipline – their mature sex-role identification is coterminous with their pre-Oedipal identification, that is, they can maintain an undifferentiated affection for their mothers and their fathers. In Parsons' view therefore the socialization *process* is fundamentally different for boys and girls. Boys must adjust aggressively to the intrusion of the father but girls do not need to do this and can remain passive and loyal family members. This may be contrasted with a more generally accepted view of differential socialization in which it is accepted only that the *content* of socialization differs for boys and girls.

Sociobiology: gender animated

The guiding principle of sociobiology is the structuralist principle that humans, like other animal species, have reproductive drives which impel them to mate, that this will create competition between them for successful mating, and that the competition will select those with the best capacity to further reproduce the species. Species reproduction impels differential behaviour for men and women:

> Genes that allow females to accept the sorts of mates who make lesser contributions to their reproductive success will leave fewer copies of themselves than will genes that influence the females to be more selective. Accordingly, genes inducing selectivity will increase at the expense of those that are less discriminating. For males, a very different strategy applies. The maximum advantage goes to individuals with fewer inhibitions. A genetically induced tendency to "play fast and loose" – "love 'em and leave 'em" – may well reflect more biological reality than most of us care to admit. [Barash 1980: 48]

This supposed propensity to different sexual behaviour is generalized by sociobiologists into non-sexual arenas so that, as in Parsons, men are impelled to be aggressive and instrumental and women to be submissive and expressive. However, such an argument makes the following problematic assumptions:

- It assumes that *genes* choose mates when in fact *people* choose mates on the basis of prior experience and social opportunity.
- It ignores the fact that each individual has a genetic inheritance from both parents.
- The range of social patterns of gender difference is enormous and genetic differences cannot explain this variation.

A more serious biological argument turns on the constraints which biological reproduction imposes on females and males. Fox (1976: 31–2), for example, argues that a primate ancestry in which females were committed to bearing and raising children and males to hunting, fighting, and making decisions, somehow transmits itself genetically and structures contemporary social arrangements. Women were thus genetically programmed to submit, and men to dominate. Fox himself admits that there may be an empirical problem for this sort of argument:

> As society becomes more technocratic, then the recruitment of suitable people to fill its many roles must mean that the net must be thrown wider than just over the males, and that women will achieve positions of dominance in some spheres. But this will usually conflict with the basic female function. [1976: 32]

Fox fails to see that it is perfectly possible to construct social arrangements (child day-care centres, for example) which ensure that there is no conflict between domestic and public life. It is also possible for some women not to bear children. The empirical fact that an increasing number of women participate fully and effectively in public life is an indication that biological explanations are difficult to sustain.

Stratification theory: malestream myopia

One of the main debates about functionalist and constructionist analyses of class and stratification which emerged in the 1970s and 1980s was about the way in which women can be located within a public-sphere system of social stratification. A major impetus for this debate was the influence of feminist thought which argued that traditional class analysis was gender-blind. The following quotations serve to confirm the point. The first comes from Parsons' functionalist analysis of social status:

> The separation of the sex roles in our society is such as, for the most part, to remove women from the kind of occupational status which is important for the determination of the status of a family. Where married women are employed outside the home, it is, for the great majority, in occupations which are not in direct competition for status with those of men of their own class.
>
> Women's interests, and the standards of judgement applied to them, run, in our society, far more in the direction of personal adornment and the related qualities of personal charm than is the case with men. [1954: 80]

The second is from Parkin's constructionist theory of class:

> [I]nequalities associated with sex differences are not usefully thought of as components of stratification. This is because for the great majority of women the allocation of social and economic rewards is determined primarily by the position of their families – and, in particular, that of the male head. Although women today share certain status attributes in common, simply by virtue of their sex, their claims over resources are not primarily determined by their own occupation but, more commonly, by that of their fathers and husbands. [1979: 14–15]

In taking such a position sociologists were able to treat the occupational status of a woman who lived with a man to be an extension of that of the man, while that of a single woman could be ignored. Consequently, women were simply not included in most of the foundational research on occupational status, including Blau and Duncan (1967), the Australian mobility survey of 1965 (Broom and Jones 1976), and Stewart et al.'s (1980) survey of British occupations, which was administered in about 1970.

Three approaches to measuring the place of women in the class system are currently available (Goldthorpe 1987: 281–96).

1   The 'conventional' approach conforms with the above assumptions, that is, it assumes that women's status is determined by that of their husbands and fathers and that, as a consequence, mobility and achievement issues for women are largely determined by the issue of whom they marry. Goldthorpe (1983) adopts and defends this position by showing that recent increases in female occupational participation are largely constituted by intermittent and part-time work, in what are elsewhere called component wage jobs. Given the contingent character

of women's status they enter into stratification analysis principally as an indicator of status closure by endogamy (see e.g. Jones and Davis 1988).

2   The 'individual approach' is the obverse of the conventional approach in so far as men and women are treated as independent sellers of labour in a market who can thus achieve personal statuses. Here the family or household is rejected as the unit of analysis. Such an approach is adopted by Heath and Brittan (1984) who show that despite intermittent and part-time, female, occupational careers, these careers are consistent across lifetimes. Indeed Goldthorpe (1987: 286), while rejecting the approach, admits that there is a high level of dissimilarity between the statuses of women and men. However, the problem remains that the approach leads one to a theoretically curious concept known as the 'cross-class family'. The concept is curious because it runs counter to all known principles of either class or stratification analysis by violating the principle of class/stratum exclusion at the most fundamental level of interactive domesticity.

3   The third possible approach is the 'dominance approach'. Broadly, this takes the view that the individual statuses of women and men are determined in the workplace but that these statuses interact competitively to determine the class position of the household according to which of the two is dominant. It employs the following rules of thumb: employment predominates over unemployment (including unpaid domestic labour); full-time employment predominates over part-time employment; and higher status employment predominates over lower status employment (Goldthorpe 1987: 290–1). This approach is not used a great deal but it bespeaks some sensitivity to the gender issue because it can accommodate an analysis of the status situations of both single and married, working and nonworking women. However, the notion of dominance can be adopted only as a matter of methodological convenience rather than as a valid representation of actual processes.

There is a genuine need for the development of a fourth, joint approach, which can take account of interaction between men's and women's work and the effect that each has on the status of the other. Thus the meaning of, for example, part-time work as a nurse is different for an unmarried twenty-year-old woman, a divorced woman with children, and the wife of a male teacher. None of the three available approaches captures the form of this gender-class interaction effect. As Garnsey (1982) indicates, what is required is a remodelling of the relationship between the fundamental division of labour and the labour market.

Feminist critiques

The above outline can serve to show that sociological theories of gender have been broadly masculine in their orientations. The attack on this inadequacy originated in the upsurge of feminist philosophy associated with the second wave of women's liberation which began in the 1960s. Here we consider three prominent and influential examples, one French and two American.

de Beauvoir: the genesis of gender

Arguably de Beauvoir's *The Second Sex* (1972) is the initiating contemporary foundational text for feminist thought. De Beauvoir rejects three prevailing masculinist explanations for differences and inequalities between men and women. First, she rejects sociobiological explanations on the grounds of widespread evidence across different species that the sexes are not differentiated in a consistent way. Second, she rejects Freudian psychoanalytic theory (e.g. Parsons) which argues that women accept their own inferiority because of 'penis envy'. In fact, she argues that there is no evidence that girls do covet the penis because: 'this outgrowth, this weak little rod of flesh can in itself inspire them only with indifference, or even disgust' (1972: 73). Moreover, Freud confuses daughterly responses to paternal domination, which has a social origin, with sexual attachment. Within each confusion, the problem is that the theory is written from a masculine point of view which allows it to collaborate in the project of reducing women to inferiority. Third, de Beauvoir also rejects Engels' historical materialism because it seeks to explain gender in terms of the masculine activities of the class struggle, although she is more sympathetic to this view than the others.

Simone de Beauvoir (1908–86)

She was born in Paris, France, to a lawyer's family and read philosophy at the Sorbonne. De Beauvoir lived a life of active social and political feminism. She refused to marry or have children, preferring the autonomy and uncertainties of a looser partnership with the philosopher, Jean-Paul Sartre, and campaigned actively for the legalization of abortion and for legal reform. She was a prolific novelist and a leading public intellectual.

Sources: Tuttle (1987: 33); de Beauvoir (1972: 1)

De Beauvoir's own theory of gender, like that of other feminist founders, claims to be a totalizing or holistic explanation, in her own terms an 'existential' explanation. There is held to be a mutually reinforcing subordination of women which runs through constructions of the body and the psyche on one hand and constructions of society and culture on the other. In fact, however, it is a two-stage theory in which the first stage is biological and genetic (historical) and the second is based on a theory of social reproduction. In the first stage, the genesis of gender differences is located in terms of the relationship between species biology and the nature of the environment under conditions of a primitive technology. In an impressionistic anthropology of early foragers she asserts:

> [M]an's superior strength must have been of tremendous importance in the age of the club and the wild beast. . . . [T]he early days of the human species were difficult; the gathering, hunting, and fishing peoples got only meagre products from the soil and those with great effort; too many children were born for the group's resources; the extravagent fertility of woman prevented her from active participation in the increase of these resources while she created new needs to an infinite extent. . . . [G]iving birth and suckling are not *activities*, they are natural functions; no project is involved; and that is why woman found in them no reason for a lofty affirmation of her existence – she submitted passively to her biological fate. . . . Man's case was radically different: he furnished support for the group . . . by means of acts that transcended his animal nature. . . . To maintain, he created; he burst out of the present, he opened the future. . . . Early man's activity had another dimension that gave it supreme dignity: it was often dangerous. [1972: 93–5, original italics]

The 'key to the whole mystery' is that the combination of biological differences with the economies of a difficult and dangerous environment in aboriginal societies 'must have led to male supremacy' (1972: 96–7).

Primitive conditions gave to men an advantage which they relinquished only once – in early horicultural societies when they allowed women briefly to till and to inherit land – but men reasserted themselves as agriculture developed and land once again became important property. Otherwise the march of masculine domination was unrelenting: in early agricultural communities men used their superior status and power to take control of land; they created religious belief systems which legitimated their domination; they established patriarchal families to ensure that property passed through male lines of inheritance; and, as societies modernized, they established abstract laws and systems of social control which affirmed their domination. This has been an incremental process of social reproduction: 'Little by little man has acted upon his experience, and in his symbolic representations, as in his practical life, it is the male principle that has triumphed' (1972: 106).

As a literary theorist, de Beauvoir is most interested in the way in which cultural products, especially literature, confirm the disadvantaged status of women but ultimately her theory is insistently materialistic: 'From humanity's beginnings, their biological advantage has enabled the males to affirm their status as sole and sovereign subjects' (1972: 109).

Friedan: the feminine mistake

While de Beauvoir tries to identify the origins of masculine domination, Friedan asks why women themselves continue to accept an inferior, powerless and exploited position. Her answer is that they are the victims of an ideology which she calls the 'feminine mystique', rather than of their own biology:

> Over and over women heard in voices of tradition and of Freudian sophistication that they could desire no greater destiny that to glory in their own femininity. Experts told them how to catch a man and keep him, how to breastfeed children and handle their toilet training, how to cope with sibling rivalry and adolescent rebellion; how to buy a dishwasher, bake bread, cook gourmet snails, and build a swimming pool with their own hands; how to dress, look and act feminine and make marriage more exciting; how to keep their husbands from dying young and their sons from growing into delinquents. They were taught to pity the neurotic, unfeminine, unhappy women who wanted to be poets or physicists or president. They learned that truly feminine women do not want careers, higher education, political rights – the independence and the opportunities that the old-fashioned feminists fought for. Some women, in their forties and fifties, remembered painfully giving up those dreams but most of the younger women no longer even thought about them. A thousand expert voices applauded their femininity, their adjustment, their new maturity. All they had to do was devote their lives from earliest girlhood to finding a husband and bearing children. [1963: 15–16]

Women, then, are the victims of a big lie perpetuated through the image of a suburban dream. The middle-class American woman had been liberated from household drudgery by technology, and therefore could devote herself to domestic 'creativity' and to perfecting her role as wife and mother. The lie is perpetrated by several agents: by the mass media, especially in its advertising and by the popular press; by psychiatric and medical practice which advises 'adjustment' and sedates where adjustment is not accomplished; by educators who dissuade female accomplishments; and by religious and political leaders exhorting family values.

The ideology claims that women are equal but different and special:

> The feminine mystique says that the highest value and the only commitment for women is the fulfillment of their own femininity. It says that the great mistake of Western culture, through most of its history, has been the undervaluation of this femininity. It says this femininity is so mysterious and intuitive and close to the creation and origin of life that man-made science may never be able to understand it. But however special and different, it is in no way inferior to the nature of man; it may even in certain respects be superior. The mistake, says the mystique, the root of women's troubles in the past is that women envied men, women tried to be like men, instead of accepting their own nature, which can find fulfillment only in sexual passivity, male domination, and nurturing maternal love. [1963: 43]

Just as Marx argues that alienation reduces humanity in general to something less than its possibilities, the feminine mystique has similar consequences for women in particular. Friedan also argues that the mystique excludes women from the creative possibilities of (nondomestic) work. This exclusion is for Friedan a relatively recent development. In a piece of somewhat dubious history, she suggests that the early immigrant women of America were independent and pioneering spirits who participated fully and equally with men in the work and politics of building a new society. The nugget of truth in this argument is the shared domestic context of labour which applied at that time, at least for farmers and petty bourgeois, if scarcely for the sweatshop ethnic working class of the Eastern states. The diminution of women occurred when men began to construct nondomestic occupations.

More convincingly, Friedan supports her argument by examining differential patterns in human pathologies. Women are more susceptible to marital dissatisfaction, neurotic behaviour, boredom and frustration, and outright mental illness than men. More importantly, unmarried women display fewer such symptoms than married ones. Friedan's conclusion is that there is a contradiction between the rewards which are claimed for monogamous marriage and the actual rewards and that this gap produces the neuroses.

More recent feminist thought would argue that female pathologies are the consequence of direct oppression and exploitation by men rather than a disjunction between ideology and actual arrangements. However, Friedan is important in alerting social scientific theory to ways in which ideology develops to accommodate changing patterns of masculine domination.

Millett: a gender agenda

If de Beauvoir identifies the fact of masculine dominance, Millett identifies its social structural form. Millett (1971) can take credit for the introduction of the term 'patriarchy' into modern feminist and social scientific discourse. She describes it as a masculine system of political domination:

> [O]ur society, like all other historical civilizations, is a patriarchy. The fact is evident at once if one recalls that the military, industry, technology, universities, science, political office and finance – in short, every avenue of power within the society, including the coercive force of the police, is entirely in male hands. [It is] the institution whereby that half of the populace which is female is controlled by that half which is male . . . [1971: 25]

In the work of Maine and Weber 'patriarchy' had been a descriptive concept, confined to premodern societies. Millett argues that it is an historical universal. More importantly, in her work 'patriarchy' became a sensitizing or 'struggle' concept to be used within feminism, much in the way that the term 'capitalism' is used within socialist ideology. It is a term with an intended counter-hegemonic content, identifying a substantive inequality which is held to be unjust, and which therefore requires active reconstruction.

It is relatively straightforward to understand why patriarchy should prevail in premodern contexts but why, Millett asks, should it be so

---

Kate Millett (b. 1934)

Millett is an American feminist writer and a sculptor. She was a founding member of NOW (the National Organization for Women) and has long been an active radical feminist.

Source: Tuttle (1987: 206)

---

persistent where women are both formally free and educated? The answer she says is that men practise an unspoken 'sexual politics', they engage in 'power-structured relationships, arrangements whereby one group of persons is controlled by another' (1971: 23). This argument is liberating because if patriarchy is a construction, it is possible for women to engage in a political struggle which aims at the reconstruction of gender arrangements.

Masculine sexual politics is broad in scale and multidimensional. It operates at least in the following ways:

- *Ideological* Sexual politics socializes both sexes in favour of patriarchy by: (i) the formation of sex-typed temperaments, 'aggression, intelligence, force and efficacy in the male; passivity, docility, "virtue" and ineffectuality in the female' (1971: 26); (ii) establishing sex-roles which assign domesticity and child-rearing to women and most areas of achievement to men; (iii) assigning inferior, 'biological' status to child-bearing women, and superior 'civilized' or 'cultivated' status to men.
- *Biological* Sexual politics promotes, through religion and popular science, the view that biological differences give rise to social differences, that gender is a reification of sex rather than a social and cultural construction which can be altered.
- *Sociological* The originating site of sexual politics is the family which establishes the general pattern of male dominance and is the chief agency of gender socialization.
- *Class* Sexual politics transcends class membership, although it varies to some extent according to class membership and thus divides women from one another.
- *Economic and educational* Women's domestic work is unpaid and often not recognized as work, while their labour in the public sphere is subjected to underpayment, discrimination, and exploitation; women are directed and encouraged into lower levels of educational performance and to educational specializations which are less occupationally marketable.
- *Force* Patriarchy is supported by legal coercion and by the threat and the fact of informal enforcement by means of rape and domestic violence.

- *Myth and religion* Christianity, in particular, casts women in the role of Eve, as the source of human suffering, connecting women with sex and sin, vilifying female seduction and lionizing male seduction.
- *Psychological* To cope, women must accept inferior personality characteristics, they must humiliate and subordinate themselves, seduce males, accept double sexual standards, attribute their own behaviour to intuition, emotion and instinct rather than to intellect, and accept continuous treatment as a sexual object.
(Millett 1971: 26–58)

Within all this, a key sociological contribution is the distinction which Millett continuously draws between gender and sex-roles. The latter had been the common sociological term to describe gender-related behaviours. It linked the biological term 'sex' with the sociological term 'role' implying that one determines the other. Rather, as Millett insists and most sociologists now accept, gender is socially constructed independently of sex.

Biological and sexual structuralist theory

Despite Millett's foundationalist separation of sex from gender, many feminist theories explicitly seek to link them. This, the first of three groups of structuralist theorists, seeks to do just that, to indicate that biological make-up is the source of social subordination and resistance and even of personality and cultural differences. The first set of two examples, by Firestone and Ortner, links cultural practice directly to biology. Similarly, Brownmiller links masculine domination to male sexual violence, the possibility of which is conferred by biology. Although the structuralism employed here can scarcely be described as a critical structuralism, we also examine the work of Brenner and Ramas which seeks to link issues of biological givens with critical themes.

Firestone; Ortner: natural inferiority

One of the most controversial analyses of patriarchy as a sex-class system is offered by Firestone (1972). Whereas Delphy (see below) and others locate patriarchal gender structures in systems of material production of commodities and services, Firestone locates it in the system of biological reproduction: '. . . the natural reproductive difference between the sexes led directly to the first division of labour based on sex, which is at the origins of all further division into economic and cultural classes . . .' (1972: 9). The imperatives of procreative biology impose dependency and subordination on women which is elaborated by men into more general forms of domination.

The view is controversial because it allows gender differences to be reified, that is treated as if they are immutable, natural patterns rather than human, social constructions: 'The immediate assumption of the layman that the unequal division of the sexes is "natural" may be well-founded' (1972: 16). However, while Firestone accepts that differences may well be natural, it is social reproduction which turns these differences into 'sex classes'.

The basic unit of biological reproduction, the family, is characterized by four fundamental 'facts':

- weaknesses in the biological constitution of women (menstruation, menopause, gestation, parturition, lactation) make them materially dependent on men;
- infants are physically dependent for relatively long periods;
- mother–infant interdependence is universal; and
- reproductive differences led to the first division of labour and thus to the first class system.
(Firestone 1972: 16–17)

We might expect that such an analysis would imply a conservative acceptance of gender differences and inequalities, as in Parsons' theory. However, it provides Firestone with the basis for a radical argument in which culture must take control of nature. Women, she argues, must repossess the reproductive processes which are the basis for their social situation. The sexual revolution must both seize control of fertility and embrace a pansexuality which transcends the distinctions between hetero- and homosexuality. To allow this development children should be bred artificially and raised communally.

A more interesting, though equally extreme, development of the argument is the view that the fundamental differences between the genders are reflected in a polarization in human culture. Culture, Firestone argues, is the consequence of humanity's attempts to grapple with the limitations which the environment places on human possibilities. There are two ways in which it can do this. It can either provide an escape into imagined worlds in which all things are possible; or it can actively engage with the environment seeking to push back its limitations. These 'idealistic/ aesthetic/humanistic' and 'pragmatic/technological/scientific' responses exist in a state of dialogue, the former offering goals and projects, the latter indicating the limits of such projects but simultaneously extending them as possibilities. In what is, again, a reification of sex, Firestone links these two cultural modes to the genders:

[T]he aesthetic response corresponds with 'female' behaviour. The same terminology can be applied to either: subjective, intuitive, introverted, wishful,
dreamy or fantastic, concerned with the subconscious (the *id*), emotional, even
temperamental (hysterical). Correspondingly, the technological response is the
masculine response: objective, logical, extroverted, realistic, concerned with the

conscious mind (the ego), rational, mechanical, pragmatic and down-to-earth, stable. Thus, the aesthetic is the cultural recreation of that half of the psychological spectrum that has been assigned to the female, whereas the technological response is the cultural magnification of the male half. [1972: 165–6, original italics]

Culture, she argues, has gone through a series of historical transformations, similar to those of patriarchy and of class, which have led it to the point where science dominates at the cost of the impoverishment of the aesthetic, and scientific dominance corresponds with masculine dominance. However, this development is riven by contradiction which will promote crisis and revolution. The principal contradiction is that science appears as a routinely empiricist, pointless, soulless pursuit. It is not integrated with human values but appears to have a life of its own. Science can now turn upon and destroy humanity, either directly by means of weapons of mass destruction or indirectly by disrupting the environment. A cultural revolution would involve not merely the merging of the two cultures as differentiated arenas of social practice but the disappearance of culture in so far as what is conceivable and what is possible become coterminous.

Like Firestone, Ortner (1974) is also concerned with the issue of the universality of female subordination. The very fact that it is universal suggests that it may have some deeply structural character which is independent of intention or even consciousness: 'What could there be in the generalized structure and conditions of existence, common to every culture, that would lead every culture to place a lower value on women?' (1974: 71).

Human culture does indeed postulate that there is a lower order of existence than itself, the order of 'nature'. This can be confirmed by the fact that culture seeks to transform and transcend the natural conditions of existence. In all societies, natural substances (dirt, rotten food, human exuviae, etc.) are understood to be polluting and contagious, and purification takes the form of culturally prescribed ritual. Symbolic action is thus used to achieve domination over natural action.

Ortner rejects a simplistic argument that women can be identified symbolically with nature and men with culture, arguing instead that women are *closer* to nature than men are. There are three facts which place women closer to nature:

- Women have a greater corporeal association with the reproduction of the species than men, indeed much of their existence is naturally controlled by their physiology, while men are free to hunt, tame and control nature through cultural practices.
- Lactation confines women to the domestic sphere, associating them with the 'natural' behaviours of children (feeding and waste disposal), and the subordinate privacy of family life, whereas men can engage in

superfamilial and public activities of politics, art, education and religion.
- The feminine psyche is more natural, emphasizing involvement with concrete things, feelings and people and emphasizing subjectivity, whereas men emphasize abstractness and objectivity.

Ortner stresses the principle that, in fact, women and men are no more and no less natural than one another. Yet women everywhere are conceived to be intermediate between nature and culture. She finally adopts a view within which the subordination of women must be seen as a self-reproducing pattern, that is as:

[A] (sadly) efficient feedback system: various aspects of woman's situation (physical, social, psychological) contribute to her being seen as closer to nature, while the view of her as closer to nature is in turn embodied in institutional forms that reproduce her situation. [1974: 87]

Brownmiller: male violence

If Firestone and Ortner identify parturition, lactation and socialization as the primary biological constraints which subordinate women, Brownmiller (1975), by contrast, focuses on the sexual relationship as the source of masculine power. The sexual relationship in the human species, she argues, is fundamentally different from that found in other animal species. In other species, even in relatively closely related primate species, females typically have an estrous cycle within which sexual accessibility is confined to certain periods ('heat' or 'rut'). Human sexual behaviour is more elaborate. It can occur at any time and involves complex psychological processes at least as much as biological ones. Males of the human species can become sexually interested in females at any time and without any need for receptivity on the part of females. The human species is therefore characterized by the possibility of rape.

More importantly, the ability to rape is asymmetrically distributed between the sexes. Men are 'structurally' capable, in a physiological sense, of doing sexual violence to women, while women are 'structurally' vulnerable. For Brownmiller, this accident of biology impels violent behaviour by men towards women: 'When men discovered that they could rape, they proceeded to do it' (1975: 14). She accepts that the first rape might have been accidental but that subsequent rape was 'indubitably' planned. Brownmiller's impressionistic anthropology centres on collective masculine violence: 'one of the earliest forms of male bonding must have been the gang rape of one woman by a band of marauding men' (1975: 14). So rape became transformed from being a means to sexual satiation to a means of domination by men over women. It became:

man's basic weapon of force against woman, the principal agent of his will and her fear. His forcible entry into her body, despite her physical protestations and struggle, became the vehicle for his victorious conquest over her being, the ultimate test of his superior strength, the triumph of his manhood. [1975: 14]

She ranks the masculine discovery of genitalia as a weapon as an event to compare in significance with the discoveries of fire and the stone axe.

The possibility and actuality of rape became institutionalized throughout history (Eisenstein 1984: 29–31). Within legal institutions it established women as property because rape was interpreted as the theft by one man of the sexual services of wives and daughters of another. Similarly, rape was understood to be a natural consequence of war and colonization in which the conquerors took control of the human property of the conquered. Rape thus entered ideology: it is not actual rape which terrorizes women but the threat of it. The rape of a few women by a few men can establish the domination of all men over all women.

> Myrmidons to the cause of male dominance, . . . rapists have performed their duty well, so well in fact that the true meaning of their act has gone largely unnoticed. Rather than society's aberrants or 'spoilers of purity', men who commit rape have served in effect as front-line masculine shock troops, terrorist guerillas in the longest sustained battle the world has ever known. [Brownmiller 1975: 209]

Brownmiller supports this view by showing that the rapist was not a peculiar or perverted deviant but similar in psychological and sociological profile to other male criminals, that is, normally rather than abnormally violent.

Brenner and Ramas: biological resistance

Brenner and Ramas (1984) seek to link occupational changes with domestic changes. Like Firestone and Ortner, they argue that the site for separation and causal efficacy of the domestic sphere is biological reproduction – however they view it as a site of resistance as well as of subordination. Their argument is historical and developmental, linking critical and constructionist themes with biological ones.

In precapitalist modes of production, production and reproduction were located within a single type of social unit, the kinship-based, household unit of economic production. Capitalism forced the differentiation of production from reproduction because of its technical division of labour, that is, high levels of specialization meant that commodity-producing workers had to be aggregated in factories. The physical constraints of gestation and lactation prevented women from participating in this public sphere. They were confined to a domestic sphere where they remained directly subordinated to men. Domesticity did, however, provide a structure for resistance to the absorption of female labour within the capitalist labour process. This prevented early capitalism from translating biological reproduction into commodity production.

However, Brenner and Ramas argue, the insatiable logic of capitalism claims the maximum exploitation of labour, and this includes female labour. In the twentieth century '[t]he sexual division of labour still has a logic. But the complex of forces pressing on women is far more contingent than in the 19th century' (1984: 82). The principal forces are:

- increasing capitalist control of the reproduction of labour power, exercised on behalf of the capitalist class by the state through its agencies, the schools and welfare bureaux, which reduce childcare responsibilities for women;
- technological developments in the area of biological reproduction (contraception, abortion, etc.), which relieve women from repeated childbirth but which increasingly place control of biological reproduction in the hands of state agencies, hospitals and medical practices;
- exploitation of the labour power of women thus released, both in commodity production and in the state agencies of reproduction, which replace their own domestic activity; and
- maintenance of the subordination of women by making them responsible for biological and social reproduction while removing control of these processes to the state, which, in turn, means that women's careers are characterized by interruptions from child-bearing and by component wage jobs.

Psychoanalytic structuralist theory

In this section we consider theories of female subordination which draw upon some of the structuralist theories outlined in chapter 4. The first, by Mitchell, links the gendered structure of the personality to its material context. The second, by Chodorow, follows a more or less conventionally Parsonsian route but seeks to fill in the arguments about gender which Freud and Parsons failed to make.

Mitchell: Althusser meets Freud

In an argument drawing on Althusserian structuralism (see chapter 4) Mitchell (1971) proposes that the structure of the situation of women is composed of four elements. Taken together they constitute a 'complex unity' but each must be examined separately because of its specific level of development at any given historical time. She outlines the four elements and their contemporary transformations as follows:

- *Production* The division of labour which consigns women to inferior work was originally the consequence of physical subordination. More recently it has become the consequence of both physical and ideological coercion. A degendered division of labour is now possible in principle but ideological constraints have proved effective and women are not making significant advances into masculine domains.

- *Reproduction of children* Biological functions have become the centrepiece of a masculine ideology which supports female subordination. A technology is available which can liberate women from this constraint but they are still defined by it.
- *Sexuality* This is the mechanism by which men, historically, have appropriated women as the property. Because women are constructed as sexual 'objects' they can thus be owned. Contemporary monogamy enshrines a contradiction between formal or legal equality and actual subordination. However, patterns of sexuality are undergoing rapid transformation under current conditions.
- *Socialization of children* As the number of children declines, and as secondary socialization is taken over by the state, early childhood socialization takes on increasing significance. Current ideology links this function to the mother thus tying her into domesticity.

Liberation can only be achieved if all four elements are transformed simultaneously. Under current conditions, liberating advances in one arena can be offset by reinforcements in others: so, for example, reductions in the constraints of biological reproduction are replaced by expectations that women will do the work of socializing children; and sexual liberation is countered by a more fixed division of labour in the public sphere of work. Masculine domination moves historically from one permutation to another. The only situation in which true liberation can occur, argues Mitchell, is when the contradictions coalesce and explode in a *'unité de rupture'* (1971: 121–2). The women's liberation movement can set the chain reaction off by attacking the structure at its weakest link, which at this moment appears to be the arena of sexuality.

The family lies at the centre of the subordination of women:

> The contemporary family can be seen as a triptych of sexual, reproductive and socializatory functions (the woman's world) embraced by production (the man's world) . . . The exclusion of women from production . . . and their confinement to a monolithic condensation of functions within a unity – the family – which is precisely unified in the *natural part* of each function, is the root cause of the contemporary *social* definition of women as *natural* beings. [1971: 148, original italics]

It is here that Mitchell makes her psychoanalytic move. The family within capitalist society makes women what they are, giving them specific personalities: 'a tendency to small-mindedness, petty jealousy, irrational emotionality and random violence, dependency, competitive selfishness and possessiveness, passivity, a lack of vision and conservatism' (1971: 162). This is the outcome, she argues, of the way in which the constraints of society return individuals to the facts of their own biology. Citing Freud (see chapter 4) she indicates that the crucial moment which sets women on this path to their social destiny is the Oedipal phase. Here, a boy must terminate affection for his mother because his penis cannot compete with that of his father, and to continue to compete would set up a risk of paternal castration. A girl faces no such risk and can continue to be affectionate to her father. She can become a 'second mother' and maternalistic in orientation. Boys must rather become a 'different' or 'alternative father'. They must externalize their orientations beyond the family, whereas girls, in a symbolic sense, can remain internal to the family and need not seek to penetrate the barriers to wider participation placed on them, by men, in the arena of production.

Chodorow: 'she's got personality'

Mitchell's psychoanalytic approach, like the socialization approach of Parsons, conforms with orthodox Freudianism. Yet Freud (see chapter 4) has always been a central target for feminist theory, especially in the work of de Beauvoir, Friedan, Millett and Firestone. This is because of the risks within Freudian thought of 'naturalizing' gender differences and feminine subordination. So some psychoanalytic feminist theories seek to remain within Freudian traditions but to 'demasculinize' them. The most prominent example is the work of Chodorow.

Chodorow's is the most Freudian of feminist theories (1974; 1989), arguing that gender identity is the product of inevitable, formative, infantile experiences. However, her argument varies considerably from Freud at several crucial points.

The first such point is the pre-Oedipal phase. Here Chodorow argues that male and female experiences are not identical. The differentiation of self from mother appears to proceed much more rapidly in boys than in girls. This is the consequence of the behaviour of mothers, who tend simultaneously to push sons away and to act seductively towards them. By contrast, mothers treat daughters as extensions of themselves.

Although the sense of separation and individuation is developed differentially between boys and girls in the pre-Oedipal phase, it is not until about the age of three that a clear idea that there are two genders emerges. The assumption of a masculine identity by boys is problematic for three reasons (1989: 51–2) (assuming traditionally gendered role-performances by adults):

- It involves a denial of attachment to and dependence upon the mother.
- It involves the repression of femininity learned in the pre-Oedipal phase.
- It involves identification with a male role-model who is only intermittently present.

Girls do not face these problems but can immediately identify with a pre-Oedipal object of affection who continues to be present, available and personal. Importantly, Chodorow argues that the establishment of the possibility of heterosexual attachments by girls is not nearly as problematic as Freud had theorized. They do not attach to the father as the consequence of penis envy but rather as a way simultaneously of escaping the domination of maternal attachments and of confirming these attachments by making the mother envious. Like Parsons then, Chodorow views the identity development of boys as discontinuous and difficult by comparison with that of girls.

All of the above are 'unconscious' developments but they become the basis for conscious sex-role learning as children mature. Girls start quite early to help their mothers around the house while boys 'escape' into peer groups. The socialization experiences of boys emphasize achievement and self-reliance, while those of girls emphasize nurturance and responsibility. Adult personalities reflect both the unconscious and the conscious processes: men tend to be oriented to individualism, objectivity, and social distance; while women are oriented to communitarianism, subjectivity and close relationships. Chodorow summarizes the differences by drawing on the Parsonsian pattern variables (see chapter 2):

> [A] quality of embeddedness in social interaction and personal relationships characterizes women's life relative to men's. . . . Their roles tend to be particularistic and to involve diffuse relationships and responsibilities rather than specific ones. Women in most societies are *defined* relationally (as someone's wife, mother, daughter, daughter-in-law; even a nun becomes the Bride of Christ). Men's association (although it may be kin-based and intergenerational) is much more likely than women's to cut across kinship units, to be restricted to a single generation, and to be recruited according to universalistic criteria and involve relationships and responsibilities defined by their specificity. [1989: 57]

The security of a female gender identity helps to explain why it is reproduced so successfully across generations, at least outside Western middle-class contexts. There is a very real problem in these latter contexts, however. Here, early separation from the mother at about the age of five leads to an immature or infantile form of dependence on the mother. This can be contrasted with a mature form of dependence where each person recognizes the other's autonomy but relies on the other for mutual support. By contrast, in immature dependence participants experience wild swings between total identification and total rejection, and between complete submission and efforts to control. This occurs at least partly because the role-model is herself a passive and dependent person with low self-esteem who invests all her psychic energy in her children rather than herself. Daughters must reject mothers in order to escape them, but can then have no basis for self-esteem. The problem thus reproduces itself.

Critical and materialist structuralist theories

The two sets of structuralist theories considered above address themselves only to one main problem: how to explain, and thus to be able to change, women's subordination to men. Theories in this third group are Marxist or socialist in character and thus must face the secondary difficulty that Engels is often criticized for failing to solve: how to reconcile a theory of gender subordination with a theory of class subordination.[3]

The single most important theoretical problem, then, for contemporary Marxist-feminist thought is that of how to analyse the intersection of patriarchy with capitalist class relations. The alternative strategies are: to view patriarchy as a purely reproductive structure, a form of ideology, which is produced by and contributes to the maintenance of capitalism; or to incorporate the domestic arena within the Marxist term 'mode of production' so that the forms of social division represented by the terms 'capitalism' and 'patriarchy' intersect. Each of these strategies is problematic. The second strategy concedes the primacy which Marxists normally assign to capitalism. The first strategy faces two contradictions: between assigning primacy to the class structure and maintaining feminist ideological commitment; and between recognizing the historical transcendence of patriarchal relationships and the historical contingency of their forms.

As we shall see, most Marxist feminists opt for the second, or dualistic, strategy but in developing their arguments they tend to retreat towards the view that patriarchy serves to reproduce capitalism.

Barrett; Eisenstein: reproductive capitalism

This dualism is well illustrated in the work of the British sociologist, Barrett (1980). On the one hand, she argues that women's oppression occurs primarily in the household:

> The family-household system of contemporary capitalism constitutes not only the central site of the oppression of women but an important organising principle of the relations of production for the social formation as a whole. [1980: 211]

On the other, patriarchy is argued to be contingent on capitalism:

> [A]lthough important dimensions of women's oppression cannot be accounted for with reference to the categories of Marxism, it is equally impossible to establish the analytic independence of a system of oppression such as the category of 'patriarchy' suggests. [1980: 249]

Barrett insists, then, on a dualistic position: while capitalist classes and domestic genders are aspects of a single formation, independent causal efficacy is assigned to each. For example, the household system is said to have contradictory consequences in relation to the bourgeoisie – it reproduces labour power but it prevents the exploitation of female labour in commodity production.

This position is worked out in her analysis of the relationship between household organization and capitalism (1980: 204–26). She begins with an assumption that the family is the site for the definition of gender identity. This is primarily an ideological process in which families both respond to and contribute to representations of the family especially in religion and the mass media. The ideology is constraining – no matter what individual family members choose to do, the representations are fundamentally gendered. However, the household is also a site of material production with a gender-specific division of labour. The assignment of child-rearing duties to women places them in a relationship of material dependence on and inequality with men.

She now makes the link between household structure and the ideology of the family on one hand and capitalism on the other. The family-household system has the following consequences:

* It prevents the revolutionary unity of working-class men with working-class women.
* The dependency of women and children on a male wage means that working-class men are less likely to engage in acts of protest or revolt.
* It provides an apparently intimate haven for men who daily face the debilitations of wage labour.
* It reproduces masculine labour-power by generating and socializing new workers.
* It provides continuity in the face of social upheavals.
* It provides a site for the maximal consumption of commodities.

So the link is essentially a functional one. The household-family system contributes to the maintenance of capitalism and, concomitantly, of bourgeois domination. It does so by making contributions to reproduction, political stability, economic demand, and ideologically induced conformity. Despite Barrett's insistence on structural duality, her theory inevitably leads to the conclusion that gender inequality is a consequence of capitalist class relations. She remains more Marxist than feminist.

A functional articulation between masculine domination and bourgeois domination is expressed even more explicitly in the work of Eisenstein (1979; 1981). Here society is conceived as the arena of commodity production; the family as the arena of (domestic) service production, reproduction and consumption. The sexual division of labour in the family provides two specific functions for society – it provides a pool of unpaid and low-paid labour and it 'stabilizes' the society (1979: 30). The practices by which this stabilization is achieved include the fulfilling of domestic roles, the biological reproduction of new workers, and consumerism (1979: 29). Within 'capitalist patriarchy' the domestic sphere takes on a particular form – a nucleated family structure and confinement of women to the domestic role as housewife. Thus the structural arrangements of patriarchy are contingent on the structural arrangements between men constituted in the class system. Patriarchy belongs to the realm of epiphenomena and ideologies – its relationship to capitalism is at the same time contingent and functional.

Christine Delphy (b. 1941)

Born in Paris, Delphy studied sociology at the Sorbonne and, as a graduate, at the University of Chicago and the University of California at Berkeley. In 1964 she left university to do civil rights work. On her return to France in 1966 she took a post at the Centre Nationale de Recherche Scientifique where she is still a tenured research fellow. She soon became active in feminist politics, participating in the major public demonstrations of 1968 which launched the movement in France, particularly within the current known as Feministes Révolutionnaires. In 1977, with Simone de Beauvoir and others, she founded the journal *Questions Féministes* and now edits *Nouvelles Questions Féministes*.

Source: Stevi Jackson, personal communication

Delphy: sex with class

By contrast with Barrett and Eisenstein, Delphy (1984) makes a rigid structural separation between patriarchy and capitalism. Whereas they view capitalist production as the primary site of exploitation in contemporary society, Delphy identifies two such sites, the domestic site and the public site. According to Delphy's analysis, both liberal economics and Marxism are gender-blind because they each fail to recognize women's work as labour. Her argument (1984: 60–74) proceeds as follows:

1 All societies depend on the unpaid labour of women whose labour services are provided within a relationship with men which is ideologically specified as one of generalized reciprocity rather than balanced exchange.[4] In many societies this includes women's work on products which are subsequently exchanged as commodities in the external market by their husbands or fathers and not by themselves. Even in contemporary society, women's labour contributions to farms and family businesses take on this character.
2 The production of domestic labour services by women and which are consumed within the family is not different from the production of commodities to be exchanged in the market.
3 Domestic labour services performed by wives are continuous with commercial production. If we take the preparation of food as an example: families can choose either to buy culinary services in a restaurant or to rely on the wife to cook; and where the wife cooks she is preparing food that has already been through one or more commerical exchanges or industrial processes.

4   However, there is a progressive restriction, under contemporary conditions, of the exploitation of women to performing domestic work and child-rearing – women are now much less likely to be producing marketable commodities.

5   The class position of women is therefore as follows:

> There are two modes of production in our society. Most goods are produced in the industrial mode. Domestic services, child-rearing and certain other goods are produced in the family mode. The first mode of production gives rise to capitalist exploitation. The second gives rise to familial, or more precisely, patriarchal exploitation. [1984: 69]

The differences between the two modes consist in the relations of production. In the capitalist mode of production, the worker performs specific services for a fixed wage; in the domestic mode of production, neither the amount of labour performed nor the benefits which are returned are fixed but will vary according to the situation of the family.

6   Married women therefore exist in a condition of exploitation. This condition can be identified as a sex-class system (1984: 25–6). Sex-classes are categories which are defined in relation to one another, and this relationship is one of exploitation and domination of women by men.

Connell: the gender fit-up

Although he is a critical theorist, Connell is much more closely associated with the cultural or humanistic Marxism of Gramsci (see chapter 6) than the structuralism of Althusser (see chapter 4). So it is somewhat surprising that he should draw upon the Althusserian elements in Mitchell's analysis to formulate his theory of gender.

Connell (1987) argues that patriarchy is constituted in a series of gender-related practices, principally to do with *power* (the ways men control women and each other), *labour* (the ways in which work is distributed), and *cathexis* (the ways in which attachments and bonds are formed between people). Connell's tripartite division conforms with the widespread sociological distinction, often found in Hegelian and Marxist sociology, between the economy, the state, and civil society.

- *Labour*   There is a division of labour between the genders. Under contemporary conditions this does not necessarily consist in explicit discrimination but in complex mechanisms which channel women into deskilled occupations with low levels of authority. Segregation of labour occurs both within occupations, in that women are assigned different tasks from men, and between occupations, in that occupations tend to be gender-specific. This division of labour is fundamentally linked with processes of making profits. Production systems promote the solidarity of men and the individuation of women; the accumulation of losses to women and of profits to men.

- *Power* Connell sketches an uneven tapestry of the power of men over women, including the fact that men have a capacity for naked violence in the form of rape and that in many social contexts kinship roles allow men to treat women as property. Nevertheless, there is always a core of masculine power in all societies which consists in: masculine control of the institutions of organized coercion, the police, courts, military, etc.; masculine control of the main means of economic production; masculine control of state agencies; and working-class cultures which emphasize physical domination of the material world.
- *Cathexis* Here Connell discusses: 'the construction of emotionally charged relationships with objects' (1987: 112) or the way in which affectual relations, the lusts and desires, of the members of a society are structured in particular ways. The normal structural pattern of heterosexuality is one in which women are sexualized as objects of desire in a different way from men. Thus heterosexual-couple relations are patterned in their idealized form as reciprocation between powerful, aggressive, conquering men and alluring, expressive, nest-building women.

These three structural aspects are organized in different ways in different institutions: for example, in the family the power of the husband is linked to his career and to the predominant role-expectation of the wife as child-raiser in the domestic division of labour; meanwhile, the state empowers men legally to enforce a dominant position in cathexis; and the street is a setting for public demonstrations of both the domesticity of women and their victimization in terms of physical and emotional harassment. There is a neat dovetailing of gender relations in these institutions:

> The conventional division of labour in working-class families in Western cities assigns most childcare and housework to the wife-and-mother; and femininity is constructed in a way that defines the work of caring for other family members as womanly. The labour market constructed by capitalist industry and the state offers some low-paid, low-status, part-time jobs; and curiously enough most of the people recruited to these part-time jobs are married women. The pattern of recruitment is justified by employers on the grounds that married women only want part-time work because of their domestic responsibilities and only need low pay because theirs is a 'second wage'. At home the much heavier domestic work of women is justified by husbands because their wives can only get part-time jobs. [Connell 1987: 134–5]

Constructionist theories

There are considerable similarities between Connell's arguments about the barriers to participation which men set up against women and the constructionist theories examined in this group. They take the view that gender inequalities are the consequence of human intention but that the structures created confer people with opportunities and limitations of various kinds. As individuals respond to these limitations and opportunities they recreate the structure (cf. Giddens' argument in chapter 4).

Constructionist theories are neoWeberian in character. They conceive of the field of social action as a competitive market in which actors will, individually and collectively, seek to maximize rewards and privileges by 'closing off' sections of it. Men will use devices of property, skills and status symbols to exclude and to exploit women. Women as an excluded group, will seek to usurp the positions of men by penetrating the barriers using moral, political, economic or symbolic means. So constructionist theory examines the processes by which men have managed to confine women to domesticity, or failing this, to low-rewarded, feminized occupations.

Kanter: the glass ceiling

Kanter (1977) focuses on the ways in which the structure of work organizations, especially those with large proportions of white-collar workers, establish women in subordinate positions, they put a 'glass ceiling' over their opportunities. Her constructionist theoretical assumptions (1977: 250–3) are, then, as follows:

- Work is a response to a more widely organized setting that is independent of the individual (and the way a person works will especially be affected by whether there is an opportunity for advancement).
- Individuals will adapt to their jobs in terms of the strategic maximization of meaning and autonomy.
- Individuals will always have some measure of 'freedom' in deciding how to perform their jobs.
- But this discretion occurs within formal limits established by the organization.
- A key issue in the distribution of persons across jobs is therefore competence, although the ability to demonstrate competence is not evenly distributed.

She asks us to understand organizational behaviour as: 'produced in the interaction of individuals, seeking to meet their own needs and manage their situations, with their positions, which constrain their options for the ways they can act' (1977: 253).

The structure of a work organization can be described in terms of three dimensions and these can then be used to explain individual-level behaviour. The dimensions are:

- *Opportunity* People who have less opportunity (e.g. secretaries) will tend to be low in self-esteem and aspiration, to be oriented to immediate rewards, and to seek the internal protections of the peer group. People with more opportunity (e.g. managers) will be competitive, oriented to the acquisition of power, committed to the organization as a whole, and have greater self-esteem.
- *Power* Kanter defines power as a capacity to mobilize resources in support of individual interests. People with low power (e.g. supervisors) tend to be authoritarian, subordinating, coercive, critical,

territorial and are not well liked. People with high power (e.g. executives) tend to be non-directive, encouraging to subordinates, helpful, morale-boosting, and popular.
- *Proportions* This refers to the social mix, for example, the racial or gender mix, at a given level in an organization. Small proportions (such as female managers) tend to be highly visible, low in credibility, highly stressed, and stereotyped. Large proportions (such as male managers) invisibly fit in with the group, find networking and the acquisition of sponsors much more straightforward, and are confident at self-presentation.

Kanter is able to draw two conclusions. First, the relative behaviours of men and women in organizations can be explained in terms of their positions rather than their gender or their individual attributes. Men do not necessarily actively discriminate. Rather, women give the appearance of not being good prospects for management because they are in jobs which encourage passivity, lack of commitment to the organization and difficulty in self-presentation. Second, the pattern is self-reproducing: tokenism will only produce an inadequate performance because the individual cannot 'relax' in the job; and because women are in low-opportunity jobs they are unlikely to perform in ways which will make them appear to be suitable for high-opportunity jobs.

Walby: publicizing patriarchy

Walby's analysis (1986; 1990) is far more general than Kanter's in that it seeks to analyse an entire structure of patriarchy. However, it bears some similarities because it attaches great significance to the organization of production. She defines patriarchy, much as Millett did previously, as: 'a system of interrelated social structures through which men exploit women' (1986: 51). Walby also incorporates Marxist themes, arguing that contemporary patterns of gender relations are constituted by an articulation between the capitalist mode of production and what she calls the patriarchal mode of production (1986: 50–69).

Walby's patriarchal mode of production bears some clear similarities with Delphy's domestic mode of production. In the patriarchal mode of production there are two classes, the class of housewives or domestic labourers and the non-producing and exploiting class of husbands. Wives labour to replenish the exhausted labour power of the husband, and to accomplish the generational production of new labourers in the form of children. Their labour power is thus appropriated by husbands and transferred to employers. The husband returns only part of his wage to her as 'housekeeping' even though she typically labours for longer hours than he does.

The patriarchal mode of production is contingent on patriarchal relations in other spheres. In particular it relies on exclusionary closure practices in the sphere of capitalist production. Here women are restricted from entering certain occupations, while in others their careers are interrupted by compulsory expulsion on marriage or childbirth. These practices ensure that women are forced back into domestic dependence and subordination. Likewise, the state excludes women from processes of political representation which would otherwise enable them to reform and redress their situation in the domestic and paid employment sectors.

This account might appear to be completely structuralist rather than constructionist in orientation. However, the crucial difference is that domestic exploitation is argued to be contingent on the exclusion of women from the public spheres of paid employment and politics. This theoretical orientation becomes more explicit in Walby's later statement (1990). Here she theorizes two phases or moments in gender relations, private patriarchy and public patriarchy. In private patriarchy there is direct exploitation of women by men by virtue of their relationships to them as husbands or fathers. Here women are excluded from the public sphere. In public patriarchy women are not excluded from the public arena but are subordinated within it. Here the expropriation of women's labour is accomplished on a collective basis in both the domestic and public arenas.

Walby's explanation for the shift is also neoWeberian. It occurred not because of the particular relationship between biology and labour in the capitalist enterprise, as argued by Brenner and Ramas, nor as a form of capitalist exploitation of the family, as in Barrett. Rather, it occurred because of usurpationary process of closure on the part of women themselves. This was the 'underrated' social movement known as 'first-wave feminism' which emerged in the Western liberal democracies in the middle of the nineteenth century. As a usurpationary strategy, it was, she argues, extraordinarily successful:

> Women won political citizenship. They won access to higher education, and hence to the professions. They won rights to legal personhood such as the right to sit on juries, to own property, whatever their marital status, and hence to have access to credit. They won the right to leave a marriage, both by legal separation and divorce.
>
> These are a considerable list of gains, which defeated the patriarchal strategy of restricting women to the private sphere of the home. Women had won access to the public sphere and claims to the rights and privileges of citizenship. They could no longer be legally subsumed [*sic*] to their husbands and fathers. [1990: 191]

In Walby's analysis, then, the public patriarchy of the twentieth century represents a very real improvement over the private patriarchy of the nineteenth.

Waters: permutations of patriarchy

Waters' analysis (1989a) bears some marked similarities to Walby. However, he divides patterns of masculine domination into four types, rather than two, and indeed argues against the use of the concept to describe masculine domination under modern conditions.

The most general term in his conceptual scheme is *gender-system*. By this he means a system of social relationships in which (biological) sex is is socially structured, institutionalized and reproduced into a stable pattern of differentiated masculine and feminine genders. It is theoretically possible for a society to be organized without, or with minimal, gender differentiation especially in an era of increasing technological control over biological reproduction, although there has been no historical instance of such a society. Typically, the relationship between the genders is structured in terms of inequality, one gender dominates the other. However, it is logically conceivable, although probably structurally unstable, for there to be differentiation between the genders without inequality. There are therefore three logical subtypes of gender system: *masculine*, in which men exercise control over women; *feminine*, in which women exercise control over men; and *neutral*, in which the genders are approximately equal in terms of their control.

In its most frequent and political usage, the term 'patriarchy' has been applied to what Waters describes as a *masculine gender-system* and this is the major concern in the rest of his analysis. He analyses the relationship between the domestic and the public spheres in terms of two dimensions. The first such dimension is the extent to which structures (and practices) are differentiated. At one pole of this dimension there are no separate structures of economics and politics but a single fused structure of kinship. He restricts the term *patriarchal* to masculine gender-systems operating under these structural arrangements, that is, to those that are structured in terms of the allocation of economic and political roles by kinship practices. By extension, at the opposite pole of the dimension, political, economic, and family practices are regarded as separable by participants, and there are differentiated structures of government, production and family relations. He now proposes the use of the new term *viriarchy*[5] to describe masculine gender-systems which occur in differentiated social contexts. In a patriarchy the senior male members of extended kinship systems have control; in a viriarchy all adult males have collective control, but not necessarily directly by virtue of their location in the kinship system.

Waters' second basis for conceptualizing the relationship between the domestic and public spheres is that of contingency, the dimension of what causes what. The first pole of the dimension is that in which the organization of gender relations in the public sphere are determined by their organization in the domestic sphere – these are direct masculine gender-systems. The opposite pole is rather more complex. Here the public sphere assumes independence and the domestic sphere is at least partially contingent. The relationship between the two spheres is one of reproduction, specifically in so far as disprivileged participation in the public sphere by women is reproduced by an unequal domestic power distribution. Masculine gender-systems organized in this way he describes as *extended* systems.

Waters' purpose in proceeding in terms of the isolation of two analytic

Differentiation of domestic/public spheres

		Low	High
Contingency	Domestically centred	Direct patriarchy	Direct viriarchy
	Publicly centred	Extended patriarchy	Extended viriarchy

Figure 8.2   *Waters' scheme of patriarchy and viriarchy*
(Waters 1989b: 1182)

dimensions of masculine domination is to develop a scheme of types. He develops such a scheme by intersecting the two dimensions, as in figure 8.2, a procedure which yields four types of masculine gender-system.

- *Direct patriarchy*   This occurs in societies in which there is little or no differentiation of the domestic and public spheres so that unequal political and economic roles are assigned within the system of kinship. Superordinate roles are heritable only by men, although the inheritance may be traced through women. Women are regarded as a form of property to be sexually consumed and to be biologically and commodity productive, and thus subject to exchange between male-dominated lineages. A system of direct patriarchy is generationally as well as gender based so that not all adult males rule – junior siblings and junior generations as well as women are excluded. Direct patriarchy therefore corresponds with the patriarchal systems described by Maine, Weber and Engels.
- *Extended patriarchy*   Extended patriarchy occurs where the kinship system is elaborated into large-scale political arrangements. Political leadership is still allocated on the basis of kinship but in extended patriarchy only the senior members of aristocratic lineages can rule. Women are absolutely confined to the domestic sphere. This subordination of women is supported by religious ideologies. The important example of extended patriarchy is European feudalism but it was to be found in all ancient settled agricultural systems.
- *Direct viriarchy*   The social context for the emergence of direct viriarchy is domestic commodity production, e.g. petty bourgeois and artisanal, family-based, production systems, domestic outwork systems, and small-scale, peasant land holdings. The predominant gender relationship is the domestic one, that is, men control women by virtue of being husbands rather than by virtue of being fathers or proto-fathers. Men have right of disposition over the labour, the bodies, and the children of women. While women are not transferred between lineages as property, their rights to freedom of action are severely circumscribed in fact and in law. The significant historical instance of

direct viriarchy is early European capitalism which was characterized by family-owned enterprises, domestic outwork and, as the system developed, full but not equal participation by working-class women in factory production.

• *Extended viriarchy* In extended viriarchy control of the public sphere is monopolized by men. This pattern is reproduced by three principal forms of practice: first, control of the material means of subsistence for families by men is used by them to control the domestic labour of women and to constrain women within domestic roles; second, men are in control of cultural representations of gender so that its idealized forms are functionally and hierarchically differentiated; and third, covert forms of discrimination are practised against women in public contexts. The structural form of extended viriarchy is therefore constituted in a gender-based domestic division of labour and power, and a segregated labour market in the public sphere. Historically, this is the type of system associated with advanced or late capitalism.

Waters' argument thus represents an elaboration relative to Walby. He divides her 'private patriarchy' into three historical phases (direct and indirect patriarchy, and direct viriarchy). A second difference is that whereas Walby sees domestic patriarchy as always contingent on public patriarchal relations, for Waters the direction of causality reverses with each historical phase shift.

Poststructuralist theories

The guiding principle of feminist sociology in English-speaking contexts is to identify patterns of female inequality and oppression with a view to emancipation. Such an emancipation would involve a reorganization of society in such a way as to ensure equal participation by women and men in the various arenas of social life. Constructionist and some critical feminist theories therefore insist that gender differences and inequalities are socially constructed rather than natural or biological because that which is social is held to be able to be reconstructed.

In this section we consider some recent French theories which take the radical position that women are different from men in a fundamental and structural sense. It follows that the relationship between the genders minimally must take the form of an equality of complementarity rather than an equality of identity. In some accounts an argument emerges for the predominance of women over men. It must be noted, however, that these theories stand radically opposed to the theories of Freud and Lacan (see chapter 4) for example, in so far as the latter legitimate a subordinate domestic role for women.

None of the arguments considered in this short section claims to be sociological – they are all literary and philosophical. Cixous, for example, communicates her position not only by means of philosophical commentary and literary criticism but also by means of fiction. Her argument centres on the notion that different styles of writing can be identified by their 'economies', by what they invest and what they hope to produce. She focuses on libidinal economies in particular:

> It is the regime of that which in the past used to be called the effect of desire, of love. It is the love of life in fact, of the sexual life, which is regulated by energy marked physically by the subject, which is lived consciously, and which can be described in economic metaphors with moments of investment in passion, love, disgust, or anything else, moments of disinvestments from subject to object. [Conley 1984: 130]

A masculine libidinal economy is grasping and acquisitive while a feminine one is 'more adventurous, more on the side of spending, riskier, on the side of the body' (Conley 1984: 133). However, these economies are not associated directly with anatomical sex because all individuals have bisexual components and each gender can therefore participate in either economy. Rather, the feminine libidinal economy is more accessible to women because they have little to lose in it and to do so means that they can thus evade participation in the phallocentric society. The danger is that women will 'become men' in order to accomplish equal participation. Rather they must insistently be themselves, expressing the feminine economy by writing and by other means.

Irigaray (1985) provides a more physiological account of this libidinal economy. She argues that female sexuality has always been defined in masculine terms. Women are inferiorized because the only elements of their bodies which have been 'sexualized' are the clitoris and the vagina – the clitoris is conceived of as a miniature penis good only for masturbation, while: 'the vagina is valued for the "lodging" it offers the male organ when the forbidden hand has to find a replacement for pleasure-giving' (1985: 23). The wordplay of her title *This Sex which is Not One* identifies female sexuality with the vaginal labia:

> This organ which has nothing to show for itself also lacks a form of its own. And if woman takes pleasure precisely form the incompleteness of form which allows her organ to touch itself over and over again, indefinitely, by itself, that pleasure is denied by a civilization that privileges phallomorphism. The value that is granted to the only definable form excludes the one that is in play in female autoeroticism. The *one* of form, of the individual, of the (male) sexual organ, of the proper name, of the proper meaning . . . supplants, while separating and dividing, that contact of *at least two* (lips) which keeps woman in touch with herself, but without any possibility of distinguishing what is touching from what is being touched. [1985: 26]

Female sexuality is continuous and everywhere and this may be, she argues, why female consciousness is continuous and everywhere. This is why women are emotional and capricious rather than logical and directed, why they can tolerate contradiction and can refuse to be trapped into 'saying what they mean', to be trapped by their own words.

Patriarchal societies repress this *jouissance* (delight) by reconstructing women as commodities (Irigaray 1985: 170–97). All exchanges in society, of commodities, of signs, and of women take place between men. Men pass women, and their sexual and reproductive capacities, between themselves according to the rule of the incest taboo. Thus society is constructed as an exclusive valorization of relationships between men – it is 'hom(m)o-sexual'[6] in its form of social mediation. Men make exchanges with other men, the substance of their exchanges are women. Men are subjects and women are objects. They are objectified and, like other commodities, fetishized in three roles: mother, because of the valorization of biological reproduction and child-rearing; virgin, because it implies an impossibility of female sexual pleasure; and whore, because it implies giving sexual pleasure and receiving none.

Kristeva (1986) sets herself apart from Cixous and Irigaray, in so far as they concentrate on the subversion of patriarchal power alone and she is concerned to undermine all monolithic power structures.[7] Nevertheless, she takes a position which is consistent with theirs. In a devastatingly creative move she establishes the differences between men and women in terms of dimensions of time. Men are in tune with a linear or cursive conception of time, an unfolding of events through history or biography which have a beginning and an end. Women's subjectivity focuses on two other dimensions: first on cyclical or repetitive time given in the biological and natural rhythms of menstruation, gestation, seasonality, etc.; second on eternal or monumental time, the dimension of the universe which is almost contiguous with space and which is cosmic, all-encompassing and infinite. Cursive time is enslaving and enlimiting while cyclical and eternal time are liberating and delightful.

Kristeva now analyses the development of the women's movement in terms of this conception. The first wave of feminism (the suffragist movement and after) sought to locate women in the linear time of the history of any given society, to give them political and social rights in its development. The second wave (post 1968) seeks to universalize the condition of women and to transcend particular historical locations by giving a voice to female psychology and its symbolic expressions. Unlike Cixous and Irigaray, Kristeva always finds psychology and symbolism to be tractable. The writings of the new feminism can draw upon feminine subjectivity to provide a counter-ideology, a new religion to displace the old ones. The desirable outcome is not an insistence on gender difference between the sexes but an interiorization of differences within every individual so that they disappear.

Conclusion

Summary

1 Historically, sociological theory has either taken the view that gender differences are natural and immutable or, more commonly, it has been

gender blind. The most important exception is Engels' argument about the development of the family which views monomgamous relationships under capitalism as a form of masculine oppression.

2   The most important contribution of feminist theory to sociological theory has been to show that gender must be considered within a debate about whether it is structurally determined or socially constructed. The principal concept which centres this debate is 'patriarchy', the current formulation of which is provided by Millett.

3   The biological structuralism of Firestone, Eisenstein, Ortner, Brownmiller and others seeks to show that masculine oppression in society and culture is the direct outcome of genetic and physiological differences. The political implication is physical reconstruction of sexuality and reproduction.

4   The psychoanalytic structuralism of Mitchell and Chodorow is more social in its orientation, linking differences in adult behaviour to childrearing practices. However, the implicit conclusion is that gender difference, if not gender inequality, is inevitable, in so far as the Oedipal phase is unavoidable.

5   The critical structuralism of Barrett, Delphy and others is the most sociological of the three structuralist approaches to gender. Its crucial theoretical problem is the reconciliation of class structure with gender structure, of capitalism with patriarchy. It often resolves this problem by adopting a dualistic approach, insisting that each has equal social efficacy. However, it also often reduces patriarchy to class by seeking to demonstrate that patriarchy performs ideological and reproduction functions for the dominant class.

6   The principal alternative to structuralist approaches is a neoWeberian social constructionism. Here men and women are conceived as differentiated interest groups. Patriarchy is re-interpreted as social closure practised by men against women. Constructionists examine the various patterns which patriarchy can take. An important political implication is that women can change their circumstances by seeking to usurp masculine social arrangements.

7   Another recently emerging alternative is poststructuralism. Here, theorists tend to view genders as symbolic orders which have the typical structuralist characteristics of inevitability and immutability. The political implication is a radical feminism which deconstructs phallocentric symbolism and seeks to replace it with a feminized symbolic order.

Critique

It is apparent from the above summary that there are three main contradictory strands in feminist theory. These have emerged serially and now present some difficult theoretical and practical choices. They are:

1 *Theories of unequal opportunity (liberal feminism)* These emerged with the suffragist movement and establish that women have an equal right to participate in public structures with men. They make no assertion about fundamental gender differences and accept masculine criteria of performance and success. In the contemporary literature they are most closely correspond with constructionist theories of closure. Their practical importance is the removal of formal and informal barriers to participation.

2 *Theories of unequal power (socialist feminism)* This stands opposed to liberal feminism by arguing that it is impossible to take advantage of opportunities where one has no potential to do so, where patriarchy holds a vice-like grip on one's consciousness. Socialist feminism sees society as organized to prevent feminine equality, either because of masculine self-interest or because such an arrangement functions in the service of capitalism. The only practical solution to female inequality is general social revolution.

3 *Theories of difference (radical feminism)* Here there are argued to be fundamental and immutable structures of difference which are reflected in masculine and feminine subjectivities and performances. Men are argued to dominate women because their subjectivities and perform-ances are oriented to power and materialism and these will always succeed over communion and emotionality. Two possible practical solutions are offered. The first is a radical degendering in which, either: genders hyperdifferentiate to the point of dedifferentiation, so that there are many more than two genders; or masculine and feminine characteristics are simultaneously developed in each individual. The second involves a female withdrawal from associations with men including the degendering of reproductive processes by the introduc-tion of 'artificial' and *in vitro* technologics.

The move towards theories of difference places feminist theory in something of a dilemma. To accept that there are fundamental gender differences provides continued legitmacy to patriarchal domination, but to deny that these differences exist is to accept phallocentric cultural defini-tions. The next consideration for feminist thought might be to examine the question of whether consciousness and performance might be disassociated and indeed whether nonmasculine standards of performance can be institutionalized.

Further reading

The most useful general introduction is H. Eisenstein, *Contemporary Feminist Thought* (1984). For anyone seriously interested in feminist theory, Brownmiller's *Against Our Will* (1975), de Beauvoir's *The Second Sex* (1972), Friedan's *The Feminine Mystique* (1963), and Millett's *Sexual*

Politics (1971) are all required reading. Engels' *The Origin of the Family, Private Property and the State* (1975) although not written by a contemporary feminist, is also a must.

For more explicitly sociological theories, see the following: on psychoanalytic feminism, Chodorow, *Feminism and Psychoanalytic Theory* (1989); on Marxist feminism, Barrett, *Women's Oppression Today* (1980) and Delphy, *Close to Home* (1984); and on neoWeberian, constructionist feminism, Kanter, *Men and Women of the Corporation* (1977) and Walby, *Theorizing Patriarchy* (1990). An approach which nicely captures the nuances of several of the positions can be found in Brenner and Ramas 'Rethinking Women's Oppression' (1984).

Notes

1 There were two waves of feminism, each involving a political movement for emancipation and an associated elaboration of feminist thought. The first wave (approximately 1860–1920) is associated with women's political suffrage and the introduction of mechanical methods of contraception. The second wave which began in the 1960s focuses on economic, familial, sexual and cultural as well as political subordination of women. Because the institutional development of sociology occurred well after the first wave had subsided, we concentrate here on contributions from the second wave because it is these which most directly affect contemporary sociological theory.

2 Given an age of majority of 21 and a nuptial age of say 25, the period of legal freedom for women does not appear to have been generous by the standards of the late twentieth century. We should also not be misled into believing that there was much *freedom* of contract in the nineteenth century – it was extremely difficult to obtain a divorce in most societies, and far more so for women than for men.

3 For a discussion of Marxist theories of class, see chapter 9.

4 Generalized reciprocity is a form of economic exchange in which each person contributes as much as they can in exchange for whatever they need.

5 The term is derived from the Latin term for adult male (though in many modern derivations the prefix is frequently taken also to mean husband) plus the suffix meaning rule.

6 This is another of Irigaray's puns, this time playing on the French word 'homme' (man) and the Latin prefix 'homo-' (same) to suggest that masculine-dominated social mediation has a similar character to a homosexual relationship.

7 Although Julia Kristeva was born in Bulgaria, she lives in France and writes in French.

9 Differentiation and stratification

If theories of gender are a recent influence on modern sociological theory, theories of differentiation and stratification are as old as the discipline itself. They were the central concerns of the classical, founding ancestors who sought to come to grips with vast changes, which we now describe as the emergence of capitalism, industrialization, democratization, rationalization and secularization, and which swept away more traditional forms of social structure.

Two features, in particular, impressed themselves on the classical, sociological imagination. First, society was much more complex than it had previously been. Individuals were the incumbents of multiple roles, and social units increasingly were specialized in their activities. In particular, kinship was no longer the central organizing principle of social lives now built around factories, governments, and schools as well as families. These were phenomena of differentiation, the separation in time and space of the components of social life into special compartments. The second feature of this new society was that it was afflicted by profound material inequalities between its members. Moreover, such inequalities came not from the fixed statuses of aristocrat and peasant but were altogether more economic in character, being bound up with property and income, and thus were class inequalities. Both class and status were phenomena of stratification, the hierarchical division of society into ranks.[1]

Differentiation takes place along broadly functional lines, so that roles, collectivities, etc. are more specialized in terms of their functional contribution to the system. Roles and collectivities move apart from one another and become, simultaneously, more formally autonomous but more materially interdependent. Differentiation is therefore often called functional, lateral or horizontal differentiation, because it does not privilege one social unit over another. A common term is 'structural differentiation'. In summary, the characteristics of differentiation theory are as follows:

1 The direction of societal change is always towards increased differentiation.
2 Differentiation implies separation between the units of social structure. Such units might include institutions, collectivities, occupations, people, positions, tasks, groups, categories or systems. The separation often implies differential location of units in time and space.
3 A central site for increasing differentiation is the division of labour, or the differential allocation of role tasks. This site has two aspects: the

social division of labour which is the allocation of social roles to persons; and the technical division of labour, which is the extent to which tasks are specialized into limited operations within roles.

4   Differentiation sets up problems of integration. The integrating cement is often theorized as a highly generalized set of ideas and values which can transcend the diversity of social experience which differentiation sets up. In some theories this is referred to as an ideology, in others as a common culture or dominant value-system.

5   Theory also focuses on exchanges of resources between differentiated social units and the way in which these exchanges are mediated and regulated.

6   The process of social change takes an evolutionary direction through a series of stages or phases in which each stage is more positive than the previous ones in material terms.

Stratification theory is usually taken up by sociologists who focus on power and structure. It is used to describe and explain the substantive phenomena which we call class, interest groups, status, racial inequality, ethnic inequality, and gender inequality. Because the preceding chapter deals with gender inequality, and because general theories of race and ethnicity are sparse, we concentrate here on theories of class and status. In point form, these argue that:

1   All societies are characterized by regular patterns of social inequality. Minimally, such social inequality consists of a series of ranks. These ranks can be conceptualized within a spatial metaphor in which there is a hierarchical ordering from top to bottom. Maximally, social inequality is a zero-sum contest between warring groups which seek to advance their own interests at direct expense to the interests of others.

2   Stratification divides society into segments which are closed off against one another so that any individual will have more in common with fellow members of their own stratum than with members of other strata.

3   Stratification always has material aspects involving differences in property ownership and/or access to material rewards.

4   Stratification also always has power aspects – some sections of society are more powerful than others and may use this power to exploit members of other strata.

5   In many theories, stratification can also be viewed as having status aspects, involving differences in the level of normative or moral approval given to different sections of society.

6   Patterns of stratification typically are stable enough to be reproduced or inherited across generations. This means that any individual's probability of access to material rewards, to moral approval and to power can be (partially) predicted by the parents' stratum membership.

7   Members of upper strata will always seek to exclude and exploit lower strata, while members of lower strata will seek either to penetrate the boundaries of upper strata or seek radically to alter the hierarchy in favour of their own stratum. Stratification systems are therefore typically characterized by contest or struggle.

DIFFERENTIATION

As is indicated above, differentiation theory emerged in the context of the fundamental social changes of the nineteenth and twentieth centuries which we have come to call the industrial and democratic revolutions (see Nisbet 1966).

The industrial revolution refers to changes in economic life in which production becomes firmly separated from the domestic arena. It was deliberately organized within large-scale collectivities using machines which were driven by inanimate sources of power, that is it was increasingly carried out in factories. However, this is something of an oversimplification because industrialization is a process which also encompasses agricultural economic activity and the production of services in office contexts. Here too the organization of economic life became more collective, more deliberately organized, more mechanized, and is equally separated from home life.

Parallel processes in the political arena are usually characterized as democratization. Democratization implies centralization of the state, coupled with an increasing accountability to its subjects who are redefined as citizens. Citizens control the state, at least theoretically, and can thus establish themselves as its clients but this, in turn, means that the state takes on an increasing load in providing for its citizens.

One of the major tasks which sociological theory has set itself is the conceptualization and explanation of these general processes of change. Differentiation is the most general and abstract sociological concept which can encompass them. Social arrangements can be held to be more or less differentiated to the extent that the component parts are separated from one another. This separation can be accomplished in several ways: in time and space, as in the case of the modern differentiation between work and domesticity; by the allocation of types of activity, as in the equally modern separation in the domestic sphere between the 'instrumental' activities of men and the 'expressive' activities of women; or by the erection of social barriers to intercourse, mobility and access to rewards, as in the example of the separation between blacks and whites in the old South of the USA.

Increased differentiation is widely understood to be pervasive and general in its scope. It encompasses, for example, interpersonal relations to the extent that many social relationships are increasingly formal, distant and anonymous so that people are no longer embedded in collective social arrangements but are more individualized. Increased differentiation also provides purchase on the issue of changes in social roles – they become more specialized in their activity. So too do the activities of collectivities as they become focused on a narrow range of operations – retail shops, Baptist churches, TV stations, and blue-collar labour unions, for example, are highly specialized in their activities. And at the level of culture, differentiation can be noted both between specialized value-spheres, for example, science, religion, art and morality, and between ranked cultural segments, such as high culture and popular culture.

The section begins in the usual way with an introduction to the classical founding arguments. These are, even more than usually, provided by the 'holy trinity' of Marx, Durkheim and Weber, but also by Spencer. Spencer and Durkheim fall into the functionalist camp, while Marx and Weber are more interested in instrumental differentiation. From there it proceeds to an analysis of modernization theory, which is the structural-functionalist version of differentiation, focusing in the modern theoretical phase on the work of Levy, Moore, Smelser and Parsons, and in the contemporary phase on the neofunctionalist offerings of Bell, Alexander and Luhmann. There is also a review of theories focusing on the syndrome of contemporary trends known as postindustrialization, postmodernization and globalization.

Founding arguments

Here we identify the origins of the concept of differentiation in the work of Spencer and trace its refinement by Durkheim. We also examined the more critical approach to differentiation taken by Marx and then Weber.

Spencer: theoretical harmony

Although Spencer's view of social change is naïve in many respects, he was responsible for the introduction of the idea of differentiation into sociology. He developed the idea by drawing an, albeit oversimplified, analogy between the evolution of society and the evolution of biological organisms. Indeed, Spencer initiated the idea of evolution, and it was his notion of 'survival of the fittest' that was later adopted by Darwin and that had such an enormous impact on biological science. Long after so-called social Darwinism died a justly deserved death, 'biological Spencerism' endures. In defence of Spencer's sociological naïveté, it must be remembered that he had little social science to draw on and was seeking to make sense of general social change that, even today, defies a complete theoretical interpretation.

Spencer makes his initial approach to the problem of change via the process of growth (1969). He was impressed by the scale of nineteenth-

---

Herbert Spencer (1820–1903)

Spencer was born in Derbyshire, England, the son of a Protestant minister. The latter inheritance meant that he was unable to attend the local Anglican school and instead received his education from private tutors. He therefore concentrated on mathematics and science rather than the classics and this led him into an early career in railway engineering. However, he also supported himself by part-time journalism, and he eventually became a subeditor for the then radical newspaper *The Economist*. A family bequest ensured that Spencer was never poor and he is also reported to have said: 'I was never in love' although he did have a short friendship with the novelist Mary Ann Evans (George Eliot) in the 1850s. Thereafter, things became both better and worse. He succumbed to a neurotic disorder which caused severe hypochondria and insomnia and led to a withdrawn and solitary life lived in the rooms of hotels. However, he also became an enormous publishing success, achieving fame and fortune in both Britain and the USA. Nevertheless he refused all scientific and university honours. When he died of old age he was a rich and well-known figure of establishment science.

Sources: Coser (1977: 102–7); Raison (1969: 76–83)

---

century society by comparison with the societies which, in evolutionary terms, preceded it. For Spencer, growth is accomplished by a historical process of compounding and recompounding – societies are viewed as progressively and more intensively joining together so that they become ever larger in scale. As they do so they become socially denser, they are not spread so thinly over a territory, and are more internally coherent and solid.

However: 'Along with that integration which is the primary trait of evolution, [societies] exhibit in high degrees the secondary trait, differentiation' (1969: 31). As they grow and become more stable and solid: 'the unlikeness of parts increases' so that a society 'to reach great size must acquire great complexity' (1969: 31). Differentiation proceeds in stages from a general to a 'special' level. The first units which separate are the coordinating agencies of government, followed by agricultural and industrial organizations, agencies of communication, and so on. Government differentiates internally into political, military and religious units, and further differentiation occurs within these subunits.

Spencer now makes a point which is critical in subsequent analyses of functional differentiation. As a society grows and differentiates, its pattern of integration changes. When the elements of a society are structurally similar, for example, if it is made up of relatively small tribes which are similarly organized, there are no relations of dependency between them. Here, society does not constitute a 'vital whole' (1969: 151) and indeed may break down in feuds and conflicts over resources. But: 'As its parts assume different functions they become dependent on one another, so that injury to one hurts others; until, in highly-evolved societies, general perturbation is caused by derangement of any portion' (1969: 151). Spencer is saying here that as the units of society become more specialized, each becomes unable to perform the functions performed by others, and each becomes dependent on the others. A natural harmony of the parts arises and they are constrained into a mutual solidarity.

This formulation enables Spencer to outline what has become his most famous distinction between 'militant' and 'industrial societies'. Militant societies are a relatively unevolved form in which the natural harmony described above has not yet emerged. Militant societies are medium in scale and moderate in their level of differentiation. Those that are fit enough to survive do so because they devote a large proportion of their resources and energies to hostile military action against environing societies. Militant societies will therefore develop central and dictatorial governing agencies which will seek to coordinate and harness resources in the direction of the defence of the society. Such coordination will result in: fixed social statuses; state ownership of collective enterprises; an absence of social mobility; and economic and political self-sufficiency.

By contrast, an industrial society is highly evolved. It is consequently large in scale and exhibits a high level of differentiation. It is a society characterized by a large measure of individual freedom and, therefore, government only exists in order to put into practice the general will of the people. Because the society is highly differentiated, any attempt to impose direction on divergent individual interests will only result in societal breakdown. Rather, interest groups must negotiate with one another in order to arrive at a consensus. Similarly: the distribution of goods and services is accomplished by free and contractualized exchange rather than by command; private ownership and control of enterprise is correspondingly favoured; occupational status is earned rather than inherited so occupational mobility becomes possible; and relations with other societies are increasingly governed by trade and diplomacy rather than by hostility, defensiveness and self-sufficiency. In general, industrial society is materially oriented, concentrating on the benefits which emerge from privately owned production and trade.

Spencer's rose-coloured vision has become extraordinarily familiar as the ideology of market democracy, and indeed has become the aspiration of millions of members of the formerly 'militant' societies of Eastern Europe which changed so radically at the end of the twentieth century. However, even at the end of the nineteenth century there had been very serious doubt about its veracity. The central difficulty is that of natural harmony between the differentiated interests of society and, as is mentioned in the preceding chapter, this matter of solidarity is the central focus of Durkheim's theory of the social system (1933). Indeed, Spencer is the main inspiration and focus for Durkheim's argument.

Durkheim: conscious of the collectivity

The critical differences between Durkheim and Spencer are twofold. First, Durkheim does not view increased differentiation as a natural concomitant of growth but argues rather that growth increases social density, which makes the struggle for existence more acute, and which in turn forces increased specialization. Second, integration between the differentiated parts of an industrial society is not the simple consequence of free contract but of new moral patterns which also specify the form and enforcement of contracts. We can now trace the threads of Durkheim's argument.

As in the case of Spencer, Durkheim's account of social change begins with a statement about growth. However, for him, the critical outcome of the growth and concentration of population, taken together with improvements in transportation and communication, is an increase not merely in the numerical density but in the *moral* density of society. By moral density Durkheim means, roughly, the number of social relationships per person. Increased moral density places people in greater contact with one another and, together with increased population volume, puts pressure on the supply of resources. Under these circumstances, Durkheim now reasons, competition for, and the possibility of conflict over resources increases. Individuals will be constrained to establish new and specialized ways of doing things, and will avoid duplicating the activities of others. In this way, the (social) division of labour, or occupational differentiation, advances. Like Spencer, then, Durkheim argues that the scale and complexity of society are correlated.[2]

A more interesting part of Durkheim's argument is concerned with the link between differentiation, on one hand, and solidarity or integration, on the other. A society which has a low level of differentiation is a segmental society, that is, it is composed of identical parts, each of which is organized on politico-familial lines as a clan. Moreover, within each clan, each member has an identical view of the world, an identical consciousness. The society is integrated by the fact that all of its members think and act in the same way. Any slight difference between clans is ameliorated by the low level of contact between them. This type of integration is called *mechanical solidarity*. By contrast, a society with a high level of differentiation can be described as an organized society. It is composed of social units which are dissimilar and which are linked with each other in complex patterns. They are harmoniously organized, but not spontaneously so. Rather, they are: 'co-ordinated and subordinated one to another around the same central organ which exercises a moderating action over the rest of the organism' (1933: 181), that is, the state.

However, Durkheim clearly became uncomfortable about this analogy between the brain and the state. Ultimately, he came to see the state as

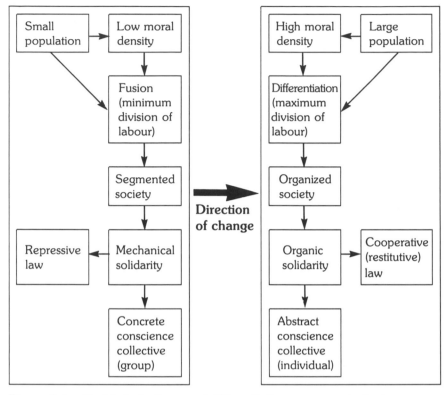

Figure 9.1   *Durkheim's theory of differentiation – arrows indicate causality*

interdependent with other units in society, but as having only a relatively privileged relationship to them. Under this argument, solidarity derives neither from the state nor from natural harmonious exchange but from shared understandings about individual autonomy and rights, and the fact that people have a moral commitment to the continuation of a society of unlike parts. This is called *organic solidarity* because society is integrated in a similar way to a biological organism. The connections between the various elements of the theory can be traced through figure 9.1.

Durkheim 'validates' his argument by an examination of different patterns of law and sanctions under mechanical and organic solidarity respectively. He finds an association between mechanical solidarity on one hand and legal systems which are penal or punishment-centred on the other. Punishment-centred law expresses society's moral outrage about the fact that some of its members have deviated and that they are no longer similar to normal members. Such societies control this deviation by meting out *repressive* sanctions of torture, incarceration, expulsion or death, which serve to exclude the deviant from normal society. By contrast, an increase in the division of labour and organic solidarity sees the emergence of cooperative law. Here the emphasis is on maintaining positive relations between the differentiated members of society by the application of civil, commercial, procedural and constitutional law. Sanctions here are *restitutive* in character, that is, they restore relationships to balance where their norms have been violated. Restitutive sanctions normally include the payment of fines or damages rather than focusing on punishment of the individual person.

These legal changes indicate alterations in the character of the *conscience collective* (for a definition and analysis, see chapter 5). Under mechanical solidarity it is highly specific and is virtually coterminous with the consciousness of each individual. However, an advance in the level of differentiation means that the collective consciousness must become more abstract in order to encompass the diversity of human experience. However, it must also release certain elements of individual consciousness, those which are specific to the individual situation, from its control. So, advances in the level of differentiation provide for a general attenuation of the *conscience collective.*

This sets up the problem that, if the collective consciousness becomes weak and generalized enough, there is just the possibility that the processes of organic solidarity might fail. The circumstances of failure are described by Durkheim as the abnormal forms of the division of labour. There are three such abnormal forms:

- *Anomic division of labour*   This is where the regulation of exchanges between the units of society fails to occur: the units may be insufficiently contiguous for their mutual interdependence to be apparent; or advances in differentiation may have been so rapid that there has been insufficient time to establish norms of exchange; or advances in differentiation may have become too extreme for the survival of the *conscience collective.*
- *Forced division of labour*   This is the term Durkheim uses to describe class conflict. It occurs where one class coerces the members of another to perform highly specialized tasks.
- *'Another form'* [bureaucratist division of labour]   This is where the differentiation of occupations by the proliferation of occupational titles occurs simply for its own sake, without adequate coordination by a leadership. Differentiated occupations are no longer goal-directed and become inefficient wasters of time and effort.

Marx: material differences

The concept of differentiation attains nowhere near the level of centrality in the work of Marx and Weber that it does in Durkheim. Indeed, each subordinates it to processes regarded as more fundamental: commodification in the case of Marx and rationalization in the case of Weber. Marx, for example, recognizes that: 'Bourgeois society is the most highly developed and most highly differentiated historical organization of production' (1977: 355). However, this outcome is purely contingent, the explanation for it being located in the social relations of production, the issue of who owns productive property and how it can be owned.

Marx views the progress of differentiation much as Spencer or Durkheim does. However, for Marx, there are two stages in the development of the division of labour. The first is what we would now call the social division of labour:

> The division of labour inside a nation leads at first to the separation of industrial and commercial from agricultural labour, and hence to the separation of town and country and to the conflict of their interests. Its further development leads to the separation of commercial from industrial labour. [1977: 161]

However, there is a second stage, more important to Marx, which is the development of the technical division of labour:

> At the same time, through the division of labour inside these various branches there develop various divisions among the individuals cooperating in definite kinds of labour. [However, t]he various stages in the division of labour are just so many different forms of ownership, i.e. the existing stage in the division of labour determines also the relations of individuals to one another with reference to the material, instrument, and product of labour. [1977: 161]

This development has two consequences. First, it separates the worker from control of the product. The fundamental source of this control is the productive power of capital which forces a division of labour on workers. Thus: 'It converts the labourer into a crippled monstrosity, by forcing his detail dexterity at the expense of a world of productive capabilities and instincts' (1977: 477). The worker is reduced by the division of labour to the status of a cog in a machine: 'the individual himself is made the automatic motor of a fractional operation' (1977: 477). The worker no longer even sees, let alone controls, the finished product, and because of this inability to produce anything independently becomes the mere tool of the capitalist. Thus differentiation is a key contributor to alienation, the condition in which a sense of self-control as a productive being is taken away.

The second consequence concerns the relationship between production and consumption (Marx 1977: 421–55). The worker produces parts of particular products yet consumes a wide range of whole products. The division of labour therefore implies exchange and exchange means that products are transformed into commodities. A product becomes a commodity when its value is established not in terms of its uses but in terms of the price for which it can be exchanged. In order for exchange to occur on a radical scale a generalized medium of exchange-values is required, hence the emergence of money. Money, in turn, allows for the circulation of commodities so that they can be exchanged and re-exchanged at a profit. The process thus allows capital to be accumulated. Meanwhile society and culture become suffused by commodities – all elements become subordinated to a cash nexus in which not only products but labour, loyalty, art, morality, sexuality, etc. become commodities which are exchangeable at a cash value.

Weber: formalities of differentiation

Weber's approach (1947: 218–65) is far more formal and less substantive than any of the other classical accounts. Weber was trying to provide a means of classifying the types of division of labour so he makes a precise separation between the technical and social divisions of labour. His discussion of the technical division of labour is relatively brief, noting that the mechanization of modern industry presupposes both a high level of functional specialization, on one hand, and calculability of the quality and quantity of human performance, on the other.

Much more is said about the social division of labour. The transition from traditional to modern society can be characterized in terms of the occupational structure. He implicitly sets up two polar types (1947: 250–1). The first is comparable with Spencer's militant type: functions are assigned and specified centrally and labour is unfree, apart from some autocephalous specialists with high levels of skill, such as artisans, physicians, etc. The second is modern or industrial: here occupational differentiation proceeds on the basis of market demand, specialization consists of a rational response to such demands, and occupations tend to be collective in character, for example, factory workers, managers, government officials.

This transformation can be subsumed under the rubric of the rationalization of society (see chapter 6). An increase in the level of occupational differentiation can be understood as part of a general drive to the institutionalization of instrumental rationality, which was itself the product of a more general process of differentiation at the level of culture – that promoted by Calvinistic Protestantism in which this-worldly concerns were differentiated from other-worldly concerns. Occupational differentiation is fundamental to the technical rationalization of social relationships, their reduction to aspects of scientific, industrial and administrative processes. Maximum occupational differentiation provides for maximum standardization of tasks and thus maximum calculability of human labour inputs. It allows organizational and physical machines to manipulate human action without reference to substantive commitment.

Modernization: the utopias of functionalism

The idea of differentiation struck a harmonic chord in mid-twentieth-century American society. Like Spencer's Victorian England, it was a society which had enjoyed enormous material and military success and it was indeed a highly differentiated society. The apparent association was irresistible and fortunately an appropriate theoretical vehicle was at hand. Just as Durkheim's ideas about system functions were carried into modern American sociology by Parsons, so also were his ideas on differentiation. In the process, Marx's and Weber's warnings about the negative consequences of differentiation received scant attention.

In structural-functionalist hands differentiation becomes modernization, not a general dimension of social systems but a unitary direction of change which is all-pervasive and whose direction is indicated by the lead given by the contemporary USA. However, the conceptual transformation was actually largely accomplished by Parsons' epigones. Only in the later part of his life did the leading structural-functionalist himself pay any serious attention to change but then in a quite masterly way which outshone preceding efforts. To begin with, however, we will concentrate on two of the early modernization theorists, Levy and Smelser.

Colomy (1990: 483) identifies the key themes of these modern differentiation theories as increased efficiency and reintegration. The assignment of similar functions to units which specialized in the performance of those functions would allow economies of scale, the development of expertise, and a concentration of resources, which reduces costs and increases benefits. At least in material terms, a more differentiated society would be a more productive and wealthy society. However, a highly differentiated society would have to concentrate some of its activities on solving the Durkheimian integration problem, the slide into anomie.

Levy: rationalizing modernization

Levy (1966) sets himself an essentially classificatory task: he seeks, in a mere 800 or so pages, to list the differences between societies which are modernized and societies which are not (hereafter described as traditional, although Levy's term is 'relatively non-modernized'). His minimum definition of modernization is highly materialistic, and roughly corresponds with industrialization: 'A society will be considered more or less modernized to the extent that its members use inanimate sources of power and/or use tools to multiply the effects of their efforts' (1966: 11). However, a more complete definition can be found in his description of the structural characteristics of any society and the ways in which these vary between traditional and modern contexts. He divides these characteristics into two categories: aspects, by which he means analytic slices or dimensions; and organizational contexts, more concrete and elaborated patterns of social relationships. Under these headings modernized societies have the following characteristics relative to traditional ones.

Aspects

- The units of society, its collectivities and roles, are highly specialized with respect to the type of activity which they perform. This means that individuals can specialize in the skills which they use in role performance.

- The units of society have a relatively low level of self-sufficiency – they must rely on other units to provide resources which they do not themselves produce.
- Value orientations are highly universalistic – they tend to stress what a person can do that is relevant to the situation rather than what they are.
- An increasing centralization of decision making is set up by the need to coordinate and control diverse, specialized activities.
- A large proportion of human relationships are characterized by rationality, universalism, functional specificity and emotional avoidance.
- A large proportion of the exchanges between specialized units takes place by means of generalized media (e.g. money) and within market contexts.

Organizational contexts

- A widespread institutionalization of bureaucracy occurs, without which the coordination and control of specialized activities would be impossible.
- The multilineal, conjugal family is established which covers a maximum of two generations, de-emphasizes unilineal descent, and focuses on the husband–wife relationship as the foundational bond.
  (Levy 1966: 38–79)

Levy makes no statement of the driving force behind modernization other than motivation at the level of the individual. For early modernizers: 'no society has members completely unable to comprehend or sense advantages in some applications of power from inanimate sources and tools' (1966: 25–6). And latecomers are highly vulnerable to the 'universal social solvent' of modernization. Once contact has been established with a modernized society, at least some members of a traditional society will want to change it in order to improve their material situation, more or less out of envy of the 'inordinate material productivity' of modern societies (1966: 125–6). Needless to say: 'United States society . . . is the most extreme example of modernization' (1966: 36).

Smelser: disturbing modernization

Levy's highly abstracted description may be compared with Smelser's more substantive theoretical statement (1968). At one level, Smelser equates modernization with economic development, which he defines in terms of four shifts: from traditional to scientifically based technology; from subsistence to commercialized agriculture; from animal power to power-driven machines; and from farm and village to urban centres (1968: 126). Familiarly such a shift promotes a new type of social structure characterized by structural differentiation which he defines as: 'a process whereby [each] social role or organization . . . differentiates into two or more roles or organizations which function more effectively in the new historical circumstances' (1968: 129). Four areas of structural differentiation are critical:

*   The removal of economic activities of production, distribution and exchange from the family-community complex.
*   The concentration of family activities on biological and social reproduction and emotional expression.
*   The separation of areas of secular concern from areas of religious concern.
*   The displacement of ascriptive status rankings (e.g. ethnicity, race, gender) by elaborate occupational hierarchies.[3]

As is indicated above, one of the central concerns in a structural-functional analysis of differentiation is the issue of the reintegration of newly differentiated units. Smelser is a key figure in bringing this issue back into the sociological agenda. He appears to view the process of change as an oscillation through time between the poles of differentiation and integration:

> Development proceeds as a contrapuntal interplay between differentiation (which is divisive of established society) and integration (which unites differentiated structures on a new basis). Paradoxically, however, the course of integration itself produces more differentiated structures – e.g. trade unions, associations, political parties, and a mushrooming state apparatus. [1968: 138, italics deleted]

Smelser is doubtless substantively correct to examine problems of, for example, exchange of employment information between firms and families, or communication between the citizen and the remote and centralized state. However, he is stumped by the paradox he nominates – newly differentiated organizations cannot replace a general sense of shared membership. The spectre of an anomic division of labour remains.

However, Smelser actually gets closer to grips with integration problems when he speaks to his third focus of interest, social disturbances. Such disturbances arise from contradictions between old and new social arrangements and the interests which represent them, either between generations or in different sectors of society. A typical response is the emergence of religious or nationalistic social movements, led by charismatic leaders and focused on a return to traditional values and the re-establishment of traditional arrangements. The process is perhaps more adequately described by Lechner (1990) as a logic of dedifferentiation in which there is a subordination of all other social arrangements to value-patterning, that is, the process is one of the 'moralization' of economics and politics.

Any routinization of such moralizations, as in contemporary, post-revolutionary Iran, indicates a progressive reconciliation between the old and the new and is indeed the resolution of an integration problem.

What Smelser had earlier described as an integration problem is one simply of establishing norms and media of exchange between differentiated institutions. His subsequent discussion of social disturbances is, in fact, much closer to the Durkheimian question of anomie. Such genuinely integrative (i.e. dedifferentiating) organizations as social movements therefore tend to be relatively short-lived – they either wilt in the face of modern forces, traditional ones having expressed themselves; or they do indeed routinize and become absorbed into an integrated modernity; or they become transformed into organizations of genuine conflict, which indicates a fundamentally malintegrated society (e.g. contemporary Lebanon or Northern Ireland).

Parsons: universal modernization

Nowhere is the treatment of differentiation as novel, developed and courageous as in Parsons. Where others view differentiation as a list of open possibilities (e.g. Levy 1966; Colomy 1990) Parsons regards it as having a specific evolutionary direction and a logic or dynamic which drives it in this direction. The logic or dynamic is adaptation: 'the capacity of a living system to cope with its environment' (Parsons 1964: 340). Differentiation proceeds in the direction of adaptive upgrading:

> If differentiation is to yield a balanced, more evolved system, each newly differentiated sub-structure . . . must have increased adaptive capacity for performing its primary function, as compared with the performance of that function in the previous, more diffuse structure. Thus economic production is typically more efficient in factories than in households. [Parsons 1966: 22]

This pattern is associated with two other developments (1966: 22–3). The first is the familiar one of integration, but Parsons gives it a new twist. Differentiation forces an upgrading of the level of integration. Because the units of society are less self-sufficient and must make exchanges, social resources (human talent, knowledge, skills, capital, commodities, etc.) must become generalized and interchangeable. This increased interchangeability provides a basis for the inclusion of out-groups within full and 'real' social membership. The second development is in the arena of the general value-pattern of the society. The value-pattern must become both more complex, so that specific elements of it can be applied to differentiated subunits, and more generalized, so as to legitimate the variety of goals and activities found in the upgraded social system.

The overarching trend of differentiation occurs in the general action system (see chapter 5) (1966: 24–5). Culture moves apart from the social system as the gods become increasingly 'dehumanized' and remote from everyday, worldly affairs; personality and social system also separate as individuals are increasingly understood to be autonomous from society and dissimilar to one another. However, Parsons is more interested in the way that this is expressed in the differentiation of any given society. In order to describe these processes we rely on two overlapping, though somewhat dissimilar sources. The first is a paper on what Parsons calls 'evolutionary universals' (1964), a concept based on the idea of natural selection in organisms. They are defined as: 'any organizational development sufficiently important to further evolution that, rather than emerging only once, it is likely to be "hit upon" by various systems operating under different conditions' (1964: 329). These developments are not only evolutionary universals but evolutionary prerequisites – universals at one level are necessary for the later emergence of higher levels of adaptive capacity.

Parsons identifies four base universals found in all, even the most undifferentiated of societies: technology, kinship, language, and religion. Then there are two universals associated with minimum evolution, stratification and explicit cultural legitimation (written preservation of tradition), and a further four associated with the emergence of modern societies: bureaucratic organization, money and markets, a universalistic legal system, and democratic association (both governmental and private).

The second source consists of two 'introductory' books on societal evolution (1966; 1971) which were later combined into a single volume (1977). Here the stress is on AGIL (see chapter 4) and the cybernetic hierarchy (see chapter 5), so that differentiation now is seen to proceed in terms of increasing specialization by AGIL function. Parsons specifies three phases in this evolutionary process: primitive society, intermediate society, and modern society. Shifts between the phases are marked by evolutionary breakthroughs in which new universals come to be institutionalized in one or more of the AGIL boxes. The discordance between this work and the 'evolutionary universals' paper is that while in the later work he specifies a quadripartite evolutionary pattern, in the earlier paper he gives four base universals and four modern evolutionary universals, but only two intermediate evolutionary universals.

A version which combines the two arguments might be constructed in the form given in figure 9.2. The main differences between this and the early 'evolutionary universals' paper is that twelve, rather than ten, universals are specified. Of the two new ones, 'abstract intellectual standards' is suggested by Parsons himself:

> The newest phase returns to concern with cultural elements. The focus is not religion but the secular intellectual disciplines and, in a special sense, the arts. Whereas philosophy was in the ascendance in the early modern phase, science has become so in the twentieth century through extending its scope to the social and behavioural fields and even to the humanities. The educational revolution has introduced mechanisms by which the new cultural standards, especially those embodied in the intellectual disciplines, are institutionalized in ways that partly replace traditional religion. [1977: 194]

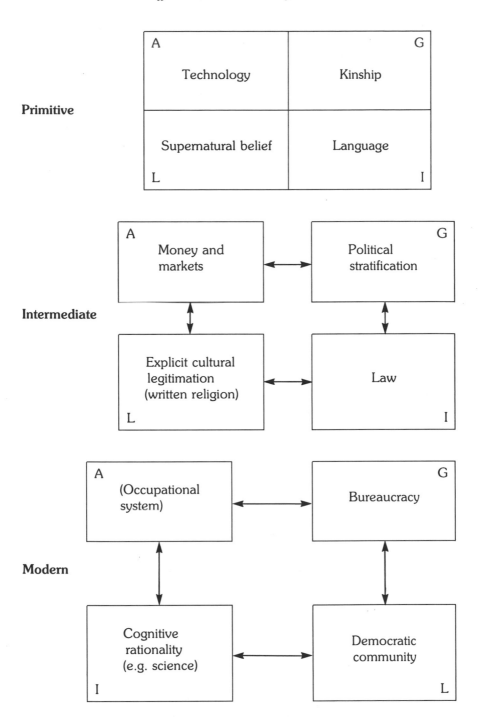

Figure 9.2 *A version of Parsons' theory of societal evolution – arrows indicate the thrust of structural differentiation*

The other new universal is 'industrial production' which develops in the modern A box, an area which is a well-known Parsonsian lacuna. In order to accommodate these new universals, we can move 'money and markets' and 'universalistic law' to the intermediate stage where they really belong. Although these are indeed prerequisites for modernity, their historical emergence pre-dates it by a long way.

The diagram should be understood as a series of layers: modern societies, for example, carry forward all the universal features of primitive and intermediate ones. Note also that evolution implies not only the emergence of new universals but that structural arrangements do indeed differentiate, they move apart. In addition, Parsons has 'resolved' the Durkheimian problem of integration by separating it into two forms: system integration (I) is the problem of normatively ordered exchange between subsystems, accomplished progressively by language, law, and then democracy; social integration (L) is the problem of establishing orderly and predictable relationships between actors and is accomplished by totemic religion, explicit cultural legitimation (priestly, hierocratic religion) and then abstract intellectual standards (cognitive rationality).

Phase shifts are marked by evolutionary breakthroughs. The consequent strains produced by each breakthrough induce the emergence of commensurate universals. Stratification is the key breakthrough in the primary move from primitive to intermediate. Lineages in economically advantaged ecological locations will be able to dominate other lineages and incorporate them as commoners subordinated to their own monarchical or noble status. This new and radical inequality must be legitimated by the development of explicit written sources which can demonstrate its divine origins. Similarly, an industrial production system based on individualized employment contracts and occupational specialization is the key breakthrough from intermediate to modern. This in turn sets up tensions of coordination and control and of commitment which induce the emergence of the other modern universals.

Luhmann: differentiating differentiation

A view of functional differentiation as a complete description of the entire course of the history of social structure is not even shared by Parsons' more recent student, Luhmann. Rather Luhmann sees differentiation as a generic concept which embraces segmentation (mechanical solidarity) and stratification as well as standard structural differentiation. He proceeds to organize these three into an evolutionary scheme which has much in common with Parsons' primitive–intermediate–modern sequence. His definitions (1982: 263) are as follows:

- Segmentary differentiation occurs when a system is divided into equal and identical subsystems. Archaic and forager societies are the main examples of segmentary differentiation.

- Stratificatory differentiation occurs when a system is divided into ranked and unequal subsystems. Ranking is a general principle. Feudal societies had stratificatory (aristocratic, religious and peasant 'estates') as well as segmentary differentiation ('manors').
- Functional differentiation occurs when subsystems are nonidentical with (different from) one another but are not ranked. Function provides the main basis for the differentiation of modern societies, although segmentary (e.g. families) and stratificatory (e.g. classes) are still present.

It must be stressed that these forms of differentiation are not mutually exclusive. Subsequent forms must 'contain' all previous ones. For example, a functionally differentiated economy might be said to contain stratificatory differentiation between managers and employees and also segmentary differentiation between firms.

However, Luhmann insists on the nonstratification of functionally differentiated units.

> No subsystem can take the place of another because no subsystem can be a functional equivalent for any other. It is impossible to order all of them together from a central position or a position of supreme authority. There is no other guarantee of the unity of society than the combination of functional closure and sensible openness to the environment on the level of the individual functional systems. That is the order that reproduces the ever-increasing complexity and lability of modern society. [1990: 432]

Here, however, the similarity with Parsons ends. There is no logic of adaptive upgrading in Luhmann. Rather the transition from one level of differentiation to the next is simply a matter of chance, and is the consequence neither of human intention nor of some general historical structuralist principle. They must be accidents, he says, because an absence of inhibitions and prohibitions is highly unlikely. Each transition has three moments – variation from the existing state of affairs; selection of the new form; and its restabilization as a new principle for the ordering of society – and could easily be arrested at any one of them.

Durkheim's problem of anomie also can easily be 'solved'. Luhmann uses a device that he calls 'the paradox of differentiated unity'. From inside any specialized unit, the social world outside appears to be unintelligibly complex and turbulent. However, this does not matter because each differentiated unit does not look outside itself for value-guidance – each becomes self-referential in terms of values. For example, business firms do not get their values from churches but from their own cultures. So long as the differentiated units can communicate with one another they do not need to share regulative values. The only functional necessity in a highly differentiated world is a system of communication: 'world society would fall apart if structural changes reversed either the primary pattern of differentiation or the system of mass communication' (1982: 248). The paradox is that the world can cohere even though its values are incoherent.

Theories of the future of differentiation

Functionalist theories set the scene for arguments about differentiation. Their vision of a rosy future of continuous economic progress and Americanization has provided a handy target not only for Marxist theorists, who view the pattern of capitalist development as something radically different, but also for those who want to view change as a lurching and bumping set of shifts rather than a smooth and gradual transformation. We make only one venture into the Marxist alternatives, one which focuses resolutely on the issue of differentiation. This is Braverman's argument about the development of the technical division of labour. We then move on to examine theories that propose that there might be something after differentiation.

Braverman: the dystopia of differentiation

Instrumentalist accounts of functional differentiation, along the lines indicated by Marx and Weber, are relatively rare. A singular and influential example is the work of Braverman (1974). Braverman is interested in the labour process, the manner in which human labour power is applied to physical objects in order to transform them into new products. His theme is the way in which, under capitalism, management is continuously oriented to controlling the labour process so as to maximize worker ouput and, in turn, to maximize the accumulation of capital. An important tool in controlling the labour process is the manipulation of the division of labour, the differentiation of work and workers.

Braverman begins by addressing the distinction which we noted had originally been made by Weber, that between the social and the technical division of labour. The social division of labour is the normal distribution of occupations or jobs to individuals and is found in all societies, e.g. the allocation of gathering to women and of hunting to men in forager societies. The distinguishing and problematic feature of capitalist societies is an abnormal technical division of labour in which occupations become fragmented into minimum component tasks. These acts of fragmentation are carried out by management which, in the process, appropriates to itself all the knowledge and skill which goes into making the product. The worker merely engages in a highly routinized, narrow, unskilled, repetitive and monotonous performance that can be regulated by the speed of a machine or the gaze of an overseer. The worker is provided with no capacity for resistance to control of work by management.

Braverman identifies two important phases in the differentiation of the labour process. The first is the application of the principles of Taylor's 'scientific management' to industrial production at about the turn of the twentieth century. Scientific management involved an analysis of the job as a series of component tasks and the experimental measurement of them so that conditions for the optimum performance of each could be established.

The tasks could then be reorganized and simplified so that workers would no longer need themselves to conceptualize the labour process. However, the key problem for scientific management was supervision and, fortunately, help was at hand in the form of the moving assembly line. This ushered in an era in which even the skills appropriate to differentiated tasks could be taken on by a machine. More importantly, because the pace of a machine could be controlled by a manager, so also could the rate of work. Scientific management and the assembly line turned manual workers into mere appendages of machines, utterly unskilled and controlled.

The second phase in the differentiation of the labour process concerns office workers. Like Bell (see below), Braverman notes the way in which a mass of office workers progressively takes over the functions of the capitalist. However, it too has been subjected to processes of scientific management and mechanization, though at a much later date. In particular, in the later part of the twentieth century, computer networks and workstations have both deskilled office workers and subjected them to an increased level of machine control. In its earliest applications the computer affected only data processing but its effects have now spread to bookkeeping, word processing, and even sales and customer relations.

After differentiation: postindustrialization and postmodernization

Bell's prognostication of the outcome of differentiating tendencies stands squarely in the 'American utopia' tradition. The outcome is a 'post-industrial' society (1973). Such a society has five characteristics:

- The differentiation of the occupational structure brings it to a point at which the number of people engaged in occupations producing services predominates over all others.
- These occupations are predominantly professional and technical in character, and they consitute the dominant class of the society.
- Theoretical knowledge predominates over practical knowledge and becomes the main source of innovation and policy formulation.
- Technological development comes within the ambit of human control and planning. Technological goals can be set and activities coordinated to accomplish them. Invention is no longer an individualized activity governed by chance.
- The most important technology is no longer physical but intellectual, so that human decisions previously based on intuitions and judgements can now be based on rational calculations within formulae.

The postindustrial society is classless, rationalized, leisure oriented, technologized, and intellectualized, a genuine American utopia.

The contrast with Braverman could not be more stark. For Bell, service workers are an emerging force, for Braverman they are being reduced to

proletarian status; for Bell, theoretical knowledge and intellectual technology are being widely dispersed, for Braverman knowledge and conceptualization functions are being concentrated in few hands; in the post-
industrial society, machines advance human possibilities, but in Braverman's proletarianized late capitalism they deskill and disempower.

Perhaps the critical problem for both Bell and Braverman is that they are
entrapped in modernist views of the differentiation process in which all
that can be conceptualized is its advance. Let us now examine a summarizing argument that draws on several other theories to suggest that the
process is not as relentless and limitless as they would suggest.

Crook, Pakulski and Waters (1992) argue that the advanced stage of
capitalism is the product of two main groups of processes. It is, in familiar
terms, a highly differentiated society exhibiting high levels of specialization
and complexity; but it is also a highly organized society exhibiting high
levels of rationalization and commodification (see chapter 6). They argue
that these two processes become so extreme that they tend to collide to
produce a societal phase-shift that can be called 'postmodernization'.

In general, they accept structural-functionalist arguments about *differentiation*. Twentieth-century, capitalist societies are made up of a series of
different types of social unit, each specialized by function. Social units
having a similar function are also similar in structure, for example:

- Manufacturing businesses have the common function of production;
  they have the common structures of human–machine teams, a separation of ownership from control and employees from managers, of
  market domination by mass production.
- Families have the functions of biological and social reproduction; they
  tend to have structures which are conjugal-nuclear and masculine
  dominated.
- States provide the function of government; they tend to be democratic
  and welfare oriented.
- Churches provide morality; they tend to embrace universalistic and
  abstract theologies.
- Political parties provide political inclusion; they tend to espouse
  multiple issues and to seek mass appeal.

However, in the contemporary period social units appear to be differentiating at the level of structure as well as of function and it is now far less
possible to read off the structure of a social unit from its function. They
term such a process *hyperdifferentiation* – that is, a very extreme level of
differentiation. Here are some examples:

- In the case of production units, mass production systems may still be
  found but so also may market-niche producers, cooperatives, techno-
  cratic partnerships, segmented organizations, subcontractors, home-
  workers, and so on.

- Families also exhibit a wide range of structures – multiple generations, lateral groupings, single parents, homosexual partnerships, childless heterosexual couples, etc.
- State functions are becoming dissipated to supernational and to local arrangements.
- Churches are broadening their functions and their media.
- Political parties are attenuating in the face of mass social movements espousing diffuse materialist values.

There is such a mixing of functions and structural possibilities, they argue, that hyperdifferentiation paradoxically moves society towards dedifferentiation.

By contrast with structural-functionalism, however, Crook, Pakulski and Waters draw on Habermas (see chapter 5) and others to argue that a second major component of modernization is an increasing level of centralized organization. The state and economic units are increasingly able to use the media that they generate, power and money, to take control of domestic and informal arrangements. The process culminates in the completion of a monocentric level of organization (hyperorganization). Here lifeworld structures (family, community and culture) are not merely dominated but completely subsumed by the centres of money and power. However, the interpenetrations of system and lifeworld can undermine the orderliness of states and economies – if organizations become 'cultural' and 'familistic' then directives will cease to be authoritative and will become mere opinions. So here too there is an ironic reversal – in so far as organization leads to hyperorganization it will also produce disorganization.

These reversals will be accelerated by a critical tension between hyperdifferentiation and hyperorganization. Even if these two processes could be sustained independently, they are not mutually sustainable. Crook, Pakulski and Waters give three grounds for this unresolvable opposition: issues associated with the sources of the media of control; issues associated with the vulnerability of objects to control; and issues associated with the reduction of distance between social units.

- If there are multiple sources for money and power, businesses and governments lose their effectivity as sources of control; put another way, self-sufficiency reduces interdependence;
- If a society is hyperdifferentiated, the consequences of a given piece of bureaucratic or economic manipulation cannot be foreseen because it becomes impossible to identify the target. States become ungovernable, economies unmanageable, and lifeworlds anarchistic.
- The intertwining of the public with the domestic negates hyperdifferentiation, reducing social units to an indeterminate mix; there are so many different types of social unit and so much individual distinctiveness that boundaries and distances collapse.

They sum up the consequences of this collision in the following terms:

> The onset of postmodernization is genuinely explosive as liberated societal components diverge rapidly from the central direction of modernity. Post-modernization is characterized by an unprecedented level of unpredictability and apparent chaos. Action is divorced from underlying material constraints (or rather these constraints disappear) and enters the voluntaristic realm of taste, choice and preference. As it does so the boundaries between determined social groups disappear. So class, gender, and ethnicity decline in social significance and so also do some of their characteristic forms of expression including class-based political action and the distinction between high and popular culture. On a more abstract level the progressive differentiation of culture, society and personality characteristic of modernity involutes so that the very idea of an independent, purely social structural realm no longer makes sense. Rather, 'society' must be understood in terms of 'culture' as patterns of signs and symbols penetrate and erode structural boundaries. The power of the large-scale social phenomena of modernity including states, monopolistic economic organizations, ecclesia, military forces, and scientific establishments is attenuated as cultural currents propagate and sweep the globe, intersecting in indeterminate ways. [1992: 35]

The onset of postmodernization for them represents a rapid and radical shift from hyperdifferentiation and monocentric organization to dedifferentiation and disorganization.

Globalization: a world of difference

All of the arguments about differentiation considered so far treat it as a social process which occurs within societies. They largely address the issue of the ways in which the component social structures of nation-states separate and drift apart. We can now move on to address analyses which focus on the world as a whole as the primary unit of analysis. Theories of globalization assess the extent to which the world as a whole is differentiating or, indeed, dedifferentiating.

Although there are several prior analyses of the world as a single system, including, for example, Lenin's concept of 'Imperialism' (1939) and 'dependency theory' (e.g. Amin 1974) which specifies a dependent relationship between centre and periphery societies, the original sociological argument for considering the world as a single system comes from Wallerstein (1974). His primary unit of analysis is the world-system, a unit which has a capacity to develop independently of the social processes and relationships which are internal to its component societies. A world-system has the following charcteristics:

- The dynamics of its development are largely internal, that is, they are not determined by events which occur outside it.
- It is materially self-contained and self-sufficient because it has an extensive division of labour between its component societies.

- It contains a multiplicity of cultures which, when taken together, are viewed by individual participants as constituting 'the world' in a phenomenological sense.
(Wallerstein 1974: 347–8)

There are three possible types of world-system:

- world-empires, in which a multiplicity of cultures are unified under the domination of a single government; there have been many instances of world-empires, for example, ancient Egypt, ancient Rome, ancient China, Moghul India, feudal Russia, Ottoman Turkey;
- world-economies, in which a multiplicity of political states, each typically focusing on a single culture ('nation-states'), are integrated by a common economic system; there has been only one stable instance of a world-economy, the *modern world-system*, integrated by a single capitalist economy (which includes state socialist societies); and
- world-socialism, in which both the nation-state and capitalism disappear in favour of a single, unified political-economic system which integrates a multiplicity of cultures; there is no instance of world-socialism and it retains a utopian status in the analysis.

Wallerstein concentrates on the emergence and evolution of the modern, European world-system which he traces from its late medieval origins to the present day. He describes the emergent phenomenon in the following way:

> In the late fifteenth and early sixteenth century, there came into existence what we may call a European world-economy. It was not an empire yet but it was as spacious as an empire and shared some features with it. . . . It is a "world" system, not because it encompasses the whole world, but because it is larger than any juridically-defined political unit. And it is a "world-*economy*" because the basic linkage between the parts of the system is economic, although this was reinforced to some extent by cultural links and eventually . . . by political arrangements and even confederal structures. [1974: 15, original italics]

The focal point of political pressure in the world-economy is the state structure – the state helps to stabilize capitalism by absorbing its costs and managing the social problems which it creates. This shifts the fundamental process of differentiation away from economic units and on to states. Thus the modern world-system differentiates into three types of state:

- core states, which have a strong governmental structure integrated with a national culture, and that are developed, rich, and dominating within the system; late-twentieth-century examples include the European Community, Japan and the USA;
- peripheral areas, which have weak indigenous states and invaded

cultures, and that are poor and economically dependent on the core states; late-twentieth-century examples include the 'newly industrializing countries' of the 'South', for instance, in Asia, Africa and Latin America; and

- semiperipheral areas, which include countries with moderately strong governmental structures, single-commodity or low-technology economies that are therefore somewhat dependent on the core states; they may be earlier core states in decline or they may be emerging from the periphery; late-twentieth-century examples include oil producers, former socialist states in Eastern Europe, and the 'young dragon' societies of South-East Asia.

There is a division of labour between states in each of these regions: 'tasks requiring higher levels of skill and greater capitalization are reserved for higher-ranking areas' (1974: 350). However, the position of the semiperipheral areas is of special theoretical importance because their existence prevents polarization and conflict between the core and the periphery.

Wallerstein is at pains to discuss the contingent connection between international differentiation and the internal class structure. He concentrates mainly on the development of social classes, in the Weberian sense of self-aware, class communities (see below), discussing, for example, the formation of a nationally restricted, bourgeois, class consciousness in the sixteenth-century European states, in response to the emerging presence of a small, but noticeable working class. Importantly, these class formations articulate with world-system formations in so far as the social relations of production stabilize the world-system. The ability of core states to remain at the centre depends on their capacity for capital accumulation.

Although some have hailed Wallerstein's theory as a precursor of more recent statements about globalization (e.g. Giddens 1990: 68–70), his argument is fundamentally at odds with true globalization theory. For Wallerstein the mechanisms of geosystemic integration are principally economic – they are constituted as trading and exploitative relationships between relatively sovereign states and relatively independent cultures. Genuine globalization theories propose a global unification of cultural orientations which 'turns on' and breaks down the barriers between national polities and economies.

The most influential theory of globalization in cultural terms is developed by Robertson (1992). He defines globalization as: 'both the compression of the world and the intensification of consciousness of the world as a whole' (1992: 8). The notion of global compression bears some similarity to Wallerstein. It refers to an increasing level of interdependence between previously independent systems. But the more important component of the definition is the notion of intensification of consciousness. Robertson means by this an increasing probability that individual phenomenologies will be addressed to the entire world rather than to a local or national sector of it. This is true not only of such apparently cultural phenomena as the mass media and consumption preferences, in which it is relatively straightforward to conceive of a globalization of tastes but also in so far as we culturally redefine issues in global terms. For example: we redefine military-political issues in terms of a 'world order'; or economic issues in terms of an 'international recession'; or marketing issues in terms of 'world' products (e.g. the 'world-car'); or religious issues in terms of ecumenism; or citizenship issues in terms 'human rights'; or issues of pollution and purification in terms of 'saving the planet'.

This rise in global consciousness increases the probability that the world will be reproduced as a single system. Thus Robertson claims that the world is becoming more and more united, although he is careful not to say that it is becoming more and more integrated. It is a single system but it is riven by conflict and there is by no means universal agreement on what shape the single system should take in the future.

In conceptual terms, globalization involves the relativization of individual and national reference points to general and supranational ones. It therefore involves the establishment of cultural, social and phenomenological linkages between four elements:

- the individual self;
- the national society;
- the international system of societies; and
- humanity in general.

Under globalization there is, for example, a tendency to define oneself, as a citizen of a national society, as affected by the planetary flow of international relations, and as an instance of humanity. Similarly, a national society is understood by its members not merely to be composed of individual citizens, but also itself to be a member of a community of nations, and to have general obligations to humanity. Expressed in these terms, globalization represents not a process of dedifferentiation but the emergence of a new framework within which differentiation continues to take place.

Robertson insists that the process of globalization is not new, that it predates modernity and the rise of capitalism. However, modernization tends to accelerate globalization and the process has moved up to top gear during the past 100 years. Moreover, European civilization is the central focus for and origin of the development. He models the path of globalization as a series of five phases:

I *The germinal phase* (Europe, 1400–1750) dissolution of medieval religious unity; development of generalizations about humanity and the individual; first maps of the planet; sun-centred universe.

II *The incipient phase* (Europe, 1750–1875) nation-state; formal diplomacy between states; citizenship; international exhibitions and communications agreements; first non-European nations.

III *The take-off phase* (1875–1925) conceptualization of the world in terms of four reference points – the nation-state, the individual, international society, and humanity; international communications, sporting and cultural links; common calendar; first ever world war, so defined; more non-Europeans in the international club.

IV *The struggle-for-hegemony phase* (1925–69) League of Nations and UN; Second World War; Cold War; conceptions of war crimes and crimes against humanity; the universal nuclear threat; emergence of the Third World.

V *The uncertainty phase* (1969–92) exploration of space; postmaterialist values and rights discourses; world communities based on sexual preference, gender, ethnicity and race; international relations more complex; global environmental problems recognized; global mass media via space technology.

(Robertson 1992: 58–60)

These developments occur independently of the internal dynamics of individual societies. Indeed, globalization has its own logic which will inevitably affect these internal dynamics.

The idea of globalization has also found its way into Giddens' analysis of modernity and its development (1990, 1991b). For Giddens, modernity is characterized by three cultural or phenomenological features:

- Time and space are separated from one another and are increasingly distanciated. Under premodern conditions time and space were calculated in relation to the immediacy of a particular place, usually in terms of where one lived. Time and space are now measured independently of any individual's location and can thus be recombined to achieve massive levels of coordination, for example, 'the best athletes in the world will meet in Sydney, Australia in the year 2000 to compete in the Olympic Games'.
- Social institutions are 'disembedded' or lifted out from local contexts and reorganized across broad stretches of time and space.[4] This is achieved by two mechanisms: 'symbolic tokens', especially money, which can mediate relationships across time and space distances; and 'abstract systems', bodies of expert technical and social knowledge which can be deployed in a wide range of contexts. Each of these implies an extension of 'trust' – we must trust both the value of valueless paper and in the ability of anonymous experts.
- The appropriation of knowledge becomes reflexive. This means that our bodies of knowledge are increasingly and self-consciously oriented to the ways in which we organize our social life. But because we continuously re-address and change our knowledge this provides us with a high level of existential uncertainty.

These three features lend a particular character to the experience of modernity: 'living in the modern world is more like being aboard a careering juggernaut . . . rather than being in a carefully controlled and well-driven motor car' (1990: 53).

The connection to globalization can now be made. Globalization is the ultimate expression of time-space distanciation: 'Globalisation can thus be defined as the intensification of worldwide social relations which link distant localities in such a way that local happenings are shaped by events occurring many miles away [and many weeks away] and vice versa' (1991b: 21). The process transforms the institutions of modernity in universalizing directions. He lists four such interrelated, modern institutions:

- capitalism;
- industrialism;
- surveillance; and
- monopolization of the means of violence.

The globalizing transformations (1991b: 55–78) which occur in each of them, respectively, are:

- the emergence of a world capitalist economy, of the type specified by Wallerstein, focused on the operations of transnational business corporations and the international expansion of markets for capital, commodities, money and labour;
- an international division of labour which stretches across the entire planet and in which there are more and less, or 'established' and 'newly', industrializing countries and in which particular state economies must be managed in terms of global interdependence;
- a system of nation-states which extends surveillance to every populated corner of the planet and which is increasingly organized through such inter-state systems as the UN; and
- a military 'world order' which is expressed in: a weapons technology which can threaten any part of the planet; a conception of the world as a global theatre of military operations; and increasing levels of military cooperation through alliances, treaties and joint peacekeeping and policing actions.

It bears restressing that theories of globalization are species of theories of differentiation. This is not because globalization implies functional integration, far from it. Rather, it is because they address themselves to processes which serve to disassemble local, fused social structures. Giddens, for example, stresses throughout that globalization can only occur in so far as state systems and economic systems are mutually insulated, that is, differentiated from one another. Indeed, the insulation of such systems can only occur so long as they are each entirely differentiated from kinship systems.

Conclusion

Summary

1 Spencer and Durkheim specify that structural differentiation is the critical process which marks the emergence of modern or industrial society. Durkheim formulates the key problem for differentiation theory, the question of how a society composed of specialized units can cohere. His own solution is a permissive and generalized collective consciousness.

2 In the modern theoretical period, differentiation is more or less entirely a proposal which comes from the functionalist tradition. It is specified as the pattern of change in the entire system. Here it is read as modernization, a progressive evolution in the direction of improved material well-being for all by virtue of the adaptive upgrading of society. Modernization is theorized as a unidirectional, evolutionary pattern.

3 In the contemporary theoretical period this theory is under attack from two directions. First, it conflicts with Marxist arguments that seek to show that capitalism develops in the direction of increased exploitation and subordination for the working class. Second, there is a considerable weight of opinion that the process of modernization is at an end and that it is being succeeded by a new set of processes variously designated as postindustrialization, postmodernization, and globalization.

Critique

Theories of differentiation can be characterized as evolutionary, unidirectional, and positive. They can be criticized in terms of each of these three characteristics.

The view that societies evolve in a patterned way is derived from an analogy with biological organisms. Thus, industrial societies are to forager societies as human organisms are to single-celled animal organisms. In the classical theoretical period, the driving force for evolution was population growth – the larger or more populous societies became the more differentiated they were likely to be. This argument clearly is spurious because large populations organized with a relatively low level of differentiation are clearly possible. Indeed, any attempt to correlate population size with societal complexity would rapidly come unstuck. Indeed the modern version of 'survival of the fittest', is Parsons' theory of adaptive upgrading. However, adaptive upgrading fails to tell us why some societies should rapidly differentiate rather than others, for example, why capitalism should have emerged in the West, why Russia 'refeudalized' in the seventeenth century, or why Bangladesh persistently remains non-modernized. The answers to these questions lie in issues to do with culture, power and stratification. If this is true, differentiation is entirely contingent.

The issue of evolution is linked to the issue of unidirectionality. Against unidirectionality it might be argued that:

- There might be many paths to a high level of differentiation; some societies have been feudal and others not while some societies have been state socialist and others not.
- The path to a high level of differentiation might depend on how early or how late the society takes the first step; being first offers major competitive advantages in material terms; however, being last might allow mimicry and rapid advancement and the avoidance of the errors of others.
- The end-point might not be identical for all societies, for example, the European corporatist societies, American market democracy, and the state-guided society of Japan are all very different.
- The question of the direction a society takes is influenced by what other societies do to it; modernization theory tells a story of mountaineers trying to reach a summit roped together and showing each other the way when in fact they might be treading on each other's fingers and trying to push each other off the cliff.

The characteristic of positivity is related to each of these. We have seen that differentiation theory, explicitly and implicitly, points to an American utopia as the positive outcome for all. Members of other societies can find ready grounds for rejecting such a model – a materialistic culture, drug infestation, decaying and crime-ridden inner cities, social division, and racism are some of the more commonly adduced ones. More formally, such a theory presupposes the homogenization of culture as the consequence of modernization when this has not been demonstrated. And lastly, the theory presupposes that the USA will remain the dominant industrial society. Current evidence suggests that this is unlikely.

STRATIFICATION

The connections between differentiation and stratification are threefold: first, they are statements about the way in which societies are internally partitioned into units or segments; second, they were of central interest to the classical sociologists; and third, they are ways of explaining or describing the fundamental social shift which is known as the capitalist and/ or industrial and/or democratic revolution. However, while differentiation is the more or less exclusive property of the functionalist tradition, stratification is a topic of interest in all theoretical traditions except utilitarianism and is a special area of interest for theorists who focus on power and structure. Before locating the theories of the classical period within their changing social context, we should begin with some definitions.

The term *stratification* has two meanings, one of which includes the other. Most generally, stratification refers to any system of inequality in which society is conceived to be organized into layers arranged in a more or less continuous hierarchy, much as geological strata are organized. In this general meaning a system of stratification may be conceived to be based on either class (economic differences) or status (cultural differences)[5]. The boundaries between the strata are conceived to be semipermeable, to be a constructed and fragile form of closure. Class strata are identified as groups within which mobility is possible, while mobility between class strata is conceived to be much more difficult. A more specific and exclusive definition of stratification confines its use only to status-based systems and regards class as something other than a stratification system.

Within this latter Marxian theoretical persuasion, *class* is a system of economic inequality, often specified in terms of the ownership and nonownership of property, in which groups of individuals live in structured and material relationships with one another. To say that they are structured usually means that the classes are interdependent and that they generate differential interests which provide a basis for actual or potential antagonisms. Classes manifest a 'zero-sum' pattern of inequality – one class's gain is another class's loss.

Status is an arrangement in which individuals or groups evaluate and rank each other differently. Here the categories or groups are not necessarily interdependent nor are they necessarily antagonistic. Status is not 'zero-sum' because the elevation of one group can be part of a restructuring of the system as a whole so that a superior group can be equalled without being displaced. Status is conceived as a potentially winnable competition between groups and individuals on a continuous dimension of mutual evaluation. However, the competition is not necessarily interminable – groups which win big can put in place a legal order which fixes and entrenches status arrangements.

Founding arguments

The founding arguments about stratification focus on the transition from a feudal system of inequality to a capitalist system of inequality. Feudalism was an agriculturally based production system based on the ownership of land. The main economic unit was the manor, a village or villages dominated by a castle or fortified house, whose head was a lord, the ruler and judge of all those who lived on the manor. He had customary rights to use the capital resources of the manor and to labouring service from peasant tenants, and he also had obligations to protect tenants. The peasants were granted the right to cultivate land and had an obligation to provide service to the lord. All of these rights were fixed by tradition, were heritable, and were supported by religious ritual.

In the most frequent tenancy arrangement, the tenant performed labour services for the knight. Agricultural land was divided into strips distributed across the manor and peasants held scattered strips and so held land of roughly equal quality. But the quantity of strips held by the knight was far greater than that held by any peasant. The peasant would divide his labouring time between his own land and that of the knight, the precise division depending on prevailing, local, economic conditions but of the order of say four-fifths to one-fifth.

There are two main sociological interpretations of stratification under feudalism. The first comes from Weber and views the various levels in the feudal order as estates or status groups (*Stände*), of which there are fundamentally three: nobility, peasantry, and clerisy (priests), although only the first two are of real significance. *Stände* were differentiated from one another on the basis of a legal or juridical specification. A person could not move from one estate to another, could not intermarry, and inherited their membership at birth.

By contrast, within a Marxist interpretation, nobility and peasantry are classes, defined by their relationship to one another rather than by the boundaries which separate them. The relationship is one of exploitation – the nobility or aristocracy expropriates the labour of the peasantry and uses it to provide for its own consumption. A critical intermediate class is the mercantile bourgeoisie which seeks to disrupt the relationship in order to aggrandize itself at the expense of the nobility. This, of course, it eventually succeeds in doing, thus ushering in capitalism.

The transformation from feudalism to capitalism is generally agreed to involve the setting up of some important new institutions: alienable private property – property that can be bought and sold rather than merely inherited and tenanted by service; contract – the idea that obligations are specific to a particular exchange, rather than for life and beyond through descendants; wage labour – the formal freedom to sell one's labour power; and commodities – freedom to exchange products for monetary prices. All of these exchanges are mediated by the use of money and occur within institutions called markets – the labour market, the capital market, the commodity market and the market for land.

In summary, industrial capitalism is a system in which capital, the means of production, distribution and exchange, is owned privately by individuals for their personal benefit. This benefit is material and it comes from the surplus of revenues over the costs ('profit'). Owners of capital theoretically compete with each other in commodity markets in order to maximize profit and they engage in rational systems of accounting in an effort to minimize cost and to maximize revenue.

These practices have two consequences for differentiation: first, an increasingly elaborated technical division of labour which serves both to increase efficiency in the extraction of labour power from workers and to increase the surveillance capacity of owners over workers; and second, a growth in the scale of economic organizations so that the social as well as the functional division of labour are elaborated, within a context in which economic power is increasingly concentrated.

The fixed status order of feudalism thus gives way to a more complex and dynamic stratification system. In Weberian terms, capitalism sees the emergence of a class system constituted of reward differentials and generated by differential market capacity. This class system is novel and is institutionalized alongside existing status patterns. Not only do capitalist societies retain both class and status systems but status systems are also highly differentiated. Thus status may be established on the basis of the material achievements of class but may also be assigned on the basis of ascribed individual qualities.

Such complexity is less apparent in Marxian analyses. Here inequality is reckoned in terms of the property–employment relationship rather than in terms of the elaborated social division of labour. All societies are class societies but capitalism sees the predominance of different classes from those found under feudalism, that is, owners and nonowners of mechanical production systems. What Weber calls status is subordinated to the social relations of production under capitalism.

The central features of economic life under capitalism then – those which form the focus for the analysis of its consequences for socioeconomic inequality – are as follows:

- *Production*   Production is predicated on ownership by a small proportion of the population and on labour by a large proportion. Labour is performed on the basis of a theoretically individualized contract in which labour power is exchanged for wages. The price of labour power is determined by forces of supply and demand given in a labour market. Property owners will seek to maximize their advantages in this market by technologically restricting their demand for labour and by standardizing jobs; while workers will seek to restrict the supply of their labour power by forming unions and by enskilling and credentializing jobs.
- *Market*   All economic goods, including products, labour, land and capital are exchanged within market institutions, that is, social contexts in which there is no formal, external constraint on the price at which the items are exchanged. So, if the members of a society are materially unequal, the proximate source of that inequality is the market, that is in the relative prices of the resources which they wish to sell and the rewards they seek to receive.[6] A consequence is an increasing commodification of all human values.
- *Occupation*   An increasingly complex technical division of labour and reward structure promotes the institutionalization of a highly differentiated structure of occupations (social division of labour). An occupation is a specialized work role with a typical career structure which carries with it a social identity. However, unlike feudal statuses, this identity is partial and is separated from personal identity.
- *Authority*   Large-scale production systems, capital concentration, increasing technical division of labour, and complex systems of exchange all contribute to highly elaborated organizational forms.

Power is typically delegated within organizations in the form of authority. Thus authority differentials may also contribute to patterns of socioeconomic inequality.

We can now examine the ways in which classical theories see the pattern of inequality developing under capitalism.

Marx: struggling about class

The beginnings of Marx's statement on the social relations of production are to be found in his well-known fragment on alienated labour where he argues that: 'The worker becomes poorer the more wealth he produces and the more his production increases in power and extent. The worker becomes an even cheaper commodity the more goods he creates' (1982: 13). Marx explains this paradoxical fact in terms of the exploitation of labour, which is spelled out in detail in the later phases of his work on labour and surplus value.

However, Marx's specific statement about the the class system which emerges from these social relations of production is primarily political and persuasive in character. It is directed at a working-class audience with the intention of raising its consciousness. Here, in the *Communist Manifesto*, he and Engels outline what has come to be known as the abstract model of class, the underlying structural pattern that determines actual class behaviour and actual class struggles. They argue that society moves towards a division into two great classes, the *bourgeoisie* and the *proletariat*. In a footnote, added much later, Engels explains these terms: 'By bourgeoisie is meant the class of modern Capitalists, owners of the means of social production and employers of wage labour. By proletariat, the class of modern wage-labourers who, having no means of production of their own, are reduced to selling their labour-power in order to live' (Marx 1982: 19n).

Even at this stage Marx recognizes the existence of 'fractions of the middle class' which are located in relation to the classes of the basic model: 'the lower middle class, the small manufacturer, the shopkeeper, the artisan, the peasant' (1982: 24). However, this *petty bourgeoisie*, as it has come to be known, is composed of residues from the decline of feudal society. It is conservative in its orientation and it will become the victim of history. Its fate is polarization, division between the historic classes, either as 'part of a bribed tool of reactionary intrigue' or as a gradual submersion into the proletariat as it becomes swamped and impoverished by competition from the industrial bourgeoisie (1982: 24–5).

The colourful polemical language of the *Manifesto* disappeared as an optimistic and romantic young Marx became more realistic about the resilience of capitalist society. A major disappointment was that the European revolutions of 1848 failed to reflect the predictions of the abstract model – society did not polarize into two classes and the proletariat proved weak. The proletariat was defeated by alliances that emerged between the new industrial bourgeoisie and the old feudal classes, that is, the landed aristocracy, the petty bourgeoisie, and, above all, the peasantry. Already then, Marx was forced to recognize not only the persistence of the intermediate classes but also the fractionalization of the historically significant classes.

In his last, and much briefer, statement on class, the unfinished, one-page fragment in *Capital* (1982: 20–1), he recognizes three great classes, wage-labourers, capitalists and landowners, whose means of subsistence are, respectively, wages, profit and ground-rent. However, the lines of demarcation between them are agreed everywhere to be obliterated by the existence of middle and intermediate 'strata'. Nevertheless, Marx continues to insist on a historical tendency towards the dichotomization of class structure entailed in: the reduction of the independent labour of the petty bourgeoisie to wage labour; and the transformation of landed property into a form consistent with the capitalist mode of production, that is, a form which produces profit rather than ground-rent.

Even so, it is clear that Marx regarded the intermediate strata as a theoretical problem. He even recognized that the middle strata were actually growing in relation to the expansion of the power of the ruling class. However, the middle class remains nonfundamental. It is parasitic relative to the system of class exploitation, providing political, military, and ideological services to the ruling class, but not making an actual contribution to the wealth of society by producing commodities (Clegg et al. 1986: 37–8). However, it is also clear that Marx did not anticipate the growth of middle strata to major proportions in society, and his theorizing of the relationship between the new middle class of white-collar workers on one hand, and the historical classes on the other, is therefore inadequate to current social complexity.

Weber: class competition

Weber responded directly to Marx's work, seeking to show that inequality was not entirely materially determined but needed to be understood in terms of the ideas and intentions of its participants. However, like Marx and other structural theorists, he also makes a distinction between underlying structural causes and concrete arrangements. He says that classes 'are not communities; they merely represent possible and frequent bases for social action' (1982: 61). These structural positions or places are differentiated from each other on the basis that they have a shared determining factor in the life chances of their incumbents. This factor is economic in character, involving the ownership of property or opportunity for income, where such ownership is 'represented' (negotiated and established) within markets for capital, commodities and labour. Because Weber stresses life chances, that is, access to scarce goods and services, his is a consumption, rather than a production theory of class. A class situation

| | **Structural dimension of class** | | **Concrete groups** |
| | | | (under capitalism) |
Level of privilege	Property ownership classes	Commercial (acquisition) classes	Social classes
Positive	Rentiers, financiers	Entrepreneurs	Privileged
Neutral	Officials, artisans, free peasants	Petty bourgeoisie, administrators	Intelligentsia and specialists
			Petty bourgeoisie
Negative	Tenant peasants	Wage labourers	Working class

Figure 9.3   *Weber's theory of class (Waters 1989c: 144)*

is one in which there is a shared typical probability of procuring goods, gaining a position in life, and finding inner satisfaction (1982: 69).

Weber agrees with Marx that property is the primary basis on which classes are established. Those who are wealthy can compete much more easily for scarce and valued goods than those who are not. Moreover, wealth can be transformed into capital in a capital market, and thus can provide access to returns on capital: ' "Property" and "lack of property" are . . . the basic categories of all class situations' (1982: 61). Ownership of property can be further differentiated according to its type and the market in which it is exchanged. Weber makes particular reference to two types of property owner: rentiers, the owners of land; and to entrepreneurs, the owners of financial and industrial capital. Likewise, nonowners are class differentiated according to the type of labour service which they offer on the labour market and particularly in terms of skill differentials. These details are given in figure 9.3.

Note that, by contrast with Marx, the market, rather than production, is the crucial concept. The potential for class membership is not real until the determining factor is used in a market to secure access to privilege:

[T]he kind of chance in the *market* is the decisive moment which presents a common condition for the individual's fate. Class situation is, in this sense, market situation. The effect of naked possession *per se* . . . is only a fore-runner of real "class". [Weber 1982: 62, original italics]

The objective class situation thus intersects with the individual at the point of the market to provide for the emergence of *social classes*, 'the totality of those class situations within which individual and generational mobility is easy and typical' (1982: 69). Social classes are concrete groups, constructed by and recognizable to participants. Weber can identify four such social classes under capitalism, each with markedly different access to rewards based on market situation, and each closed to the others in mobility terms:

(a) the working class as a whole – the more so, the more automated the work becomes,
(b) the petty bourgeoisie,
(c) the propertyless intelligentsia and specialists (technicians, various kinds of white-collar employees, civil servants . . .),
(d) the classes privileged through property and education. [Weber 1982: 71–2]

The particular characteristic of these social classes is not simply that some have reward and opportunity advantages over others but that they are able to maintain and even enhance these advantages by excluding the members of inferior groups. This is achieved by monopolizing access to property and to credential-granting institutions. It is also achieved by reducing possibilities for advancement on the part of inferiors. Thus Weber accepts from Marx the idea that the labour process homogenizes the working class and he also anticipates the major current controversy in relation to Marx's class theory, that of the emergence of the middle class. For Weber, the middle class is structured in a stable fashion, whereas for Marx it is problematic.

Critical structuralist theory: possession is all

This issue of the new middle class, called new because it supposedly was not present at the emergence of capitalism, has become the crucial problem for Marxist theories of class. Here we examine some attempts to accommodate the enormous growth of the middle class in the twentieth century to a theory which admits to only two historic classes.[7]

Poulantzas: abstract models

Poulantzas (1982) emphasizes Marx's distinction between an underlying structure, the social relations given in the mode of production (e.g. the capitalist mode of production), and the actual and apparent set of class processes and events, the conjuncture or *social formation*. The underlying mode of production determines class behaviour: 'classes are groups of social agents, of men defined principally but not exclusively by their place in the production process . . .' (1982: 101). These places are not independent of one another. They are associated with divergent and fundamentally antagonistic interests that promote a continuous struggle of control against resistance between the classes.

Of all neoMarxist theorists, Poulantzas clings most firmly to Marx's dichotomous model. This obliges him to engage in a dualism in order to take account of the complexities of the actual formation. The following is a statement in which Poulantzas simultaneously asserts the existence both of two classes and of more than two classes under the historic formations of capitalism:

> [I]f we confine ourselves to modes of production alone, examining them in a pure and abstract fashion, we find that each of them involves two classes – the exploiting class, which is politically and ideologically dominant, and the exploited class, which is politically and ideologically dominated . . . bourgeois and workers in the capitalist mode of production. But a concrete society (a social formation) *involves more than two classes*, in so far as it is composed of various modes and forms of production. No social formation involves only two classes: but the two fundamental classes in any social formation are those of the dominant mode of production in that formation. [Poulantzas 1982: 106, original italics]

Poulantzas is also forced by the facts of historical experience to make certain reformulations in Marx's theoretical categories 'ownership of the means of production' and 'labour process'. He respecifies ownership as real economic ownership. The exploiting class does not merely own the means of production, in a narrow legal sense, but *possesses* the means of production. 'Possession' means the capacity to put the means of production into operation, that is, control over the means of production (1982: 102). Thus, in capitalist societies, exploiting classes are not the shareholders of large companies but the controlling managers of those companies; in state socialist societies, the owners of the means of production are not the citizens but senior Party officials and bureaucrats (1982: 103). This parallels Carchedi's identification of the membership of economic classes as those who perform the functions of capital and labour respectively (1977).

Marx had emphasized the development of technology and the technical division of labour (on the basis of task specialization) as the process by which labour was controlled and immiserated. For Poulantzas this process is subordinate to the social division of labour between exploiters and exploited: 'it is the relations of production which have primacy over the labour process and the 'productive forces' (1982: 105). Only those who produce surplus value by the direct production of commodities can properly be understood to be the members of an exploited class. So Poulantzas is unwilling to amend Marx's definition of the proletariat and thus continues to exclude nonmanual workers from the working class.

Because the social division of labour takes precedence over the technical division of labour, exploitation operates not only at the level of production but also at the levels of politics and ideology. As is noted above, Poulantzas assigns to production the principal role in determining class. But he contradicts himself by saying that: 'purely economic criteria are not sufficient to determine and locate social classes . . . it becomes absolutely necessary to refer to positions within the political and ideological relations of the social division of labour' (1982: 107). This admission is particularly important in theorizing the fragmentation of classes in a social formation

along political or ideological lines. Unproductive (non-commodity producing) labour of an intellectual kind, for example, is in a contradictory
position because it is exploited in relation to capital but exploitative in
relation to workers. It thus comes to constitute a special class fraction, the
'new petty bourgeoisie'.

However, the problem of the historical significance of these emerging
occupational groups remains. Poulantzas' theory of the class structure
recognizes two dominant 'economic' classes, but also residual (e.g.
peasant) or emergent (e.g. professional-managerial) social classes[8] which
overlay them. He also says (1982: 108–9) that classes are split into fractions
and strata:

- 'Fractions' are differentiated *places* in the system of exploitation –
  artisans, for example, are a less exploited sector of the proletariat, and
  finance capitalists have a different basis for exploitation than do the
  industrial bourgeoisie.
- 'Strata' are differentiated status groups, groups with differentiated
  ideological positions – for example, some sectors of the middle class are
  pro-capitalist and conservative, others are radical and pro-worker.

Each of these is a 'social' class phenomenon, and recognizable within the
experience of agents.

Classes become fractionalized and stratified because structure develops
in an uneven way. Here Poulantzas draws on Althusser's idea of different
levels of structure (see chapter 4). The persistence of the overall structure
depends on differential alignments between these levels. So the maintenance (reproduction) of economic classes depends on the persistence of
political fractions and of ideological strata.[9] Political strata (e.g. social
democratic parties) displace conflict away from the area in which it might
fundamentally rupture the system. Equally, such ideological strata as the
intellectuals can express dissent in a non-threatening way. The exploitative
system of production remains untouched.

Wright: a duodecotomous structure

While Wright (1978) takes his main cues from Poulantzas' analysis of the
class structure, he finds Poulantzas to be inadequate in specifying the
boundaries between the classes, and in particular rejects the notion of
fractions and strata. In disassembling the criteria for class membership (i.e.
economic, political, and ideological) Wright finds that it is possible to be
dominant on one or more criteria while being subordinate on others.

These possible situations are called 'contradictory class locations'. He
maps a class structure with three consistent class locations, two of which
are defined within the capitalist mode of production in its pure form, the
familiar bourgeoisie and proletariat, with the third being defined by simple
commodity production (production using one's own labour), the petty

bourgeoisie (see figure 9.4). Between these are the three contradictory locations:

- Managers, technocrats and supervisors are located between the bourgeoisie and the proletariat – they have some possession but minimal actual ownership, and their labour is at least partially exploited.
- Small employers are located between the bourgeoisie and the petty bourgeoisie – as well as employing others they also perform some labour on their own behalf.
- 'Semi-autonomous employees' are located between the proletariat and the petty bourgeoisie – these are professional employees who have some level of possession.

Unlike Marx, Wright does not expect processes of polarization/ proletarianization to occur. The class structure is stable and there will be no absorption of simple commodity production into the capitalist mode of production, nor will there be a progressive technologization of the work of semi-autonomous employees. Rather, Wright sees these processes as cyclical, so that the progressive employment of new techniques and the absorption of autonomous producers creates new problems of control of the labour process. These, in turn, lead to a hierarchization of production enterprises. All of these processes imply stability for this structure of class positions.

However, two things appear to have changed Wright's mind about the contradictory locations argument. First, there was considerable theoretical debate which suggested that the contradictory class locations should not be considered as internally contradictory because they are, in fact, quite stable and consistent at the level of the agent's experience (see e.g. Holmwood and Stewart 1983). For example, semi-autonomous employees (professional workers) receive moderate rewards, have moderate levels of control/autonomy, and are moderately exploited. Second, Wright's own empirical research on the changing American class structure produced notably 'negative' results. The majority of the labour force was in the 'contradictory' rather than the 'historic' locations and the trend was towards an increase in this imbalance (see Wright and Martin 1987). Wright was thus forced to admit a theoretical failure: 'Capitalist societies cannot be analyzed concretely as simple embodiments of the abstract capitalist mode of production; they are always complex combinations of a variety of mechanisms of exploitation and accompanying forms of class relations' (Wright and Martin 1987: 24).

Wright therefore abandons production as the sole source of class exploitation. On the basis of a reading of Roemer's theory of exploitation (see chapter 3) he suggests an expansion of the concept of exploitation to a range of resources which operate in parallel with the means of production (Wright 1985). Two such resources are important within capitalism: organizational assets and credentialized skills.

The first model

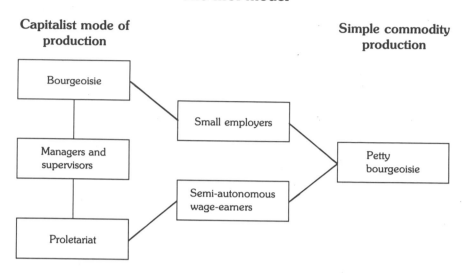

Capitalist mode of production

Simple commodity production

Bourgeoisie

Small employers

Managers and supervisors

Semi-autonomous wage-earners

Petty bourgeoisie

Proletariat

The second model

Means of production

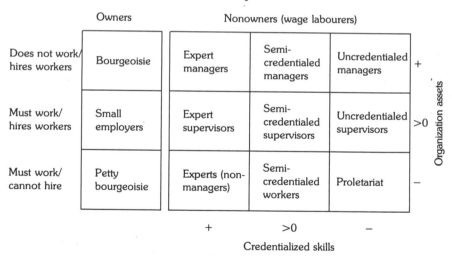

	Owners	Nonowners (wage labourers)			
Does not work/ hires workers	Bourgeoisie	Expert managers	Semi-credentialed managers	Uncredentialed managers	+
Must work/ hires workers	Small employers	Expert supervisors	Semi-credentialed supervisors	Uncredentialed supervisors	>0
Must work/ cannot hire	Petty bourgeoisie	Experts (non-managers)	Semi-credentialed workers	Proletariat	−
	+	>0	−		

Organization assets

Credentialized skills

Figure 9.4 *Wright's models of the class structure of advanced capitalism (Wright 1978: 63; 1985: 88, adapted)*

The specification of organizational assets is an extension of Poulantzas' idea of possession: that it is possible to control productive resources without actually owning them. However, Wright also suggests that organizational assets, the capacity to appropriate and plan the distribution of surplus, are distributed downward through bureaucratic hierarchies. In state socialist societies, the distribution of organizational assets displaces property as the primary basis for distribution of surplus; in capitalist societies it operates in a parallel though subordinate way to property. Here, senior managers, entrepreneurs and owners possess the means of production and the major share of organizational assets but the latter are distributed down bureaucratic hierarchies and are also distributed in non-economic, especially state, organizations. The main difference between capitalist and state socialist systems in this regard is that in the latter case capital cannot be valorized.[10]

Credentialized skills are capable of being distributed far more evenly than the means of production or organizational assets. They nevertheless offer the possibility for the appropriation of surplus by rendering certain forms of labour scarce. Credentials are subordinate both to the means of production and to organizational assets but operate in parallel to them under both capitalism and state socialism. Wright envisages a technocracy, a pure type of non-state socialism, prior to communism, in which credentials are the only dimension on which class differentiation occurs.

Wright's new map of the class structure (see figure 9.4) thus intersects the dimension of possession of property with these two newly introduced dimensions that are reminiscent of Weber, credentialized skills and organizational assets. This produces a scheme of twelve class locations. The fundamental division is still between owners and nonowners of the means of production. Owners are internally differentiated according to the extent to which they own sufficient capital to exploit the labour of others. Nonowners are internally differentiated on the basis of organizational assets and credentialized skills. The possession of organizational assets provides a priority basis of power and exploitation over credentials.

Constructionist theory: market forces

There is no statement of class exploitation in Weber except in so far as it can be accommodated within a more general set of processes known as 'closure', the capacity to monopolize market segments and to resist the entry of members of other classes. These are the central concerns for British neoWeberian sociologists of class for whom the major focus of debate is the extent to which property remains a central aspect of class closure. The parallel American theory is called 'dual labor market' theory and we also consider that in this section.

British neoWeberians: closing arguments

Giddens (1973) focuses on the 'decisive moment' in Weber's thought, the way in which the market transforms objective potential into actual patterns of inequality. He calls this closure process structuration. As we saw in chapter 2, he distinguishes between two forms of structuration: mediate and proximate.

Mediate structuration is located in the market: 'the structuration of classes is facilitated to the degree to which mobility closure exists in relation to any specified form of market capacity' (1973: 107, italics deleted). The specified forms of market capacity which he identifies are familiar: ownership of the means of production; educational and technical credentials; and manual labour power. These yield: 'the foundation of a basic three-class system in capitalist society: an "upper", "middle", and "lower" or "working" class' (1973: 167). Giddens stresses the possibility of further stratification within this basic structure, particularly of the petty bourgeoisie and within the working class according to skill level. However, there remains, for Giddens, a decisive separation between manual and nonmanual work.

However, because the capitalist market is without formal or legal limitation on individual mobility there must be mechanisms which maintain the separation between groups in face-to-face or micro-contexts. These are the sources of *proximate structuration*, and they are threefold.

- The first is the division of labour within the enterprise, the most important aspect of which is industrial technique. This creates an important separation between manual and nonmanual workers.
- The second source is the division of authority in the enterprise (similar to Wright's organizational assets) which reinforces structuration on the basis of property in the upper ranges of the class structure.
- The third source is distributive groupings: 'those relationships involving common patterns of the consumption of economic goods' (1973: 109) – by these he means such forms as class-segregated neighbourhood communities.

So Giddens' theory of class is spectacularly multidimensional, perhaps indecisively so. Class stratification is the consequence of property, credentials, labour power, the technical division of labour, authority differences, and consumption patterns.

Parkin is rather more equivocal than Giddens about the role of property in the class structure. In an early theory he focuses exclusively on the occupational order: 'The backbone of the class structure, and indeed of the entire reward system of Western society, is the occupational order' (1971: 18). This spine is a hierarchy of occupational categories which represents the distribution of social and material rewards. However, the hierarchy is linked to: 'an approximate hierarchy of skills – or at least the kind of skills in demand within an industrial order' (1971: 21). Parkin can therefore conclude that: 'marketable expertise is the most important single determinant of occupational reward, and therefore one of the key elements in the system of class inequality' (1971: 21).

Actual classes are formed on the basis of distinctive breaks in the hierarchy across which mobility is problematic. These breaks are enforced by closure practices in relation to class boundaries. The most important cleavage is between the nonmanual occupational categories at the top and the manual ones at the bottom. The boundary is marked by major differences in material rewards, including not only income but also job security, pensions, vacations, health and disability insurance, promotion opportunities, and physical working conditions. Importantly, there is no propertied upper class in Parkin's analysis. His reasons for excluding property as a basis for class formation are: first, that property represents a declining proportion of the sources of income; and second, that property has been redistributed down the occupational order in the modest form of personal, nonproductive property (e.g. houses, cars) and thus subordinated to that order – access to property depends on occupation.

In a subsequent book (1979) Parkin changes his mind and admits that both property institutions and credentials are ways in which dominant classes can exclude subordinate ones. However, he extends the notion of property to possessions (equivalent to Wright's concept of organizational assets). But note that, as in Weber rather than Marx, property is only a means of exclusion and not a means of exploitation (1979: 53). Moreover, property and credentials are seen as interchangeable and equivalent assets.

Piore: two markets are better than one

An important development in market theories of class is the idea that the market for labour power, that is the working-class labour market, can be internally segmented. Piore (1975) proposes that there is a dual labour market with primary and secondary sectors. The *primary sector* develops in instances where the supply of labour power can be controlled in some measure by those providing it in the market. For example craftworkers can effect such control by monopolizing skill, especially where this monopoly is enforced by legal sanction. But it can also be effected by the operation of trade unions, especially in capital-intensive industries where the cost to employers of a withdrawal of labour might be high. The primary sector is internally segmented into an upper tier of professional, administrative, managerial and white-collar workers, and a lower tier of skilled workers and other blue-collar workers in large-scale monopolistic organizations.

The *secondary sector* operates in industries which are characterized by small, labour-intensive firms, in competitive situations, requiring low levels of skill – 'sweatshop' manufacturing, retailing and personal service industries are particularly relevant. Such ascriptively statused 'outsiders' as women and ethnic minorities tend to be consigned to this secondary sector. This may be attributed to the sharing of interests between: highly capitalized firms that typically rely on the maintenance of low-income component, service, and distributional suppliers; and unionized, male, majority group labour on the other. The general tendency on the part of these two groups is to try to expand the secondary sector as much as possible.[11]

Functionalist theory: class as status

This last of the three groups of theories of stratification is the least critical. It views social inequality as a necessary component of the system. Indeed, it denies that class exists at all and that economic inequality is best theorized as occupational or socioeconomic status (SES). The most apologetic functionalist theories of stratification emerged in the USA after the Second World War. More recently, they have been adopted by British and other European sociologists, but in this context they have been merged with a Weberian class stratification approach.

The functionalist theory: ability receives its just reward

Whereas in Weber status is independent of class, Parsons (1954) and other functionalists use the terms interchangeably. Parsons' main concern is, therefore, why in capitalist societies some roles (positions) have higher status and are thus able to monopolize greater levels of reward than do others.

Parsons theorizes the status dimension in terms of two premises: first, that evaluation is a universal aspect of social practices and where evaluation occurs there must also be a system of ranking; and second, that the stability of society requires a common value-system (culture) that integrates constituent social units. Therefore, roles are ranked in terms of their cultural significance, as specified in the common value-system (1954: 388–9). Whereas in Marx and Weber values are associated with particular interest groups, so that the value-commitments of the upper class and the working class are viewed as differentiated, in Parsons values integrate the commitments of differentiated interest groups – they are common to people with different statuses.

There are four types of value that are of possible significance: economic values, political values, integrative values, and socialization/social control values (1954: 394–8) which correspond with the AGIL scheme (see chapter 4). Any one of these value-types may be paramount in any given society. In capitalist societies, economic values tend to be paramount – society coheres predominantly on the basis of its members' shared commitment to economic advancement. So the principal dimension of inequality in capitalist societies is the structural subsystem which corresponds with this value, the occupational structure. By contrast, in state socialist societies, political values are paramount and here rewards vary with membership of political roles (e.g. party elite [*nomenklatura*], party members, citizens).

However, Parsons does not address the issue of why some occupations are rewarded more highly than others. This was attempted by his students,

Davis and Moore (1945). They accept Parsons' view that the occupational structure has a functional relationship to the society as a whole – it is a universal necessity for societal survival. Differential rewards are necessary because some occupations are more important for societal survival than others and people must be motivated to enter the more important ones. In a statement replete with teleology and contradiction, they assert that:

> Social inequality . . . is an unconsciously evolved device by which societies insure [*sic*] that the most important positions are conscientiously filled by the most qualified persons.
>   In general those positions convey the best reward and hence have the highest rank, which (a) have the greatest importance for society and (b) require the greatest training or talent. [1945: 243]

In summary, Davis and Moore's theory makes the following related propositions:

1 Some positions or roles (usually occupations) are more functionally important to the social system than are others.
2 These roles require special skills, talents, and abilities in order to be performed competently.
3 Talent is in short supply, and competence requires time-consuming and expensive training.
4 Differential rewards must therefore be provided so that the talented can be attracted into the most needed positions and so that the young will commit themselves to the expensive training required.

From status mobility to class inheritance

Parsons and Davis and Moore still provide the main theoretical assumptions of non-Marxist and non-Weberian accounts of economic inequality. If one accepts that occupations are ranked by processes specified neither by production nor by a legal order, then they must be ranked or evaluated in terms of conscious negotiation between human beings. Indeed, so confident are such occupational status theorists as Blau and Duncan that this is indeed the real process, that only the occupations are real, the structure is merely epiphenomenal.

> The occupational structure in modern industrial society not only constitutes an important foundation for the main dimensions of social stratification but also serves as the connecting link between different institutions and spheres of inequality . . . The hierarchy of prestige strata and the hierarchy of economic classes have their roots in the occupational structure; so does the hierarchy of political power and authority, for political authority in modern society is largely exercised as a full-time occupation. [Blau and Duncan 1967: 6–7]

However, the methodological process for the construction of the Blau and Duncan occupational scale indicates that occupational prestige, as opposed to differential rewards and power, is not just the primary concern but the sole one. They construct a scale of occupations that measure their relative prestige as indicated by occupation and income. In so doing Blau and Duncan assume that: 'the occupation structure is more or less continuously graded in regard to status rather than being a set of discrete status classes' (1967: 124).

A fundamental shift in empirical stratification research occurred in the 1970s. As methodological procedures became more capable of disentangling the grounds for any particular individual's location in the stratification system, so perceptions of it as a subjectively ordered reality began to shift in a more structuralist direction. In part this came from the comparative finding that patterns of circulation mobility were more or less common to all capitalist societies, and conceivably to state socialist societies as well. This, the now famous Featherman-Jones-Hauser (FJH) hypothesis, states that: 'the genotypical pattern of mobility (circulation mobility) in industrial societies with a market economy and a nuclear family system is basically the same. The phenotypical pattern of mobility (observed mobility) differs according to the rate of change in the occupational structure, exogenously determined . . .' (Featherman et al. 1978: 340). More importantly, Featherman and his colleagues assert that the structural basis of the similarity is socioeconomic in character rather than being based on occupational prestige (1978: 357).

Status theory thus began to take the Weberian step of demarcating clusters of occupational statuses as classes, identified by relatively high levels of internal mobility and by external closure. Goldthorpe and his colleagues' influential analysis (1987) of the genotypical class structure in Britain does just this. In a departure from its earlier empiricist emphasis on prestige scaling (Goldthorpe and Hope 1974) this procedure incorporates a large dose of theoretical intuition. Goldthorpe regroups the scaled occupations into an *a priori* 'sevenfold class schema' which combines aspects of market and work situations.[12] Market situation consists of levels of income and other conditions of employment, job security, and promotion opportunities; while work situation consists of organizational assets (authority and autonomy) (Goldthorpe 1987: 40).

Goldthorpe is careful to say that the schema is not hierarchical because there are status overlaps between the classes but, given a consistent order of presentation in which professionals are placed at the top of the page and unskilled operatives at the bottom, it would be difficult to accept this conceit. More importantly, Goldthorpe seems to have several ideas in mind when he uses the term 'class'. He says: classes I, II, and III can be taken together as 'white-collar' classes; classes III, IV, and V are the 'intermediate class' between the service and working classes; and classes VI and VII are the working class. So it is unclear whether Goldthorpe intends a seven-class model or a three-class model, although the seven-class model receives most attention.

These possibilities are purely intuitively based. The actual shape of the class structure, the real boundaries of social classes, are given in Goldthorpe et al.'s research on the actual extent of mobility closure between classes. This discussion of closure represents a considerable theoretical shift from measuring the movement of individuals in a vertical status continuum to trying to understand the overall fixity of the structure, the extent to which it is generally in motion, its 'social fluidity'.[13]

Goldthorpe (1987) reaches three substantive conclusions:

- There is a marked level of intergenerational closure at the peak of the class structure. There is only a small chance that professional, managerial and senior administrative origins will lead to dissimilar destinations. The further down the hierarchy a person's parents are the less likely it is that they will move up to class I. This indicates a considerable effect for the inheritance of credentials and of organizational assets.
- While this high solidity declines lower down the hierarchy, it does so in an irregular way. In particular, the proprietorial petty bourgeois group also exhibits a high level of solidity. So property continues to be effective in structuring class.
- While there is a historical increase in working-class mobility, it is limited in its range, so that there is a significant barrier between white-collar and blue-collar occupations.

Goldthorpe's conclusion now looks rather like Weber's analysis of social classes. He is specifying an upper or service class, a petty bourgeoisie, a white-collar middle class, and a manual working class.

Conclusion

Summary

1   The two classical statements about stratification come from Marx and Weber. For Marx, class is determined by the social relations of production. Under capitalism this yields two great historic classes, the owners and the nonowners of the means of production. For Weber, class stands alongside status groups and parties as part of a triple pattern of stratification. Class stratification is based on market capacity, and differential market capacity is determined both by property ownership and the acquisition of credentials.
2   The most important neoMarxist stratification theory is structuralist Marxism. Here, Poulantzas and Wright extend the notion of property ownership to 'possession'. Each seeks to come to terms with the existence of 'intermediate' or nonhistoric classes. Poulantzas theorizes that they are fractions or strata within the historic classes, determined by politics or ideology. Wright argues that they inhabit 'contradictory' class locations between the historic classes as specified by Marx,

although he later abandons this position to take a line which is much closer to Poulantzas.

3 The critical problem in neoWeberian theory is whether property continues to structurate class. For Giddens, property stands alongside credentials and labour power as a source of market capacity; for Parkin, property is subordinate to occupation; while for Piore property is not worth mentioning. In each case the stress is the capacity of class groups to effect closure on access to privilege by outsiders.

4 Functionalist theories of stratification (which owe an inchoate debt to Durkheim) view social inequality as a positive contribution to the social system. In its most extreme statement, Davis and Moore argue that differential rewards are necessary in order to motivate talented people to enter occupations with long training. Here then, stratification was conceived as a continuous hierarchy of occupational statuses. More recently, Goldthorpe and others have tried to show the ways in which occupations cluster into groups separated by mobility barriers. Functionalist theory has thereby been subsumed into neoWeberian theories of market closure.

Critique

Each of the types of stratification theory considered here has its weaknesses.

The weakness of Marxist theory is its continuing insistence on the reality of class structure and the epiphenomenal status of class experience. Historical experience is accommodated by the theoretical construction of social classes. The more that historical developments escape from the nineteenth-century model of a class structure posited by Marx, the more tenuous does the theoretical connection specified for the relationship between structure and experience become. The general retreat from Althusserian, structuralist Marxism, i.e. the move from Poulantzas to Wright, is a clear indicator of this failure.

The critical weakness in neoWeberian analysis is the absence of a clear specification of an upper class. Whereas Marxist analysis made a straightforward transition from legal ownership to possession of property as the basis of upper-class membership, statements about property have remained equivocal in neoWeberian analysis. The critical theoretical problem appears to lie in separating those possessing significant amounts of property from those in command of organizational assets – to Weberians these groups appear to be continuous. The key to this problem is the Weberian emphasis on closure and the denial that exploitation at the level of capitalization is a qualitatively distinctive form of closure. The theoretical requisite for the specification of an upper class is the concept of a capacity to put the means of production or reproduction into operation in such a way as to exploit the assets of others in order to accumulate capital, and Weberian theory fails to meet such a requisite.

The critical problem which remains in developing social fluidity models into a theory of class is that the class categories are indeed a priori. For example, what Goldthorpe describes as the 'service class' (in more conventional terms, the upper class) includes such diverse locations as CEOs in large-scale corporations and senior politicians and bureaucrats in the state sector on one hand and laboratory technicians, librarians, and shop-floor supervisors on the other. Likewise, the petty bourgeoisie includes both capitalists, who exploit labour in the strict Marxist sense, and the self-employed. The use of intuitively constructed occupational categories may well mask class boundaries which exist within them. Notwithstanding Abercrombie and Urry's claim that the functions of capital (control of labour power, reproduction of labour power, and conceptualization) are increasingly subsumed within this 'service' class (1983: 122–5), this subsumption is by no means uniform and many of the locations identified as professional, administrative and managerial receive small return in the market and experience high levels of subordination in the work situation.

Nevertheless, the apparent convergence between Marxist models, as found in Wright, and Weberian and functionalist ones, as found in Goldthorpe, suggest that very real theoretical progress is being made in this area. It is instructive that in both instances theory is explicitly constructed as an accommodation of research findings. If this theoretical integration can be made convincing, stratification theorists will have the opportunity to move on to seeking a unification of class theory with theories of gender and ethnicity, the other key stratification orders.

Further reading

Differentiation

The classic text is Durkheim's *The Division of Labor in Society* which can also serve as an introduction to Spencer. A good secondary source is either Thompson's *Émile Durkheim* (1982) or Giddens' *Durkheim* (1978). The various arguments about functionalist approaches to change are canvassed in Demerath and Peterson (eds), *System, Change and Conflict* (1965). The most important example, of course, is Parsons, *The Evolution of Societies* (1977). A good critical review of theories of industrial and postindustrial society is Kumar, *Prophecy and Progress* (1978). More recently developed analyses of differentiation can be found in Alexander and Colomy (eds), *Differentiation Theory and Social Change* (1990b).

Stratification

Classical theories of the transition from feudalism to capitalism are reviewed by Giddens in *Capitalism and Modern Social Theory* (1971). He reviews Marx's and Weber's theories of stratification as well as presenting his own in *The Class Structure of the Advanced Societies* (1973). The best selection of excerpts from all the theories discussed here is *Classes, Power and Conflict* (1982), edited by Giddens and Held. A wide-ranging and more detailed review can also be found in Waters, *Class and Stratification* (1990).

Notes

1 Generally, Marxist theories of class would not accept that they are species of stratification theory. This is because they accuse stratification theory of merely describing inequality and failing to pay appropriate attention to the formation of classes as real groups which struggle against one another. For organizational purposes, however, theories of class can be thought of as theories of stratification in the terms of economic inequality.

2 As an empirical generalization, this argument about a positive correlation between scale and complexity is insupportable, whether proposed by Spencer or Durkheim. Highly differentiated, small-scale societies are perfectly possible, e.g. Andorra, Liechtenstein. And history is replete with examples of large-scale societies which had relatively low levels of differentiation, e.g. the ancient societies of Rome, China, India, Egypt, etc., and the feudal societies of medieval Europe and premodern Japan.

3 The claims about race and gender, in particular, are unacceptable by contemporary standards.

4 This is Giddens' preferred version of differentiation. He prefers it because differentiation misses the characteristic expansion of time and space distances in each individual's perceptual horizon.

5 A variety of status attributes may become the basis of a status stratification system. Occupational status is the most common theoretical specification but it may also be based on ethnicity, gender, religious status, age, generation, kinship, or race. Other nonstatus, nonclass, stratification systems may be based on military force, political power, or ideological monopolization (Mann 1986). This part of the chapter, however, focuses on socioeconomic inequality.

6 No assumption is made here that markets are either noncontingent or free. The capacity of individuals to secure advantage in a market is entailed in a priori inequalities.

7 Bourdieu's theory of class is also critical and structuralist. However, because it is oriented to the cultural reproduction of class differences it is included in chapter 6 on culture and ideology.

8 The situation of unproductive labour is viewed as similar to that of the petty bourgeoisie. Professionals are excluded from the upper class on the grounds that they do not own the means of capital accumulation; and they cannot be included in the working class because their labour is 'unproductive', it produces no surplus value, and it therefore cannot be exploited. It is because professional work is to some extent self-directed but does not lead to capital accumulation that, in Poulantzas' scheme, the professional workers of the new middle class are said to constitute a *new petty bourgeoisie*.

9 For an elegant critique of Poulantzas' position on this structural arrangement, see Connell (1982). Connell is particularly concerned to show that Poulantzas' explanation for the existence of fractions and strata is a functional one – they exist 'for the purpose of reproducing classes'. Poulantzas' explanation for stratification therefore has about the same level of credibility as the functionalist accounts of Parsons and Davis and Moore (see below).

10 That is, it cannot be invested and thus made to grow in value.

11 Because of the continuing political manipulation which seeks to ally working-class tories/Reagan democrats with bourgeois interests, the distance between the two segments has increased. In the USA, for example, the ratio of primary to secondary segment income increased from 1.14 in 1947 to 1.56 in 1977 (Gordon et al. 1982: 196).

12 Goldthorpe's seven classes are:

Class I: Large proprietors; higher professionals; higher administrators and managers. (Service class.)

Class II: Lower professionals; technicians; lower administrators; small business managers; supervisors of non-manual workers. (Cadet level of the service class.)

Class III: Clerks; sales personnel.

Class IV: Petty bourgeoisie.

Class V: Lower technicians; foremen and shop supervisors.

Class VI: Skilled manual workers.

Class VII: Semi- and unskilled manual workers. (Goldthorpe 1987: 40–3)

13 The shift has also been marked by a change in methodological procedure, from regression analysis of determinants of individual mobility, to log-linear modelling, which superimposes a map of actual positions (destinations) on a map of what would be expected if there were no social fluidity (origins) and allows the differences to be quantified.

10 Conclusion: the past and the future of sociological theory

Most surveys of the theoretical literature in sociology conclude with an embarrassed apology, or perhaps an uncertain triumphalism, about its inability to offer a unified set of answers about 'why society?' or 'why social order?' or 'what is the meaning of social life?' Having identified theory as the product of a series of schools of thought, it then becomes necessary to confess that this multiplicity of approaches is less than desirable. Here are some such confessions:

> For anyone wanting cut and dried answers, answers 'off the peg', sociology is certainly not the subject to take up. For it is a subject area best characterized by its lively disputaciousness, its conflicting approaches and versions, and, vitally, by its questions. [Cuff et al. 1990: 230]

> [I]f the hat is the social world, the world studied by sociology, we can pull out not only a variety of rabbits but any number of other animals, many of them weird and wonderful. [Craib 1992: 247]

Some hold this to be the consequence of oppositions derived from the classics:

> In the higher realms of sociological theory . . . not only is there no recognizable paradigm, but often sociologists seem not to aspire to acquiring one. In textbooks on the history of sociological thought, the great thinkers of the past are divided up into schools and played off against each other. . . To the present day, new sociological sects arise from time to time, loudly proclaiming their own final solution to the sociology problem, denying any merit in rival approaches, yet remaining minority sects. [Mennell 1974: 3]

Others regard the lack of a theoretical centre as the product of a fundamental break from the classical tradition:

> Sociological theory at present consists largely of reified conceptual debris from the project of Weber, Durkheim and Marx. Gone, for the most part, are the broad theoretical views which were intended as the basis for the development of an integrated stance toward whole societies and relations among societies. Gone is the kind of discourse which moved frequently and fluidly between discussions of moral, political and economic structures. [Wardell and Turner 1986: 17]

Evaluations of this theoretical diversity are themselves equally diverse. Embarrassment is primary for some:

> There are many different theoretical approaches . . .; within and between these general theoretical perspectives are profound disagreements on substantive issues . . . Sociological theory is thus a highly eclectic activity, and this gives it a sense of being problematic when viewed as a whole. [Turner 1991: 638]

Others try to find virtue in diversity:

> This [renewed] focus [on theory] does not mean that we have, or are likely to have in the near future, a single integrated theory or the breakout of peace among warring theorists. It is not even clear that it would be a good idea. . . . When it comes to analyzing a particular area of social life . . . different perspectives offer different and often complementary insights. [Wallace and Wolf 1991: 377]

The pleasures of complementarity notwithstanding, theories which contradict one another cannot all be correct or true. At least, they cannot be unless one accepts that the diversity is found not only in theory but also in social experience, that is, to take the view that the social world, rather than sociological theory, is intrinsically problematic.

> I propose that action should be conceived not as either instrumental or normative, but as both. Furthermore, this action should be conceived as ordered both through internal and external structures. Only such a dialectical criticism of the presuppositional dilemma enables us to conceive of social theory in a multidimensional way, and multidimensionality is the standard by which I propose to evaluate theoretical logic. [Alexander 1982a: 123]

If Alexander wants a sociological theory which is multidimensional, i.e. which accepts its own contradictions because it views the social world as contradictory, then that is certainly available in general, although the various individual theories which make up the overall corpus are not themselves individually multidimensional.

At least Alexander is explicit in his acceptance of the problem. Others feel able to speak of various dimensions or levels of social reality while simultaneously denying their existence. An early example specifies two levels of theorizing:

> Most sociological theory which is of any value deals with one of two levels of social reality, though some tries to deal with both. The first level is that of social action and interaction; the second is that of social structure or system. [Cohen 1968: 236]

But the proposal is for theory that, by the author's own standards, is of no value because it does not confine itself to one level.

[W]hen one 'demystifies' much of what is said about social action, interaction, social structure and social systems, it is possible to explain, or to suggest ways of explaining, why social systems persist and change, why they vary their characteristics; and that one can do this without taking sides in rather pointless debates concerning the limitations of the 'structural-functional' as opposed to some other models of society, or the merits of the 'integration or consensus model' . . . as opposed to the so-called 'conflict-coercion model'.[1] [Cohen 1968: 237]

A more recent example is even more explicit in its contradictions. Here the author makes a bald statement that:

[T]he social world is not really divided into levels. [Ritzer 1992: 667, italics deleted]

However, he is not going to allow his analysis to be constrained by social reality:

Although the idea of levels is implicit in much of sociology, it has received relatively little explicit attention. In concentrating on levels here, we are doing little more than making explicit what has been implicit in sociology.

The close of this Appendix will offer a conceptualization of the major levels of social analysis. [Ritzer 1992: 667]

Ritzer is scarcely culpable because, as he says, his view is widely shared and he would doubtless defend it by saying that the levels are purely analytic slices of reality. Here is another example that does just this.

The distinctions among micro, macro and meso [levels] are in the theorists' heads. If one looks at the world 'out there', one does not see a world composed of levels or layers – that is, micro, meso, and macro. The social world is more seamless and continuous; when we partition theories into micro, meso, and macro, we are doing so for analytical convenience. [Turner 1991: 591]

It needs to be said that a theory of the social world which denies the reality of its own terms, analytic or not, invites even more ridicule than one which cannot find agreement. We must surely move beyond assessing the validity of theory in terms of its convenience or utility.

Three diagnoses

Because sociology is a highly reflexive discipline, the extent of self-diagnosis of these problems has been considerable, not merely in the pages of books and academic journals but in countless coffee-room conversations, conferences and graduate seminars. The following are three of the best examples.

Merton: the hunt for grand theory

In everyday terms, Merton's view (1968: 39–72) is that sociology is trying to run before it can walk. Sociology is for him a young discipline not nearly so developed as, even though contemporary with, modern physics. At this point in intellectual history, attempts to develop unified theories from which all subsidiary theories can be derived will only result in arguments which are the equivalent of early philosophies of the universe. Thus, it would probably not be too difficult to identify the sociological equivalents of a world carried on the back of a turtle, supported by four elephants, or perhaps, a Ptolemaic system of wheels within wheels within wheels. Merton was remarkably prescient, writing in 1949, in predicting that the route to general theory would become clogged up if each 'charismatic sociologist' tried to develop their own general theory: 'The persistence of this practice can only make for a balkanization of sociology, with each principality governed by its own theoretical system' (1968: 51).

He recommends instead that we concentrate on 'theories of the middle range', theories which stand between the minutiae of everyday findings of empirical research, on one hand, and overarching (or is it undergirding?) theoretical paradigms which claim the inclusion of all the events in the social world. He summarizes his arguments (1968: 68–9) about middle-range theory as follows:

- Middle-range theory focuses on limited areas allowing specific hypotheses to be derived from them.
- Middle-range theories can, in principle, be later consolidated and integrated into wider theoretical networks.
- They are sufficiently abstract to transcend specific events and configurations.
- They cut across the micro/macro distinction.
- They would provide the explanations which so-called general or grand theories fail to do because these are in fact conceptual schemes rather than explanations.
- Middle-range theories are consistent with several of these grand conceptual schemes and can therefore link them together.
- Many middle-range theories are legacies of the classical tradition.
- Middle-range theories are most important in identifying areas of sociological ignorance.

Merton is suggesting, then, that we should return to the classical tradition of addressing particular substantive events and problems.

Alexander: positive barbarism

If Merton's view is that theory has, in a sense, been too 'theoretical', Alexander's is that it is not theoretical enough. Since the Second World

War, he argues, sociology has moved in the direction of what he calls a
'positivist persuasion' which absolves it from genuine theoretical and thus
intellectual endeavour. Positivism involves four postulates:

- There is a radical separation between empirical and nonempirical
  statements.
- The most generalized nonempirical statements, metatheory and philosophy, have no fundamental significance for sociological practice.
- Since natural science also eschews metatheory, sociology must model
  itself on natural science.
- Therefore, theory can be reduced to statements of empirical generalization: it must be derived inductively; its disagreements must be
  resolved empirically; and there can be no logical basis for scientific
  disagreement.
  (Alexander 1982a: 5–15)

The baleful effect of the positivist persuasion, Alexander claims, is to
impoverish sociology in intellectual terms and, in effect, to deny its special
contribution as a discipline. For Alexander, it is not surprising that a
unified theoretical system has failed to emerge in sociology when so few
sociologists are making an effort at theory.

However, this is not the only reason for the balkanization of theory.
Alexander also diagnoses a problem within a problem. Sociology, he
argues, has a particular presuppositional structure which locates its
activity. This presuppositional structure is outlined in the quotation above
and in figure 8.6.[2] Various attempts at theory have failed to overcome the
positivist persuasion precisely because they have been guilty of 'conflationism' within this presuppositional structure – they have tended to offer
unidimensional theoretical accounts when social life is, and theory therefore must be, multidimensional. As we saw in chapter 8, Alexander's view
is that, in the modern period, only Parsonsian theory comes remotely close
to the standard of multidimensionality.

Holmwood and Stewart: contradictory dualism

What Alexander holds to be a virtue, Holmwood and Stewart (1991) hold
to be a vice. His multidimensionalism is, in their terms, a contradictory
dualism, an assertion that mutually exclusive theoretical categories are
real. Social life, they argue, cannot simultaneously be subjectively generated and creative on one hand and external and constraining on the other.
The balkanization of theory is for them the consequence of a failure to
come to terms with and reformulate such contradictions.

These contradictions appear when sociologists are confronted by facts
which do not fit the theory proposed (1991: 42–4). At such points,
sociological theory tends to be afflicted by a universal fallacy – it assumes
that the recalcitrant fact can be absorbed into the theory without there

being any need to alter the theory. They identify two versions of the fallacy, horizontal and vertical. Theorists guilty of the horizontal fallacy take the view that contradictory elements of a theory are experienced separately in different parts of the society. Weber might be seen as guilty of such a fallacy in arguing that some actors experience the objective constraints of class while others engage in status competition. Holmwood and Stewart would argue that some new terms in a theory of inequality, other than class and status, might need to be constructed if this contradiction is to be resolved. Theorists guilty of the vertical fallacy take the view that while actors' experiences may contradict the theory, the contradiction can be absorbed and 'explained away' by a set of superseding terms. The most obvious example is Marx's view that there is a contradiction between workers' alienation and exploitation, on one hand, and their apparent acceptance of capitalism on the other. The contradiction is 'explained away' by the superseding concepts of ideology and false consciousness.

The reason why theoretical perspectives multiply and compete is that none can succeed. The reason none can succeed is because they are guilty of the common fallacy of not adapting theory to reality. In the contemporary theoretical phase, as we have seen, various strategies for resolving contradictory dualisms have been applied:

- Giddens opts for elision: structures are said to be enabling *and* constraining.
- Alexander goes one better and effects the double elision of multi-dimensionality – the social world is both instrumental *and* normative, and it is both subjective *and* external.
- Elster cannot cope with norms and retreats to a proposal of limited rationality.
- Habermas engages both in a horizontalist partition between system and lifeworld and in a verticalist view of the corrigibility of actors' versions of their experience in the notion of 'systematically distorted communication'.

None of these solves the problems of theory and more attempts seem bound to be made.

The accomplishments of theory

It would be an absurdity to propose a series of easy fixes which would magically transform sociological theory into a universal and complete answer to any question about the social world. However, it would be an equal absurdity to dispense entirely with a vital and vigorous intellectual tradition which has managed simultaneously to refuse the easy temptations of either an anxiety-free positivism or a purely opinionated and interpretive social philosophy or the withdrawn scholasticism of metatheory. Any worthwhile development in sociological theory must draw upon a pattern, established in its classical instances, of coming to grips with the substantive and practical problems which face contemporary humanity in its social existence. Sociological theory must involve the development of a set of intellectual resources which are useful to sociologists and which, possibly in an attenuated form, provide substance to wider public debate. Any other course would be self-indulgent and morally bankrupt.

The preceding chapters of this book are an attempt to sum up what sociological theory can say and do, what might be the basis for any move forward. In summary, its statements are as follows. Any good theory of the social world must somehow put together four irreducible proposals which are characterized by the terms, agency, rationality, structure and system. It will make its own decisions about which of the proposals has priority, about whether it wishes to conflate one proposal to another, but we are now in a reasonable degree of agreement that it must address all of them. Ideally, doubtless at some distant future point, we may be able to supersede these proposals with a more unified set. However, as they stand at the moment, the proposals are that:

• Humans are conscious and aware beings who act in terms of meanings and motives and their individual actions both have consequences for, and are taken account of, by other humans; they act as if they have the capacity collectively to construct the social world.
• Humans also have interests both in building their own resources and in material consumption, and they will act, individually and collectively, investing and spending the resources which they already possess, in terms of maximizing these interests; maximizing one's own interests will often constrain or reduce others' ability to realize their interests.
• There are, at least limitations on, if not determinations of, the acquisition of meaning and the maximization of interests, which come from what might be called the arrangement of possibilities given in actually being human and in being located at a particular temporal (historical or biographical) or spatial or biological or social juncture.
• There are generalized, organized and bounded totalities which are independent of the intentions of individual human beings and which contain collective knowledge, aspirations and preferences; humans are obliged to draw upon the guidance of this totality in formulating their individual projects in relation to others, to their resources, and to the possibilities conferred on them by their situation.

However, this book does not confine itself to proposals about how we should look at the social world but what we can actually say about it. It does not claim to offer an exhaustive inventory of what sociology can say about the social world. Indeed, such an inventory would not be possible in principle. However, it does indicate the most important things that can be said about it at the present moment in the development of the discipline. It limits itself to five such statements:

- The social world is suffused by shared ideas and values. These ideas and values intersect and interact with one another to constitute a systemic reality that can be called a culture. Culture is progressively becoming more separate from actual social relationships and from the individuals who participate in them. As it becomes so it is becoming more autonomous, so that social action increasingly can be conceived of as guided by culturally provided possibilities and decreasingly as constrained and controlled.
- The pattern of constraint and control which we call power nevertheless remains a fundamental social process. The process operates both by proaction and prohibition, and both at the level of intention and below the level of awareness. Under contemporary conditions power might be seen as being absorbed by culture and thus increasingly located within its communicative and discursive symbolizations.
- An important site for the operation of both power and culture is the field of gender. Here, men and women exhibit differential patterns of behaviour which are subject to cultural guidance; their situations are fundamentally unequal in terms of the distribution of material and nonmaterial resources; and men control and constrain women in both domestic and nondomestic contexts in the direction of subordination and exploitation.
- A second important site for the operation of power and culture is the field of socioeconomic stratification. This is a major arena for the distribution and allocation of resources. This distribution tends towards inequality. Society is thus characterized by groups which are internally homogeneous but externally unequal on the basis of access to resources of property, credentials, organizational position, occupational and income opportunity, prestige, and social approval.
- The social world experiences a continuous process of organization and reorganization in which patterns of action progressively become more pervasive and narrow, as opposed to concentrated, local and diffuse. Social participation thus progressively moves towards a series of layered memberships (e.g. spouse, parent, citizen, client, voter, worker, consumer, audience, student . . . etc.) and away from singular, personal identity-statuses.

Moving forward

The fact that very many sociologists can agree that all or most of these statements are true, even if they cannot completely agree on the relative importance of each, indicates that sociological theory has made an important contribution to the coherence of the message which the discipline gives to the wider community. The problem is how to move theory more certainly in a positive direction by refining the message and maximizing the level of agreement. One thing is clear, that sociology should not, once again, seek to develop a grand theory of everything because to do so can only result in the related failures of dualism and conflationism or vertical and horizontal fallacies. Rather, the move forward needs to occur in a detailed and incremental way. In summary, there are several present practices which theory needs to avoid:

1 Conceptualizing social reality as a series of levels, layers or dimensions in any guise. These seduce the theorist into tolerating discrepancies between theory and reality (not least the fundamental one that that social reality is itself not layered) as well as into tolerating internal theoretical contradictions. It encourages dualism and conflationism.

2 Treating theory as an analytic framework, perspective or paradigm. Such an approach discourages reality tests. So long as a theorist can say: 'There are multiple perspectives on the social world and mine is as useful as any of the others' we shall continue to risk being trapped in an endless war between the schools.

3 Trying to explain everything within a unified theory, and even demanding that any piece of theory should be evaluated against a standard of being able to explain everything. The discipline is simply not at a stage in its development where this is possible.[3]

4 Accepting that interpretivist descriptions or minimalist behavioural formulae are theory. These fail to meet a normal definition of theory and if we deny the possibility of theory we lose our intellectual tradition and thus our claim to being an identifiable discipline.

5 Accepting that philosophical meta-arguments about the possibility of theory are theory. These divert us from the goal of making sense of and explaining the social world. Entertaining and diverting brain-teasers they may be but that is all they are and they should be left to those interested in counting dancing angels on pinheads.

6 Asking the big questions first. While we always need to keep in mind the ultimate goal of explaining 'the lifeworld, universalism and everything', the answers to the big questions are unlikely to emerge within the lifetime of any single person. After well over 2,000 years, physics has yet to accomplish the unification of particle theory with cosmic theory, although it is widely reckoned to be very close. Why, then, should sociology be able to reconcile structure with agency after only 100 years or so of trying, and with far fewer resources?

There are also certain complementary practices that sociological theory should proactively engage in, including:

1 Reconceptualizing the notion of general theory. The implicit under-

standing of the term 'general theory' is identical with what natural scientists call a 'unified theory', that is an integrated set of propositions that one can use to explain any event in a specified universe. However, a more appropriate meaning of the term 'general theory' might be that it is a set of propositions which claims that there is a specified universal process and all events of that type can be explained by reference to its propositions. The 'general theory of relativity' does not claim to explain all events in the physical universe, nor does the 'general theory of evolution' claim to explain all events in the biotic universe. Sociology could equally have general theories of power, and rationality, and exchange, and ideology, and class without such theories being integrated with one another and without claiming to explain all events in the social universe. General theory does not need to be thought of as 'grand' theory.

2   Embracing a substantive realism. Theory needs to privilege the social world and its constraints, to regard it as penetrable and orderly rather than as an unyielding complexity which has to have order imposed upon it by the sociologist. Theory needs to allow the world to speak to it, importantly by means of research, but also by means of a simple and sensitive perceptiveness and lack of conceit.

3   Remaining resolutely theoretical. Sociologists must insist on continuing to make statements which are general, conceptual and abstract but which above all seek to be explanatory. Such an orientation need not embrace a formal structure of propositions as is proposed in many positivistic philosophies of science, but should seek to make clear why behaviour falls into particular social arrangements. It is critically important that theory should not be self-limiting in terms of a lack of concepts or of findings. In seeking to explain particular problems theory will generate appropriate questions and resources in the long term.

4   Accepting that theoretical problems are *theoretical* problems. This means accepting that theory sometimes can fail. It implies that when a contradiction arises that this is a theoretical problem, not a difficulty in perception on the part of subjects, or that actors are contrary beings who sometimes act one way and sometimes another, or that if we could only get our measurements right then the theory would be confirmed. There must be a constant willingness to reformulate, revise and even abandon the statements which our theories make.

5   Addressing the practicalities of human experience. One of the assumptions we can make is that human beings are natural, practical problem-solvers. We should never deny what our subjects tell us because their statements have to make sense of the worlds in which they move. In any of the limited theoretical fields in which we work we therefore ought at least to be able to accommodate and explain subjective statements. If we do, sociological theory can become a resource not only for ourselves but for those fellow human beings whom we study. Sociology should

never be: 'The study of those who don't need it by those who do'. If it can avoid this particular epithet then it can open up genuinely emancipatory possibilities across the social realm.

The final question now arises as to whether this book moves us forward on any of these dimensions.[4] The answer must be: not a great deal, but possibly a little, and every little bit helps. In introducing sociological theory it has sought to identify the critical weaknesses which, if addressed, might engender positive developments. More importantly, it has sought to regroup theory in relation to a series of topics which might provide the main directions for future development. Its task is to indicate what theory has said so far, but in undertaking this reorganization it necessarily indicates what it is possible for theory to say in the future. What theory does say might take the form of responses to limited questions within each of the themes specified here.

Notes

1 The author's claim that the debates are pointless must, on this quotation, be grounded in a view that they are already resolved in the direction of structural or system-conflation.

2 Indeed, a version of Alexander's presuppositional scheme is an organizing principle for this book.

3 Alexander's proposal of multidimensionality as the standard may therefore be regarded as both unrealistic and misleading. Within our current knowledge it simply is impossible to make an agreed and unified statement about agency, rationality, structure and system.

4 I have tried to direct my own efforts at theorizing precisely at the level recommended here. For those sufficiently interested, see my work on collegiality and other nonbureaucrative administrative systems (1989b; 1993) and issues of class formation (1990; 1991).

References

Abercrombie, N., S. Hill and B. Turner (1980) *The Dominant Ideology Thesis*. London: Allen & Unwin.

Abercrombie, N., S. Hill and B. Turner (1984) *The Penguin Dictionary of Sociology*. Harmondsworth: Penguin.

Abercrombie, N. and B. Turner (1978/1982) 'The Dominant Ideology Thesis', *British Journal of Sociology* 29(2): 149–70, and in A. Giddens and D. Held (eds), *Classes, Power and Conflict*. Berkeley: University of California Press: 396–414.

Abercrombie, N. and J. Urry (1983) *Capital, Labour and the Middle Classes*. London: Allen & Unwin.

Adorno, T. (1978) 'Freudian Theory and the Pattern of Fascist Propaganda' in A. Arato and E. Gebhardt (eds), *The Essential Frankfurt School Reader*. Oxford: Blackwell: 118–37.

Adorno, T. and M. Horkheimer (1979) *The Dialectic of Enlightenment*. London: Verso.

Alexander, J. (1982a) *Theoretical Logic in Sociology*, Vol. 1, *Positivism, Presuppositions, and Current Controversies*. London: Routledge.

Alexander, J. (1982b) *Theoretical Logic in Sociology*, Vol. 2, *The Antinomies of Classical Thought: Marx and Durkheim*. London: Routledge.

Alexander, J. (1983) *Theoretical Logic in Sociology*, Vol. 3, *The Classical Attempt at Theoretical Synthesis: Max Weber*. London: Routledge.

Alexander, J. (1984) *Theoretical Logic in Sociology*, Vol. 4, *The Modern Reconstruction of Classical Thought: Talcott Parsons*. London: Routledge.

Alexander, J. (1985) 'Introduction' in J. Alexander (ed.), *Neofunctionalism*. Beverly Hills: Sage: 7–18.

Alexander, J. (1988) *Action and its Environments*. New York: Columbia University Press.

Alexander, J. and P. Colomy (1990a) 'Neofunctionalism Today' in G. Ritzer (ed.), *Frontiers of Social Theory*. New York: Columbia University Press: 33–67.

Alexander, J. and P. Colomy (eds) (1990b) *Differentiation Theory and Social Change*. New York: Columbia University Press.

Althusser, L. (1977a) *For Marx*. London: New Left.

Althusser, L. (1977b) *Lenin and Philosophy and other essays*. London: New Left.

Althusser, L. and É. Balibar (1970) *Reading Capital*. London: New Left.

Althusser, L. and É. Balibar (1972) 'Marx's Immense Theoretical Revolution' in R. De George and F. De George (eds), *The Structuralists: From Marx to Lévi-Strauss*. Garden City: Anchor: 239–54.

Amin, S. (1974) *Accumulation on a World Scale*. Hassocks: Harvester.

Anderson, P. (1976) *Considerations on Western Marxism*. London: New Left.

Arato, A. and P. Breines (1979) *The Young Lukács and the Origins of Western Marxism*. Sydney: Pluto.

Arato, A. and E. Gebhardt (eds) (1978) *The Essential Frankfurt School Reader*. Oxford: Blackwell.

Archer, M. (1988) *Culture and Agency*. Cambridge: CUP.

Arendt, H. (1986) 'Communicative Power' in S. Lukes (ed.) *Power*. Oxford: Blackwell: 59–74.

Arrow, K. (1963) *Social Choice and Individual Values* (2nd edn). New York: Wiley.

Bachrach, P. and M. Baratz (1962) 'Two Faces of Power', *American Political Science Review*: 56: 947–1052.

Bachrach, P. and M. Baratz (1963) 'Decisions and Nondecisions', *American Political Science Review*: 57: 941–1051.

Bachrach, P. and M. Baratz (1970) *Power and Poverty*. New York: OUP.

Bannock, G., R. Baxter and R. Rees (1971) *The Penguin Dictionary of Economics* (3rd edn). Harmondsworth: Penguin.

Barash, P. (1980) *Sociobiology*. London: Souvenir.

Barrett, M. (1980) *Women's Oppression Today*. London: Verso.

Baudrillard, J. (1983) *In the Shadow of Silent Majorities . . . or the End of the Social and Other Essays*. New York: Semiotext(e).

Baudrillard, J. (1988) Selected Writings. Stanford: Stanford University.

Becker, H. (1963; extended printing 1973) *Outsiders*. New York: Free Press.

Beilharz, P. (1991) *A Guide to Central Thinkers in Social Theory*. Sydney: Allen & Unwin.

Bell, D. (1973) *The Coming of Post-Industrial Society*. New York: Basic.

Bell, D. (1979) *The Cultural Contradictions of Capitalism* (2nd edn). London: Heinemann.

Bernstein, R. (ed.) (1985) *Habermas and Modernity*. Cambridge: Polity.

Berger, P. (1966) *Invitation to Sociology*. Harmondsworth: Penguin.

Berger, P. and T. Luckmann (1967) *The Social Construction of Reality*. London: Allen Lane.

Blackburn, R. (ed.) (1972) *Ideology in Social Science*. Glasgow: Fontana.

Blau, P. (1964) *Exchange and Power in Social Life*. New York: Wiley.

Blau, P. and O. Duncan (1967) *The American Occupational Structure*. New York: Wiley.

Blumer, H. (1969) *Symbolic Interactionism*. Englewood Cliffs: Prentice-Hall.

Bottomore, T. (1966) *Elites and Society*. Harmondsworth: Penguin.

Bottomore, T. and R. Nisbet (1979) 'Structuralism' in their *A History of Sociological Analysis*. London: Heinemann: 557–99.

Bourdieu, P. (1977) *Outline of a Theory of Practice*. London: CUP.

Bourdieu, P. (1984) *Distinction*. London: Routledge.

Bourdieu, P. and J-C. Passeron (1977) *Reproduction*. London: Sage.

Bowie, M. (1979) 'Jacques Lacan' in J. Sturrock (ed.), *Structuralism and Since*. Oxford: OUP: 116–53.

Branson, J. and D. Miller (1991) 'Pierre Bourdieu' in P. Beilharz (ed.), *Social Theory*. Sydney: Allen & Unwin: 37–45.

Braverman, H. (1974) *Labor and Monopoly Capital*. New York: Monthly Review.

Brenner, J. and M. Ramas (1984) 'Rethinking Women's Oppression', *New Left Review* 144: 33–71.

Broom, L. and F. Jones (1976) *Opportunity and Attainment in Australia*. Canberra: Australian National University Press.

Brownmiller, S. (1975) *Against Our Will*. New York: Simon and Schuster.

Brubaker, R. (1984) *The Limits of Rationality*. London: Allen & Unwin.

Bryant, C. and D. Jary (eds) (1991) *Giddens' Theory of Structuration*. London: Routledge.

Buchanan, J. (1978) 'From Private Preferences to Public Philosophy' in J. Buchanan et al. (eds) *The Economics of Politics*. London: IEA: 1–20.

Burnham, J. (1941) *The Managerial Revolution*. New York: John Day.

Carchedi, G. (1977) *On the Economic Identification of Social Classes*. London: Routledge.

Chodorow, N. (1974) 'Family Structure and Feminine Personality' in M. Rosaldo and L. Lamphere (eds), *Woman, Culture, and Society*. Stanford: Stanford University Press: 43–66.

Chodorow, N. (1989) *Feminism and Psychoanalytic Theory*. New Haven: Yale University Press.

Clark, J., C. Modgil and S. Modgil (eds) (1990) *Anthony Giddens*. London: Falmer.

Clegg, S. (1989) *Frameworks of Power*. London: Sage.

Clegg, S., P. Boreham and G. Dow (1986) *Class Politics and the Economy*. London: Routledge.

Cohen, P. (1968) *Modern Social Theory*. London: Heinemann.

Coleman, J. (1990) *Foundations of Social Theory*. Cambridge: Belknap.

Colomy, P. (1990) 'Revisions and Progress in Differentiation Theory' in J. Alexander and

P. Colomy (eds), *Differentiation Theory and Social Change*. New York: Columbia University Press: 465–96.

Conley, V. (1984) *Hélène Cixous*. Lincoln: University of Nebraska Press.

Connell, R. (1982) 'A Critique of the Althusserian Approach to Class' in A. Giddens and D. Held (eds), *Classes, Power and Conflict*. Berkeley: University of California Press: 130–47.

Connell, R. (1987) *Gender and Power*. London: Allen & Unwin.

Cook, K., J. O'Brien and P. Kollock (1990) 'Exchange Theory' in G. Ritzer (ed.), *Frontiers of Social Theory*. New York: Columbia University Press: 158–81.

Coser, L. (1977) *Masters of Sociological Thought* (2nd edn). New York: Harcourt.

Craib, I. (1984; 2nd edn 1992) *Modern Social Theory*. Hemel Hempstead: Harvester Wheatsheaf.

Crook, S. (1991) *Modernist Radicalism and its Aftermath*. London: Routledge.

Crook, S. and L. Taylor (1980) 'Goffman's Version of Reality' in Jason Ditton (ed.), *The View from Goffman*. London: Macmillan: 233–51.

Crook, S., J. Pakulski and M. Waters (1992) *Postmodernization*. London: Sage.

Cuff, E., W. Sharrock and D. Francis (1990) *Perspectives in Sociology* (3rd edn). London: Unwin Hyman.

Culler, J. (1979) 'Jacques Derrida' in J. Sturrock (ed.), *Structuralism and Since*. Oxford: OUP: 154–80.

Cutler, A., B. Hindess, P. Hirst and A. Hussain (1977) *Marx's 'Capital' and Capitalism Today*, Vol. 1. London: Routledge.

Cuzzort, R. and E. King (1980) *20th Century Social Thought* (3rd edn). New York: Holt.

Dahl, R. (1957) 'The Concept of Power', *Behavioural Science* 2: 201–5.

Dahl, R. (1961) *Who Governs?* New Haven: Yale University Press.

Dahl, R. (1986) 'Power as the Control of Behavior' in S. Lukes (ed.), *Power*. Oxford: Blackwell: 37–58.

Dahl, R. (1991) *Modern Political Analysis*. Englewood Cliffs: Prentice-Hall.

Davidson, A. (1977) *Antonio Gramsci*. London: Merlin.

Davidson, A. (1991) 'Antonio Gramsci' in P. Beilharz (ed.) *A Guide to Central Thinkers in Social Theory*. Sydney: Allen & Unwin.

Davis, K. and W. Moore (1945) 'Some Principles of Stratification', *American Sociological Review* 10: 242–9.

de Beauvoir, S. (1972) *The Second Sex*. Harmondsworth: Penguin.

De George, R. and F. De George (eds) (1972) *The Structuralists: From Marx to Lévi-Strauss*. Garden City: Anchor.

Delphy, C. (1984) *Close to Home*. London: Hutchinson.

Demerath, N. III and R. Petersen (eds) (1965) *System, Change and Conflict*. New York: Free Press.

Denzin, N. (1971) 'Symbolic Interactionism and Ethnomethodology' in J. Douglas (ed.), *Understanding Everyday Life*. London: Routledge: 285–94.

Ditton, J. (ed.) (1980) *The View from Goffman*. London: Macmillan.

Downs, A. (1957) *An Economic Theory of Democracy*. New York: Harper & Row.

Durkheim, É. (1915) *The Elementary Forms of the Religious Life*. London: Allen & Unwin.

Durkheim, É. (1933; 1964) *The Division of Labor in Society*. New York: Macmillan/Free Press.

Durkheim, É. (1951) *Suicide*. New York: Free Press.

Durkheim, É. (1964) *The Rules of Sociological Method*. New York: Free Press.

Durkheim, É. (1972) *Selected Writings*, ed. A. Giddens. Cambridge: CUP.

Eisenstein, H. (1984) *Contemporary Feminist Thought*. London: Allen & Unwin.

Eisenstein, Z. (1979) *Capitalist Patriarchy and the Case for Socialist Feminism*. New York: Monthly Review.

Eisenstein, Z. ([1981] 1986) *The Radical Future of Liberal Feminism*. Boston: Northeastern University Press.

Ekeh, P. (1974) *Social Exchange Theory*. London: Heinemann.

Elias, N. ([1939] 1978/1982) *The Civilizing Process* (2 vols). Oxford: Blackwell.
Elster, J. (1989a) *Nuts and Bolts for the Social Sciences*. Cambridge: CUP.
Elster, J. (1989b) *The Cement of Society*. Cambridge: CUP.
Emerson, R. (1981) 'Social Exchange Theory' in M. Rosenberg and R. Turner (eds), *Social Psychology*. New York: Basic: 30–65.
Engels, F. (1975) *The Origin of the Family, Private Property and the State*. New York: International.
Featherman, D., F. Jones and R. Hauser (1978) 'Assumptions of Social Mobility Research in the US', *Social Science Research* 4(4): 329–60.
Field, G. and J. Higley (1973) 'Elites and Non-Elites', Module 13. Andover: Warner Modular: 1–38.
Field, G. and J. Higley (1980) *Elitism*. London: Routledge.
Firestone, S. (1972) *The Dialectic of Sex*. London: Paladin.
Foucault, M. (1979) *Discipline and Punish*. New York: Vintage.
Foucault, M. (1980) *Power/Knowledge*. Brighton: Harvester.
Foucault, M. (1981) *The History of Sexuality*, Vol. 1, Harmondsworth: Penguin.
Foucault, M. (1982) 'The Subject and Power' in H. Dreyfus and P. Rabinow, *Michel Foucault*. Chicago: University of Chicago Press: 208–26.
Fox, R. (1976) *Kinship and Marriage*. Harmondsworth: Penguin.
Frankfurt Institute for Social Research (1973) *Aspects of Sociology*. London: Heinemann.
Freud, S. ([1924] 1952) *A General Introduction to Psychoanalysis*. New York: Washington Square.
Freud, S. ([1950] 1965) 'The Ego and the Superego' in T. Parsons, K. Naegele, E. Shils and J. Pitts (eds), *Theories of Society* (one vol. edn). New York: Free Press: 733–8.
Friedan, B. (1963) *The Feminine Mystique*. London: Gollancz.
Frisby, D. (1981) *Sociological Impressionism*. London: Heinemann.
Garfinkel, H. (1967) *Studies in Ethnomethodology*. Englewood Cliffs: Prentice-Hall.
Garnham, N. and R. Williams (1980) 'Pierre Bourdieu and the sociology of culture', *Media, Culture and Society* 2: 209–23.
Garnsey, E. (1982) 'Women's Work and Theories of Class and Stratification' in A. Giddens and D. Held (eds), *Classes, Power and Conflict*. Berkeley: University of California Press.
Geras, N. (1972) 'Althusser's Marxism', *New Left Review* 71: 57–86.
Giddens, A. (1971) *Capitalism and Modern Social Theory*. Cambridge: CUP.
Giddens, A. (1973) *The Class Structure of the Advanced Societies*. New York: Harper Torchbook.
Giddens, A. (1976) *New Rules of Sociological Method*. London: Hutchinson.
Giddens, A. (1977) *Studies in Social and Political Theory*. London: Hutchinson.
Giddens, A. (1978) *Durkheim*. Glasgow: Fontana.
Giddens, A. (1979) *Central Problems in Social Theory*. London: Macmillan.
Giddens, A. (1981) *The Class Structure of the Advanced Societies* (2nd edn). London: Hutchinson.
Giddens, A. (1982) *Profiles and Critiques in Social Theory*. London: Macmillan.
Giddens, A. (1984) *The Constitution of Society*. Cambridge: Polity.
Giddens, A. (1987) *Social Theory and Modern Sociology*. Cambridge: Polity.
Giddens, A. (1990) *The Consequences of Modernity*. Cambridge: Polity.
Giddens, A. (1991a) 'Structuration Theory: Past, Present and Future' in C. Bryant and D. Jary (eds), *Giddens' Theory of Structuration*. London: Routledge: 201–21.
Giddens, A. (1991b) *Modernity and Self-Identity*. Cambridge: Polity.
Giddens, A., and D. Held (eds) (1982) *Classes, Power and Conflict*. Berkeley: University of California Press.
Glucksmann, M. (1974) 'The Structuralism of Lévi-Strauss and Althusser' in J. Rex (ed.), *Approaches to Sociology*. London: Routledge: 230–45.
Goffman, E. (1959) *The Presentation of Self in Everyday Life*. London: Allen Lane.
Goffman, E. (1974) *Frame Analysis*. New York: Harper.
Goldthorpe, J. (1983) 'Women and Class Analysis', *Sociology* 17(4): 465–88.

Goldthorpe, J. (1987) *Social Mobility and Class Structure in Modern Britain*. Oxford: Clarendon Press.

Goldthorpe, J. and K. Hope (1974) *The Social Grading of Occupations*. Oxford: Clarendon Press.

Gordon, D., R. Edwards and M. Reich (1982) *Segmented Work, Divided Workers*. Cambridge: CUP.

Gramsci, A. (1977a) *Selections from the Political Writings (1910–1920)*. New York: International.

Gramsci, A. (1977b) *Selections from the Political Writings (1921–1926)*. New York: International.

Gramsci, A. (1985) *Prison Notebooks: Selections*. New York: International.

Habermas, J. (1971) *Toward a Rational Society*. London: Heinemann.

Habermas, J. (1972) *Knowledge and Human Interests*. London: Heinemann.

Habermas, J. (1974) *Theory and Practice*. London: Heinemann.

Habermas, J. (1976) *Legitimation Crisis*. London: Heinemann.

Habermas, J. (1979) *Communication and the Evolution of Society*. London: Heinemann.

Habermas, J. (1981) 'Modernity versus Postmodernity' *New German Critique* 22 (Winter): 3–14.

Habermas, J. (1984) *The Theory of Communicative Action*, Vol. 1, *Reason and the Rationalization of Society*. Boston: Beacon.

Habermas, J. (1986) 'Hannah Arendt's Communications Concept of Power', in S. Lukes (ed.) *Power*. Oxford: Blackwell: 75–93.

Habermas, J. (1987) *The Theory of Communicative Action*, Vol. 2, *The Critique of Functionalist Reason*. Cambridge: Polity.

Habermas, J. (1989) *The Structural Transformation of the Public Sphere*. Cambridge: Polity.

Harker, R., C. Mahar and C. Wilkes (1990) *An Introduction to the Work of Pierre Bourdieu*. Basingstoke: Macmillan.

Harvey, D. (1989) *The Condition of Postmodernity*. Oxford: Blackwell.

Hawkes, T. (1977) *Structuralism and Semiotics*. London: Methuen.

Heath, A. (1976) *Rational Choice and Social Exchange*. Cambridge: CUP.

Heath, A. and N. Brittan (1984) 'Women's Jobs do Make a Difference', *Sociology* 18(4): 475–90.

Held, D. (1980) *Introduction to Critical Theory*. London: Hutchinson.

Held, D. and J. Thompson (eds) (1989) *Social Theory of Modern Societies: Anthony Giddens and his Critics*. Cambridge: CUP.

Hindess, B. (1988) *Choice, Rationality, and Social Theory*. London: Unwin Hyman.

Holmwood, J. and A. Stewart (1983) 'The Role of Contradictions in Modern Theories of Stratification', *Sociology* 17(2): 234–54.

Holmwood, J. and A. Stewart (1991) *Explanation and Social Theory*. Basingstoke: Macmillan.

Homans, G. (1961) *Social Behaviour*. London: Routledge.

Horkheimer, M. (1978a) 'The End of Reason' in A. Arato and E. Gebhardt (eds), *The Essential Frankfurt School Reader*. Oxford: Blackwell: 26–48.

Horkheimer, M. (1978b) 'The Authoritarian State' in A. Arato and E. Gebhardt (eds), *The Essential Frankfurt School Reader*. Oxford: Blackwell: 95–117.

Hughes, H. (1979) *Consciousness and Society*. Brighton: Harvester.

Hunter, F. (1953) *Community Power Structure*. Chapel Hill: University of North Carolina Press.

Irigaray, L. (1985) *This Sex which is Not One*. Ithaca: Cornell University Press.

Jameson, F. (1972) *The Prison-House of Language*. Princeton: Princeton University Press.

Jameson, F. (1984) 'Postmodernism: Or the Cultural Logic of Late Capitalism', *New Left Review* 146: 53–92.

Jay, M. (1973) *The Dialectical Imagination*. London: Heinemann.

Jay, M. (1984) *Marxism and Totality*. Cambridge: Polity.

Jessop, B. (1982) *The Capitalist State*. New York: New York University Press.

Joll, J. (1977) *Gramsci*. Glasgow: Fontana/Collins.
Jones, F. and P. Davis (1988) 'Class Structuration and Patterns of Social Closure in Australia and New Zealand', *Sociology* 22(2): 271–91.
Jones, G., M. Löwy, G. Therborn, J. Merrington, A. Gorz, R. Aronson, N. Geras, A. Glucksmann and L. Coletti (1977) *Western Marxism*. London: New Left.
Kanter, R. (1977) *Men and Women of the Corporation*. New York: Basic.
Keat, R., and J. Urry (1975) *Social Theory as Science*. London: Routledge.
Kolakowski, L. (1981) *Main Currents of Western Marxism*, Vol. 3, *The Breakdown*. Oxford: OUP.
Kristeva, J. (1986) *The Kristeva Reader*. Oxford: Blackwell.
Kumar, K. (1978) *Prophecy and Progress*. Harmondsworth: Penguin.
Lacan, J. (1968) *The Language of the Self*. New York: Delta.
Lash, S. (1990) *The Sociology of Postmodernism*. London: Routledge.
Lash, S. and J. Urry (1984) 'The New Marxism of Collective Action', *Sociology* 18(1): 33–50.
Lash, S. and J. Urry (1987) *The End of Organized Capitalism*. Cambridge: Polity.
Leach, E. (1974) *Lévi-Strauss*. London: Fontana.
Lechner, F. (1990) 'Fundamentalism and Sociocultural Revitalization: On the Logic of Dedifferentiation' in J. Alexander and P. Colomy (eds), *Differentiation Theory and Social Change*. New York: Columbia University Press: 88–118.
Lenin, V. (1939) *Imperialism*. New York: International.
Levine, D. (1959) 'The Structure of Simmel's Thought' in K. Wolff (ed.) *Georg Simmel, 1858–1918*. Columbus: Ohio State University Press: 9–32.
Lévi-Strauss, C. (1969) *The Elementary Structures of Kinship*. Boston: Beacon.
Lévi-Strauss, C. (1977) *Structural Anthropology*. Harmondsworth: Peregrine.
Lévi-Strauss, C. (1978) *Structural Anthropology 2*. Harmondsworth: Peregrine.
Levy, M. Jr (1966) *Modernization and the Structure of Societies*. Princeton: Princeton University Press.
Lichtheim, G. (1970) *Lukács*. London: Fontana.
Lockwood, D. (1976) 'Social Integration and System Integration' in G. Zollschan and W. Hirsch (eds), *Social Change*. Cambridge: Schenkman: 370–83.
Lofland, J. (1980) 'Early Goffman: Style, Structure, Substance, Soul' in J. Ditton (ed.), *The View from Goffman*. London: Macmillan: 24–51.
Luhmann, N. (1982) *The Differentiation of Society*. New York: Columbia University Press.
Luhmann, N. (1990) 'The Paradox of System Differentiation and the Evolution of Society' in J. Alexander and P. Colomy (eds), *Differentiation Theory and Social Change*. New York: Columbia University Press: 409–40.
Lukács, G. (1968; trans. R. Livingstone 1971) *History and Class Consciousness*. London: Merlin.
Lukes, S. (1974) *Power: A Radical View*. London: Macmillan.
Lukes, S. (1975) *Émile Durkheim*. Harmondsworth: Penguin.
Lukes, S. (1978) 'Power and Authority' in T. Bottomore and R. Nisbet (eds), *A History of Sociological Analysis*. London: Heinemann: 633–74.
Lukes, S. (ed.) (1986) *Power*. Oxford: Blackwell.
Lyotard, J-F. (1984) *The Postmodern Condition*. Manchester: Manchester University Press.
MacIntyre, A. (1970) *Marcuse*. London: Fontana.
Maine, H. ([1861] 1963) *Ancient Law*. Gloucester: Peter Smith.
Malinowski, B. (1939) 'The Group and the Individual in Functionalist Analysis', *American Journal of Sociology* 44: 938–64.
Mann, M. (1982) 'The Social Cohesion of Liberal Democracy' in A. Giddens and D. Held (eds), *Classes, Power and Conflict*. Berkeley: University of California Press: 373–95.
Mann, M. (1986) *The Sources of Social Power*, Vol. 1. Cambridge: CUP.
Marcuse, H. (1964) *One Dimensional Man*. London: Paladin.
Marshall, A. ([1890] 1961) *Principles of Economics* (9th edn), Vol. 1, *Text*. London: Macmillan.
Marx, K. (1954) *Capital*, Vol. 1. London: Lawrence & Wishart.

Marx, K. (1977) *Selected Writings*, ed. D. McLellan. Oxford: OUP.

Marx, K. (1982) 'Selections' in A. Giddens and D. Held (eds), *Classes, Power and Conflict*. Berkeley: University of California Press: 12–49.

Marx, K. and F. Engels (1970) *The German Ideology* (Part One). New York: International.

Marx, K. and F. Engels (1979) *Pre-Capitalist Socio-Economic Formations*. Moscow: Progress.

McLellan, D. (1977) *Engels*. Glasgow: Fontana.

Mead, G. (1934) *Mind, Self, and Society*. Chicago: University of Chicago Press.

Meisel, J. (1962) *The Myth of the Ruling Class*. Ann Arbor: Ann Arbor Press.

Meltzer, B., J. Petras and L. Reynolds (1975) *Symbolic Interactionism*. London: Routledge.

Mennell, S. (1974) *Sociological Theory*. New York: Praeger.

Mennell, S. (1992) *Norbert Elias*. Oxford: Blackwell.

Menzies, K. (1977) *Talcott Parsons and the Social Image of Man*. London: Routledge.

Merquior, J. (1985) *Foucault*. London: Fontana.

Merton, R. (1968) *Social Theory and Social Structure* (enlarged edn). New York: Free Press.

Michels, R. (1958) *Political Parties*. Glencoe: Free Press.

Miliband, R. (1969) *The State in Capitalist Society*. London: Weidenfeld and Nicolson.

Miliband, R. (1983) *Class Power and State Power*. London: Verso.

Millett, K. (1971) *Sexual Politics*. New York: Avon/Equinox.

Mills, C. (1959) *The Power Elite*. New York: Galaxy.

Mills, C. (1970) 'The Power Elite' and 'The Structure of Power in American Society' in M. Olsen (ed.), *Power in Societies*. New York: Macmillan: 241–61.

Mitchell, J. (1971) *Woman's Estate*. Harmondsworth: Penguin.

Mosca, G. (1939) *The Ruling Class*. New York: McGraw-Hill.

Nagel, E. (1961) *The Structure of Science*. London: Routledge.

Nisbet, R. (1966) *The Sociological Tradition*. New York: Basic.

Niskanen, W. Jr (1971) *Bureaucracy and Representative Government*. Chicago: Aldine.

Norris, C. (1987) *Derrida*. Glasgow: Fontana.

Olsen, M. Jr (1965) *The Logic of Collective Action*. Cambridge: Harvard University Press.

Ortner, S. (1974) 'Is Female to Male as Nature is to Culture?' in M. Rosaldo and L. Lamphere (eds), *Woman, Culture, and Society*. Stanford: Stanford University Press: 67–87.

Pareto, V. (1966) *Sociological Writings*. London: Pall Mall.

Parfit, D. (1986) 'Prudence, Morality and the Prisoner's Dilemma' in J. Elster (ed.), *Rational Choice*. Oxford: Blackwell.

Parkin, F. (1971) *Class Inequality and Political Order*. London: McGibbon.

Parkin, F. (1979) *Marxism and Class Theory*. London: Tavistock.

Parkin, F. (1982) *Max Weber*. Chichester: Ellis Horwood.

Parry, G. (1969) *Political Elites*. London: Allen & Unwin.

Parsons, T. (1937; 2nd edn 1949; pb edn 1968) *The Structure of Social Action*. New York: McGraw-Hill/Free Press.

Parsons, T. (1954) *Essays in Sociological Theory*. New York: Free Press.

Parsons, T. (1964) 'Evolutionary Universals in Society', *American Sociological Review* 29: 339–57.

Parsons, T. (1965) 'An Outline of the Social System' in T. Parsons, K. Naegele, E. Shils and J. Pitts (eds), *Theories of Society* (one vol. edn). New York: Free Press: 30–79.

Parsons, T. (1966) *Societies*. Englewood Cliffs: Prentice-Hall.

Parsons, T. (1970) 'The Monopoly of Force and the "Power Bank"' and 'The Distribution of Power in American Society' in M. Olsen, *Power in Societies*. New York: Macmillan: 54–7, 269–78.

Parsons, T. (1971) *The System of Modern Societies*. Englewood Cliffs: Prentice-Hall.

Parsons, T. (1977) *The Evolution of Societies*. Englewood Cliffs: Prentice-Hall.

Parsons, T. (1978) *Action Theory and the Human Condition*. New York: Free Press.

Parsons, T. (1986) 'Power and the Social System' in S. Lukes (ed.), *Power*. Oxford: Blackwell: 94–143.

Parsons, T. (1991) *The Social System* (2nd edn). London: Routledge.

Parsons, T. and R. Bales (1955) *Family, Socialization and Interaction Process*. New York: Free Press.

Parsons, T., R. Bales and E. Shils (1953; reprint 1981) *Working Papers in the Theory of Action*. Glencoe: Free Press/Westport: Greenwood.

Parsons, T. and G. Platt (1973) *The American University*. Cambridge: Harvard University Press.

Parsons, T., E. Shils, E. Tolman, G. Allport, C. Kluckhohn, H. Murray, R. Sears, R. Sheldon and S. Stouffer (1951; pb edn 1962) *Toward a General Theory of Action*. New York: Harper.

Parsons, T. and N. Smelser ([1956] 1968; 1984) *Economy and Society*. London: Routledge.

Piore, M. (1975) 'Notes for a Theory of Labor Market Stratification' in R. Edwards, D. Gordon and H. Reich (eds), *Labor Market Segmentation*. Lexington: Heath: 125–50.

Pollack, F. (1978) 'State Capitalism' in A. Arato and E. Gebhardt (eds), *The Essential Frankfurt School Reader*. Oxford: Blackwell: 71–94.

Poulantzas, N. ([1968] 1973) *Political Power and Social Classes*. London: New Left.

Poulantzas, N. (1978) *State, Power, Socialism*. London: New Left.

Poulantzas, N. (1982) 'On Social Classes' in A. Giddens and D. Held (eds), *Classes, Power and Conflict*. Berkeley: University of California Press: 101–11.

Poulantzas, N. (1986) 'Class Power' in S. Lukes (ed.), *Power*. Oxford: Blackwell: 144–55.

Pusey, M. (1987) *Jürgen Habermas*. Chichester: Ellis Horwood.

Radcliffe-Brown, A. (1952) *Structure and Function in Primitive Society*. London: Cohen & West.

Raison, T. (ed.) (1969) *The Founding Fathers of Social Science*. Harmondsworth: Penguin.

Ritzer, G. (1992) *Sociological Theory* (3rd edn). New York: McGraw-Hill.

Robertson, R. (1992) *Globalization*. London: Sage.

Rocher, G. (1974) *Talcott Parsons and American Sociology*. London: Nelson.

Rock, P. (1979) *The Making of Symbolic Interactionism*. London: Macmillan.

Roemer, J. (1981) *Analytic Foundations of Marxian Economic Theory*. Cambridge: CUP.

Roemer, J. (1982) *A General Theory of Exploitation and Class*. Cambridge, Mass.: Harvard University Press.

Rowley, C. (1978) 'Market "Failure" and Government "Failure"' in J. Buchanan et al. (eds), *The Economics of Politics*. London: IEA: 29–43.

Schütz, A. (1962) *Collected Papers*, Vol. 1, *The Problem of Social Reality*. The Hague: Martinus Nijhoff.

Schütz, A. (1964) *Collected Papers*, Vol. 2, *Studies in Social Theory*. The Hague: Martinus Nijhoff.

Schütz, A. (1972) *The Phenomenology of the Social World*. London: Heinemann.

Sciulli, D. (1986) 'Voluntaristic Action as a Distinct Concept', *American Sociological Review* 51: 743–66.

Simmel, G. (1959a) 'The Problem of Sociology' in K. H. Wolff (ed.), *Georg Simmel, 1858–1918*. Columbus: Ohio State University Press: 310–36.

Simmel, G. (1959b) 'How is Society Possible?' in K. H. Wolff (ed.), *Georg Simmel, 1858–1918*. Columbus: Ohio State University Press: 337–56.

Skinner, B. (1953) *Science and Human Behavior*. New York: Free Press.

Skinner, B. (1974) *About Behaviourism*. London: Jonathan Cape.

Smelser, N. (1968) *Essays in Sociological Explanation*. Englewood Cliffs: Prentice-Hall.

Spencer, H. (1969) *Principles of Sociology*. London: Macmillan.

Stewart, A., K. Prandy and R. Blackburn (1980) *Social Stratification and Occupations*. London: Macmillan.

Sturrock, J. (ed.) (1979) *Structuralism and Since*. Oxford: OUP.

Taylor, L., P. Walton and J. Young (1973) *The New Criminology*. London: Routledge.

Thompson, K. (1982) *Émile Durkheim*. Chichester: Ellis Horwood.

Turkle, S. (1979) *Psychoanalytic Politics*. London: Burnett.

Tuttle, L. (1987) *Encyclopedia of Feminism*. London: Arrow.

Turner, J. (1991) *The Structure of Sociological Theory* (5th edn). Belmont: Wadsworth.

Turner, R. (ed.) (1974) *Ethnomethodology*. Harmondsworth: Penguin.

Walby, S. (1986) *Patriarchy at Work*. Cambridge: Polity.

Walby, S. (1990) *Theorizing Patriarchy*. Oxford: Basil Blackwell.

Wallace, R. and A. Wolf (1991) *Contemporary Sociological Theory* (3rd edn). Englewood Cliffs: Prentice-Hall.

Wallerstein, I. (1974) *The Modern World-System*. New York: Academic.

Walliman, I., H. Rosenbaum, N. Tatsis and G. Zito (1980) 'Misreading Weber: The Concept of "Macht" ', *Sociology* 14(2): 261–75.

Wardell, M. and S. Turner (eds) (1986) *Sociological Theory in Transition*. Boston: Allen & Unwin.

Waters, M. (1989a) 'Patriarchy and Viriarchy', *Sociology* 23(2): 193–211.

Waters, M. (1989b) 'Collegiality, Bureaucratization and Professionalization', *American Journal of Sociology* 94(5): 945–72.

Waters, M. (1989c) *Sociology One*. Melbourne: Longman Cheshire.

Waters, M. (1990) *Class and Stratification*. Melbourne: Longman Cheshire.

Waters, M. (1991) 'Collapse and Convergence in Class Theory', *Theory and Society* 20: 141–72.

Waters, M. (1993) 'Alternative Organizational Formations: A Typology of Polycratic Administrative Systems', *Sociological Review* 41(1): 54–81.

Weber, M. (1947) *The Theory of Social and Economic Organization*. New York: Free Press.

Weber, M. (1949) *The Methodology of the Social Sciences*. Glencoe: Free Press.

Weber, M. (1976) *The Protestant Ethic and the Spirit of Capitalism*. London: Allen & Unwin.

Weber, M. (1978) *Economy and Society*. Berkeley: University of California Press.

Weber, M. (1982) 'Selections' in A. Giddens and D. Held (eds), *Classes, Power and Conflict*. Berkeley: University of California Press: 60–86.

White, S. (1988) *The Recent Work of Jürgen Habermas*. Cambridge: CUP.

Winch, P. (1958) *The Idea of a Social Science and its Relation to Philosophy*. London: Routledge.

Wollheim, R. (1971) *Freud*. London: Fontana/Collins.

Wright, E. (1978) *Class, Crisis and the State*. London: New Left.

Wright, E. (1985) *Classes*. London: Verso.

Wright, E., and B. Martin (1987) 'The Transformation of the American Class Structure', *American Journal of Sociology* 93(1): 1–29.

Wrong, D. (1976) 'The Oversocialized Conception of Man in Modern Sociology' in L. Coser and B. Rosenberg (eds), *Sociological Theory* (4th edn). New York: Macmillan: 104–12.

Index